"What we are, what we can know, and how we fit into the world turn centrally on the analysis of perception. In *The Metaphysics of Perception* Paul Coates teases apart the tensions that have systematically confused philosophers of perception and defends a sophisticated form of the causal theory of perception. In his detailed responses to recent Realist arguments and his careful consideration of modern psychology of perception and the growing body of empirical results, Coates has essentially re-invented Critical Realism, revising, expanding, filling in, and deepening the proto-theory found in Sellars' pére et fils. Coates's theory is the only one I know that is at home accounting for the fact that perception is first-personal and qualitative and yet subject to empirical, scientific investigation. It will become a landmark in the philosophy of perception."

Willem deVries, Professor of Philosophy, University of New Hampshire

"Steering a lucid course between sense-data theory and Direct Realism, Coates delivers a nuanced, up-to-date version of the Critical Realism associated with Wilfrid Sellars. This is a timely and important contribution that successfully integrates scientific, philosophical, and first-person perspectives on the nature of perception and the relation between experience and its objects."

Andy Clark, Professor of Logic and Metaphysics, University of Edinburgh

"The publication of this book is a major event in the philosophy of perception. Paul Coates develops a deeply thought out theory and makes powerful criticisms of alternative accounts. It merits attention from everyone interested in its topic."

Paul Snowdon, Grote Professor of Mind and Logic, University College, London

The Metaphysics of Perception

This book challenges contemporary Direct Realist theories of perception and defends a version of the causal theory that the author locates in the Critical Realist tradition of which Wilfrid Sellars is the main recent exponent. The author highlights the difficulties Direct Realists face in providing a coherent positive account of their view. He develops an analysis of perceptual experience derived from the later writings of Sellars. According to this account experience involves both low-level concepts and a distinct sensory component. This view makes sense of the various notions of non-conceptual content appealed to in current discussion, and provides, in addition, solutions to the conceptual problems raised by recent experimental work on attention and change blindness. An important feature of this theory is the dynamic navigational account of perception and action, which points to an underlying continuity between common sense, scientific and philosophical accounts of perceiving.

Paul Coates is Reader in Philosophy at the University of Hertfordshire, UK.

Routledge Studies in Twentieth-Century Philosophy

The Metaphysics of Perception
Wilfrid Sellars, Perceptual Consciousness and Critical Realism

Paul Coates

Routledge
Taylor & Francis Group

NEW YORK AND LONDON

First published 2007
by Routledge
270 Madison Ave, New York, NY 10016, USA

Simultaneously published in the UK
by Routledge
2 Park Square, Milton Park, Abingdon, Oxon OX14 4RN, UK

Routledge is an imprint of the Taylor & Francis Group, an informa business

Transferred to Digital Printing 2009

Typeset in Times New Romans by Taylor & Francis Books

Library of Congress Cataloging in Publication Data
Coates, Paul.
  The metaphysics of perception : Wilfrid Sellars, critical realism, and
the nature of experience / Paul Coates.
     p. cm. – (Routledge studies in twentieth century philosophy ; 20)
  Includes bibliographical references and index.
  1. Perception (Philosophy) 2. Sellars, Wilfrid. 3. Critical realism. 4.
Metaphysics. 5. Consciousness. I. Title.
  B828.45.C63 2007
  121'.34–dc22
    2006033165

British Library Cataloguing in Publication Data
A catalogue record for this book is available from the British Library

ISBN10: 0-415-28445-7 (hbk)
ISBN10: 0-415-87447-5 (pbk)
ISBN10: 0-203-50382-1 (ebk)

ISBN13: 978-0-415-28445-5 (hbk)
ISBN13: 978-0-415-87447-2 (pbk)
ISBN13: 978-0-203-50382-9 (ebk)

For Jen

Contents

Preface

For almost as long as I have been studying philosophy, I have been absorbed by questions about the nature of perception. My interest grew at a time when the prevailing philosophical view had turned against the classical sense-data tradition that postulated inner, mediating, conscious states as the direct objects of perception. The deeper I explored the issues, however, the more convinced I became that the commonly held Direct Realist reaction to the tradition, whilst rightly rejecting the idea of sense-data, was an over-reaction to the faults of that general position. Although, clearly, there is a sense in which we do see external physical objects directly, an adequate theory of perception needs to take a proper account of the subjective aspect of perceptual experience. I also felt, as did others, that attempts to explain away the troublesome facts of hallucination were largely unsuccessful. In exploring the tension between the conclusions of arguments suggesting that perception is in some ways an indirect process, and the claims, arising largely from the phenomenology of perception, that experience presents us with the direct awareness of external objects, I came to realize that there is a way of reconciling the two views. The solution, which I set out in this book, turns upon, first, recognising the internal complexity of perceptual experiences, and second, developing an adequate account of the way that low-level classificatory concepts are exercised, both within, and also sometimes about, our experiences.

Shortly after coming to this realization, I discovered that some of these ideas had already been anticipated in the writings of the American school of Critical Realists, who formulated their views in the early part of the twentieth century. I also became aware of the challenging and important work of Wilfrid Sellars, the inheritor of the Critical Realist tradition. I was fortunate enough to meet and study briefly with Sellars at a time when he was refining his later views and returning to a consideration of problems of perception and consciousness. These early discussions with Sellars, and a prolonged subsequent study of his work, provided the stimulus for further development of my own thoughts about the nature of perception, and I began to develop plans for an extended work on the subject. For a number of reasons, chief of which was a serious illness that took several years to diagnose and cure, work on this project had to be postponed. Only more recently have I had the opportunity to return to this study of perception and complete it.

This book aims to show that Critical Realism provides a coherent framework for developing a satisfactory analysis of perception. However, adoption of this basic framework leaves many issues unresolved. Critical Realism is a version of the causal theory of perception, and at a superficial level there appear to be several major objections to it, all of them calling for reply: I summarize these objections at the end of Chapter 2. Although the present work starts by defending the standard Critical Realist dual-component analysis of experience, the arguments I advance in the remaining chapters, in which I consider the various objections to the analysis, are all original. In presenting these, I explain in detail how the Critical Realist theory can be reconciled with our fundamental intuitions about the nature of perception, and with the phenomenology of experience.

There are many people and organizations I wish to thank for their support in helping me to complete this work. The Arts and Humanities Research Council kindly funded me on a one-year matched-leave award in 2002–3. For useful comments, and for providing opportunities for wider discussion of early drafts and ideas, I would like to thank Stephen Brearley, Andy Clark, Adrian Haddock, Jane Heal, John Hyman, Jakob Lindgaard, Andrew McGonigal, Duncan Pritchard, Anthony Rudd, Peter Simons, David Smith and in particular, Jerry Valberg. My colleagues at Hertfordshire, especially Dan Hutto, Brendan Larvor, and Richard Menary also made many helpful comments and suggestions. I am grateful to Paul Snowdon, who read Chapter 8, and to Willem deVries, who read several chapters, for detailed critical comments. Kim van Gennip read the whole manuscript and made some useful suggestions. Steve Torrance looked at some early drafts, and provided much generous support along the way. Bruce Kuklick and John Rose have been constant friendly critics throughout the evolution of this work and I would like to record warm thanks to both for enjoyable discussions on various philosophical topics over very many years, discussions that have helped shape my own philosophical thinking. I would like to thank Tigran and Joanna for the illustrations. My deepest thanks are to my wife Jenny, whose support and critical suggestions have been as valuable as ever and have improved my work more than I can say.

Perception is an age-old topic. However, the arguments I present here are mainly new, although parts of some chapters are adapted from my own previously published work. Chapter 1 extends the argument of my paper 'Wilfrid Sellars, Perceptual Consciousness and Theories of Attention' in *Essays in Philosophy,* 2004; Chapters 3 and 4 are a substantial reworking of my inaugural address, 'Perception and Metaphysical Scepticism', in the *Proceedings of the Aristotelian Society, Supplementary Volume*, 1998; and a part of Chapter 6 is based upon my paper 'Deviant Causal Chains and Hallucinations: A Problem for the Anti-Causalist', in *The Philosophical Quarterly*, 2000.

But although the conceptual framework of physical color is in this sense ontologically grounded in visual impressions, the conceptual framework in terms of which common sense conceives these impressions is itself an analogical offshoot from the conceptual framework of physical color and shape. To put the matter in Aristotelian terminology, visual impressions are prior *in the order of being* to concepts pertaining to physical color, whereas the latter are prior *in the order of knowing* to concepts pertaining to visual impressions.

Wilfrid Sellars, 'Scientific Realism or Irenic Instrumentalism', Chapter XIV in his *Philosophical Perspectives* (1967)

... even if a person were shut up in a private gallery with respect to all the sense-modalities he possessed, he could and would arrive at essentially the same view that we have of the material world, and would take his perceptions to be direct perceptions of it in just the same sense as we so take ours. His perceptions too would be judgementally direct, though (as we could see) causally mediated.

John Mackie, *Problems From Locke*, Chapter 2 (1978)

Introduction

1 The problem of perceptual experience

This book defends Critical Realism, a version of the causal theory of perception. In developing the Critical Realist account, I aim to show that it provides the metaphysical analysis of perception best able to make sense of a whole range of problematic perceptual phenomena. These include both traditional puzzles arising from perception, and also more recent discoveries in cognitive science about the complex nature of attention.

Two connected sets of questions are central to the metaphysics of perception: the first set concerns the cognitive structure and ontological nature of perceptual experience; the second involves questions about the relation between our perceptual experiences and the physical objects we perceive. Our initial reflections about the nature of perception can give rise to conflicting views about what, essentially, is involved. When we try to formulate clear answers to these questions, we find ourselves pulled in opposing directions, the reasons for which this introduction will set out.

No matter how one considers it, perception is a complex affair, and there are tensions inherent our thinking about what goes on when we perceive the world. These tensions are manifested in the different sorts of claims we feel entitled to make about the overall process and about the role of experience in perception. They arise in part because of the difference between the first-person and third-person perspectives on perceptual experience. This leads to a number of familiar problems. Even our common-sense grasp of experience indicates that appearances are not always a reliable guide to the nature of our physical surroundings. Normally, we take ourselves to perceive objects as they really are, but various non-standard perceptual phenomena raise prima facie puzzles about the relation that holds between our subjective experiences and the physical objects we perceive in the surrounding world: in perceptual illusions the way an object appears is, by definition, at variance with how it really is; in hallucinations, there may be no objects in the surrounding scene that correspond to the way things subjectively appear to be; while in double vision, an object seems to be situated in more than one location relative to the subject.

There are two contrasting ways of trying to make sense of such problematic phenomena: on one line of thought, experiences are *inner* states, distinct from the objects we perceive. Reflections upon common sense, and in particular, upon scientific extensions of common sense, suggest the idea that perception is an essentially causal process linking the subject's inner experience to physical objects in the surroundings. According to this conception, when we consider perception from an external point of view, and think about what is going on when some *other* person is perceiving, then it is natural to think of the process of perception as involving a series of distinct, causally related events. When observing the subject of some experiment on vision in a laboratory, we are able to make some sense of a distinction between the fact that a given object is situated in front of the subject, and the visual experience that the subject has as a result of looking in the direction of that object.

This external perspective on perception suggests the idea that perception involves a number of separate stages, linking what is situated outside the subject, by a causal chain that includes neurophysiological events, to the culminating inner phenomenal experience, which supervenes upon the subject's brain state.[1] We can combine this thought with the idea that an experience with the same phenomenal content could have been caused in an abnormal manner, without the external object being present – the subject could, for example, have had a hallucinatory experience of the same kind, triggered by quite different distal causes (such as the ingestion of a drug), but resulting in the same proximal brain state. This way of considering perception, called by Valberg 'the problematic reasoning', suggests that a person's experience in perceiving an object is something logically distinct from that particular object. This reasoning is not dependent upon any particular detailed set of scientific theories about perception. It arises at a very general level.[2]

According to the problematic reasoning, hallucinatory and veridical experiences are both types of *inner experience*, belonging to a common ontological kind. The notion of an 'inner experience' will be further refined in the course of this book, but the following description will, I hope, suffice here: an experience is an *inner* experience of a person if it is a conscious state with phenomenal qualities, and in a logical sense could occur independently of the existence of any *particular* object outside the subject's skin. Should any given particular external object be taken out of existence then, as a matter of logic, the inner state need not vary. In this sense, hallucinatory experiences, pains and other sensations are inner experiences of different kinds. Whether or not we should accept the problematic reasoning, and regard veridical perceptual experiences as inner experiences, and of the same ontological kind as hallucinatory experiences, is a question that will be examined in much greater detail in Chapters 3 and 4.

The above line of thought is also supported by some phenomenological considerations relating to our first-person, subjective point of view. The idea that all perceptual experiences are inner states is based in part upon the fact that experiences of different kinds share a degree of intrinsic resemblance.[3] It is possible for cases of veridical perception, perceptual illusion, and hallucination to be subjectively similar. From the standpoint of the subject, such situations can be, at least on some occasions, phenomenologically indistinguishable from each other. Even if an awareness of the surrounding context enables subjects to realize, in most cases, that they are hallucinating, it does not negate the fact of the intrinsic resemblance. Thus, for example, if a subject is visually aware of something red and round, so that it seems that an apple is visually present, it is at least epistemically possible that the subject is suffering from an illusion, either of a green apple, or of some other object; or is simply having a hallucination of an apple. There may therefore be no physical object situated in the subject's environment that possesses the phenomenal qualities that the subject seems to see. Nevertheless the qualities of redness and roundness seem in some way to be immediately present in the subject's experience, in a manner different from mere belief. Such considerations have in the past been adduced as reasons for postulating sense-data. We shall see later on, in Chapter 9, why such an inference is *not* warranted, and why sense-data should *not* be introduced as inner objects. Nevertheless, it will be argued that it still makes sense to postulate a common class of *inner experiences*, present in both veridical perception as well as in hallucination, in order to make sense of the subjective similarity.

The phenomenological considerations cut both ways, however. There is an alternative conception of experience, which rejects the idea that veridical perception involves conscious inner states, and several lines of argument point towards this different position. In normal everyday perception the subject becomes directly aware of the physical objects in the surroundings without making any inferences, and without being aware of any inner mediating entities. From a phenomenological point of view, what are present in my experience are just the very objects I perceive. Sitting at my desk, I am directly aware of several books, paper, writing implements, a word-processor, and so on; my perceptual beliefs about the objects in my surroundings come to me spontaneously, without effort and without conscious inference. Veridical experience, it is claimed, is transparent. Experience is not an item in consciousness: it is a condition that enables me to be directly conscious of external physical objects. Or, to put the point another way, the objects I see are essential constituents of my perceptual experience: if the objects I perceive are removed, then it follows necessarily that the identity of my experience is fundamentally altered.

Third-person considerations can also be appealed to in support of this object-involving conception of experience. According to the ecological view of perception originally developed by Gibson, it is wrong to think of perception in terms of inner processing that essentially involves inner experiences.[4] Perception involves the direct pick-up of information in the surrounding world – it is an active, exploratory process, whereby the perceiving subject acquires knowledge of the world directly. A number of exponents of this approach to perception, known either as the enactive theory or the sensorimotor contingency view, have recently developed Gibson's ideas.[5] The central thought is that we should *not* analyse perception as a series of causally connected – yet discrete – stages, but instead treat it as relational. Perception, according to this alternative approach, does not essentially involve inner states of any kind, neither in the sense of nonconscious sub-personal representations, nor in the sense of conscious sensory experiences that are distinct from external objects. Work in robotics and animate vision, which suggests ways in which systems can successfully explore and manoeuvre around their environments without needing to form complex inner representations, is also taken to support this approach. It is claimed that subjects do not, in the normal case, have *inner* experiences when they see objects in front of them – they are directly related to the external objects, in a manner that allows them to act in appropriate ways. Perception does not require the construction of *inner* experiences. It is a skill by means of which we actively explore the world.

Thus on the very central questions about perception there are conflicts contained within our common-sense picture of things, conflicts that go deeper than can be resolved by straightforward scientific experimentation. It is because of the tension between these two lines of thought that the metaphysics of perception is so problematic. We need to examine the conceptual and methodological underpinnings of our theories, in order to try to reconcile the opposed intuitions about conscious experience. No account of perception that fails to do justice to the insights of both positions can be considered satisfactory.

For a theory of perception to be satisfactory, it must put forward a *synoptic account*: that is, one which makes some sense at least of these contrasting intuitions. It must incorporate an analysis of experience which takes into account the phenomenology, and which makes sense of the directness of our perception of external objects, while at the same time doing justice to the various arguments that suggest that experiences involve an inner conscious aspect.[6]

In this book I attempt to provide such a synoptic account, and I defend a version of the causal theory of perception in dealing with these questions. Specifically, I defend a Critical Realist version of this theory which derives from the work of Wilfrid Sellars.[7] Critical Realism, it will be argued, makes sense both of the first-person, subjective nature of experience, and also of the third-person conception we have of perception as a means whereby humans, and other creatures, engage directly with their surroundings, and act appropriately so as to satisfy their needs.

According to Critical Realism, in perceiving a physical object, the subject has a perceptual experience. This experience is an *inner* state that is, in important ways, distinct from, and caused by, the particular object perceived; yet in having an experience, we perceive objects directly. These two claims are compatible because, according to Critical Realism, perceptual experience involves two contrasting components. First, the subject's experience contains a conceptual component, a thought or 'perceptual taking' that refers directly, without conscious inference, to the external object or event perceived – usually a physical object in the nearby surroundings of the subject. This conceptual component may be of a 'low-level' kind (as will be subsequently explained), but it will always involve a form of classification. Second, the experience also contains a phenomenal, or sensory, component. This is an inner state to which phenomenal qualities belong.[8] I shall defend this analysis of the structure of experience in Chapters 1 and 2. For now, the important point to note is that the inner phenomenal state prompts, and guides, the perceptual taking; it is not, however, the focus, or object, of it. According to Critical Realism, we have to acknowledge the existence of such inner phenomenal states in perception, but the overall perceptual experience should not be identified with a purely phenomenal state.

In defending Critical Realism, I shall be arguing against the different forms of Direct Realism currently much in vogue. This general view comes in various different guises, and under a variety of different labels, including 'the disjunctive view' and 'naïve realism'. Something very close to it, I shall argue in Chapter 5, underpins the view known as 'the enactive approach', or 'the sensorimotor contingency' account of perception. The central tenet of Direct Realism is that, in normal perception, we perceive the external objects in our surroundings without being conscious of any mediating entities. If I see an object in normal circumstances, then that very object is immediately present in my consciousness; the phenomenal character of my experience is constituted by certain observable properties belonging to the very physical object I see. Perception involves some kind of direct or simple relation between the perceiver and the object.[9] There is an important truth that Direct Realism emphasizes. Those who favour this tradition are right to claim that our perceptual experiences focus directly on the physical objects that we perceive to be physically present in our surroundings. Nothing at the *conceptual* level (which includes low-level concepts) mediates our direct perception of physical objects.[10] I shall, nevertheless, argue that Direct Realism is mistaken in its treatment of the phenomenal component of experience.

2 Perception and metaphysical issues

It is important to appreciate that the tension between the two contrasting pictures of perceptual experience outlined above is independent of epistemic considerations, although these have often exacerbated the tension. The tension points to a metaphysical puzzle about the nature of perception. I use the term 'metaphysical' here to capture the thought that we need to examine the nature of the fundamental categories we use to make sense of perception. We need to explore at a very general level the structure of the conceptual framework we use in our thinking about perception and perceptual consciousness.

The issue of what is involved in the veridical perception of a physical object is problematic for a number of reasons, and there is a tendency for related, though distinct, questions to be conflated. Two of these are:

(1) What analysis, if any, can we provide of what it is veridically to perceive a physical object?

(2) Does veridical perception ever take place?

These questions clearly concern different issues and it can be argued that they are largely independent from each other.[11]

It might be thought that the second question, which raises epistemological problems, is closely connected with the first, for the reason that certain ways of analysing perception are particularly open to the kinds of challenge made by a philosophical sceptic. However, sceptical possibilities can arise on any analysis of perceiving. It is a mistake to suppose that Direct Realism offers a better defence against the sceptic than the causal theory. Even for the Direct Realist there is a prima facie possibility that we are dreaming all the time. If there are valid transcendental arguments which refute the sceptic, it is arguable that they can be applied as readily to a reasonable form of the causal theory, as to the rival Direct Realist view. Such arguments are neutral between the two theories.[12]

Traditional approaches to perception and epistemology therefore often conflated two distinct projects. The first of these projects concerns the nature of knowledge in general, and the specific way in which knowledge arises in the context of perception. This raises *normative* questions about our entitlement to perceptual knowledge: whether we are justified in our perceptual claims, and whether such perceptual claims in turn justify further claims about the nature of the physical world.

The second project concerns the *metaphysics* of the perceptual situation. This involves issues about how we are related to the world through perception: this aspect of epistemology raises questions about the structure of perceptual and other kinds of similar experiences, about what it is to perceive a physical object, and about how physical objects are connected with perceptual experiences. This book takes the metaphysical issues as the more fundamental, and therefore concentrates mainly on the questions arising from the second project, about the analysis of perceiving, questions that are to a large extent independent of what we may justifiably claim to know.[13] But although I concentrate on the metaphysical issues, I shall nevertheless argue, in Chapter 10, that the form of causal theory that I endorse does not render physical objects unknowable. The causal theory is not undermined by epistemological considerations.

One advantage of taking the metaphysical aspects of perception to be more fundamental is that this approach frees us from excessive concentration on the first-person approach to perception. The full concept of perception arises from the two perspectives that we adopt towards ourselves as persons: the first-person, subjective perspective, and the third-person, objective perspective. Much insight into the nature of perception can be gained from considering what it is for another creature (person or non-human animal) to perceive and negotiate a way through their surroundings. As I shall argue in Chapter 7, we can only make sense of the complex ways in which *other* humans behave when perceiving the objects in their surroundings, if we take them to have inner states *causally linked* to those objects. Such inner states guide a person's complex responses to their surroundings. By considering perception from this external, third-person, perspective we gain important insights into the way that it is essentially connective with action.

But of course perception also involves a crucial first-person perspective. Indeed, it is arguable that perception only becomes a philosophical problem because of the fact that perceptual experiences involve the element of first-person subjective *consciousness*. When an object is perceived, it in some way enters into the experience of the subject: some aspect of it becomes present to the subject's consciousness. The central metaphysical problems of perception arise from the need to combine these two different perspectives into a coherent overall account.[14] The idea that we should explore the notion of perception from these two perspectives will be an important feature of my overall argument, and exactly what each involves will be elaborated in the course of this work.

As we have noted, problems about the nature of perception originate in tensions in our common-sense view of the process. Yet the various sciences of physics, physiology, neurology, psychology, etc., provide a great deal that philosophers can learn from. Although there is no settled view about the precise nature of conscious experience, experimental investigations into phenomena such as change and Inattentional Blindness, blindsight, and Anton's syndrome[15] have a lot to tell us about the constraints on a synoptic account of perception; moreover, at any level there are conceptual issues that are central to structuring and interpreting the kinds of investigations we make. A further feature of the view I adopt here is to show that there are important continuities between common sense, scientific and philosophical notions of perception. In arriving at a satisfactory synoptic view, we should be receptive to their various different contributions.

It is an irony that, despite renewed interest in both the philosophy of Sellars and also in the topic of perception generally, Sellars's own writings on perception have not been given the close attention they deserve. Footnotes citing Sellars's work on such matters as the Myth of the Given appear with increasing frequency, but there has been little systematic attempt to engage at length with his position. One important exception is McDowell's recent work, but that is largely critical of Sellars.[16] The version of Critical

Realism I defend here is partly an attempt to remedy this situation, to show the importance of the position he advanced.

It has to be acknowledged, however, that much of Sellars's writing on perception is dense and programmatic, and needs to be supplemented not only by an account of our understanding of perceptual concepts, but also by detailed discussion of many points that Sellars simply took for granted, such as his dismissal of the Direct Realist view. While acceptance of the basic Critical Realist framework leads me to advocate a position close to that of Wilfrid Sellars, much of the argumentation in this book is original. It also has a different focus from Sellars's work. I aim to show here, by a detailed examination of the central issues, how the Critical Realist version of the causal theory can be turned into a full and satisfactory account of perception. In articulating the central dual-component account of experience, I draw largely upon Sellars's work, both in EPM, and also as set out in his later and less well-known papers.[17] However, in much of the subsequent argument defending the causal theory against the Direct Realist view, what I shall have to say develops in significantly more detail the framework provided by Sellars, and deals with more recent lines of objection to the theory.[18] Those who are familiar with Sellars's writings will be aware of how extraordinarily rich and subtle his philosophy is. In presenting a defence of the Critical Realist analysis of perception, I am drawing upon only one facet of his complex metaphysical system.[19]

There is one important point that needs to be emphasized. The Critical Realist position allows an essential role for inner sensory episodes in perception. However, as noted above, this position should be clearly distinguished from those versions of the sense-data view that also acknowledge a role for inner states, in making sense of the phenomenal aspect of experience. In contrast to the sense-data view, Critical Realism does not treat the inner sensory state as the *object* of perception; the difference between the two accounts of experience is spelt out in much greater detail in Chapter 9. As a consequence, Critical Realism is not committed to a foundationalist account of knowledge. One of Sellars's central achievements in EPM is to show how we can avoid the foundationalist theories normally associated with empiricism, and yet preserve the insight that phenomenal, or sensory, experiences are inner states. They are states that can be distinguished from the sensible objects we perceive, but the manner in which we grasp them is conceptually dependent on our understanding of the physical object framework. As Sellars writes:

> ... the fact that each of us has a privileged access to his impressions, constitutes a dimension of these concepts that is *built on* and *presupposes* their role in intersubjective discourse. It also makes clear why the 'privacy' of these episodes is not the 'absolute privacy' of the traditional puzzles. For, as in the case of thoughts, the fact that overt behaviour is evidence for these episodes is built into the very logic of these concepts ... [20]

However, as we shall have reason to note in Chapter 4, when rejecting certain externalist lines of argument for the Direct Realist view of experience, we need to distinguish carefully between the different kinds of conceptual links that hold between the inner and the outer.

3 Outline of the overall argument

The first half of this work, in Chapters 1 to 5, consists in showing why some form of the causal theory of perception is necessary. This general view has frequently been rejected on the grounds that it is open to a number of insuperable problems. In the remainder of the book, in Chapters 6–10, it is shown how Critical Realism is able to provide solutions to them all.

In Chapters 1 and 2 the Critical Realist account of the structure of experience is set out and defended. Five central objections often raised against the theory are then outlined at the end of Chapter 2. Each of these is taken up in turn, and analysed in depth, in the ensuing chapters. A careful examination of the resources open to the Critical Realist shows that not one of the objections is cogent.

In Chapters 3, 4, and 5 it is argued that no version of the Direct Realist account of experience succeeds in providing a clear alternative to the Critical Realist analysis. The underlying problem for Direct Realist views is that they fail to provide a clear and coherent positive account of what perception is. In purporting to provide such an account, Direct Realism trades implicitly upon our understanding that perception is an essentially causal process, which links the subject's experience and the perceived object.

In the second half of the book, in Chapters 6 to 10, I explain how the causal theory of perception can be formulated in a way that resists the objections traditionally raised against such theories. This task involves explaining the precise nature of Critical Realist version of the theory. It requires that we provide an account of the unity of perception, and of perceptual experience, from both a first-person, and also a third-person, point of view. In Chapters 6 and 7, I explore our understanding of the nature of perception from an external, third-person perspective. In these chapters connections are drawn between our common-sense understanding of perception, as the means whereby we succeed in moving around and coping with the environment, and the scientific discoveries about the nature of the processes that enable us to do so.

In Chapters 8 and 9 phenomenological issues are brought to the fore, in conjunction with an analysis of the claim that perceptual experience is 'transparent'. It is explained how our direct, first-person, experience of the world through of perception is compatible with a causal account. In Chapter 9, a comprehensive examination is carried out of a whole variety of perceptual and related phenomena, in which the phenomenology of perception is explored in depth. The conclusions drawn here provide strong support for the Critical Realist account of experience, and indicate that there is no conflict between that theory and our pre-reflective grasp of perception. Finally, in Chapter 10, it is shown why the Critical Realist version of the causal theory is not committed to a foundationalist view, and how it is compatible with the acquisition of knowledge relating to the external world.

1 The structure of perceptual consciousness (1)

Phenomenal qualities and the two-component view

1 The nature of Critical Realism

In considering perception in this book, the focus will be upon forms of distance perception. There are good reasons for considering the various types of distance perception together, as forming a distinctive class, for reasons that will be made clear in Chapter 7. Amongst these different modes are seeing and hearing, and also other forms of perception such as the echolocation system employed by bats, and the electromagnetic perceptual systems employed by some sharks and certain other kinds of fish.[1] Examples will be taken mainly, but not exclusively, from visual perception, to illustrate this general form of perceptual encounter with the world.

According to Critical Realism, perceptual experiences and hallucinatory experiences belong to a common kind. Suppose that in seeing one of the black and white cats that share my home, I have a visual experience with a certain content – it appears to me as it normally does when I see a black and white cat. It is hard to dispute the claim that I could have the same qualitative *type* of experience without there actually being a cat that I see – this is established by the possibility of matching hallucinations.[2] It is only because of the qualitative similarity between veridical and hallucinatory experience that I am able to describe the character of a hallucinatory experience. The Critical Realist makes a further, ontological, claim. My perceptual experience is a conscious *inner* state; it does not differ intrinsically from a hallucinatory experience. I might have had exactly this same *token* experience, even if the physical thing, the particular cat I actually happen to see, had been removed. This is because my actual *token* experience supervenes upon my internal neural states. If we subtract the current distal causes of my perceptual experience, then the proximal cause, my neural state, is *sufficient* for the production of the experience I am having now.[3] In the course of the next few chapters I shall expand upon these ideas in order to clarify the precise sense in which experiences are inner states.

Critical Realism is therefore a version of the causal theory of perception. When I see an object, it is the cause of my having an *inner* experience, a conscious state that is distinct from the physical object I perceive. Perceptual and hallucinatory experiences differ only in their causal ancestry. This claim about the ontological status of experiences is contentious, but I will postpone the defence of it until Chapters 3 and 4. In this chapter and the next it will be assumed that visual experiences can be understood in this way, as *inner* states belonging to the subject.

Visual experiences are complex. They have a phenomenal character. This involves the vivid awareness of a sensory manifold, an array of colours and shapes. Experiences also have a conceptual representational aspect: they classify the physical objects and events the subject takes to be in the surroundings. The central tenet of Critical Realism is that we should explain the complex character of experiences by analysing them as having two components. One component is the nonconceptual *phenomenal* state, in virtue of which the subject is aware of the presence of phenomenal qualities, a presence in consciousness that accounts for the fact that seeing something is fundamentally different in kind from merely thinking about something. In arguing that experiences have a distinctive phenomenal character, I shall sometimes, for convenience, follow Sellars in referring to the phenomenal component as the sensory component to which the phenomenal qualities belong.

But there is a second component in visual experience. Seeing is also a cognitive process, whereby creatures represent their surroundings. Seeing involves conscious classification, an awareness of kinds. Even at the most primitive level of consciousness, the subject has a grasp of how the current experience differs from other possible experiences. On one plausible view, this grasp involves the exercise, in experience, of low-level classificatory concepts. These concepts refer directly to features of the external world, to objects, properties and events in the surroundings of the perceiver, such as books, pens, apples, trees, sunsets, people and car-crashes. It is due to the exercise of such concepts that all perceptual experiences have a 'what kind' and a 'where'. A visual experience cannot count as perceptual unless the subject of that experience grasps (possibly mistakenly) that what is seen has a certain kind of character, and has a certain location relative to the subject's body. The exercise of classificatory concepts in experience generates expectations about the likely course of future experiences, and can guide potential action. This accounts for the intentional directedness of perceptual experience, as I shall elaborate in Chapter 9.

The distinctive feature of the Critical Realist version of the causal theory of perception is its claim that the concepts exercised by the perceiver in perceptual experience refer *directly* to the external physical objects perceived. When I look in normal circumstances at a red apple, I am nonconceptually aware of a red phenomenal quality, which belongs to my inner phenomenal state. But I do not usually attend to my inner state, and it is not what I see. I see the apple, I classify it directly as such. As Mackie pointed out, perception is judgementally direct, though causally mediated by my inner phenomenal states.[4]

Before examining the Critical Realist analysis of experience in depth, however, the terminology needs to be clarified. Because of various confusions and ambiguities in the terms 'conceptual' and 'nonconceptual', I need to explain how they are employed in this book. Various kinds of conceptual activity can be distinguished, their differences corresponding roughly to the degree of sophistication manifested by subjects in exercising concepts: at one end of the spectrum there is the conceptual activity of a subject characterized by reference to higher-level abilities, which include the ability of subjects to make judgements that they can rationally reflect upon and defend, to grasp the inferential connections of the concepts they employ, and to be self-aware. Towards the other end of this spectrum is the lower-level classificatory ability of subjects who can recognize *kinds* of objects and act appropriately in consequence, but may lack some or all of the other abilities previously identified. Subjects who manifest such simple recognitional abilities, yet lack the higher-level range of abilities, are often said to exhibit states with 'nonconceptual content'.[5]

David Smith makes a useful distinction between 'high' and 'low' accounts of conceptualization by reference to the abilities exercised by the subject. Smith's terminology has advantages, since, as will shortly be explained, there are several different kinds of nonconceptual content. Subjects, including animals, can be said to exercise concepts of a low kind when they manifest recognitional behaviour in the absence of more sophisticated higher-level abilities. The considerations that motivate the attribution of some kind of low-level classificatory concepts derive from a third-person perspective on humans and other animals. We explain certain kinds of behaviour in creatures by appeal to such low-level classificatory representational states. Such states have a *representational* kind of nonconceptual content. Low-level concepts – or alternatively, states with 'nonconceptual content' – form part of the explanation of how an animal or infant can recognize a certain kind, and act accordingly.[6] This third-person account, however, does not appeal directly to notions of phenomenal consciousness; it is independent of the subjective view of experience.

The notion of nonconceptual content is also invoked by several writers in order to explain facts about our awareness of the 'fineness of grain' of our experiences: the fact that we can discern fine differences in degree of qualities such as colour and shape. But we need to make a further distinction here. Abstracting from phenomenal experience, we can *think* about distinctions of quality with any number of fine differences, and mathematicians have provided us with the appropriate concepts. However, when we introduce the idea of low-level, or nonconceptual content in order to explain the fineness of grain of what is *experienced*, we are appealing to specifically first-person, subjective considerations. We justify claims about fineness of grain, because we are in some sense aware of what it is like to be conscious, for example, of many fine differences in the shades of red that may be co-present in one phenomenal experience, differences that outrun our ability to grasp and remember them each individually in a manner that supports subsequent recognition of 'exactly the same shade again'. The fine differences we are aware of are differences in *phenomenal* nonconceptual content (although, importantly, as we shall see in the following chapter, we need to employ concepts of some kind, in order to come to be consciously aware of such fine-grained differences at the phenomenal level).

This ability to be aware of the subjective experience of fine differences between phenomenal qualities in consciousness needs accounting for. When we employ the term 'nonconceptual' to apply to the phenomenal content in which we discern such differences, it is not at all clear that we are referring to the same kind of low-level conceptual activity that is involved in explaining, from a third-person point of view, the discriminatory behaviour displayed by a person or creature. The two notions of nonconceptual content may be connected, but mere discriminatory behaviour on its own need not be conscious. So it is arguable that there are at least two ideas of a 'nonconceptual state' in play. The first I equate with the notion of a representational state that is involved in the exercise of *low-level* concepts; the second I equate with the notion of the *phenomenal* aspect of experience, an aspect that distinguishes perceiving from merely thinking. To defend the claim that this phenomenal aspect constitutes a distinct component in experience is the main task of this chapter.

Clark has also argued that there are two different notions of low-level or nonconceptual concepts, but for different reasons.[7] Clark's first sense of nonconceptual content relates to representational states that are required for the 'recognition, recall and reasoning', and are employed in the planning and guiding of extended action sequences aimed at some goal of which the agent is conscious. The second is involved in the fine online control of immediate actions such as grasping and catching, behaviour associated with activity in the dorsal system. There is strong evidence, as Clark notes (citing the work surveyed by Milner and Goodale), that the second kind of fine discriminatory behaviour is not conscious.[8] But the distinction I defend here, between representational nonconceptual content and phenomenal nonconceptual content, is different from Clark's. I accept that concepts of a low-level kind are required to explain extended actions based upon the recognition of kinds; and also that different kinds of representational states need to be introduced to explain the online fine control of grasping and similar actions, as Clark argues. But both of Clark's notions are introduced from a third-person perspective. As Clark notes, we speak of agents being conscious of their plans, but this is not the same as speaking of the consciousness of phenomenal qualities. I am therefore suggesting that we need to recognize in all *three* different senses of 'nonconceptual content': (i) the nonconceptual content involved in the fine online control of actions that are carried out by the dorsal system; (ii) the nonconceptual content belonging to representational states that involve the exercise of low-level concepts, in explaining certain patterns of complex extended behaviour in infants and animals; and (iii) the phenomenal nonconceptual content that belongs to the phenomenal (or sensory) component of experience. The task of the present chapter is to establish that this phenomenal component is in fact distinct from the (low-level or higher-level) conceptual component.

Throughout this book I shall use 'concept' to refer to both low-level, merely classificatory concepts, and also to the higher-level concepts associated with judgements. I shall reserve the term 'nonconceptual' to refer to the specifically phenomenal, or sensory, aspects of experience.[9]

The Critical Realist's essential claim about the structure of experience is this: the purely phenomenal nonconceptual component of experience, in virtue of which the subject is consciously aware of sensible qualities such as the colour red, or the smell of coffee, is distinct from any conceptual representational activity, even of a low-level kind. In being actual, and having a fairly determinate structure, and also being non-intentional, the phenomenal aspect of experience differs fundamentally from the conceptual aspect. Concepts, in contrast, are essentially dispositional in nature; they are involved in the exercise of intrinsically representational states of mind, states of mind that are directed onto possible states of affairs in the world.[10] The exercise of concepts (perhaps of a low-level kind) accounts for the intentional aspect of experience. Their employment leads the subject to form expectations about the behaviour of physical objects seen in the local environment, and about potential changes in their position relative to the subject. Their exercise also involves, through the workings of our imaginative faculties, an implicit understanding of potential changes of the phenomenal qualities belonging to the sensory component of experience. Their exercise guides the subject's behaviour towards objects in the world. For example, in exercising the concept of an apple in respect of my phenomenal state, I set up a range of expectancies about the surfaces I cannot directly see, and how I might pick the apple up as a single object, and what I will experience if I bite it, and so on.[11]

None of these claims about the twofold nature of experience, however, should be taken to imply that states of pure phenomenal or sensory consciousness can exist on their own. Since all conscious awareness is the awareness of kinds, phenomenal states only enter into consciousness through their connection with the exercise of concepts, of at least a low-level kind. As I shall argue more fully in section (4), in order to be consciously aware of a phenomenal state, the subject must to some extent grasp or appreciate the kind of experience they are having.[12]

As the above reflections indicate, discussions about the nature of perception are frequently complicated by the many different kinds of distinction that are appealed to in characterizing experience. To avoid misunderstandings, it will help to summarize the specific commitments entailed by the version of Critical Realism that will be defended here, and to explain how they relate to the issue of perceptual content.

(1) Veridical, illusory, and hallucinatory experiences (henceforth simply: 'perceptual experiences'), of the type that occur normally in distance perception, belong to a common ontological kind. From a *subjective* viewpoint they are in principle indistinguishable from each other, even though in practice contextual clues are normally sufficient for subjects to know what kind of experience they are having. Such experiences are conscious *inner states* of the subject, in the sense that a token experience of a given type (e.g. a visual experience as of a cat) can occur in the absence of causal input to the sense-organs from an external physical object.

(2) Perceptual experiences contain two components:
   (i) A phenomenal nonconceptual component;
   (ii) The exercise of conceptual states, possibly at a low level, in a 'perceptual taking', in virtue of which the subject represents aspects of the physical surroundings.

(3) There are at least three different kinds of content, understood in a broad sense, which can be said to belong to experience:
   (i) *Intrinsic phenomenal* content, or phenomenal character, belonging to the phenomenal component that the perceiver is nonconceptually aware of, subjectively, in having that experience;[13]
   (ii) In virtue of the phenomenal component, experiences have, in addition, a form of *informational representational* content. This is a form of scenario content.[14] It is important to note, however, that such informational content does not necessarily determine the full nature of the intrinsic phenomenal content that is subjectively available to the subject. It may be that the most we can say is that a certain type of phenomenal state has informational representational content for a given subject, *modulo* a given environment over a period of time.[15]
   (iii) There is a different form of representational content that belongs to the experience by virtue of the classificatory *concepts* exercised in the form of perceptual takings and which accounts for the intentional directedness of perceptual experience. As noted in the previous section, this form of *conceptual representational* content may arise from the exercise either of low-level concepts, or of concepts at a higher level.[16]

(4) It is the distinction between (3)(i) the phenomenal content, or character, and (3)(iii) the conceptual representational content (high or low), which is of particular significance in experience. On the version of Critical Realism defended here, it will be argued that these two different kinds of content of experience can vary independently from each other. There can thus be differences between the phenomenal contents of distinct visual experiences that are not reflected in differences in their conceptual contents, and vice versa.[17]

(5) The representational content of the conceptual component of visual consciousness is distinct from a further kind of nonconceptual, action-

guiding content that is plausibly associated with processing in the dorsal system (and which may be non-conscious).

(6) A perceiver does not *perceive* the phenomenal component of the experience. In having an experience that includes a phenomenal state, the subject perceives an external physical object. Critical Realism must therefore be distinguished from the sense-data theory with which it is sometimes confused. The Critical Realist view is not committed to any form of foundationalism; nor is it committed to a dualist conception of phenomenal states.

As noted in the introduction, the Critical Realist two-component analysis explains why perceptual experiences have both direct and indirect aspects. My perception of the black and white cat is mediated by my inner phenomenal states. These states account for the phenomenal qualities of my experience, the phenomenal aspect that distinguishes conscious experience from the kind of consciousness that arises in mere thought. But in perception, my concepts, in the form of perceptual takings (or perceptual thoughts), relate directly – without inference – to the external physical objects I see.[18] As also noted, in interpreting experiences as involving inner states, the Critical Realist disagrees with the Direct Realist over the question whether the phenomenal component in experience is distinct from the actual cat situated in my physical surroundings. That ontological issue will be taken up in subsequent chapters. The topic of the present chapter concerns the two-component structure of experience.

2 Sellars's Subtraction Argument: the phenomenal component of experience

The Critical Realist two-component analysis of experience has been criticized in two contrasting ways.[19] These criticisms are to a large extent independent of the ontological issue about the *inner* status of the phenomenal aspect.[20] Proponents of the "representationalist", or "intentionalist", interpretation of experience attack the analysis by denying that the phenomenal content belongs to a separate component, of a quite different kind from the conceptual representational state involved. Visual experience, they claim, is a unified state, in which a state of affairs is represented in a uniquely visual manner. Experiences are exhausted by their conceptual representational content (or, alternatively, they have a special kind of 'nonconceptual' content, understood here as a form of intentional content, rather than purely phenomenal).[21] Interpreting experiences as purely representational solves two problems. It explains the intentional directedness of experiences, and also the fact that experiences can have indeterminate contents.

The Critical Realist two-component model of experience has also been attacked from the opposite direction. David Smith, for example, has argued that perceptual awareness does not necessarily involve concepts of any sort, either of a 'high-level' form that can enter into judgements, or of a 'low' form that is equivalent to nonphenomenal, nonconceptual content.[22] For Smith, the intentional directedness of perceptual experience is independent of the employment of concepts, and derives from quite different sources.

I begin my defence of the Critical Realist analysis of the structure of experience by explaining why I believe the two-component view is preferable to the representationalist view of experience. Smith's criticisms are examined in the following chapter.

Why should we accept the Critical Realist view that experience contains two contrasting types of consciousness? The central reason for the distinction stems from the fundamental phenomenological difference between seeing and thinking. The difference between these mental episodes is not to be equated with the phenomenal/conceptual distinction, but provides a route to an understanding of it. Superficially, it might be supposed that conscious mental states or episodes belong on a common continuum; the idea would be that they are distinguished by features such as spontaneity, liveliness and complexity. This view of experience, however, leads to all kinds of incoherence. As Kant stressed, the phenomenal (or sensory) and the conceptual belong to two different orders: there can be no single continuum.[23] Purely conceptual episodes can be simple or complex, forceful or lacking in force, and also involuntary, in a manner that parallels perceptual states; but they do not in themselves involve the presence of any actual phenomenal qualities. The difference between seeing and thinking lies in the fact that visual experiences contain an additional component, a distinctive phenomenal aspect that is not present in mere thought. I will defend this two-component view of experience through an examination of Sellars's arguments for the distinction.

Throughout his career, Sellars's writings on perception and experience contain a line of thought that draws upon this Kantian insight. I shall label it the 'Subtraction Argument'. In outline, the argument is simple, and has the following schematic form:

(1) Perceptual episodes such as seeing something (or seeming to see something) when considered as a whole, belong to the framework of representational states, and have *propositional contents* that can be expressed in the form:
    'S sees (or seems to see) that there is an F in front of her.'

(2) For any such perceptual episode there is a matching *pure* propositional episode – a thought or belief (occurring without accompanying imagery) – that has the same content, but involves no phenomenal aspect:
    'S thinks that there is an F in front of her.'

(3) There is an essential difference between *seeing* (or *seeming to see*) that something is the case, and merely *thinking* that something (i.e. the same thing) is the case.

(4) This essential difference is accounted for by analysing perceptual episodes as involving, in addition, what Sellars calls the 'descriptive content': a non-propositional component, that is, a phenomenal or sensory state (a *sense-impression* or "*sensing*"). This component Sellars construes as an inner state of the perceiver.

A succinct illustration of this argument occurs in SK, where Sellars writes, ' ... there is all the difference in the world between *seeing* something to be a pink ice cube, and *merely* thinking something to be a pink ice cube.' He goes on to state: 'over and above its *propositional* character ... [perceptual] thinking has an additional character by virtue of which it is a *seeing* as contrasted with a *mere thinking*.'[24]

Sellars's conclusion is, like Kant's, that an important distinction should be drawn within visual experience. Experiences contain two components. First, there is a sensory component of consciousness, a 'brute reality' – some aspect that is actual, even if not necessarily physical.[25] In modern terminology, this has become known as the *phenomenal* aspect of experience. Perceptual experience, it is claimed, involves some aspects of the scene made manifest in a unique and vivid way.[26] As Valberg expresses the point, in experience, something is made *present* to the subject.[27] The phenomenal aspect that is available in consciousness underpins and guides the higher cognitive processes, and enables successful demonstrative reference to be made. This phenomenal component Sellars refers to as, variously, 'a sensory state', 'a sense impression', 'a sensation', or 'a sensing'. The term 'phenomenal' will mostly be used here to describe this nonconceptual component, although occasionally, so as to clarify the relation to texts by Sellars, I shall also use the term 'sensory'.

Second, experience involves some employment of categories on the part of the subject, an intentional (or representational) awareness of the kind of object to which the mind is directed. This intentional component involves, at a minimum, some sort of *classification*, the employment of *low-level concepts*. Such low-level concepts are to be understood, as Sellars spells out in the late paper MEV, as inner episodes that contribute to guiding complex behaviour; their employment may not support inferential connections of a sophisticated kind that the subject is able to assess rationally, but they share some important features with fully fledged concepts.[28] In many respects Sellars's employment of the idea of such low-level concepts comes close to the form of nonconceptual content that Peacocke describes as 'proto-propositional' content.[29] Central to this account is the following claim: for a creature – a non-human animal, or a human being – to constitute a representational system employing low-level concepts, the states of that creature must be integrated in 'a form of perceiving –

inferring – wanting – acting organism'. To ascribe a state with proto-propositional content to the subject helps to explain a pattern of guided behaviour over time, in focusing upon an object of a certain kind, even if there are reasons for denying that such states are fully conceptual in the sense that entails an ability to form judgements.

The Subtraction Argument turns on the fact that there is an essential difference between, on the one hand, mere conceptual activity, even of a low-level form, and on the other, the richer conscious activity involved in perception.[30] In what follows I shall therefore not be concerned with the distinction between low-level and fully fledged concepts, and for ease of exposition shall employ the term 'concept' to cover both forms.

3   The third-person version of the Subtraction Argument

I shall argue that the Subtraction Argument is fundamentally sound. But there are several aspects of the argument that need to be examined before we can embrace its conclusion. Care needs to be taken here over exactly what Sellars means, and also over what is, and what is not, essential to the argument's conclusion.

One issue concerns the ontological status of the phenomenal non-conceptual component in experience. For reasons connected with his wider metaphysical concerns, Sellars tends to run together two distinct philosophical theses in his various formulations of the Subtraction Argument. The central claim, as far as the two component model of experience is concerned, is that experiences involve some kind of irreducible phenomenal, or sensory, aspect. Sellars in fact always interprets the phenomenal component as an *inner state* of the subject, a sense-impression or sensing that is distinct from the perceived object.

Strictly speaking, however, there are two distinct claims at issue in Sellars's analysis of experience: (i) the claim that visual experiences are to be distinguished from mere thinkings by virtue of containing some kind of *additional* phenomenal component, and (ii) the further, and logically independent thesis, that there is a *common* ontological component contained in all types of experiences, and this always constitutes an inner state of the subject. The Subtraction Argument relates specifically to the *first* claim, i.e. that experiences of all kinds necessarily involve a distinct phenomenal, or sensory, nonconceptual component. Sellars combines this with the second claim, relating to what I term the 'Common Content Argument', which is that the phenomenal aspect in experience always belongs to the same ontological kind, which is an *inner* state of the subject. Although Sellars interweaves the two arguments, they are separable. In advancing the Common Content Argument, Sellars goes beyond the plausible claim that there is an essential qualitative similarity in veridical, illusory and hallucinatory experiences. He gives little in the way of a direct argument for the Critical Realist view that there is a common content, and many who accept the qualitative similarity between veridical and hallucinatory states would reject it. For example, on the Direct Realist or disjunctivist view of perception, no distinct phenomenal states of the subject mediate the awareness of physical objects in veridical experience; there is no inner phenomenal state common to all types of experience. Phenomenal qualities belong to external objects. Whether we can make sense of the Direct Realist view of 'non-inner experiences' in explaining veridical perception is a matter postponed for examination until Chapters 3 and 4.

A second issue that needs to be examined, in order to fully understand Sellars's position, concerns the precise nature of the last two steps in the Subtraction Argument; in particular, we need to clarify the specific reasons Sellars has for interpreting perceptual episodes to be radically different from mere thinkings. The central claim here is about the *fact* of a difference between ostensible seeings and mere thinkings, a difference that is independent of conceptual content. Although seeings and thinkings can share the same conceptual content, seeings must in some way involve a further non-propositional (or phenomenal) component, in order to account for this difference.

Sellars consistently argues that we do not discover this phenomenal component by direct inspection of our own mental states. This strategy fits with his criticisms of the Myth of the Given, as I shall spell out in the following section. He does not, however, always make entirely clear the grounds for the key claim that there is a difference between seeing and thinking, nor how these grounds support the account he offers concerning the nature of the extra component. In some sections in EPM Sellars simply asserts that there is a nonconceptual descriptive residue to seeing, which remains when we subtract the propositional content (i.e. the conceptual aspects), and when we put to one side the issue of whether the propositional claims involved in seeing are, or are not, endorsed.[31] This descriptive residue is the phenomenal (or sensory) component.

When we carefully examine the exact reasons Sellars offers for asserting a radical difference between seeing and merely thinking, it transpires that he appeals to what are, in effect, two different versions of the Subtraction Argument. This is a point that is not always appreciated. I shall explore each version of the argument in turn.

A first version of the Subtraction Argument figures prominently in the earlier writings, especially in SM.[32] According to this version, what motivates the introduction of phenomenal states is the existence of important differences between distinct general types of conceptual episode, differences that are grasped from an external perspective. The (higher-level) concepts *about* the differences involved can be grasped by third parties who, as observers, witness the activity of another subject. The idea is that from this standpoint, we come to distinguish between the complex representational states that occur in perception (that is, perceptual experiences), and other kinds of representational states, such as pure beliefs (i.e.

beliefs that occur without any accompanying imagery). We can then apply this understanding to our own case. Such differences include the fact that perceptual experiences (understood in the broad sense, as containing concepts) tend to arise in certain typical ways, and are involved in learning. Normally they occur in the presence of the objects they are about, and contribute in a direct way to actions, so that the subject is able to move in appropriate ways around her environment. They tend also to be relatively independent of other beliefs.

The argument therefore runs as follows: in order to explain the distinctive nature of perceptual beliefs, we should view them as connected with a further component, that is, a distinct class of inner episodes which (in the normal case) mediate causally between them and physical input from the physical objects we see. These inner episodes are components of the overall perceptual experience, and we can label them sense-impressions, or phenomenal states.[33]

Yet it has to be conceded that this argument for a phenomenal nonconceptual component in experience is rather weak. It is essential to Sellars's conclusion that phenomenal, or sensory, states are considered as *conscious* states – as he subsequently makes quite explicit in the third Carus Lecture:

> Consciousness is a many-splendoured thing, but as used in the title it refers to sensory consciousness, the sort of consciousness we have in virtue of feeling a pain or sensing a cube-of-pinkly.[34]

However, the problem on this third-person version of the Subtraction Argument is that phenomenal states, introduced in terms of their causal-explanatory role in the manner described, need not be understood as *conscious* states. Third-person, objective characterizations will not help us to grasp the full nature of subjective phenomenal, or sensory, consciousness. McDowell rightly objects to this version of the Subtraction Argument in his Woodbridge lectures:

> ... it is not clear why we should suppose that our explanatory need can be met only by finding a sameness at the level of visual sensations – items in consciousness – between the members of such a trio [of veridical, illusory and hallucinatory experiences], as opposed to sameness at the level of, say, patterns of light impinging on retinas.

McDowell's conclusion is that nonconceptual sensations (that is, phenomenal states) 'look like idle wheels'.[35]

The fundamental problem for what I am calling the first version of Sellars's Subtraction Argument is that third-person, objective considerations are not going to deliver any conclusions about the nature of subjective consciousness. This reasoning is of a piece with the reasoning for the existence of an 'explanatory gap' between our concepts of the phenomenal qualities of subjective experience, and of the objective properties that belong to physical systems.[36] There do not seem to be any straightforward entailments between descriptions of the physical and behavioural facts about a person, and descriptions of their conscious states. An objective description of what is going on in a person, couched in physical or functional terms, fails to capture the essential aspect of consciousness.

4 Perceptual experience and phenomenology

There is, nevertheless, a further dimension to Sellars's argument for a phenomenal component in experience, which McDowell's criticisms fail to engage with. It is possible to reconstruct from Sellars's writings another, significantly different version of the Subtraction Argument. This second version is articulated more clearly in the later writings, but is already suggested in EPM, when Sellars points out that the evidence for sense-impressions includes the fact that experiences are introspectible inner episodes: *lookings that* such and such is the case.[37] The second version of the Subtraction Argument appeals to subjective, phenomenological considerations, and as such is not open to the criticisms directed at the first version. Before spelling out this argument more fully, I need first to deal with a preliminary worry about the appeal to phenomenology.

It is a familiar point that one central theme of EPM is the attack Sellars makes on what he characterizes as 'the Myth of the Given'. It may therefore come as a surprise to some philosophers that Sellars should appeal in this way to subjective phenomenological considerations about the nature of experience. Before explaining why there is no inconsistency in Sellars's views on this issue, it will help first to provide some examples of Sellars's later claims.

In his SK, referring to what is involved in the 'total experience' of seeing, Sellars claims:

> Now I think it is clear that, phenomenologically speaking, there is such a non-propositional component.[38]

In the key later paper, SRPC, he argues that phenomenology has an important role to play in the analysis of experience, whilst also acknowledging its limitations:

> Sufficient to the occasion is an analysis of the sense in which we see of the pink ice cube its very pinkness. Here, I believe, sheer phenomenology or conceptual analysis takes us part of the way, but finally lets us down. How far does it take us? Only to the point of assuring us that *something, somehow* a cube of pink in physical space is present in the perception as other than as merely believed in.[39]

In the Carus Lectures, he is more emphatic:

> The one thing we can say, with phenomenological assurance, is that whatever its 'true' *categorial* status, the expanse of red involved in an ostensible seeing of the redness of an apple has *actual existence* as contrasted with the *intentional in-existence* of that which is believed in as believed in.[40]

Sellars admits at the start of the Carus Lectures that in his earlier writings on the Myth of the Given: 'Some formulations were at the very least misleading, and, in general, the scope of the concept of the Given was ill-defined.' Nevertheless, he claims that his afterthoughts ' ... invariably turned out to be variations on the original theme.'[41] To reject the appeal to phenomenology as inconsistent with his earlier criticisms is to misunderstand the whole thrust of Sellars's attack on the Given.

The Myth of the Given, for Sellars, arises from a confused nexus of ideas relating to the supposed foundations of knowledge. As it applies to empiricist views about knowledge and experience, the Myth concerns a number of false conceptions about the *relation* between phenomenal nonconceptual experience and our beliefs about the things we are aware of. In its most basic form, the Myth involves the idea that when a subject has a phenomenal state of kind F, this *entails* that the subject thereby entertains a concept of the category properly applicable to that kind F.[42] So at root, what Sellars opposes is the view that there is some kind of logical or quasi-logical connection between phenomenal and conceptual states.

This confusion about the relationship between the phenomenal and the conceptual is what underlies many of the various conceptions of the Given that Sellars's criticizes throughout EPM.[43] At one extreme, it is manifested in the 'mongrel idea' that Sellars criticizes in Part I. This is the idea that directly conflates the phenomenal and the conceptual components of experience. On this view, 'being aware of something red' is treated as a unitary episode, an episode that is both a kind of sensation, yet also a form of knowing. For Sellars, however, as for Kant and Wittgenstein, the phenomenal and the conceptual differ fundamentally, and cannot be equated in this way.[44] A phenomenal state is an occurrent state of consciousness, whereas a conceptual episode is essentially dispositional, and also has distinctive normative aspects.[45]

But confusion about the relation between the phenomenal and the conceptual could also arise in other ways, for example, if it were claimed that perceptual beliefs are *inferred* directly from phenomenal states. According to Sellars, since the phenomenal and the conceptual belong to quite different categorial orders, there can be no such logical relation of entailment between them. Most importantly, we cannot appeal to the idea of '*direct examination*' of phenomenal experience in order to justify a belief about it.[46]

In order properly to comprehend Sellars's views about the nature of the phenomenal component in experience, it is necessary therefore to distinguish between three questions:

(1) Is there a distinct conscious phenomenal nonconceptual component in experience?

(2) Is it possible to discover such a phenomenal component, independent of the employment of concepts, by some kind of direct confrontation with experience – by some kind of direct inspection and abstraction, or attentive perceptual reduction?

(3) Can some of the results of phenomenology – understood in a broad sense as a way of exploring the totality of what is present in consciousness experience – be used as *indirect* evidence for distinctions in consciousness, and thus of the fact that experience contains phenomenal nonconceptual states?

It is incontrovertible that on Sellars's view, experience does contain a conscious, nonconceptual, phenomenal component. This is why he claims:

> It is clear that the experience of seeing that something is green is not *merely* the occurrence of the propositional claim 'this is green' – not even if we add, as we must, that this claim is, so to speak, evoked or wrung from the perceiver by the object perceived. ... The something more is clearly what philosophers have in mind when they speak of 'visual impressions' or 'immediate visual experiences'.[47]

For Sellars, 'propositional' here has the meaning of: conceptual. The answer to the first question therefore has to be in the affirmative. Sellars does not object to the notion of a phenomenal, nonconceptual component in experience as such, but, as deVries and Triplett point out, 'rather to the idea that we can simply find such a thing by attentive examination of our experiences.'[48]

It is the second question that raises problematic issues. The idea of perceptual reduction, or the direct confrontation with phenomenal experience, is one of Sellars's main targets in EPM. An *understanding* of the phenomenal component of experience is not something arrived at directly, through some special act of inspection whereby the subject enters into a special kind of immediate apprehension of what is given, *independently* of the application of concepts. But we should be careful to note exactly what is wrong with such an approach. An important paper by Firth contains passages that encapsulate some of the ideas that Sellars is objecting to in his criticisms of the Given.

Firth contrasts the *direct inspection* of experience with a special act of attending, employing a process of *perceptual reduction* aimed at the phenomenal content of experience.[49] His principal line of criticism is, in fact, independent of ontological claims about the status of sense-data, and is directed against all two-component interpretations of experience. His positive view is that perceptual consciousness is a unified state. In having a perceptual experience, according to Firth, we do not find any distinction between the ways that properties are presented to us. Inspection does not reveal any difference. What we find in perceptual experience is a single thing, 'an ostensible physical object'. For Firth the conclusion is 'that it is impossible to discover in perception ... two types of consciousness'; ' ... all those things that are in *any* way present to consciousness in perception are present in *exactly* the same way.'[50]

One of Firth's principal arguments is a phenomenologically based criticism, to the effect that there is no coherent process of perceptual reduction that would allow a subject to become aware of a 'sensory core', or distinct phenomenal component, that underlies the levels of interpretation and belief involved in normal perceptual awareness. Firth is not completely explicit about the nature of this process, but it appears from his examples that it involves subjects attending to, and reflecting upon, their current state of perceptual consciousness in a special way, and abstracting from it all the beliefs and conceptual elements. Perceptual reduction is supposed to be 'a procedure for cleansing perceptual consciousness of its non-sensory constituents.'[51] After I have performed this process I can then describe my state of phenomenal consciousness as revealed by direct inspection.[52] Firth's assessment of perceptual reduction is worth quoting from:

> But when this last stage is reached, or perhaps before, there is a second effect: a radical change takes place and a new object of consciousness appears and grows more determinate. ... the operation of perceptual reduction destroys the state of perceptual consciousness on which it is performed; it is an operation, to be precise, which has the effect of replacing a state of perceptual consciousness by a state in which we are aware of sense-data.[53]

However, Firth is at the same time both overly critical, and also too concessive, in his assessment of perceptual reduction. He is right to object to the idea of perceptual reduction and inspection, but he does so for the wrong reasons. By claiming that the process of perceptual reduction replaces the original perceptual state of consciousness involved in seeing a physical object by another, different state of consciousness in which the subject makes out the bare properties of colour and shape, he can be accused of overstating the extent to which concepts determine the phenomenal content. It is certainly arguable that the phenomenal aspect of experience can remain much the same while the concepts employed to categorize it vary significantly; a change in the overall character of experience is for the most part accounted for simply in terms of a change in the way that it is organized by the concepts exercised when the subject conceptualizes something differently. Such organization can in turn be explicated dispositionally, in terms of the expectancies of the subject, as I shall show in detail in Chapter 9. Thus the subject may group aspects of phenomenal experience together, as a potential unity underlying possible further changes. Conceptualizing what I see as a cat behind a fence makes me more prepared for the way the cat will move as a whole. (This is not to deny that there may be some top-down feedback from concept employment that can affect the character of lower level phenomenal states).

But, more importantly, Firth concedes too much to the traditional view of sense-data in allowing that it could make sense to speak of some kind of awareness of entities, when experience takes the stripped-down, concept-free form envisaged. For Firth, the conscious state that is produced at the end of a process of perceptual reduction is one that the subject is somehow nonconceptually aware of; the subject is supposed to grasp the phenomenal content laid bare, *independently* of the exercise of any classificatory concepts. What is objectionable about the notion of perceptual reduction is the very idea that it can result in states of *awareness* whereby perceptual consciousness is, as Firth expresses it, 'cleansed of its non-sensory constituents', that is, whereby the subject has a pure awareness of the phenomenal component, achieved without the exercise of any kind of concepts.[54]

The fundamental problem with the idea of the Given is that conscious awareness implies some kind of understanding, and therefore the exercise of concepts; this conflicts with the idea that the final state of mind, which is allegedly arrived at after the process of reduction, is supposed to be free of concepts. Merely *having* a phenomenal state is not the same as *understanding what kind* of state it is.[55] There is no way we can, somehow, 'bypass' the concepts we exercise in experience, so as to grasp the pure phenomenal content without classifying it in some way. To grasp the phenomenal state is necessarily to employ concepts of some rudimentary kind. This fundamental point, which Sellars emphasizes throughout his attack on the Given, is independent of whether what remains of the phenomenal or sensory core is changed or unchanged by the process of reduction.[56]

Suppose, for example, I was in a purely phenomenal state that consisted in the visual consciousness of two red patches next to a blue patch. How would I grasp the fact that one of the items was different from the other two? To do so, I would have to classify the items in some way. True, I need not classify them as being coloured, or as having the particular shades they have. I need not be aware of the number of patches. But I would have to be aware of the two red patches as similar to each other, as somehow sharing some respect that they do not share with the blue patch. But to do this is to begin to think of the patches in some way, to conceptualize them (perhaps at a very primitive classificatory level). In other words, I would be beginning to employ some rudimentary concepts in order to appreciate or grasp the fact of the difference.

In being aware of what kind of thing is in my experience, I am classifying it in some way, for example as a red patch; my awareness of my experience is still conceptual, whether or not the concepts that I employ, and what they apply to, have changed.[57] A *purely phenomenal* state of the kind supposedly arrived at after a process of perceptual reduction would be, as Kant saw, effectively *blind*. It would not involve any kind of cognitive awareness, nor any grasp or appreciation of the kinds of phenomenal content involved. Accordingly, the (nonconceptual) awareness we have of the purely phenomenal aspect of consciousness leaves undetermined the manner in which we come to conceptually classify what is present at the phenomenal level.[58]

These ideas lie at the heart of Sellars's attack on the Myth of the Given in its empirical manifestations. Sellars is not denying that there are distinctive phenomenal states in experience; indeed, the central strand of argument in EPM concerns their nature, and how we can come to form concepts about them, without being committed to foundationalism. Nor, in attacking the Myth of the Given, is Sellars directly concerned with advancing a claim about the ontological nature of the phenomenal component in experience. His attack is equally applicable to forms of Direct Realism, as he points out at the very start of EPM.[59] We may summarize the thrust of his argument against the Given as containing at least three central strands:

(1) In order for subjects to have any conscious awareness of their own phenomenal experiences, they must employ classificatory concepts of some sort; a pure unconceptualized awareness on its own would not be a state in which the subject grasps, appreciates, or notices anything at all.

(2) The concepts the subject employs in coming to be consciously aware of phenomenal experience are not logically 'inferred' from that phenomenal state. Nor do they need to 'match' the category to which phenomenal experience actually belongs. Subjects must employ concepts of some kind in order to have a grasp of the fact that they are having an experience of some kind, but the categorial nature of phenomenal experience does not impose itself at the conceptual level.[60]

(3) In addition, Sellars claims that any beliefs subjects have to the effect that they are having some kind of experience are in part causally prompted by their phenomenal states, but also have presuppositions. A subject's 'basic observational beliefs' are conceptually connected with that subject's background beliefs.[61]

5 The first-person version of the Subtraction Argument

Sellars's criticisms of the Given point to the following conclusion: if having a purely nonconceptual phenomenal state, such as a red shape, is considered as one component in experience, such a state cannot, on its own, directly provide an inferential route to a conceptual grasp of its nature. Phenomenal states of consciousness are not 'self-intimating'. Our understanding of the claim that there is a phenomenal component in experience cannot be supported by an appeal to direct inspection.[62]

The question now arises as to how we arrive at any sort of understanding of the general nature of phenomenal experience, if this is not obtained by direct examination. We need to clarify how having first-person experiences is connected with our understanding of the concepts we apply to experiences. How, for example, is the fact that a sighted person has experiences of colours connected with the ability to understand fully what it is to see something red? We must find a way of doing justice to the common-sense fact that a person cannot acquire the full concept of experiential colour without being able to have colour experiences.

Fortunately, there is another means by which we can defend the idea of there being a distinct phenomenal component in experience, and explain how we attach a sense to claims about it. Sellars is, in effect, claiming that we may have *indirect* phenomenological reasons for thinking that not all the properties that arise in experience are involved in the same way. There are indeed two components in experience, but we do not arrive at an understanding of this fact by direct inspection. There is a big difference between phenomenology, understood in a broad sense as dealing with the entirety of our perceptual consciousness, and the idea of direct inspection of nonconceptual phenomenal states. A failure to understand this difference can lead to a confusion over the views Sellars expresses about experience in his later work.

In broad terms, phenomenology deals with those features of perceptual consciousness that the subject is aware of from a subjective standpoint. Phenomenology, in this sense, appeals to the entirety of our perceptual experience, and does not restrict itself to a narrow focus on the purely phenomenal aspects of experience.[63] Considering the nature of perceptual experience from a phenomenological standpoint, provides us with a first-person version of the Subtraction Argument that avoids the difficulties that attach to the third-person approach considered above.

The most obvious fact about experiences, considered subjectively, is that they are rich conceptualized episodes that differ from purely conceptual episodes such as belief. Visual and other experiences are conceptualized episodes that manifest the *presence* of phenomenal qualities in a manner that is quite different from the way qualities are *represented* in pure thought. Phenomenologically, there is all the difference in the world, as Sellars notes, 'between *seeing* something to be a pink ice-cube and *merely* thinking something to be a pink ice-cube'.[64] No amount of philosophizing can argue away the brute difference between the way qualities such as the shape or colour of an object are actually present, phenomenally, in experience, and the way such qualities occur when merely thought of, when they have only intentional 'in-existence'. The fact of the difference between perceptual experience and thinking is not based upon some kind of 'direct inspection' of an unconceptualized raw 'Given'. It is established by a second-order reflection upon differences in our conscious conceptualized states.

Once this phenomenological point is established, it can then be combined with the conceptual consideration that thoughts and visual experiences (understood in the broad sense) are in important respects similar: they can share exactly the same conceptual representational contents. Just as I can think that there is something red and triangular (in front of me, etc.), or think that there is a book on the table, or think that Gandini is juggling five clubs, I can see that there is something red and triangular (in front of me, etc.), or see that there is a book on the table, or see that Gandini is juggling five clubs. At a very basic and simple level, there is a difference between thinking that there is a uniform creamy surface situated at some indeterminate distance in front of oneself, and having a visual experience with the same representational content, as experiments on the *Ganzfeld* have established; hence this difference has nothing to do with the detail or complexity of the conceptual contents involved.[65]

It follows from these considerations that a first-person version of the Subtraction Argument is vindicated. If I compare what it is like to have the overall – conceptualized – experience of seeing a red and triangular shape with merely thinking about a red and triangular shape, I am aware not only of a similarity in the conceptual content, but also of some further difference between the two states. The experience, considered overall, must have a further phenomenal nonconceptual aspect that accounts for the difference between the two: the red triangular shape is *present* in my conscious, as a visual expanse, in a manner that is very different from the way that it is *represented* in a thought about a red triangle.[66] The argument generalizes: if, for any perceptual experience with a given conceptual content, there can be a corresponding thought with the same content, then the conceptual content cannot exhaust the experience state. So we have indirect grounds for claiming that experience involves a component that is not conceptual, but phenomenal.

No claim is made here that we arrive at an understanding of the nature of phenomenal states simply through a process of perceptual reduction, or that we find out about our phenomenal nonconceptual states by some kind of direct inspection. The subject does not directly compare having a conceptualized state with having a pure, nonconceptualized phenomenal experience. For the reasons outlined above, such a comparison does not make sense, because we cannot grasp directly what a purely phenomenal state is like. Rather, we arrive at the conclusion that there is a nonconceptual phenomenal aspect indirectly, by reflecting on the general differences and similarities pertaining to experience and belief. What are compared are different kinds of conceptualized states: states that are purely conceptual, such as thought, and conceptualized experiences, complex states that involve both thoughts and a further phenomenal component. In drawing phenomenological conclusions, we employ higher-level conceptual states about the manifest differences in consciousness between these radically different kinds of lower-level conceptualized states. The phenomenology is in harmony with the central concepts we find it natural to use in reflecting about our own states of mind, when we contrast sensations and thoughts. In doing so, we appeal to the kinds of self-ascription that we find ourselves employing in common-sense usage. Before considering replies to the Subtraction Argument, in the next section I shall first say something about the nature of our understanding of phenomenal states.

6 The nature of phenomenal states

This way of formulating the Subtraction Argument provides an answer to questions about the nature of our understanding of phenomenal non-conceptual experience – the central problem that Sellars is concerned with throughout EPM. On Sellars's account we have an explanation of what it is that we *understand* when we say of other subjects that they are having experiences that involve phenomenal nonconceptual states of a certain kind, or when we apply the concept of an inner experience in our own case, as for example, when I notice I am experiencing a red after-image. Phenomenal states are states of the kind that can arise in various perceptual situations, and normally result in perceptual beliefs about the surroundings, and in propensities to act in various appropriate ways.

Claims about such phenomenal states have a sense for us because, as Sellars points out in EPM, they are understood as both evidentially and conceptually connected with both their input and their output.[67] The conceptual connections that contribute to our grasp of the nature of phenomenal states are, therefore, twofold. The first kind of connection is straightforwardly with the type of physical object that normally causes the type of phenomenal state in question. A phenomenal nonconceptual experience of red, for example, is in part characterized by reference to its informational representational content, as the kind of state that arises in normal circumstances as a result of input from red physical objects. A second kind of connection is with our perceptual beliefs about the environment. Typically, the phenomenal experience of red, caused by looking at a red object in normal circumstances, will cause the subject to be inclined to believe that there is a red object present, and to act accordingly. The general conceptual connections with physical input, and the final behavioural output that perceptual beliefs can give rise to, are what enable us, in practice, to communicate about our phenomenal states. We inherit a capacity to report directly upon them, and are inculcated by social training into the practice of doing so.[68] We learn to attribute phenomenal states to others, and also to ourselves.

When we report upon our inner phenomenal states *as such*, we do not produce such reports because we can introspect our raw, unconceptualized states, as we noted above in criticizing Firth's account. Prior to developing the appropriate concepts that refer to them, phenomenal states exist in conscious experience, but subjects only become conscious of them indirectly, in forming concepts about physical objects and their appearances. Initially, at the stage when our mythical ancestors only have concepts of physical objects, phenomenal states are not recognized for what they are.[69] When, subsequently, our concepts for inner states have developed, we come to have what Sellars terms 'such introspectible inner episodes as its looking to one as though there was a red and triangular physical object over there', episodes which we can introspect and distinguish from a mere thought with the same content *because* we now have the appropriate concepts relating to inner states. By virtue of exercising the concept of an inner state, I become able to grasp the nature of a phenomenal state for what it is – a state having such-and-such phenomenal character, for example, as a red after-image. As Sellars notes in EPM, we could not notice our inner phenomenal states (our 'impressions') until we had formulated a language for such states, i.e. before we had formed the relevant concepts.[70] In Chapter 9, I shall spell out precisely what is involved in conceptualizing our inner states as such in considerably more detail.

The evidential links with physical input and fully conceptualized perceptual experiences directed at kinds of external objects *fix the reference* of our phenomenal vocabulary, and enable us to characterize inner experiences in terms of their informational representational content.[71] By providing us with a way of thinking about the phenomenal component of experience, they allow us to attach a general sense to phenomenal concepts. But this view allows for the possibility that our understanding of the nature of phenomenal states can be extended. The claims we make about our inner phenomenal states are not just avowals, but (conceptual) reports about what we are aware of, nonconceptually, in our conscious experience. Once we have acquired the general concept of an inner phenomenal state, we develop in more detail concepts relating to the *intrinsic* phenomenal characters of the various types of such inner states. We learn more about their intrinsic nature.

We exercise concepts about the intrinsic nature of phenomenal consciousness in becoming conscious of the very fact that phenomenal nonconceptual states are present in experience. By employing such concepts, we become aware of what is immediately available in experience, that is, of what is immediately present, from a subjective point of view, which enables us to distinguish *lookings* from mere *thinkings*. We also become able to attend to the nature of the intrinsic phenomenal content or character. We are thus able to characterize such states in terms of properties that are understood by analogy, as closely mapping the resemblances and differences between physical objects.[72]

Strawson has objected to the idea that our concepts of inner experiences are distinct from those that we would apply to the public world. His claim is that we cannot give a veridical description of an experience without reference to the conceptual contents of the perceptual judgement it involves. The perceptual judgement is 'internal to the characterization of the experience' in virtue of which I come to make that judgement.[73] The suggestion is that the concepts we apply in our normal perceptual judgements about the world exhaust the characterization of their contents; there are no independent phenomenal states that we can report upon. Strawson's claim is correct for the *conceptual* component of experience – as it applies to the perceptual taking that is a part of the way I experience the world. All I can say to characterize my state of belief that there is a red apple in front of me is to report the content it has. But descriptions of the phenomenal aspects of experience are more various. Sellars does not deny a conceptual connection between concepts of the physical, and concepts of the inner, as we have noted above. But his claim is that these connections do not exhaust the nature of the inner *phenomenal* states. He writes:

> Thus, 'impression of a red triangle' does not simply mean 'impression such as is caused by red and triangular physical objects in standard conditions,' though it is true – *logically* true – of impressions of red triangles that they are of the sort which *is* caused by red and triangular objects in standard conditions.[74]

The general idea of the phenomenal nonconceptual component of experience is indeed conceptually connected with an acceptance of the broadly common-sense, realistic conception of the objective physical world, as Strawson asserts. Within a given environment, we may have principled grounds for selecting certain conditions as optimal for perceiving. This in turn will provide a basis for general claims about the informational representational content of experiences; we are be able to identify experience *types* in terms of their normal (informational) content, by reference to the normal causes of states of such a type.

That such general conceptual connections hold is quite compatible with the following set of claims: if I have a token perceptual experience state on a given occasion, it has an intrinsic phenomenal content. This type of content is not fully identified by reference to the contents of the specific perceptual belief about the world that I have at that moment, nor even by my general beliefs about the properties of objects in the world. Nor is the phenomenal content of experience necessarily correctly specified by reference to properties of the actual external object that I am seeing on that occasion, because of the phenomenon of perceptual constancy, and the possibility that I may be suffering from an illusion.[75]

It is indeed true that I often characterize my experience as a whole in terms that mirror the way I would express the perceptual judgement involved. So in seeing a Persian carpet, I may describe my experience as an experience of seeing a Persian carpet. But, as noted, I may also have reasons for focusing more narrowly on the phenomenal component of my experience, and in doing so I might find out more about it. To draw attention to the phenomenal component is not to deny Strawson's claim that perceptual experience presents itself as 'an *immediate* consciousness of the existence of things outside us'. This immediacy (better, this 'directness') arises from the perceptual taking or belief. But perceptual consciousness has the further phenomenal or sensory character that belief alone lacks.

Moreover, there are good reasons for holding that most perceptual experience has a rich complexity that far outruns the content of the perceptual judgements it involves. I can reflect on the fact that my perceptual experience contains, as Brian O'Shaughnessy notes, a mass of 'teeming detail'.[76] I do not, and cannot attend to every aspect of it.[77] The point is that there is usually too much that is immediately present in my experience in a single moment for me to attend to and conceptualize every aspect. The concepts that naturally spring to mind when I contemplate my surroundings in no way exhaust what is present in a phenomenal nonconceptual way. This point about the *richness* of experience, it should be noted, is distinct from the question of the *fineness of grain* of phenomenal experience, a feature that has also been cited as distinguishing phenomenal and conceptual content, and which I shall discuss in the next chapter.

The general criteria for assertions about the content or character of the phenomenal component of my visual experience are based upon two kinds of fact: facts about the sort of object I believe myself to be seeing, and facts about what kind of object I actually am seeing, and which is causing me to have a visual experience. Because of the two-fold nature of the conceptual connections with the phenomenal component, these criteria can come into conflict.[78] We can therefore make sense of the idea that, when I look at a Persian carpet, the phenomenal component of my visual experience is not completely identified by my perceptual thoughts – it can also be identified by reference to the physical input that leads to it. Unless I am an expert, different but similarly patterned carpets can lead to identical judgements about them.[79] But because the physical input from the two carpets differs, there are grounds for claiming that the phenomenal components of the two experiences are different in kind. This is *not* to say that I implicitly *notice*, in a conceptual sense, the character of my phenomenal nonconceptual experience. Strawson rightly criticizes Ayer on this point. The claim is, rather, that much of the detail of the carpet is present in my phenomenal consciousness, even though I may not conceptualize all that is present in this way in my experience.[80] Phenomenal content outruns our attentional capacities. There is more going on in my overall experience than I am conceptually aware of.

Thus I may say of another perceiver that she must be having an experience of a certain visual kind – meaning that her experience has a certain type of phenomenal nonconceptual content – on the grounds that she is facing a certain scene, and with her eyes open. My reasons for asserting this claim about her visual experience are the physical criteria, together with certain implicit background assumptions to the effect that she has normal eyesight, is not suffering the effects of some drug that impairs vision, and so on. Such physical criteria may occasionally come into conflict with what may be termed the belief criteria – the subject's own beliefs, as expressed in her reports, about what she sees. So when the subject says she cannot see any turquoise colour in the carpet in front of her, I may claim that although she fails to notice it, there is in fact an area of that colour almost directly in front of her, and, moreover, that it is immediately present in her experience. My attribution of a certain feature to her phenomenal experience may then be vindicated, when after a brief further moment she does come to notice the turquoise colour in her visual field.[81]

An extreme case in which subjects are in error about the character of their own phenomenal states is provided by Anton's syndrome. The unfortunate sufferers from this rare condition have damage to the visual areas of the cortex, so that they are unable to see; that is, they do not have visual phenomenal states. However, they deny their disability, and claim to be able to see normally. They confabulate responses to questions such as: 'Is the light on in this room?', even though they are completely unable to tell whether the room is light or dark. It appears that there is a dissociation between the phenomenal component of experience and the concept applied. All the evidence clearly shows that such subjects are mistaken about their ability to see; and they may indeed eventually come to acknowledge this fact.[82]

It is true that the physical criteria we employ for claims about phenomenal states of others are defeasible. The background assumptions implicitly relied upon are testable. I may wrongly claim of someone that he has a phenomenal nonconceptual experience of two different shades of colour, because I am unaware of the fact that he is colour blind. In other words, a physical condition affecting input rules out a certain kind of phenomenal nonconceptual experience. But such cases will manifest themselves by the general way in which the subject fails to discriminate physical inputs across a whole range of cases (as in Anton's syndrome).

7 Objections to the Subtraction Argument

The Subtraction Argument turns on the claim that perceptual experiences and 'pure' intentional episodes such as thought can share exactly the same conceptual representational content, yet still be significantly different, because thoughts are lacking in phenomenal qualities. In replying to this argument, the representationalist has to explain the grounds of the essential difference between perceptual experiences and pure intentional episodes, without embracing a position that covertly appeals to the distinct content or character belonging to a phenomenal component in experience. I shall consider four responses by representationalists.

Reply (1)

It might be suggested that while the conceptual representational content of, say, my seeing (or seeming to see) a blue screen in front of myself is identical with the content of thinking about there being a blue screen in front of myself, the representational contents differ in their 'mode of presentation'. In the case of seeing, this content is represented in a visual manner. The notion of a mode of presentation was introduced by Frege, who says little about its precise nature. It is not clear precisely what a mode of presentation involves, aside from its use in connection with the idea of sense.[83]

The problem with this response is that none of the interpretations of the notion provides support for the representationalist case.

First, we may interpret a mode of presentation along the lines suggested by Evans, as 'a way of thinking about something'. So, for example, it may be that I think, or am inclined to think, of the fact of there being a blue screen in front of me as connected with a physical screen in a showing of the film by Derek Jarman, in a certain cinema, and so on. But, clearly, if this is the way we should explicate the idea of a mode of presentation, then it could not be used to account for the distinctively *visual* nature of my representations. All that is involved is the addition of a potential further thought, with further conceptual representational content to add to the original content. If we interpret a mode of presentation as a means of being in principle able to identify what the thought is about, we encounter a similar difficulty. I may associate 'this blue screen' with some Russellian definite description; but again, we have not shown what is distinctive about representing a state of affairs *visually*.[84]

We could, alternatively, interpret 'mode of presentation' as involving something more than a disposition to entertain further connected thoughts. It might then be claimed that the case of *seeing* the blue screen case is distinctive, because the *act* of seeing has, itself, some property which distinguishes it from the *act* of thinking about a blue screen. Seeing and thinking can still both conceptually represent exactly the same state of affairs; nevertheless, it is the difference between the nature of the *acts of representing* the situation that accounts for the difference between thinking and seeing. However, to argue in this way is to locate the additional phenomenal quality of blue, which I am aware of in the visual case, *outside* the representational content, and this involves a capitulation to the two-component view. According to the representationalist, if I am representing a blue screen visually, the phenomenal blueness I am conscious of should belong *in* the representational content, not *outside* it.

The dilemma for the representationalist who adopts this reply is this. If we try to account for the distinctive nature of acts of seeing by appealing to some further feature of the *content* of what is represented by such acts, such as a tendency of the subject to associate or identify some item referred to in the original representation by a distinguishing feature, then we are only adding more representational *content*, without explaining how representing that overall content visually differs from the case of pure thought. But if we go outside the representational content and claim, instead, that there are distinctive qualities in consciousness, qualities that account for the difference in the *manner* in which the representational content is presented, then we have capitulated to the two-component analysis. The phenomenal quality of visual experience is separated from the representational content.[85] Talking of phenomenal qualities as 'ways' in which sensible qualities are presented in experience seems to be, as Block suggests, 'closet phenomenism' – it is tantamount to an acceptance of the two-component view.[86]

Reply (2)

A second reply appeals to the notion of nonconceptual content. Here again we encounter an ambiguity. As we noted at the start of this chapter, 'nonconceptual' can be used in different ways. If 'nonconceptual content' is intended to refer to a distinctively phenomenal state, of a different kind from the representational component of experience, then the resulting position is equivalent to the two-component view of experience. If, on the other hand, by 'nonconceptual' is meant: the kind of state involved in conceptual classification of a low kind, then no account has been provided about what is distinctive about visual experiences. Just as it is not possible to convert thinking into seeing by increasing the complexity of the conceptual representational content, it is not possible to do so by reducing the form of conceptual content to classification of a more primitive kind. We can appreciate this point by considering a further example from adapted from Evans.

In discussing cases of hearing sounds, Evans allows that a subject may be in a state with nonconceptual content when she hears a sound as coming from a particular direction.[87] So consider this comparison: (i) a subject, in the dark of night, hears her bedside clock to be in a certain direction in her egocentric space; (ii) the same subject is simply aware of her clock in the dark, without hearing, and 'nonconceptually'; that is, at a low level, she represents her clock as being in a certain direction. In each case her nonconceptual grasp is manifested by the fact that she could reach out and pick up the clock, even though she is not capable of conceptually articulating her grasp of the precise direction of the clock. Yet only in the first case, when she hears the sound, is the subject consciously aware of the phenomenal quality of sound. Two representational states can thus be alike in their nonconceptual representational content, yet there can still be a further *phenomenal* difference between them. This example shows that the Subtraction Argument can apply at the level of nonconceptual content, when that content is understood as cognate with the exercise of low-level concepts.

Reply (3)

Frank Jackson has offered a different line of reply to the Subtraction Argument.[88] Jackson's idea is this. The representational contents of experience are different from those of pure beliefs for the following combination of reasons:

(i) When a subject has a perceptual experience, she represents how things are in her vicinity in rich, though not necessarily determinate, detail. In seeing something, she will represent the colour shape and location of an object.

(ii) The subject also represents the fact that she is tracking a world that causally affects her; she represents the fact that in representing objects in her environment, she is causally responding to them – for the idea of there being a causal connection, Jackson claims, is part of what is involved in the notion of perception.

(iii) Finally, she represents the above features directly, and not in virtue of representing anything else. (This last requirement is to rule out states of belief inferred from things a subject sees directly.)

Apart from the fact that seeing does not always involve the representation of detail, a problem that arises for Jackson's suggestion is that we may imagine a scenario in which someone is hooked up to a special helmet, a device that I shall call a 'belief machine', that prompts beliefs about the environment without any accompanying phenomenal states. This thought experiment is suggested by the phenomenon of blindsight.[89] Subjects who have had a long experience of blindsight learn to prompt themselves about the spatial nature of objects in their surroundings. They come to form beliefs that are not inferred from other beliefs, nor based causally upon phenomenal states. It therefore makes sense to claim that it is in principle possible to construct a belief machine that transmits information directly from the environment, causing neural states in the subject's brain that give rise to pure beliefs about the surroundings, in a manner that bypasses the visual cortex. We can imagine a subject who by this means represents the visual qualities of the objects in her vicinity, but lacks visual phenomenal states.[90] Moreover, because she has been told about how the belief machine works – she may have tried it out many times before – she believes that the beliefs acquired in using it causally track the environment. This case fits the analysis provided by Jackson, yet the subject has no phenomenal states. Therefore Jackson's appeal to the idea of 'directly caused beliefs' fails to account for the difference between seeing and believing solely in terms of the distinctive character of the representational contents involved in perceptual experiences.

A variant of Jackson's proposal is to attempt to account for the essential difference between seeing and thinking by amending the causal condition (ii). The revised proposal would include the claim that what is distinctive about the representations involved in seeing is that they include a representation to the effect that the objects represented as being in the surroundings cause the subject to have an experience. This suggestion does not help the representationalist view, however. If by 'experience' we mean simply: having representational states, then clearly, we are no nearer to accounting for the essential difference between seeing and thinking. If, on the other hand, we mean to refer to a state that includes a distinct phenomenal component, then the variant proposal is no longer a form of representationalism about experience.

Reply (4)

The final line of reply I consider arises from claims made by McDowell.[91] Following Sellars, McDowell notes that there is a sense in which perceptual episodes are involuntary, or passive. I may direct my sense organs and attention so that I perceive certain things in my surroundings, but the actual content of those experiences derives, causally, from the fact that certain kinds of objects are situated there. Nevertheless, as McDowell acknowledges, this involuntariness is not what accounts for the fact that, when I am having a visual experience, I am in a conscious state that has a distinctive character, different in kind from other sorts of conceptual representational state. The reason is that sudden thoughts, and obsessive thoughts, can also be involuntary.

McDowell argues that there are two ways in which the representational states constitutive of visual experiences are distinctive, and different from those involved in ordinary beliefs. First, he claims that experiences are 'shapings of visual consciousness', and 'conceptual episodes of a special kind, already conceived as conceptual shapings of sensory, and in particular, visual consciousness'.[92] Visual experiences contain their representational claims 'as ostensibly visually imposed or impressed on their subject'.[93]

Perhaps because McDowell is concerned with Sellars's claim that hallucinatory and veridical experiences have a common content, and with explicating Sellars's ideas about intentionality, he appears to overlook the fundamental question that Sellars is concerned with in EPM, which is that of providing a proper account of the phenomenal dimension in conscious experience. He therefore rejects Sellars's claim that there is a phenomenal, or sensory, element in consciousness that is 'outside the space of reasons', as he expresses it. McDowell assumes that perceptual experiences are fully accounted for in conceptual terms, and are therefore completely enclosed in the space of reasons. But McDowell is already helping himself to the notion of a '*visual*' state and a '*visual*' object, in accounting for what is special about the representational states involved in seeing. He thus overlooks the force of the first-person version of the Subtraction Argument. On McDowell's own account, it is left unclear how a *visual* representation is to be distinguished from the kind of representation that occurs in thinking. Both, for McDowell, are conceptual episodes. But we are still owed an account of what distinguishes visual consciousness from the kind of consciousness that is involved in mere thought, one that may be involuntary.

Perhaps the second way in which McDowell refers to the difference is supposed to provide the explanation. He claims that visual experiences are evoked 'by an ostensibly *seen* object'. The use of 'ostensibly' here is intended to capture the possibility that the experience might be a case where the subject merely seems to see something, but nothing matches her experience. But the use of 'seen' then begs the question. What is 'ostensibly *seeing*'? How does it differ from merely thinking? Obviously there is a causal, *external* difference in the way that the states arise, in that if an object is seen, it follows that it must actually exist, and be causally responsible for the subject's experience. However, this does not help us to understand what constitutes the essential *subjective* difference between seeing and thinking that is manifest in the first-person consciousness. For someone to see a physical object, it is not sufficient that the object exists, suitably placed in front of them. They must have an experience of the object, an experience that differs from merely thinking about it.

In having a perceptual experience nothing intrinsically present in that experience indicates to the subject that it is genuine. The external presence of an object in the surroundings cannot ground the subjective difference between visual consciousness and thought. This follows for the same reason that the third-person version of the Subtraction Argument fails; external considerations bring us no nearer to understanding subjective differences. The difference we are searching for must be a difference between seeming to see, and thinking (possibly falsely). On McDowell's account, we are again left with the bare claim that experiences and thinkings differ subjectively, but with no account of the phenomenological ground of the difference. McDowell's attempts to capture the essential distinguishing feature of experience leave us none the wiser. Sellars's two-component analysis of experience, on the other hand, offers prospects of accounting for its distinctive nature. Experiences straddle the divide between the conceptual and the phenomenal nonconceptual – experiences are therefore both 'in the space of reasons', by virtue of their conceptual content, and also outside of it, by virtue of having a further, phenomenal component.

8 Why representationalism cannot provide a satisfactory account of experience

The reason why the representationalist accounts of experience cannot succeed stems from the fundamentally different logical character of sensations and conceptual states. Phenomenal, or sensory, states, by their nature, essentially involve phenomenal qualities that are immediately present in consciousness. This phenomenal dimension accounts for the 'what it is like' of experiences.

Representational states such as thought, on the other hand, do not essentially involve anything of a phenomenal nature. Such states may give rise, contingently, to inner images of various kinds. If I have a sudden thought, such as 'I have left the cat out', I may rehearse inwardly the inner word images which reflect the verbal behaviour that such a thought could give rise to. But the thought itself should not, of course, be identified with any particular inner images. For a non-English speaker, the same thought will give rise to different inner word images. It is not even necessary that I have any word images. In many cases what I am thinking will be directly manifested in what I do, without my needing to say anything inwardly. Thoughts and other purely representational states refer beyond themselves, and are directed onto possible states of affairs. Thoughts are in this way genuinely transparent. When I reflect on the nature of my thought, I find nothing of a phenomenal kind essential to that thought actually present in my consciousness.[94]

The sense of 'actually present' needs to be carefully explained. By saying that something is actually present, I am describing how things are from the subject's subjective point of view, independently of whatever is the case in the public world around her. Even to hallucinate is to have something actually present in experience, in a manner that is different from thought. Consider three cases:

(i)   I actually see a red patch before me on the wall;
(ii) I hallucinate a red patch, by having an after-image of something red;
(iii) I close my eyes, and think, without accompanying imagery, of there being some red patch on the wall before me (there may not be any physical patch that corresponds to my thought).

In the first case (i) there is a material object, the physical patch on the wall, which I am in some way perceptually related to. It exists, but its existence is independent of the fact that I experience it. When I reflect on my experience, I am aware of a red phenomenal quality in experience that is, in fact, something distinct from the patch on the wall.[95] In the second case (ii) there is, again, something going on in my experience – something is immediately present in consciousness, so that I am aware in a distinctive manner of the phenomenal quality of redness. In a hallucination, the red patch is not *seen*, because it is not a physical object external to the subject. Nevertheless, it is still something that exists (perhaps as a *state*, and not as an individual object), something the subject is nonconceptually aware of. The red patch has actual existence, in a manner that is lacking in case (iii), whatever its true ontological status happens to be. In the third case, what I am aware of is sometimes referred to as an 'intentional in-existent object'. But such intentional objects lack any real existence; they are nothing but ways of describing the content of the belief. Nothing exists in the third case that has the phenomenal quality of red.[96]

On the 'act-object' model of experience and thought accepted by Moore it is claimed that there always is an object present to consciousness, an object that has real existence. For Moore, if I am aware of a red sense-datum, then it must exist, even if I am hallucinating; being acquainted with a sense-datum involves a unique, real relation to a real entity.[97] Moore treated the awareness, or 'apprehension' of thoughts along the same lines. If the intentional act of *thinking* is mistakenly conflated with Moore's act-object model of awareness, then the objects of thought might be supposed to have some kind of real existence. However, the representational acts involved in belief and experience must be clearly distinguished from the kinds of acts that Moore accepted. Intentional objects are not real entities. The way that representational acts have contents cannot be modelled on the kind of act-object view that Moore upheld. Representational acts of mind cannot explain phenomenal experience.[98]

As Bennett points out, the reason that representational acts such as belief do not involve states that have actual existence is that they are essentially dispositional in nature.[99] They are states that are connected with guiding the subject to respond to the environment. Representational acts essentially refer beyond themselves to something else, to something that may be left indeterminate, as we noted at the outset. They do not contain in themselves anything actual – rather, they are ways of shaping and responding to what is *actually* present at the phenomenal level. In perception, the exercise of concepts is a way of organizing the phenomenal material present in consciousness.[100] These considerations suggest that representational states of an *intentional* kind are the wrong sort of episodes to appeal to in attempting to account for the intrinsic phenomenal content of perceptual experiences.

9 Inattentional Blindness and connected empirical objections

According to the two-component account of perceptual experience we have been considering, there are aspects of the perceiver's phenomenal experience that are independent of conceptual representational content. Phenomenal features may be present in her consciousness, even if she is not attending to them. The claim is that these features exist, even if the subject does not fully conceptualize all aspects of her experience. I have argued that this claim is not defeated by *a priori* argument. The question arises whether the two-component view of experience is consistent with empirical work on vision. Certain recent experiments on the limitations of visual attention have been interpreted by some philosophers and cognitive scientists to undermine the kind of account offered here.

Some surprising results have been produced by a cluster of experiments on Change Blindness, Inattentional Blindness and associated phenomena. According to one plausible characterization, these results show that we consciously take in far less of the visual world than it seems to us that we are aware of. It is worth briefly summarizing the results of two recent sets of experiments, in order to give a flavour of this work. Simons and Chabris describe a striking example of *Inattentional Blindness*.[101] Subjects were asked to perform a task that involved watching a video of a casual basketball game that lasts for about one minute. The task involves counting the number of passes between two members of one team. While the ball is being thrown from player to player, something unexpected takes place: a person dressed in a black gorilla suit walks through the play, stops briefly in the centre of the picture, thumps his chest, and then walks off. Although most subjects correctly record the number of passes made by the team, more than half of the subjects fail to notice the gorilla-suited interloper, who is visible for about nine seconds in all. When shown the video sequence a second time they are amazed to observe what they had previously overlooked.[102]

In *Change Blindness* experiments, a subject is asked to attend to a picture of a scene, for example of two people in the foreground, with a number of buildings clearly visible in the background. A brief flicker, or *transient*, interrupts the display, which then returns with one substantial change – a large building in the background is no longer visible. This display remains visible for a few seconds, and then again the flicker occurs and the switch is made, returning to the original picture. It may take many such alternations between images before the subject finally notices the large scene change not previously attended to; again, this produces surprise on the part of the subjects, when they realize they have overlooked an apparently obvious change. What is agreed by all theorists is that the phenomena of Change and Inattentional Blindness are well established. These experiments provide strong evidence about the limits of attention. Exactly what they show about the overall nature of visual experience is less clear.

One straightforward reaction to the experimental work is to interpret it as showing something about the limitations of our concept-forming processes and memory, rather than about the impoverished nature of our of experience. The idea in the more simple-minded versions of this response is that a subject does indeed take in and process information relating to most of the scene in front of her, but then rapidly forgets the details that are not connected with her plans and projects. So formulated, this 'instant forgetting' response offers an implausible account of why unusual features of scenes are overlooked, as Andy Clark notes.[103] I shall return to Clark's views shortly.

However, there are more subtle variants of this approach, as we shall see in due course. In order properly to assess these, it is first useful to appreciate why some alternative responses canvassed are not satisfactory.

As it turns out, there is strong empirical evidence for the claim that a considerable amount of information from items in a complex visual scene is at least physically registered by the subject, even when she is unable to report on it all directly. This evidence is of two kinds. First, there is much evidence that unattended features of visual displays have priming effects. Mack and Rock give a number of examples of this in their work on Inattentional Blindness. In one experiment cited, a group of subjects failed to notice the written word: 'flake', when being asked to attend to a distracting task. A significantly higher than average percentage of these subjects subsequently chose a picture of a snow-flake from a display of five different objects. Mack and Rock claim that this experiment 'seems to provide clear evidence of semantic priming, because a stimulus that was not consciously perceived seems to have a determining influence on the choice of the picture made by a significant number of subjects'. They conclude that there is 'clear evidence of the implicit perception of stimuli to which subjects are inattentionally blind.'[104] A second source of evidence consists in the very common place fact that attention can be attracted by changes in the scene that are unmasked – movements on the periphery of the visual field will cause eye saccades and attract attention. Some event is registered as taking place *before* we attend to and classify it.

It may still be claimed that these cases do not show anything about conscious experience, even if they do show, pretty well conclusively, that at some level the subject is registering much of the data in the surroundings. But there is further evidence to show that data from the unattended parts of the visual field enter into conscious experience. In the experiments on Inattentional Blindness, attention is highly focused, and background phenomena are ignored. But in other, more normal, contexts, subjects are able very rapidly to ascertain the *gist* or 'general sense of a complete scene'. So a subject becomes able, in a very short space of time – in the order of 120 milliseconds – to report on the overall type of scene they see: whether the scene shown is, for example, a party, a garden, a harbour, and so on. In addition, subjects are also able to report rapidly upon the overall *layout* of a scene, even when they cannot report much of the detail it contains. We can absorb the information from events in the environment for certain purposes rather more quickly than seems to be required for detailed conceptual awareness of specific aspects of the scene.[105]

These objectively verifiable abilities support the idea that conscious experience does indeed contain a considerably greater amount of structure than is conceptualized. This means that, in a sense, the structure of the background phenomenal state is still attended to; the attention is, however, largely *unfocused,* so that distinct objects are not individuated and conceptualized as such. The point is that the concepts employed do not relate to all the detailed features present in phenomenal experience; the concepts do not reflect all the distinct objects experienced. But the concepts employed do relate to different overall kinds of scene that, necessarily, differ from each other in 'gist' only *because* the experiences of the scenes contain differences at a more detailed level.

We may speculate that our subjective experience of a rich and moderately detailed background, situated around the central foveated area to which we normally attend in seeing, is intimately connected with the low-level stages of vision that are a central feature of information-processing accounts of vision. One important theory of attention in harmony with Sellars's two-component conception of phenomenal, or sensory, experience is the model recently developed by Rensink, who builds on the general framework originally formulated by Marr and others.

Rensink argues that there is considerable evidence for the formation of a 'low-level map-like representation' at an early stage of visual processing. On Rensink's account, the low-level, map-like representation is not a stable structure, but an extremely volatile one that is being constantly updated: it is 'largely created anew after each eye movement'.[106] Representations at the lower level are categorized only by their spatial features and location. They play a crucial explanatory role in accounting for changes in fixation and attention, in priming, and in our knowledge of the overall layout, and of the gist of scenes. It is only at higher levels of processing, where *focused* attention is brought into play, that a 'coherence field' generates the specific representations (involving higher-level conceptual categories) of individuated physical objects in the environment. At this level we come to grasp and form beliefs about the stable world of objects in our surroundings.

It is plausible to claim that Sellars's two-component view of experience is consonant with the kind of information-processing account of seeing defended by Rensink and others. On Rensink's, and similar models of attention, there are two key stages in the overall take up of information that contributes to higher-level decision making, based upon beliefs about the objective nature of the surroundings. Initial unconscious processing leads to a low-level stage at which the map-like array is formed. This is the essentially spatial structure of 'proto-objects', that is, 'relatively complex assemblies of fragments that correspond to localized structures in the world'.[107] Such proto-objects provide the raw material on which the attentional processes act. This leads on to the second stage. In attending to some part of this spatial array, we conceptualize aspects of the scene as forming a coherent unity across time, as an object of some kind. These two stages correspond to the phenomenal and the conceptual components of conscious experience. It is arguable that phenomenal experience supervenes, at least in part, upon the low-level map-like array postulated on Rensink's account.

We can build upon this model of experience to provide a variant of the 'rapid forgetting' response to the experimental evidence for Change Blindness. Andy Clark's criticisms of this response are worth quoting more fully. He writes:

> Some element of forgetting may, I accept, be involved in some of these cases. But overall, the hypothesis strikes me as unconvincing. First of all, it is not really clear whether 'seeing-with-immediate-forgetting' is really any different from not seeing at all. (Recall Dennett's 1991 discussion of Stalinesque versus Orwellian accounts.) Second, we know that only a very small window of the visual field can afford high resolution input (Ballard 1991), and we know that attentional mechanisms probably limit our capacity to about 44 bits (plus or minus 15) perglimpse (see Verghese and Pelli (1992), Churchland *et al.*, (1994). So how does all that fleeting richness get transduced? And lastly, as Simons (2000) nicely points out, the inattentional amnesia account seems especially improbable when the stimulus was an opaque gorilla presented for up to 9 seconds. Could we really have been consciously aware of that and then had it slip our minds?[108]

The two-component model of experience allows a satisfactory reply to be made to Clark's objections. The main thrust of this reply is that, on a model of experience such as Rensink's, although the sensory information from the whole scene in front of the observer is initially processed to a rudimentary level, little of it is categorized at a higher conceptual level, hence little of it is available for storage in the memory system. The key insight is that detailed information about specific events in the scene is not forgotten, *because most of it is never conceptualized by the subject in the first place.* A full higher-level conceptual representation of the scene, complete with a classification of its all elements, is never constructed. Nevertheless, *low-level information* about the objects that are before the subject is represented, in an informational sense, in a volatile map-like spatial array, a visual field that is constantly regenerated. As Rensink points out, even though many observers in the Simons and Chabris experiment fail to see the gorilla, 'they could still have experienced the stimulus itself – as an array of colours and lines, for example'.[109] This low-level spatial array, it can be argued, accounts for the phenomenological qualities immediately present in consciousness.

Clark's objections can be responded to in more detail. First, there is no 'seeing-with-immediate-forgetting'; the subjects who fail to report the gorilla-suited figure never conceptualized input from the figure as forming a unified coherent object. The input does indeed contribute to the map-like array so that the subjects were aware that they were seeing, and not just thinking. The input from the gorilla suit may be processed in terms of a low-level array of shapes and colours. Crucially, however, the input leading to the formation of the map-like array is not classified at any higher level. Being processed no further, a representation of a gorilla does not reach even the subject's short-term memory. There is no representation of a unified object. If you do not come to believe, and store, information in the first place, you cannot be said to forget it. This reflects an important and necessary feature of any information-processing system, which is that detail must be sacrificed to allow complex higher-level classification at a subsequent stage. Second, it is not denied that only the central foveated area of the visual field affords high resolution input; so we may admit that the surrounding areas in the low-level spatial array do not contain structures articulated in great detail, although they do contain a certain amount of structure. Third, only a fraction of that structure in the low-level array feeds into the attentional mechanisms; limitations on the capacity of those mechanisms do not affect the amount that is processed earlier on in the perceptual system.

10   Conclusion

Phenomenal states, I have argued, are to be distinguished from the conceptual representational realm. Sellars's two-component analysis of experience points to a way of understanding perceptual experience that allows a degree of autonomy to the phenomenal, or sensory, component. If there are two quite different kinds of component in experience, we are conscious of them in different ways; or, in other words, consciousness takes two different forms. If phenomenal experiences are distinct from conceptual representational states, this makes intelligible the thought that a subject may have a phenomenal state that she is not conceptually aware of, and that she therefore does not necessarily know she is in. To adapt a case that Evans mentions, I may be aware at the phenomenal level of ten lights arranged in a circle, but fail to grasp conceptually how many points of light are present in this way in my experience.

It is plausible to claim that in order to count as being a part of consciousness, a phenomenal state must at least be classified at some minimal level. Looking at a given scene, I may be conscious of a rich array of colours and shapes. Perhaps I conceptualize much of what I see in considerable detail, noticing instantly that what I am looking at is a Shiraz carpet, and that there are many detailed figures. But it is not plausible to say I conceptualize it all, as the Change Blindness experiments demonstrate. Necessarily, much of what I see is not fully conceptualized; I may look at the carpet and notice only that something coloured is physically situated near me. But so long as I apply some concepts (perhaps of a 'low' kind) to the array of features present at the phenomenal level, those features form part of my consciousness.

It follows, therefore, that in perception a rich and detailed phenomenal, or sensory, state may be present as one component of conscious experience, even if the subject does not conceptually grasp every aspect of that state. The presence of such rich and detailed phenomenal states in consciousness accounts for the impression that there is more in perceptual experience than we can attend to at any given moment (this impression is itself a state that involves further conceptualization).

One further reason for accepting the two-component model is that it allows an understanding of much of the complex phenomena connected with the different general ways in which we can conceptualize our experiences, and also of the fact that experiences of the same scene can be conceptualized in different ways. As we shall explore in Chapter 9, experiences can be conceptualized at different levels of explicitness, to different degrees of complexity and detail, and in terms of different ontological categories. The way that such differences can be made sense of according to the two-component model will provide further strong reasons for accepting the model.[110]

2 The structure of perceptual consciousness (2)

Concepts and the awareness of fineness of grain

1 Concepts and experience

The discussion of the Critical Realist analysis of experience has so far concentrated upon a defence of the claim that there is a distinctive phenomenal (or sensory) nonconceptual component in experience. In seeing an object such as a tree, I am conscious of phenomenal qualities such as greenness in my experience. These qualities belong to my visual sensations (although I may not appreciate this fact). However, the mere existence of phenomenal states on their own is not sufficient for perceptual experience.[1] As Kant observed, unless the understanding is involved in the overall experience, the subject is effectively blind.[2]

The term 'experience', as it is used throughout this book, refers to the subject's overall experience, in the full sense that includes both phenomenal and conceptual components. Where reference to the phenomenal component alone is intended, the qualification will be made explicit. The Kantian insight is that experience, in the full sense of there being a conscious state involving features that the subject is aware of, always involves something more than the mere phenomenal states. It contains a second component, which is the exercise of concepts, where this is understood in the wide sense, explicated at the start of the previous chapter, as including low-level concepts. It is only in virtue of this second, conceptual, component in experience that subjects can have any grasp of what they are seeing, or seeming to see. To be consciously aware that there is some sort of object nearby involves the exercise of classificatory conceptual states. For such reasons Sellars claims in EPM:

> For we now recognise that instead of coming to have a concept of something because we have noticed that sort of thing, to have the ability to notice a sort of thing is already to have the concept of that sort of thing, and cannot account for it.[3]

I shall not attempt here to present a full account of what it is for something to *be* a concept, nor of what it is to *have* a concept. The number of conflicting views on this issue testifies to its complexity. A detailed examination of the nature of concepts is outside the scope of this book. My defence of Critical Realism will mainly be concerned with what it is to *exercise* concepts in experience, in the sense that includes low concepts, as explained previously. So the account I sketch out here is not intended as anything like a comprehensive account. It is intended only to introduce and lend some background support to the ideas I shall develop about the complex ways in which concepts are employed when we perceive objects.

I shall start from a set of plausible assumptions. Concepts are constituents of states like thought and belief, and are exercised when we classify items. In being aware of what I see, I must think of it as belonging to a kind. On an austere view, concepts might be identified by reference to what is believed, without any further commitments to ontology.[4] But any full account of a notion such as belief ought to say something about how beliefs function as psychological episodes in explaining behaviour. Beliefs are not only involved when we think about the things we currently perceive, they also play a key role in our mental life by representing the world in a way that facilitates action. At a fundamental level, concepts are introduced as components of states such as belief, in order to explain the way that humans, and perhaps certain other animals, behave in complex discriminating ways, and can engage in the kinds of extended actions that require representations of the world. As Sellars argues in MEV, the root idea is that what enables a given state, such as a belief, to represent an object or feature is that it is connected with other structures that make up a representing system in an agent, and, in virtue of such linkages, that state is the focal point of strategies for finding the represented object or feature.[5]

If one thinks of concepts as kinds of representations in this way, it is necessary to distinguish two aspects of them. A concept can be understood as a representational vehicle, possibly some physical structure within the subject's body, which plays a causal role in the production of behaviour. A concept also has a representational content, which is the aspect of a state of affairs that the concept represents as being the case. In order to identify the concept type we need to know the state of affairs that it correctly represents. One development of this idea is the thought that, at least for some concepts, there is an intimate connection between the identity of that concept and the conditions in which we can *recognize* that the concept in question is correctly applied.[6]

Even if it is accepted, as Sellars suggests, that all concepts are indirectly linked in some ways with strategies for action, this does not mean that every concept is directly linked to recognition conditions. We have concepts of abstract objects for which the notion of recognition conditions does not seem to have any immediate application. Aside from such obvious examples, for any given subject, there will be countless items that he or she has not learnt to apply in experience, even in optimal circumstances. It is arguable that, for many concepts, there is a referential component involved in their employment that we inherit from other members of our society, in ways made familiar through the writings of Kripke, Putnam, Burge and others. So I may use the concepts of, e.g. beech tree, or alpha particle, without being able to recognize instances of the relevant category. Physicists with sufficient training are able to apply the concept of an alpha particle directly to what they see when looking at a cloud chamber; but many of those who have even a quite sophisticated grasp of physics will lack this ability.

Nevertheless, for any subject there will be many concepts that he or she can apply directly, without inference, in having an experience – that is, on the basis of sensory input, and depending upon the particular package of background beliefs, interests and attentional set that they may have in addition. To establish this point does not require a detailed examination of concept possession. All that needs to be claimed is that, at a minimum, a subject must be capable of applying some concepts to experience non-inferentially, in virtue of being able to perceive and act upon the physical world. Unless the exercise of at least some concepts was connected directly with phenomenal experience, we would have no means of increasing our store of empirical knowledge. We would be unable to embark upon the more sophisticated kinds of planned action, with respect to the objects in our immediate environment, on the basis of perceptual knowledge gained by direct observation.

Hence for any subject there must be some concepts which at a given time count for them as observational, at least to this extent: their exercise is prompted directly, and noninferentially, by sensory input. Subjects must directly recognize some items in experience which fall under observational concepts, and make use of them; they must know the conditions under which it is correct to apply such concepts directly. Such direct recognition is defeasible, and involves presuppositions.[7] In principle, there seems to be no restriction on the empirical concepts that may count as observational in this sense. Thus, in the appropriate circumstances, not only sub-atomic particles, but also such matters as the emotional states of other people, might rank as observational items.

The fundamental point, however, is this. There is no full perceptual awareness of any item independently of the use of concepts. Phenomenal states are necessary for perceptual consciousness, but not by themselves sufficient. In order to have any appreciation of what it is I am seeing, I have to understand what kind it belongs to. This is because to be aware of something is to be aware of what kind it is, as was noted in the discussion of perceptual reduction. I cannot grasp what I am experiencing unless I am aware both of what kind of thing it is, and also what it is not. Awareness is not a simple registering of phenomenal items in experience; it essentially involves classification.[8]

But we must be careful also to note that the concepts exercised in classi-fying experience can be very general and indeterminate in nature. The position I shall call '*modest* conceptualism' does not endorse the idea that the phenomenal and the conceptual are in strict correspondence. It was argued in the previous chapter that I may see a Persian carpet as a carpet, without noticing and classifying each separate feature. I am consciously aware, nonconceptually, of various fine details present at the phenomenal level in my experience, which I do not classify *as* such. Yet such differences at the phenomenal level contribute causally to my classifying the overall pattern as belonging to a certain kind.

According to Dretske's version of Direct Realism, the unattended non-conceptual differences in my phenomenal consciousness are qualities of the physical carpet that I experience without realizing it. On Sellars's Critical Realism, these differences are differences at the level of inner phenomenal, or sensory, states, which mediate my classification of the overall type of pattern. On both accounts, my concepts relate directly only to some of the differences in features of the physical object. I can take in the broad features of the carpet, by noting its general colour and shape, and so on; and I can also attend to and grasp a selected few of the fine differences of detail. But since my capacity to attend to the details of what is present at the phenomenal level is limited, it is impossible for me to take in all the detail at once. I do not conceptualize every detail of what is present in a phenomenal nonconceptual sense.

Nevertheless, the detailed elements present at a phenomenal level in experience *collectively contribute* to informing my conceptual representation of the whole, without each individual element being separately conceptualized *qua* separate element. This view is supported by recent psychological work on vision, which indicates that subjects can rapidly absorb the gist and layout of a scene, without necessarily discerning each distinct element as such.[9] Purely *phenomenal* (non-conceptual) awareness is not the same as *perceptual* (conceptualized) awareness, nor need they be strictly correlated.

There are, therefore, good reasons for holding that the subject need not be aware in a *conceptual* sense of all the visible features of the objects they see, and which give rise to differences in their consciousness at the non-conceptual phenomenal level. The *modest* version of conceptualism need only be committed to the following claim: the features of the physical scene that are currently *perceptually* discriminated by the subject are discriminated by virtue of the fact that the subject is exercising some (perhaps low-level) classificatory concept. In order to give sense to his general position, the modest conceptualist must acknowledge that there should be some, at least indirect, evidence for the existence of unconceptualized features present at the *phenomenal* level; but this evidence need not take the form of the simultaneous employment of concepts in respect of *all* of those features. It can be cashed out by reference to dispositional claims about what the subject could come to conceptualize under different slightly circumstances, when for example, attending differently. The position also does not rule out the additional claim that experiences are only discriminated because they also involve a further aspect, namely, differences in their intrinsic phenomenal content. The critical claim is that such phenomenal content can only be discriminated through the exercise of concepts of some kind.

So the claim that all experiences involve concepts is a minimal claim in two senses. First, as indicated in the preceding chapter, the use of 'concept' here implies only that some kind of, at least low-level, concepts are exercised. The subject need not have any of the higher level capacities associated with the employment of concepts in a full sense. The subject can see and classify things into kinds, without necessarily being able to draw inferences from the way she classifies what she sees. Second, the subject need not classify *every* aspect of what is present in a phenomenal manner in her consciousness. The exercise of some kind of classificatory component in experience is necessary for full perceptual consciousness, but it is not necessary that each and every aspect that is immediately present at a phenomenal nonconceptual level is separately conceptualized. Nor, indeed, is it clear that this would be an intelligible requirement, since it is arguable that such conceptualization, if it covered all relational aspects of the phenomenal component, would be potentially unlimited.

2   An objection to the role of concepts

This minimal account of the role of concepts has been challenged recently by David Smith. Smith attacks what he terms 'conceptualism', a thesis he characterizes as follows:

> ... the claim that every perception, as such, necessarily involves the exercise of some concept, and that it is only in virtue of this that perception is anything more than mere sensation.[10]

In objecting to this view, Smith argues that 'concepts are simply irrelevant to perception as such. ... they are irrelevant to the intentionality of perception, to its basic world-directedness'. Smith claims that features can still be 'perceptually registered' – which implies being in the subject's consciousness – even if the subject is not able to classify them in any way conceptually. According to Smith, ' ... our senses themselves are competent to direct us intentionally to the world, independently of the offices of the understanding or intellect.'[11]

Smith claims that conceptualism, when interpreted to refer to concepts in the 'low' sense adopted here, is ' ... either incoherent, or empty and unilluminating.'[12] In defending the Sellarsian model, I shall acquit the low account of concepts of the charge of incoherence. I shall also show why the position is not empty and unilluminating, but in fact supports an important insight into the most fundamental way that we classify our experiences.

Smith rejects even the *modest* version of low-conceptualism. He therefore objects to the weak thesis 'that in order to perceive you need to possess at least one concept'.[13] Smith accepts that perceptual experiences contain, minimally, phenomenal, or sensory, qualities. But, he claims, perceptual consciousness does not result from the integration of phenomenal qualities with concepts of any kind. I now show why Smith's argument fails. We can defend a modest low-conceptualism.

Smith's central criticism of conceptualism is connected with what has become known as the problem of the 'fine-grained' nature of experience. His argument is based upon two claims that, in themselves, are very plausible. The first is that the exercise of a genuine concept must involve a recognitional capacity. To have a concept of a given perceptible kind F means being able to recognize, on separate occasions, things belonging to that kind as the 'same again', independently of any sample. This means that we cannot defend conceptualism by appeal to the exercise of perceptual-demonstrative concepts expressed in such terms as 'that shade', in explaining our perceptual discrimination. Our grasp of 'that shade' is tied to the present experience, and is too short-lived, and so lacks the independence required for the operation of a genuine concept.[14]

The second claim is that, as a matter of basic empirical fact, our ability to make fine-grained discriminations of features such as colour shades far outstrips our ability to grasp determinate shades and recognize them as the same again after a discernible interval of time, even when we interpret this grasp according to the low-conceptualist view. The reason is that the number of genuine concepts I can grasp relating to fine differences in shades of red is restricted by the capacity of my memory. Human beings simply do not have sufficient low-level, recognitional conceptual capacities corresponding to the several million colour shades that we can discriminate.[15] Smith therefore concludes that because we don't have enough colour shade concepts, we cannot be employing genuine concepts in perceptually discriminating between fine grain differences of colour shades: low-conceptualism collapses into incoherence.

3 Hybrid relational concepts

However, Smith's argument involves a *non sequitur*. Smith, along with others who have discussed this topic, overlooks an important category of concepts. These are *hybrid relational* concepts that have both demonstrative and recognitional aspects. It is true that we do not have genuine recognitional concepts corresponding to all the fine distinctions we can discriminate at the phenomenal level in experience. But it is invalid to conclude from this fact that we therefore cannot be employing *any* recognitional concepts at all when we directly respond to phenomenal experience. We can, and do, exercise recognitional concepts in making discriminations of the fine-grained phenomenal differences in experience, without those concepts corresponding to the differences in a one-to-one fashion.

The concepts we employ in making fine-grained discriminations are not concepts of *monadic* qualities. We exercise more general concepts of certain kinds of qualitative differences. These are *relational* concepts that have demonstrative aspects, but are nevertheless also genuinely recognitional. In order to illustrate this, consider a subject S who visually distinguishes two patches of slightly different shades of red, the situation being partly described as follows:

(1) S has a phenomenal experience of a patch of Red_{31} to the left of a patch of (the slightly different shade) Red_{32}.

The subject will subsequently be unable to identify either of the precise shades of red displayed. So in visually discriminating the shades, the subject does not appeal to specific *monadic* colour shade recognitional concepts. But, pace Smith, the subject still exercises a conceptual ability, and discriminates the shades by employing a *relational* concept with a genuinely recognitional element:

[this ...] has a slightly different shade of colour from [that ...]

This type of relational concept has both recognitional and demonstrative components. It incorporates a demonstrative component, because its use is essentially tied to what is present in experience as a phenomenal non-conceptual constituent. To illustrate this, suppose I claim, 'This cherry, on the plate alongside several other cherries, is a slightly darker red than the others.' Someone now shakes the plate, so that the cherries move around. I am able to keep track of and select the cherry I have identified. I distinguish it as an individual by virtue of its spatial boundaries and location. But what essentially matters in keeping track of it, so that know it is the same cherry that I originally identified, is that I can recognize the slight difference in shade that is manifested in my experience of the cherries – I can identify the cherry that is darker than the others. In so far as my use of 'this' connects with an ability to locate the cherry in space, my use conforms to Evans's requirements for demonstrative identification.[16] But the hybrid relational concept also has a genuinely recognitional aspect. In exercising it, I make use of an ability that, of its nature, I am able to exercise again in distinguishing between *other pairs* of slightly different shades.

Thus the subject who visually discriminated Red_{31} from Red_{32} can go on to apply the same relational concept to a distinct phenomenal array, containing different shades:

(2) S has a phenomenal experience of a patch of Red_{33} to the left of a patch of Red_{34}.

The subject can employ the concept of *slightly different shade* to distinguish between any number of pairs of shades. This relational concept is distinct from the concepts of *slightly different size*, or *very different shade*.

Relational concepts of this kind are genuinely recognitional; they are not anchored by any particular current experience. The same hybrid relational concept can apply to quite different pairs of items, which have different phenomenal characteristics. It is arguable that such concepts constitute the most fundamental of the concepts we employ in acting upon the world.[17] Typically, the use of such recognitional relational concepts helps us keep track of one amongst a number of closely resembling items. The exercise of this ability allows us to discriminate items even though we may be unable to exercise one-place property concepts in respect of any determinate colour shade.

Smith attacks the two component theory of experience because he does not think that our conceptual grasp can do justice to the appreciation of fine-grain differences at the phenomenal level. This objection overlooks the way that we exercise relational concepts. Their use explains how the fine detail present at the lower, phenomenal level is integrated with the exercise of conceptual or classificatory abilities at a higher cognitive level. Perceptual discrimination must involve the exercise of at least some genuinely recognitional, low-level concepts. How, otherwise, would the subject be able to appreciate the way in which the particular object that they are attending to differs from others in the environment, so that they are able to act upon it?

The fact that we employ recognitional relational concepts vindicates Sellars's two component analysis of experience. However, it provides no support for the *strong* conceptualist position that is the converse of Smith's, and which is advocated by McDowell. Such recognitional relational concepts have a demonstrative element, as noted above. But their employment presupposes that the phenomenal aspects of experience are antecedently available.[18] They are exercised upon the phenomenal nonconceptual component of conscious experience, a component that has a *complementary* nature. Concepts, understood as abilities, are essentially dispositional, and thus contrast with the phenomenal aspects of experience, which involve phenomenal qualities that are actually present.[19]

A subject cannot apply a hybrid concept such as 'lighter than' unless there are elements present in their experience that they can demonstratively single out and compare. Such elements have to be present at the phenomenal nonconceptual level. In exercising the relational concept of *lighter than* the subject is disposed to act in various ways so as to respond selectively to the objects experienced as present in his or her environment. For such reasons, according to Sellars, there must be a component in perceptual consciousness which is, in McDowell's terminology, 'below the line', that is, nonconceptual.[20]

On the modest conceptualist view – in contrast to the strong conceptualist position – there will be many aspects present at the phenomenal level that are not taken up conceptually by the subject. If a presentation of the two different pairs of situations (1) and (2) above is made sequentially, separated by a brief flicker, as in Change Blindness experiments, the subject will not realize that their overall experience of the first pair of shades, Red_{31} and Red_{32}, differs from their overall experience of the second pair, Red_{33} and Red_{34}. From the subject's point of view, it will seem as if there are two identical presentations of the *same* pair of closely resembling red shades. This point might seem superficially to lend support to McDowell's account, in which he claims, ' ... we must not suppose that receptivity makes an even notionally separable contribution to its co-operation with spontaneity'.[21] Thus, according to McDowell, there would be no conscious difference *of any kind* between the subject's experiences on the two occasions, because the same concept is applied in each case (even though the experiences might be individuated by reference to external differences, these would not be available subjectively).

There are, however, reasons for rejecting McDowell's position, since there are arguments that suggest we should distinguish between the two experiences. The difference in visual input from the distinct pairs of shades provides indirect grounds for claiming that there are differences in the subject's overall conscious experience of the two successive displays, even though she may not be fully aware of such differences at the conceptual level. Such differences are grounded in the different *phenomenal* nonconceptual awareness of the shades present in experience, caused by differences in input.

Notice, moreover, that when all four slightly different shades, Red_{31}, Red_{32}, Red_{33} and Red_{34}, are brought together in the *same* display at a subsequent stage, the subject will then able to discriminate them all from each other, again by using the same hybrid relational recognitional concept that demonstratively refers to the shades of the objects perceived. The different objective shades physically present are causally responsible for subjective, phenomenal differences in experience. But *until* all four shades are brought together in the same display, the subject does not appreciate that there are two different pairs of shades – four shades to be distinguished, not simply the same two. The subject lacks the resources to conceptualize each shade independently when the four different shades are presented as separate pairs, but once they are displayed simultaneously within one conscious experience, the subject is then able to notice the nonconceptual phenomenal differences in shade – by using relational concepts. This again strongly suggests that such phenomenal differences can exist in consciousness, even when not taken up at the conceptual level.[22]

What I have called the modest conceptualist position therefore offers a natural explanation of facts about our grasp of the fineness of grain in experience, and provides a satisfactory way of avoiding the extreme positions of Smith and McDowell. It is not an unilluminating thesis. It explains the fundamental fact that I can know that I am aware of fine differences in my experience, without implying that I must possess recognitional concepts for every difference in shade and shape that I can discern. It supports the central Sellarsian insight that in order for me to be consciously aware of anything, I need to be conceptually aware of kinds; the appeal to the primitive hybrid relational concepts of differences explains such awareness. I conclude therefore that the Sellarsian two-component analysis of experience is correct. We are entitled to claim that all experiences have a conceptual component, in addition to the phenomenal component.

4 The Critical Realist analysis of perception

With the defence of the two-component analysis of *perceptual experience* completed, we are now in a position to make a preliminary appraisal of the Critical Realist analysis of the overall nature of perception. Critical Realism is a version of the causal theory of perception. According to the Critical Realist, we can provide something approaching an analysis of what it is to see a physical object along the following lines:

At a first approximation, a subject S sees a physical object X, if and only if:

(1) X exists

(2) S has an inner visual experience E, comprising:
    (a) a visual phenomenal state
    (b) a perceptual taking, an episode that involves the exercise of concepts.

(3) The object X causes E, in the appropriate manner for seeing.

Let me make clear straight away that at this stage I am concerned with the broad outlines of the analysis, and not with the specific details. There is much in the above set of conditions that could be developed further. In particular, there are complex issues about the way the concepts exercised in perceptual experience relate to the category of object seen. Clearly, I can be said to see an object even if I do not recognize what kind it belongs to. A child seeing an elephant for the first time sees the elephant, even if that child does not know what an elephant is, or even that it is an animal. I may be said to see a horse at dusk, even if I take it to be a cow, or a bush. All I am committed to here is the claim that subject must exercise some concept in relation to the object seen.[23]

It is also true that we often speak of perceiving things other than physical objects. We can be said to see physical events such as explosions and car-crashes; we can also see rainbows, shadows, holes in the ground, the joy or sadness in a person's expression, and so on. I shall assume that the analysis of such cases can be derived in fairly obvious ways from the paradigm situation of perceiving a physical object situated somewhere in the subject's surroundings; and for the most part I shall concentrate on the central type of case of seeing physical objects such as apples, trees, juggling balls, rivers, clouds, humans, dogs and other animals, and the like.

A more serious issue for the analysis concerns the well-known difficulty about what it means for an object to cause an experience in the manner that is *appropriate* for seeing. This raises the issue of how we can avoid the problem of deviant, or non-standard chains, without introducing a circularity into the analysis. This issue, and other deeper problems that relate to the overall form of the analysis, and in particular the central claim that the experience is an inner state, distinct from the perceived object, are what really matter in the analysis of perception.

The two-component analysis of experience defended by the Critical Realist explains much about perception that would otherwise be problematic. But the causal structure of the overall analysis of perception also gives rise to a number of well-known criticisms. These objections to the analysis come from different directions. The five main objections I shall focus on in this work are as follows:

(1) The ontological objection

According to this objection, phenomenal experiences are not inner states. The claim is that the Direct Realist is right to hold that perception involves some kind of direct relation to the object perceived. In so far as the subject is aware of phenomenal properties in experience, in the normal case these belong to the physical objects in the subject's surroundings. The redness of the apple I see is a sensible quality of the apple, and not a quality in my mind.

This ontological objection is said by some to be supported by scientific considerations. According to the enactive approach to perception, and the related sensorimotor views, perception is direct – it involves the direct pickup of information that is out there in the environment; it is a way of exploring the environment. An alternative way of expressing the view is to say that perceiving does not consist in having inner states, but instead is something we *do*, it is a 'species of skilful bodily activity'.[24] It is a mistake, according to this approach, to attempt to 'decompose' perception into a series of causally linked, separate stages, involving an inner experience. Perceiving is inextricably connected with action.

(2) The conceptual objection

If we analyse perception as involving a separate inner experience, distinct from the object perceived, then we run into serious difficulties in trying to analyse the nature of perception. The specific problem lies in trying to fit the components back together again, once we have separated the process into distinct stages. According to causal accounts, the particular object perceived is that which produces an inner experience, one that in some way matches that object. There are, however, well known problems for causal accounts, which arise when we try to specify, without circularity, exactly what type of causal connection links the subject with the perceptual object. Providing a precise list of sufficient conditions for perceiving has been a major hurdle for causal accounts of perception. So the objection is that once we have separated the perceptual object from the subject's experience, we cannot bring them back together again.

(3) The phenomenological objection

An important issue in perception theory, and one that has recently become a focus of attention, concerns the claim that perceptual experiences are 'transparent'. This claim, which goes back at least to Moore, arises in part from phenomenological considerations. In normal perceptual situations, we do not need to make inferences about the sensible qualities of the objects we perceive. Objects, and their qualities, are simply presented to us directly in experience. Hence, the objection runs, postulating an inner phenomenal experience as an essential stage in perception, a stage that is distinct from the perceptual object, cannot be right.

(4) The semantic objection

On the basis of our perceptual experiences, we succeed in making demonstrative judgements that refer directly to physical objects. But if experiences involve inner, phenomenal states of the subject's mind, how is that possible? The semantic objection is that a causal account of experience renders direct reference to external objects impossible, because we can only refer to what is made directly available in experience.

(5) The epistemic objection

The final major objection to Critical Realism is that, because it is a causal theory, it allows the possibility that our experiences may not faithfully reflect the nature of reality. If our experiences are distinct from the objects that cause them, it may be that there are no external objects corresponding to them. So the objection is that the theory can lead to scepticism about the external world.

The plan of the remainder of this book is as follows. In Chapters 3, 4 and 5, I discuss the ontological objection. Direct Realism is often assumed to be something like a *default position* in perception, a position we have to adopt because all the other positions encounter insuperable difficulties. The idea is that on the Direct Realist account, we are able to avoid all the objections raised above. This thought, however, turns out to be an illusion, as is the assumption that common sense supports the Direct Realist view. Direct Realism is a philosophical chimera. In what I refer to as the 'core argument', I show that the Direct Realist view cannot be given any positive content; we can make no *sense* of the position, neither in its philosophical garb, nor in its more scientific versions. Direct Realism is not false; it is incoherent. The upshot of this is that some version of the causal theory of perception is necessary.

In the second half of this book I show how a causal theory of perception is possible. A Critical Realist version allows satisfactory answers to the objections listed above. In Chapter 6, I explain, first, why causality is essentially bound up with our understanding of what perception is. In Chapter 7, I develop what I term a 'navigational theory' of perceiving, and show how the common-sense, scientific and philosophical understanding of perception all relate to the same underlying conception of perceiving as a *dynamic* process, which enables a creature to move around its world, and to carry out extended sequences of planned actions. Through empirical investigation, we can discover the nature of actual processes involved. We can therefore in principle produce a sufficient set of conditions for perceiving an object, for any given perceiver. This allows a solution to the problem of deviant causal chains.

In Chapters 8 and 9, I take up the phenomenological objection, and show why perceptual experience is only partly transparent. These chapters in some ways form the heart of the book. I consider in turn a number of disparate non-standard perceptual phenomena, and, for each case, I explain how the subject's inner phenomenal state is unified with concepts exercised directly about the objects in the environment, through the use of the imagination. It is then shown how this same unifying process integrates our inner phenomenal states with the concepts we exercise when perceiving external objects normally. The account explains why the Critical Realist view is not at odds with our common-sense views about the nature of perception.

In Chapter 10, I focus mainly upon the semantic objection, and show why the Critical Realist view does not render impossible demonstrative judgements aimed directly at external objects. I also discuss briefly the epistemic objection, which raises issues of a rather different order from the remaining objections. I argue first, that Critical Realism, unlike other versions of the causal theory, is not committed to a foundationalist theory of knowledge. Second, I suggest that when it comes to problems connected with scepticism, the Critical Realist view is no worse off than the rival Direct Realist position. As indicated at the beginning of this work, epistemic issues are relatively independent of the metaphysical issues concerning the proper analysis of perception.

3 Hallucinations, illusions and the challenge of metaphysical scepticism

1 The causal-scientific argument against Direct Realism

According to Critical Realism, in veridical perception the subject's conscious experience is an inner state that is distinct from the perceived object. In seeing a beech tree in full leaf, the phenomenal qualities I am aware of, such as the irregular green shape in my experience, mediate my perceptual thoughts about the tree I see before me. This general treatment of perception contrasts with the position termed 'Direct Realism', which has been the subject of several recent defences.[1] According to Direct Realism, perception should not be analysed along the lines proposed by the causal theorist, as involving an inner experience: perception involves a direct relation between the subject and the perceived object. Perceptual experience is transparent. There are no intermediary entities, such as sense data or sense-impressions, intervening between the subject and what is perceived. In cases of genuine perception, it is the physical object itself, or some fact involving the physical object, that is immediately present to the perceiver.

Suppose I am seeing a tree. For the Direct Realist, perceptual experience does not merely involve thoughts and concepts directly related to the tree I see; it also involves a direct phenomenal awareness of that very tree, and of the greenness of its leaves. According to McDowell's disjunctive version, in veridical perception ' … the object itself is presented to one's awareness.'[2] Admittedly, subjects are capable of having other types of experience, for example when they hallucinate, and such experiences are in principle qualitatively indistinguishable from the experiences that occur in veridical perception. But the fact of such qualitative likeness should not obscure the point that not all experiences belong to the same ontological type. There is, McDowell expresses the point, no 'highest common factor' that is shared by both cases of hallucination and veridical perception. The common aspect of hallucination and perception is not ontological, but *epistemic* – it consists only in the fact that from the subject's point of view there can, in principle, be a perfect similarity in how things appear.[3] Veridical perception should not be considered, in the way that Descartes and other causal theorists think of it, as a process built up from materials already present in hallucination.

In this chapter and the following I will explore a line of argument that I shall refer to as 'the core argument', which supports the Critical Realist interpretation of experience. I shall begin with some reflections on the comparison between veridical and hallucinatory experience. There is a long scientific tradition that treats perception as comprising a series of stages, which in outline goes back to Descartes's work in *The Optics*. The idea on this view is that perception is a causal process, connecting the physical object in the environment to neural events in the perceiver's brain, and ultimately to an *inner* state of consciousness. In veridical perception, the subject is in a state of conscious awareness that is distinct from the perceived object. The proximal cause of the conscious state of awareness is the subject's brain state.[4]

The central idea on this causal-scientific account of perception is that when the subject has a visual experience, which includes an awareness of phenomenal qualities, this experience is either identical with, or supervenes upon, the subject's brain state, or at least upon her bodily state alone. The brain state, and hence the visual experience, is indirectly caused by the perceived object, and is independent from it. But since all that is required to bring about that experience is the proximal brain state, it must be considered as a distinct occurrence from the distal object perceived. Perception, on this account, should be interpreted as a series of stages which select, refine, organize and transmit information about the physical objects in the subject's vicinity, information that is taken up in neural processes at the sub-personal level and, depending upon the perceiver's attentional set, results finally in beliefs at the personal level about the kinds of objects that are physically present, and about their location relative to the perceiver.

This way of looking at experience is supported by common-sense facts about hallucination, as Valberg and Robinson have argued. We know from our own subjective point of view that hallucinations can occur which are in principle indistinguishable from veridical experiences. Bodily states, independent of any particular external physical objects, are sufficient for experiences *as of* physical objects. It therefore follows that if we take away the distal cause of the brain state that occurs in ordinary perception, and replace it by some quite other kind of cause, then – provided that the proximal brain state is unchanged – the subject will continue to have an experience that is of the same intrinsic type as the veridical experience that she was having.[5] This fact, in conjunction with the causal story that scientific experimentation reveals about the perceptual systems, points to the conclusion that veridical and hallucinatory states belong to a common kind. They are both inner states, and differ merely in their causal ancestry.

2 A possible response: two levels of description

Persuasive as the above line of argument is, I am not assuming at this stage that it is water-tight. I will shortly examine it in more detail, and develop it in a way that I believe does, however, provide a conclusive argument against Direct Realism. Before embarking upon this task, and making some necessary clarificatory remarks, there is one important kind of response that I need to mention first. Many writers have argued that the causal argument sketched out above trades upon a confusion of personal and sub-personal levels. Hurley, for example, warns against a simple mapping of what goes on in experience at a personal level, at the level at which we can ascribe conscious states to ourselves, and the sub-personal processes involved in physical input to the sense organs.[6] Hurley is right to point out that there is no simple correlation between *perceptual input* and the perceiver's experience. But that is not what a defender of the causal argument should claim. For a number of reasons, the same input can lead to different neural states, and hence to different phenomenal states; moreover, the same phenomenal state can be conceptualized in a variety of different ways. The important correlation is between the subject's *neural state*, on the one hand, and the *phenomenal* component of experience, on the other. There is strong empirical evidence from brain imaging experiments for such a correlation.[7]

Nevertheless, it is plausible to claim that we employ a different conceptual framework when speaking of what takes place in a subject's conceptualized consciousness, in contrast to the framework we use in speaking about what takes place in the brain. So one response to the Valberg-Robinson argument can be formulated in this way: the physical distinction between the external object and the subject's brain states is of no relevance to the account we give of the place of the perceived object in conscious experience. The conceptualized experiences occurring in normal perception, at the personal level, give us an immediate awareness of physical objects. The disjunctivist version of Direct Realism defended by John McDowell and others is connected with this idea. McDowell argues that we need to distinguish two different logical spaces: 'the logical space of reasons and justification' and 'the logical space of causal relations to objects, and the realm of law'.[8] In seeing an object, there is no conscious experience in the inner, mediating sense. Experience should be conceived as openness to the world: 'we, and our seeing, do not stop anywhere short of the fact'.[9] I shall return to this particular claim subsequently.

According to the Direct Realist, when I see a tree, *this* experience that I have involves the tree *directly*, as a necessary part. The experience should not be conceived of as a separate entity *contingently* related to the tree via a chain of causal intermediaries; my veridical experience involves the very tree itself, as a constituent. If I had been hallucinating, this very experience could not have existed, even though some other qualitatively similar experience might have done. Perceiving is an unanalysable relation holding directly between physical objects and experiences; it cannot be divided into discrete stages. The causal story is simply inappropriate to the story we tell at the level of an experiencing self.

The Direct Realist can concede that from the perceiver's subjective standpoint, hallucinatory and perceptual experiences may be indistinguishable.[10] It is only if we grant an at least close subjective similarity between hallucinatory and veridical experiences that we can make sense of the fact that we are able to describe qualitative *kinds* of hallucinatory experiences, by reference to the type of physical situation that normally produces the corresponding veridical experience that is subjectively like it. Importantly, we classify the phenomenal component of veridical and hallucinatory experiences by appealing to the common content that, in principle, they can share.

Nevertheless, according to the Direct Realist, sentences involving the term 'looks' and its cognates, when used to describe the phenomenal aspects of experience, are made true by two different categories of states of affairs, even though epistemically the subject may not be in a position to tell them apart.[11] The phenomenal aspects of experiences that belong in different categories can give rise to the similar descriptions. Consider a claim such as 'There looks to be a red patch on the wall in front of me'. In the hallucinatory case, the description is made true by the existence of a subjective experience, perhaps an after-image. In the veridical (and, perhaps, the illusory cases), where there is a physical object seen, what grounds the truth of the description is the immediate presence of the physical object itself. In ontological terms, phenomenal experiences differ radically.

The Direct Realist is therefore committed to a general distinction between a *qualitative* sense of 'experience', and an *ontological* sense: we need a way of characterizing the phenomenal nonconceptual component of experience which, in the light of the indistinguishability mentioned above, leaves open the question whether the experience is hallucinatory or veridical. In speaking of experiences in an ontologically neutral sense, I shall speak of 'the *qualitative* character' of experience, in describing the qualities of the phenomenal component that the subject is immediately aware of in having an experience. This is intended to contrasts with talk of 'the *ontological nature*' of experience, where the description entails an essential commitment to the ontological status of the individual entity involved in the experience.[12] Thus the mere claim that the subject has 'a qualitative experience of something red', leaves it open whether the phenomenal character described belongs to an inner state, such as an after-image, or (if the Direct Realist is correct) an external object or feature, such as the red surface of an apple, which is immediately present in the subject's consciousness as a result of the perceiver standing in a direct visual relation to the external physical object. This distinction between the two conceptions of experience appealed to here is compatible with the separate point defended in Chapter 1, that a subject may make an error of a different kind about their own experience, if they fail to *notice* some qualitative aspect of the phenomenal experience.[13]

By invoking the above distinction between qualitative and ontological senses of characterizations of experience, the disjunctivist is able to resist the causal theorist's claim that all experiences must belong to the same ontological category, and are inner experiences. The disjunctivist's reply thus relies on the following principle:

> *The Qualitative Indistinguishability Principle*: The qualitative character of the subject's experience does not, in itself, imply anything about the ontological nature of that experience; in particular, sameness of experience in the qualitative sense does not guarantee sameness of experience in the ontological sense.

On the basis of this principle, the Direct Realist can claim that two experiences may be indistinguishable because they appear qualitatively the same, yet one of them could be an inner experience, and the other a non-inner experience, involving the very physical object that is immediately perceived.[14] I shall return to an important consequence of *The Qualitative Indistinguishability Principle* in the following chapter.

Although it appears that the Direct Realist can in this way form some sort of counter to the causal argument, the price he has to pay is high, and it leaves him with two interconnected problems. He needs to provide a *positive* account of the unique relation that holds between the subject's perceptual experience and the physical object perceived, and he also needs to explain what kind of evidence we have for the existence of such a unique relation, evidence that would rule out the type of causal analysis that the Critical Realist upholds.

It is important to realize here what is essential to the Direct Realist view is not the mere fact that there are two levels of description of the perceptual process. The Critical Realist can also accept a distinction between personal and sub-personal levels of description. The crucial element in the Direct Realist view is the resulting conception of experience as '*non-inner*', as a state that includes the object perceived. Unless this conception of perceptual experiences can be explicated, the appeal to different levels of description is not going to help the Direct Realist.

According to the Critical Realist, distinguishing between the personal-level account, at which we speak of the subject's conscious experience, and a sub-personal level at which we refer to mere brain activity, is perfectly compatible with a causal account of perception. The Critical Realist will argue that the experience occurring at the conscious level is self-contained, in the following sense: my perceptual experience, when I veridically see the tree, is a state such that, if it does in some way necessitate the existence of anything physical, includes at most just those proximal physical parts of my brain causally necessary for an experience of that kind. The experience I have of the tree is still a distinct existence from the actual tree in my surroundings, just as a hallucinatory experience is.

The Critical Realist holds, also, that it is unclear what it could *mean* to claim that my experience also includes other physical states or events which extend further back along the causal chain to the external object. All we need to say in order to account for veridical perception is that the experience is caused to come about by the external object (in the appropriate way). The causation of visual experiences is analogous (as Descartes pointed out) to the manner in which pains are caused to come about by external objects, although the kind of concepts exercised differ. To explain why a given experience counts as perceptual requires that we make reference to the perceived object and its causal role in producing the experience. But in accounting for the nature of the experience, *qua* experience of a general type, we need only refer to the proximal brain state.

The Direct Realist's denial of the causal analysis of the perceiving therefore amounts to the claim that perception involves a unique, primitive, and unanalysable relation holding directly between the subject's consciousness and the physical object he perceives. The problem that confronts the Direct Realist is whether we can make sense of such a relation.

3   Can there be complex indiscriminible hallucinatory phenomena?

Before turning to the core argument, there is a different kind of objection to the causal argument we must consider. Certain writers – such as, for example, Noë – have rejected the basis of the causal argument, the claim that veridical experiences and hallucinations can be at least qualitatively indistinguishable. His objection is that the types of experiences that supervene upon the brain alone are at best impoverished, sketchy, and lacking in detail. It is very unlikely, he asserts, that such internally generated experiences can match the rich complex experiences typical of normal perception.[15]

Noë provides two main sets of reasons for this negative thesis. First, he claims that there is little empirical evidence in support of the claim that veridical and hallucinatory experiences can be identical. Second, he claims that there is evidence suggesting that complex visual experiences physically require temporally extended interactions between the subject and their environment: perceptual experience is produced by a tight coupling with the environment. Noë claims, 'Experience isn't something that happens in us. It is something we do, it is a temporally extended process of skilful probing.'[16] I shall consider Noë's positive views about the nature of seeing in Chapter 5. Here I concentrate upon his scepticism about the possibility of complex hallucinations.

Dreams, according to Noë, provide no support for the qualitative indistinguishability claim. Dream sequences are poor in detail, and lack stability. These points may be conceded. Yet, surprisingly, Noë does not consider the much more compelling evidence based upon the phenomena of hallucinations. Noë's consideration of hallucinations goes only as far as a brief discussion of the simple kinds of hallucinations that have been generated by external stimulation in experimental conditions. He states:

We are now able to produce very simple sensations such as the illusion of the presence of flashes of light by means of direct neural stimulation ... At the present time, however, we are not able to generate directly more complicated experiences.[17]

In fact Noë's claim on this point seems to be contradicted by the work of Penfield and his associates. Complex visual and auditory hallucinations can be produced by stimulating the different parts of the brain.[18] In any event, the kinds of experiences we are presently able to produce by using a few electrical probes tells us little about the way that visual hallucinations depend upon the brain. One might, analogously, try to argue that no computer could play chess well, because we cannot create a good chess playing program in one simply by poking the insides with a screwdriver. It is very likely that complex visual hallucinations depend upon complex patterns of correlated activity in different regions of the brain. It is of no significance that we are at present unable to produce complex hallucinations in subjects, given the limitations of our current knowledge of the workings of the visual system in the brain. What has much more relevance to the argument is that the brain is capable of producing spontaneous hallucinatory experiences, resulting from internal activity alone.

There is now extensive evidence for the existence of complex visual hallucinations, sometimes known as the Charles Bonnet Syndrome (CBS). Such complex hallucinations, which may be of rich and detailed scenes, often arise in otherwise normal patients who have suffered some deterioration in their vision. Strangely, Noë fails to address this important phenomenon. Hallucinations occur with various degrees of complexity. Fairly simple hallucinations include the visual aura that are usually associated with migraine, but which can also occur independently. These often take the form of bright spots, flashes, and geometrical forms, one common pattern being referred to as 'fortifications' in virtue of its zigzag shape. Even such geometrical visual disturbances have a degree of complexity.

Typical descriptions refer to such aura as 'scintillating', or 'shimmering'. These scintillations occur at the rate of around 10 flickers a second. A typical pattern of aura takes the form of a scintillating crescent-shaped boundary that enlarges gradually, usually over a period of about twenty minutes to half an hour, and eventually disappears off the periphery of the visual field. Because the change in size is gradual, at any moment the overall shape may appear fixed relative to the visual field. When the disturbance is located centrally it is hard to avoid attending to it, and reading or similar pursuits can be difficult or impossible; sometimes it is accompanied by loss of vision in part of the visual field. As the aura moves away to the side, direct attention to the crescent shape becomes difficult, although the flickering or shimmering quality still makes it hard to ignore altogether.[19] Oliver Sacks cites a number of descriptions and provides illustration derived from subjects who have experienced them. A paradigmatic account cited by Sacks is the following:

A bright stellate object, a small angled sphere, suddenly appears on one side of the combined field. ... it rapidly enlarges, first as a circular zigzag, but on the inner side, towards the medial line, the regular outline becomes faint, and, as the increase in size goes on, the outline here becomes broken, the gap becoming larger as the whole increases, and the original circular outline becomes oval.[20]

Such migraine aura tend to be fairly simple. But more complex hallucinations also occur. Patients who suffer from CBS hallucinations may experience hallucinations varying in richness of detail.[21] Such hallucinatory experiences can have lifelike complexity. They involve the apparent perception of people, buildings, animals and other complex scenes. The current view is that this phenomenon is considerably more widespread than formerly appreciated. CBS hallucinations tend to occur in otherwise completely normal patients suffering from macular degeneration in the eye who, as a result, experience visual deprivation. Since the condition is usually age-related, it tends to occur in elderly people, who are reluctant to report the hallucinations they experience. In their review article of the phenomena, Manford and Andermann cite a number of cases, including a case of one woman patient who hallucinated 'small silent white dogs running around her room'; another patient is described as becoming aware of 'numerous cats. ... They were black or brown and moved silently around the room. One jumped onto his knee and he was able to stroke it; he later recalled the sensation of its fur.'[22]

There is no doubt that such complex hallucinatory phenomena do occur. One recent attempt to construct a classificatory schema for complex hallucinatory and related illusory phenomena provides evidence of their dependence on increased neurophysiological activity. Having drawn attention to the range of complex visual hallucinations, the authors conclude:

> The classification is not intended to be complete and it is descriptive rather than explanatory. We hope that it provides a theoretical framework of use to both clinicians and neuroscientists and that the spectrum of disorders we have described will begin to be recognized as *common clinical findings* rather than rare neurological and neuropsychiatric curiosities.[23] (My italics)

In sum, there is overwhelming evidence for the existence of complex hallucinations. The proximate, and sufficient, causes of these appear to be complex neurological activity inside the subject's brain. In many cases, the context may make it apparent to subjects that what they appear to be experiencing has no real existence as an external physical thing. Nevertheless, on other occasions subjects are uncertain about the status of what they appear to see. Contrary to Noë's claims, the clinical evidence shows that the brain alone can act as the subvening basis for experiences that, in themselves, are qualitatively indistinguishable from veridical experiences. This strongly suggests that perceptual experiences do indeed supervene solely upon what is inside the skull, given the assumption that the same internal mechanisms are involved. Internalism about experience is not a dogma, as Noë claims. On the contrary, it is extremely well supported by the scientific evidence.

4 Background assumptions about perception

In order to set the stage for an examination of the respective merits of Critical and Direct Realism, I first need to clarify certain matters which are broadly agreed to be common ground between them. As Armstrong and others have pointed out, perception is a process, involving the senses, whereby we are enabled to arrive at largely true beliefs about our environment.[24] This does not mean that on every occasion when we perceive something we ineluctably arrive at correct beliefs. Rather, perception is a process that in general leads to knowledge about objects, even if on occasion we may be misled as to the exact nature of our physical surroundings. As it stands, this account of perception is not sufficient, as I shall show in Chapter 6; distance perception is an essentially dynamic process that is integrated with action. It does not merely lead to true belief, but to successful movement through an environment, allowing perceivers to satisfy their needs.

Although it is fairly clear that the end product of perception is *belief* and *action* directed onto some aspect of our environment, it is the nature of the intervening processes making up perceptual *experiences* that constitutes the main problem. Few nowadays would accept Armstrong's analysis solely in terms of beliefs and inclinations to believe: as has been argued, to perceive that something is green is radically different, phenomenologically, from merely thinking or being inclined to believe that something is green. We have argued that this difference shows that there is a distinct phenomenal component in experience. The dispute between the Critical Realist and the Direct Realist concerns the ontological status of this phenomenal component.

Whatever its specific analysis and ontological status, it is in virtue of this phenomenal component that we are entitled to speak of a person seeing an object in something approaching an *extensional* sense. Standing on a hillside and looking at a distant village, I may be aware that there looks, in a phenomenal sense, to be some brown rectangular object present, without realizing what kind of object it is, let alone *which* particular object it happens to be. In such a case it might truly be said of me: 'He sees the house that Bernard Shaw lived in, but does not realize it'. Walking along a country path in a fog, I may see a vague dark shape looming ahead of me, that I take to be a person, when in fact it is a small tree. Such examples, which can be multiplied indefinitely, indicate that a person can properly be said to perceive an object, despite being radically mistaken about its nature. The concepts that the perceiver applies to the object seen do not have to be correct, so long as there is some underlying way in which that object looks to be. For *seeing* to occur, in what I shall take here to be a basic extensional sense, all that is necessary is that the following be the case: first, that the subject must, at most, entertain some minimal conceptual component in experience – perhaps merely to the effect that there is something present in the surroundings; and second, that there be some sort of relation between the phenomenal aspect of the subject's experience and the object perceived, in virtue of which it is correct to say that there is a particular given object which looks a certain way to the subject.[25] Nothing I have said about extensional seeing is intended to prejudge the debate between the Critical Realist and the Direct Realist. What precisely seeing is, in this basic extensional sense, is the problem we are concerned with.

One last set of remarks is necessary before I tackle the main issue with which this chapter is concerned, the debate between the Direct Realist and the Critical Realist. Any putative analysis of our ordinary concept of perception has to conform to certain general constraints.

First, an analysis of perception has to show how the concept that it purports to give an account of can be employed by the layperson. No account can do justice to our understanding of the ordinary concept if it makes direct reference to scientific matters outside the knowledge of the average person. But while this means ruling out the kind of causal account which refers explicitly to detailed physiological and other similar matters, there is no reason why an account cannot make reference to more general causal notions, such as the idea that there should be a causally based functional covariance between the perceiver's experience and the perceived object; moreover, as I shall show in Chapters 6 and 7, there can be indirect arguments for the claim that the concept of perception would be incoherent unless it incorporated some general notion of a causal relation.

Second, an analysis of perception must give some explanation of the fact that someone who understands the concept of a particular sense modality, such as seeing, has a grasp of the sense of the concept by virtue of which its application can be extended to novel situations. If someone claims to have seen an object unfamiliar to me, my understanding of their claim is not in general limited: I know, in principle, how the concept of seeing should be applied in the new situation. The different modes of perception, such as seeing, form kinds, which we can apply to unfamiliar cases.

This principle has an important consequence. If someone says to me that she can see some object – a blade of grass, a nearby bird on a tree, a cloud, or a distant star, I understand her claim to be singling out some particular object as the one seen. Part of what determines which particular object is seen is the fact that the subject distinguishes, through the use of attention, one particular object from an array of objects that she may be perceptually related to. But for present purposes it is not the attentive processes that matter (though in a later chapter we shall be returning to these) but the general difference between those objects which are in experience, so that the subject sees them, and those which are out of view. In knowing what it is for someone to see an object, I know that there is a difference between those objects currently seen, and those objects not seen, because they are not experienced; in principle, I know what this difference consists in. In what follows, I shall for simplicity speak of the perceptual object, as if there is just a single physical object that a person is seeing at any given time. This will make the arguments easier to follow, but will not otherwise affect matters. Knowing what seeing is entails knowing, in principle, what makes it the case that someone is seeing *some particular object* and not another, perhaps similar object, which is hidden.

Finally, a proper analysis of perception must allow that it makes sense to perceive something when suffering a perceptual illusion. If Armstrong's outline account of the notion is accepted as a starting point, illusions clearly fall into the category of perceptual cases, since in nearly all cases of illusion the subject acquires at least some rudimentary knowledge of the environment. As Robinson points out, even if without my glasses everything appears blurred, I am still able to see things in my surroundings, to track those objects I identify in my experience, and so on.[26] Moreover, it should be noted that the line between normal perception and illusion is indeterminate: how, for example, should one classify the fact that distant hills appear bluer than those nearer to the perceiver? There is no clear basis upon which to decide between classifying this case as an illusion, on the grounds that blue would not be the colour seen when close up, or as normal because all things look bluer at a distance.

5 The sceptical challenge

In the light of the above claims, a necessary condition for any adequate account of perception is that it provides an explanation of what it is for a subject to perceive some particular object, rather than the other objects in the surroundings that are out of view. In the extreme case, it should tell us what the difference is between *seeing* something, and merely *hallucinating*. I shall now introduce what I term 'the core argument', which is designed to show that Direct Realism is unable to meet this essential condition.

I propose to put on one side any epistemic doubts about whether there is a physical world, and simply take it for granted that in an ordinary sense physical objects, tables, chairs, trees, earth, and humans and other creatures, and so on, do exist, and that much of the time people do perceive such things. Yet even if we grant all this, there is still a form of metaphysical scepticism that can be raised concerning perception, an examination of which will allow us to take the debate between causal theorist and Direct Realist further, and which should, I suggest, enable us to understand what is problematic about the Direct Realist view.[27]

Imagine a situation as follows. I am standing in an apple orchard with a friend, who has climbed up a ladder and is picking apples. I look up and point to a red apple I see above me, on a branch within her reach, and say something to the following effect:

'I can see a ripe apple at the end of that branch.'

Normally such a claim would strike one as unremarkable; as noted above, our grasp of the concept of perceiving allows us to apply it in an indefinitely large number of ordinary situations. Now, however, let us probe this claim, by envisaging a bizarre sceptic, who questions the claims we make about *which* particular object we are seeing.

The sceptic argues as follows:

> You believe that the question of which object you are now seeing is unproblematic, that you are seeing a particular red apple that is physically located a few feet away, above and ahead of you, within your companion's reach. But *what fact* about your current situation makes it the case that you are indeed seeing *that particular object*? Is this fact based solely upon the nature of your subjective experience? There is a sense, we may allow, in which a person's experience can 'match' an object that can be seen. But there are many red apples in this orchard that look just like the one your friend is about to pick, and any one of them could be said to match your experience. Moreover, as we are all aware, perceptual illusions can occur; so perhaps what you are seeing is not the ripe apple just a few feet in front of you, but another apple, further away and slightly to the left? Yet we know from past experience that illusions can take strange forms – there can be visual illusions of colour, shape and location. If we extrapolate from such possibilities, what prevents us from claiming that you are actually suffering from some very strange illusion? Although it looks to you as if you are seeing something red and round in front of you, perhaps you are actually seeing the blue, oval cushion at the foot of the ladder that your friend is standing on?

In short, the sceptic is suggesting in any situation where someone is held to be perceiving a given nearby object of a certain kind, nothing in the experience or the physical situation rules out the possibility that the object perceived is different from that assumed by common sense. It might be the case that what is perceived is some remote object, of a radically different kind from any of those located in front of the subject.

I will shortly elaborate on this scepticism and consider the different responses it might elicit. But I want to emphasize again the point that the immediate focus of the scepticism is metaphysical, and not epistemic. The sceptic is not *directly* confronting the issue of whether there is a physical world, or whether we are justified in claiming to have knowledge of that world. A sceptical challenge about any philosophical area draws attention to the need for a positive account of the subject matter raised. In the case of metaphysical scepticism, what is required is metaphysical analysis of perception, which accounts for the relevant distinctions between veridical perception, illusion and hallucination.

The main challenge that the sceptic is raising concerns the ontological nature of the seeing relation: *what fact of the matter* about my situation and the way I am placed in the world makes it the case that I am seeing, in a normal way, one particular object X, and not misperceiving some different object Y which happens also to be located somewhere in my surroundings?

Scepticism about which physical object a person is currently perceiving in having an experience bears some similarities to the type of scepticism that Kripke has raised about meaning and rule-following. In Kripke's original discussion there are two aspects to the sceptic's metaphysical challenge. Kripke's sceptic asks, 'What fact about my past use of a word justifies me in using it in a certain way on a future occasion so that such use can be said to be correct or incorrect'.[28] Kripke is raising both a version of the symbol grounding problem – what fixes the extension of a term for an individual at any given time – and also issues of normativity and justification, relating to what determines a person's intention to continue using that term in the same way.[29] A parallel distinction can be advanced in respect of the perceptual case. Thus, arguably, there is a first question about what it is that links a subject's experience with a particular physical object at a certain time, so that he or she is aware in a phenomenal manner of that object, in the basic *extensional* sense discussed earlier. There is a second question about how being the subject of an experience, linked in such a way to the object, makes the subject justified in claiming to have prima facie *perceptual knowledge* about an aspect of the physical world, and justified in classifying the object perceived as belonging to a certain category. As well as such parallels with meaning scepticism, there are also, I believe, some important differences, but I shall not attempt to explore the further question of justification here.[30]

Although the sceptical challenge is of use in highlighting the theoretical requirement that we need to explain what fact of the matter links someone's experience with the perceptual object, it is worth noting that the problem can arise at a practical level. Cases can be constructed where we are apprised of all the facts available at an ordinary common-sense level – facts that are independent of detailed investigation into precise causes – but where it is not possible to say which object the subject perceives:

(1) Looking down into the water at an angle, while drifting in a small boat along the still surface of a shallow lake, I see a single object glinting below. It looks to me as if there is a metal object amongst the stones on the floor of the lake. On diving down, I find several coins. Which one did I see?

(2) I am talking to a colleague in a crowded room full of people. I suddenly hear someone nearby say a word that sounds to me like 'Capablanca', only I am not sure if I hear the word correctly. A film enthusiast nearby was in fact talking about the film *Casablanca*; however there was also a chess expert nearby discussing the world champion who was beaten by Alekhine. Which utterance did I hear?

(3) I am walking in a hot desert, and seem to see a few trees in an oasis far head of me in the shimmering haze. There may be more than one clump of trees in my approximate line of sight. Because of the well-known 'desert-mirage' phenomenon, it is not clear which trees I am actually seeing.

(4) I am in a hall where there are many mirrors, arranged so that multiple reflections of objects are possible. There are also a number of lit candles situated around the hall. Looking in one of the mirrors, I see the flame on one of the candles flicker. It may be very hard for me to work out in practice which candle I am looking at in the mirror.[31]

In none of these cases is it possible to determine which particular object or event is perceived by appealing only to matters that are in principle available to common sense, in the absence of a more detailed investigation into precise causal connections. The overall context, specified in ways that do not refer to causal connections, leaves it open which object is perceived.

6 Answering the sceptical challenge

The sceptic challenges us to say what facts about a perceiver in her surroundings determine *which* of the objects she is seeing. What is required is an account of what I shall term '*the linking fact*', using the word 'fact' in its broadest sense. Let me spell out briefly what the challenge means. The facts that are not in question include the ordinary 'common-sense' physical facts about the nature of the objects in the environment of the subject, and their spatial and causal relations to her body.[32] It may also be agreed that there are facts of some kind which relate to the phenomenal character of the subject's experience, and the subject's perceptual takings. Such facts about perceptual experiences seem to be at the least closely bound up with the subject's brain states. When a subject sees an object, it is physically *necessary* that activity in the brain is involved.[33]

Thus the sceptic is allowing that we may take for granted facts of the following form:

(1) It seems to S, visually, as if there is an object of kind F at some position P relative to S's body.

And

(2) There are objects of various kinds situated at various positions relative to S.

We may assume that the reports that subjects make about their current visual experiences are reasonably reliable. Scepticism about *which* object is experienced is therefore in principle independent of the subject's own point of view. The same problem will arise from the perspective of a third party who is apprised of all the facts about the subjective, qualitative nature of the subject's experience, and also of the objective facts about the subject's bodily state, and the physical objects in the vicinity. So the problem about *which* object is currently perceived by that subject is independent from a particular point of view. It is also independent of general ontology: it arises for dualism as well as for physicalism. The sceptic's claim is that the facts above – described by (1) and (2), on their own – leave open *which* object, if any, S is seeing.[34]

There would appear to be five different possible ways in which one might attempt to ground the claim that a particular object is seen, and explain what it is that constitutes the linking fact:

(1) Some aspect of the conscious perceptual experience itself and the subject's body; in other words, what links the subject to the perceived object is based upon facts about the phenomenal features of experience available, subjectively, from a first-person point of view, or more broadly, upon facts that include some set of properties belonging to the subject's body.

(2) Some set of non-causal features of the subject's physical surroundings, and in particular such matters as the spatial layout of the physical objects relative to the subject's body and, in particular, to the subject's sense-organs.

(3) Some form of conceptual, or logically necessary link, for example, that the subject's overall perceptual experience is necessarily individuated by reference to the physical object that is perceived in having that experience (a claim that might involve externalist considerations).

(4) Some form of intrinsic (and non-causal) connection which links the subject's perceptual experience (including the phenomenal qualities that the subject is conscious of) with the perceived object, in a manner that is metaphysically necessary, such that the existence of the former is dependent on the existence of the latter.[35]

And finally

(5) A certain kind of causal relation linking the perceiver's conscious experience and the physical object seen, which treats the experience as an inner state, having a logically distinct existence from that particular object.[36]

The immediate consequence of the illusory possibilities raised by the sceptic is that the first and second types of fact, even if combined, cannot provide an answer to his challenge. The sceptic's central point can be expressed in the following way. Perceiving an object always involves a 'which' and a 'how': *which* particular object it is that looks some way to S, and *how* the object looks to the subject S (and also where it looks to be). These dimensions of perception can vary independently of each other. The sceptic therefore insists that it is irrelevant how the object appears to the subject; the qualities of which she is conscious in experience do not determine which particular object is seen. Nor will any appeal simply to the way physical objects are located in relation to the subject help matters, because of the possibility of illusions.

Many accounts of perception overlook this elementary point. Alan White, in reply to Grice's original article, claimed:

> ... the existence of an X and the fact that it looks to me as if there were an X or as if there were other than an X provide the necessary and sufficient conditions of my seeing an X.[37]

In the light of the sceptical view outlined above, these facts clearly do no such thing.

The straightforward informational account at one stage offered by Dretske is similarly defective. After criticizing the causal theory, Dretske claims:

> What *makes* it X (rather than Y) that we see is that the information these internal events [in the experience of the subject] carry is information about X (rather than Y).[38]

This view leads him to assert that we could, in theory, see an object at the far side of a brick wall, 'as long as visual information about X is getting through'. However, this way of formulating the analysis begs the question: what grounds the fact that the information is getting through *from X*? Suppose there are two different objects, X and Y, behind the wall. Dretske's simple informational account is unable to distinguish between case (1) where S sees X normally, and case (2) where S sees Y but, because of some kind of distortion, Y appears as X normally does. We are given no account of what it is that makes the information *about X*, rather than about some other object. In later work Dretske amends the analysis by allowing that the perceptual object is identified by a combination of causal and informational facts, thus providing a possible candidate for the linking fact.[39] This move, however, builds a causal relation into the analysis.

Appealing to the alleged intentionality of perception, on its own, is no help here – a point that is often overlooked. Suppose seeing were analysed along the lines favoured by the representationalist view, as follows:

S sees an object X of kind F, if and only if:

(a) S has a visual experience with a certain intentional representational content that represents the world as being in a certain way; in other words, S has a visual experience *as of* an F;
(b) The world is such as to match that intentional content; an object X physically present nearby is of kind F.

If the representational content of the experience is determined in a manner that an *internalist* about experiential content would accept – by what is available from a subjective view – then this proposed account will not work. Like the pure informational account, it will encounter problems with illusions and the Gricean examples of matching hallucinations. Having an experience with a certain intentional content, when interpreted on internalist lines, leaves open *which* existing physical object is the *material* object of perception, the one the subject sees. To claim that the particular physical object seen is the 'relevant material object', which can be described by the same expression that gives the intentional object, will not necessarily succeed in pinpointing the particular object seen. The appeal to what is 'relevant' simply begs the question. Again, the insufficiency of the analysis is established by the possibilities that there could be more than one F present, or that S is hallucinating in the presence of an F. In any event, this internalist form of the representational theory appears to accept the central Critical Realist claim that the experience is a distinct object from the physical object seen.

These considerations suggest that there are three, or possibly four, serious candidates for explaining what the linking fact is that determines the particular perceptual object.[40] One possibility is that the linking fact is some kind of causal connection, of the kind appropriate for seeing, as suggested by the option (5) outlined above. This is the form of account put forward by the Critical Realist. The perceiver's experience is treated as distinct from the object seen. The Direct Realist can try to avoid a causal account in one of two main ways:

(i) By defending a version of (3) above, and appealing to externalist considerations in support of the Direct Realist view, in either a representationalist form, or a two-component version.

Or, alternatively

(ii) By developing a different form of Direct Realism, one that is based upon a direct intrinsic relation that obtains between the subject and the perceptual object, as indicated in account (4).

There is perhaps a further possibility open to the Direct Realist, which it is appropriate to call a 'mixed account'. The idea would be to try to combine

Direct Realism with aspects of the causal account. Veridical experiences, according to the mixed view, contain the very object perceived as a constituent; yet what determines that a particular physical object counts as the perceptual object is the causal relation that holds between it and the subject's experience.[41] In the next chapter, in developing the core argument, I shall explore these different attempts to clarify Direct Realism, and discuss the very considerable problems they face. I shall argue that no clear sense can be made of Direct Realism.

4   The incoherence of Direct Realism

1 Externalism and phenomenal experience

At the end of the last chapter Direct Realist views were faced with a challenge. This was to provide a positive account of the relation that links a perceiver's experience to the physical object perceived. The core argument against Direct Realism is that it is unable to clarify the nature of this relation. There is no coherent non-causal account of the linking fact that connects conscious experiences with external objects.

I shall begin by considering whether Direct Realism can meet this challenge by appealing to some kind of *externalist* view. It might be suggested that the linking fact could be based upon some sort of logical or conceptual relation that connects experience and object. Now, it is of course trivially true that a *perception* of object X logically includes X; a description of the entire perceptual relation necessarily involves reference to its object. But the issue raised by the metaphysical sceptic concerns the subjective aspect of the perceptual relation – the subject's perceptual experience – and the way that this is related to the world. It is not immediately clear why we should say that the experience, considered in itself, contains the perceptual object – the very object seen by the subject in having it.

Any attempt to argue for an externalist treatment of perceptual experience needs to be based upon a general picture of the underlying nature of perception. It is useful to compare experiences with thoughts in this respect. Consider some of the familiar lines of argument. I am able to think about water, or H_2O, because that is a natural kind that is in my vicinity, and to which I am causally related, whereas my double on Twin-Earth has beliefs about twater, or XYZ, because that is what he is in causal contact with. It is not just a matter of the subject being in the context of the natural kind to which his thought relates, where 'context' is understood in a purely spatial sense. There could be XYZ, superficially indistinguishable from ordinary water, flowing beneath my feet in hidden underground rivers, for all I know; but that would be irrelevant to what I mean by 'water'. For me to know about water, and hence to be able to entertain thoughts about water, what matters is that I, or members of my community, actually come into causal contact with the stuff.[1] In describing matters in this way I do not intend to endorse any simplistic appeal to crude causal accounts of content; no doubt many complex factors involving the holistic character of thought and other issues come into play here. The point is that at some stage the content of a thought must connect with features of some part of the world; the only plausible candidates for what that connection could be will involve some reference to causal notions (other than by appealing to some direct and non-causal relation of the kind that a Direct Realist might uphold, which I shall shortly examine). Even evolutionary or historical accounts will at some stage have to appeal to causal links – perhaps involving actions – between the subject's thoughts and what is in the environment, or in the local environments of others in the same community.

On similar general grounds, it might be argued that a subject's experiences will in some way involve perceptual objects as constituents, because of the fact that those experiences stand in various causal relations to features of the world the perceiver inhabits. I don't think that such arguments can succeed. There are indeed general links between experience *types* and the kinds of objects and properties in the subject's surroundings. This fact, however, is perfectly compatible with a causal theory of perception. When I see a red juggling ball in normal conditions, I have an experience of something red. I can describe the nonconceptual phenomenal component of my experience as a phenomenal experience of red, because that experience is a token of a certain type of experience – one that is normally caused in seeing red things.[2] But my token experience is not conceptually tied to any particular red object.

When I identify the kind of experience I am having, my identification of the phenomenal component is not dependent upon the existence of any specific external red object. It is only tied, more broadly, to the general kind of external feature that normally causes such experiences. I could have a qualitatively indistinguishable experience of something red if I were hallucinating, or having an illusory experience of an orange ball seen in non-standard lighting conditions.

It was suggested earlier that we can distinguish two kinds of content that hold of the phenomenal component of experience: intrinsic phenomenal content or character, and informational representational content. The intrinsic phenomenal content that is available to me, when I hallucinate a red ball, is necessarily independent of any particular object in the surroundings. But I am aware of the same kind of phenomenal content in other cases, where I do see external objects. Necessarily, veridical, illusory and hallucinatory experiences share some *common* phenomenal content.

Only if we assume that the phenomenal content shared by experiences of different kinds is independent of context can we make sense of the fact that we are able to identify the type of phenomenal content present in hallucinations, and in qualitatively similar veridical cases. How the phenomenal component is caused on any given occasion is irrelevant to the way that the subject becomes aware of it in their experience. Hence, in the veridical case, the qualitative aspect of my phenomenal experience is not logically tied to the object I am seeing, and which happens on that occasion to cause it. It is only connected with the general *type* of experience that occurs when I see objects veridically. A weak externalism of this form is therefore compatible with the causal analysis of perception, and does not help to explicate Direct Realism.[3]

Somewhat similar considerations apply if we consider the informational representational content of my experience. Again, such content is held in common by veridical, illusory and hallucinatory experiences. When I describe the informational representational contents of experiences, I am characterizing them in general terms, by reference to *types* of features in the environment. The phenomenal component of a token experience need not be identified by reference to the actual object or feature perceived in having that experience. This is shown clearly by the facts of illusions and perceptual constancy, as was noted in Chapter 1. Thus neither the appeal to intrinsic phenomenal content, nor to informational representational content, can help to establish a strong form of externalism, in which the object perceived is held to be present in experience as a *phenomenal* constituent. As far as these lines of argument go, they are compatible with a causal theory of perception, in which my experience is not essentially connected with the actual object I see.

2 Externalism and the role of demonstrative thoughts

The Direct Realist might try to defend the position by appealing to the role of the demonstrative thoughts that form part of the overall perceptual experience. Suppose it is conceded to the externalist that a demonstrative *thought* about a particular object perceived contains that object in a 'logical' sense, as a constituent. On this assumption, the perceptual experience contains the perceived object as a formal constituent, by virtue of the conceptual aspect of the experience – because of the perceptual taking it contains. It is of the utmost importance here to recognize that the Direct Realist still has more work to do, to defend the view. In order to provide an alternative possible candidate for the linking fact, the Direct Realist must argue for the stronger externalist thesis: that a token perceptual experience somehow involves the individual object perceived in a manner that determines the *phenomenal* nature of that experience. The problem is to show that in perception, the very individual object perceived – or some aspect of it, such as its sensible properties – is not just present in the subject's experience formally, as some kind of logical constituent, but is immediately present as a *phenomenal* constituent, in a manner that contributes to the qualitative nature of perceptual consciousness.

The Direct Realist might try arguing that the phenomenal component of an experience is identified by reference to the *demonstrative thought* that the subject entertains in having such an experience, and that this thought will in turn involve its object as a constituent. Suppose we allow that the overall experience has some kind of individual content. For example, if Max throws me a juggling ball, and I think 'this ball is red', then which particular ball I am perceptually identifying is determined by the fact there is a particular ball actually present that I see, catch, and think about. If I later see a different red juggling ball, I can be mistaken in thinking that it is the one I was looking at earlier. *Which* ball I initially represented in my overall experience is determined in part by external matters, and not solely by what was subjectively available in my experience.

But *how* I see the ball to be seems to be determined in a different manner. From my subjective point of view, the ball seems to be red. In seeing it, I am aware of an intrinsic phenomenal content or character of a certain kind, belonging to the nonconceptual component of my experience (although to be so aware of this component, I exercise concepts relating to how things look, as I shall explain in more detail in Chapter 9). As noted above, what determines the nature of such phenomenal content is independent of the *actual* ball I see.[4] A certain type of phenomenal content can be held in common by both veridical and hallucinatory experiences. At the same time as veridically seeing the red ball I could also be aware of a matching red after-image. I could subjectively compare the two shades immediately present in my experience. My grasp of the subjective nature of my experience is not determined by shade of the physical colour property of the actual ball present; it is a grasp that I can extend to other possible experiences. So in this respect the phenomenal content or character of experience is not externally determined in the strong sense required to support Direct Realism. I identify that phenomenal content independently of my thoughts about any particular object that I happen to see.

If the above line of argument is correct, the perceptual object cannot be present in experience as a *phenomenal* constituent, for as we have already seen, the kind to which the phenomenal content belongs is determined only by the general links between experiences and their surroundings. The qualitative phenomenal content or character of a given token experience is logically independent of the particular object – if any exists – perceived in having that experience. It is at most connected with objective feature types. As far as the arguments we have so far examined are concerned, the fact that we identify the phenomenal components of experience by reference to context is perfectly compatible with the Critical Realist view that perceptual experiences are inner states, causally related to the objects perceived.

There are additional reasons for thinking that we should resist the view that experiences are necessarily identified by reference to the demonstrative thoughts they give rise to. As we noted in Chapter 1, the phenomenal content of a perceptual experience far outstrips any content belonging to the actual demonstrative thought entertained. Perceptual experience is just too rich to be fully captured by the demonstrative thoughts actually entertained.[5] Any attempt to appeal to the demonstrative thoughts to which an experience *would* give rise is likely to be question-begging and will depend upon the specific features of the envisaged counterfactual circumstances.

In any event, there is a further serious problem. An account is still required about which fact of the matter determines that some particular object is the focus of the subject's perceptually based demonstrative thought.[6] But this demand returns us to the question of how, in principle, it is determined which particular object is seen, and this leads to a threat of circularity in the Direct Realist's position. We can express this difficulty in the following way. Underlying the externalist view we have just been considering seem to be three interconnected theses:

(1) The *perceptual thought* I have as part of my overall perceptual experience is a thought about the object X I see (and not some matching object), because my experience makes X *available* as the object of my perceptual thought;

(2) My experience makes X *available* as the object of my perceptual thought, because in having that experience I am *seeing* the object X;

(3) I am *seeing* the particular object X, in virtue of the fact that it is the object X that is a constituent of the *perceptual thought* that forms part of my overall experience.

Clearly, if this is all we could say, we would be trapped in a vicious circle; it would never be clear what the actual connection is between X and my experience, which *determines* that X is the ball I see. No connection has yet been offered to account for how my experience is linked to the object X to make it available to figure in the content of my perceptual thought. The obvious way to avoid the problem is by appealing to some kind of causal relation, and thus to interpret the experience as an inner state or event, as the Critical Realist suggests.

As Davidson observed, the existence of a causal connection between events is compatible with the existence of a conceptual connection that arises because of the way that we describe them.[7] We could claim that what makes the particular ball X a *logical* constituent of the perceptual thought is precisely the fact that the perceptual thought is prompted by a phenomenal experience caused (in the appropriate manner) by X in the first place. In this way we can explain the intimate connection between perceptual experience and demonstrative thought. This way of defending the externalist position does not help to clarify Direct Realism, however. We reach this conclusion that X is a *logical* constituent of the perceptual thought independently of any claim about the ontological status of the *phenomenal* component of experience. It has not yet made it clear how, according to Direct Realism, the subject's phenomenal experience makes X available.

On the Critical Realist causal view, experiences relate to external objects indirectly. That is, the external object X that I see causes an *inner* phenomenal experience, which in turn causes me to have a thought about the object X that is physically nearby, perhaps in front of me. It is X that does the causal work, but we do not need to claim that X is immediately present in my experience because it is part of my phenomenal state. All that matters is that I succeed in forming a thought about X, and think of it in some way as, for example, the object in front of me now.[8] We need to appeal to the causal connection in order to explain why it is that X is seen, and not some other object Y, but this does not establish that X is immediately present in experience as a phenomenal constituent.

These considerations show that there are two different notions in play here, which need to be carefully distinguished. On the one hand, there is the idea that some kind of causal connection links the object perceived and the subject's demonstrative perceptual thought; this causal connection underpins a conceptual connection between the two. The perceived object is therefore a *formal* or logical constituent of the subject's perceptual taking. On the other hand, there is a claim about the phenomenal component of experience, and how this relates to the perceived object. On the Critical Realist view, the formal point about the constituents of the perceptual taking is compatible with interpreting the experience as an inner state. We have not yet found any argument to show that the phenomenal component of experience should be identified with the perceived object, as the Direct Realist claims. Because phenomenal content can be held in common by qualitatively similar veridical and hallucinatory experiences, it appears that *phenomenal* content is independent of any particular object perceived. It pertains to types of experiences. This means that there are no externalist grounds at all for claiming that the perceived object is immediately present as a phenomenal constituent of the subject's conscious experience.

One alternative account that might be offered by the Direct Realist to determine the linking fact – between experience and object seen – appeals to the subject's behaviour. It has been suggested that the content of experience is tied directly to a person's capacity to discriminate and single out or locate one particular object from amongst others in the environment.[9] But what is it to single out or locate an object? We cannot appeal here to such notions as 'attending to or focusing upon what is given in one's immediate visual experience', on pain of circularity: the sceptic's challenge is to provide an account of what it *is* for an object to be in the subject's experience. Singling out an object must therefore be interpreted physically, as involving some kind of behavioural capacity guided by experience, such as the physical ability to move directly towards and select the object located. But because of the possibility of motor error of various kinds, and also because of illusions, such an account is unlikely to succeed.[10] In any event, such a view can again establish at best that some kind of general conceptual connection holds between the subject's experience, and the object seen; it is compatible with the causal theorist's view that the perceptual experience is a distinct entity from the perceived object.

This concludes the first part of the core argument against Direct Realism. Externalist considerations are unable to establish the claim that the physical object perceived is present in experience as a phenomenal constituent. Taken on their own, logical or conceptual considerations about the necessary preconditions for the identification of phenomenal experiences are insufficient to establish anything stronger than a form of weak externalism about experience types, or a form of externalism about the subject's perceptual thought. But what it is for the perceived object to be a *phenomenal* constituent of the experience is still left unexplained. It means that such considerations fail to explain what connects the experience and the object, and are parasitic upon a more substantive account of the linking fact.

3 The idea of an intrinsic connection

If the Direct Realist account is to be vindicated, it must be shown that we can make sense of a relation of intrinsic connectedness. Many Direct Realists try to explain the nature of perceptual experience by appealing, either covertly or explicitly, to the idea of a unique non-causal relation of a special kind. The simplest version of such a relation would be that of partial identity: the perceived object is taken to be, literally, a part of the subject's experience. Not all those who reject the causal theory in favour of a relation of intrinsic connectedness would express the point in this manner; all, however, accept the idea that the experience is necessarily bound up with the object perceived, and is not a logically separable inner entity.

This basic idea is formulated in a number of ways. Some opponents of the causal theory may argue for a version of the position that William Child labels 'Compatibilism'. This view concedes that causality is involved to some extent in seeing, but denies that the experience is distinct from what is seen: the object X which is seen causes an experience that is construed as 'the complete state of affairs' of X looking some way to the subject S.[11] What it is for a particular object to 'look some way' is, crucially, left unexplained (this position is equivalent to that previously termed 'the mixed view'). In a number of papers defending the disjunctive view, Paul Snowdon rejects the causal theorist's claim that the concept of perception is to be analysed as involving a logically distinct experience, and claims that seeing involves an 'experiential relation R' which is conceptually primitive and unanalysable.[12]

McDowell, in defending his version of the disjunctive view, speaks of the 'unmediated openness of the experiencing subject to external reality', and in a number of places makes claims reminiscent of Heidegger's view that, standing in some sense 'outside science', we find ourselves in perception 'face to face' with objects.[13] Despite other differences, Michael Martin makes the same appeal to a non-causal relation in defending his version of the disjunctive view. He labels his version naïve realism, and claims that in a literal sense 'the actual objects of perception, the external things such as trees ... partly constitute one's conscious experience ... '.[14]

What all these views have in common is the thesis that a perceptual experience is necessarily, or intrinsically, connected with the object perceived in having it. This position is the fourth of the main replies to the sceptic identified at the end of the last chapter. In contrast with the weak externalist position that interprets the necessity as arising at the conceptual level from characterizations based upon a contingent relation (when, for example, it is stated that an individual X is 'necessarily related' to Y because X is identified as the murderer of Y), this position, as exemplified by many versions of Direct Realism, interprets the necessity in a metaphysical sense, as arising from some basic feature of the world (for example, when Y is a part of X).[15] The object is a constitutive part of the experience, and not merely contingently connected with it. The Direct Realist is therefore committed to the idea of some unique relation of acquaintance between mind and world: a mind-independent entity, a physical object, is somehow brought into the subject's consciousness. The claim is that the object perceived is intrinsically related to the perceptual experience, and is immediately present to phenomenal consciousness, so that the subject becomes aware of it. Yet at the same time the object is not an episode in the subject's consciousness, in the way that the subject's thoughts, sensations and other mental state are. The problem for the Direct Realist is whether we can make sense of this idea.

In the remainder of this chapter I shall take 'Direct Realism' to refer to the view that in perceiving an object, the subject's conscious experience is somehow intrinsically connected to that very object, so that it is immediately present in the experience as a phenomenal constituent. The first strand of what I have termed the 'core argument' was aimed at establishing that Direct Realism could not be defended by appeal to externalist considerations. The second strand in the core argument, which I shall now develop, argues that we cannot make sense of the intrinsic connectedness version of Direct Realism. The basic problem for this variant of Direct Realism consists in trying to clarify the nature of the relation that, it is claimed, connects a subject's conscious state of mind with an item that is not, in itself, a conscious entity, but a mind-independent object.

4   The problem with 'independent Direct Realism'

Different versions of the Direct Realist's intrinsic connectedness thesis can be developed, according to the way that claims about what is involved in the subject's perceptual experience are supposed to harmonize with the underlying physical story that could be told about the causal relations between the object perceived and the subject's brain states. A first version, which I will label 'Independent Direct Realism', or 'I-Direct Realism' for short, treats the two accounts as relatively independent. The explanatory space of conscious perceptual experience is not constrained by the explanatory space of physics and neurophysiology.[16] The experiential relation which connects the subject with what she sees is interpreted as being independent of all causal factors. To see an object X is just to be directly connected with it in a manner which cannot be reduced or explained in other terms. I am not sure that this version of the intrinsic connectedness thesis is susceptible to a clear refutation.[17] Nevertheless, it is not sufficient for the upholder of I-Direct Realism to describe his position purely negatively, merely as a denial of the claim that the experience and the object are logically distinct; we are owed a *positive* account of the intrinsic connection involved. Although the issue is a metaphysical one of what facts ground perceiving, the Direct Realist must provide some sort of story about how we might come to *understand* such facts about perception and perceptual experience, so that we can attach sense to his claim. In addition, the Direct Realist has to provide some account of the facts that determine *which* particular object is seen on any given occasion. Just as the causal theorist has to square his account of seeing with our ordinary, common-sense understanding of seeing, so also the Direct Realist must meet the same requirement.

It would appear that there are only two ways in which the upholder of I-Direct Realism might attempt to clarify his view about the nature of the intrinsic connectedness. These relate, roughly, to the differences between the first-person and the third-person viewpoints. Both, I shall argue, fail.

The first attempt is based upon what might loosely be termed subjective or phenomenological considerations. It is sometimes argued that the very experience of perceiving is sufficient to establish the Direct Realist View that we are directly aware of the physical objects we perceive, and that anyone who denies this is refusing to accept the compelling evidence, provided by the senses, of the way the world is given in experience. The Direct Realist View is supposed to be the common-sense view.[18] We are, it is claimed, in direct contact with the physical world: what is presented 'is a matter of *the fact itself being disclosed* to the perceiver'.[19]

But when we strip the metaphors away, what does this line of argument amount to? It is true that there is an immediacy in our perceptual grasp of the objects in our surroundings which points up the artificiality of theories that posit rapid processes of inferences from beliefs about our phenomenal states of mind to beliefs about physical objects. But on a Critical Realist version of the causal theory it is held that our conscious thoughts are not based upon inferences. They are caused to refer directly to the physical objects we perceive.[20] At the conceptual level, our thoughts relate directly to the physical objects we see.

But this fact about the directness of perceptual takings tells us nothing about what is present at the phenomenal level. It leaves open the question of what kind of entity we are immediately *aware* of, in our *phenomenal experience*. Is it true, as the Direct Realist urges, that there is simply no place for a conception of the phenomenal component of experience as something inner, which is additional to, and distinct from, the physical object perceived? If there is any subjective basis for this assertion, it can only amount to this: just the way in which things appear to us in phenomenal experience when we perceive physical objects provides grounds for claiming that our perceptual experiences and the physical objects we perceive are related in some direct way that connects them intrinsically. The claim is that we have subjective grounds for rejecting the Critical Realist view that perceptual experiences are only causally connected with the physical objects we perceive. It is arguable, however, that these subjective grounds cannot be sufficient.

The reason for this has already emerged during the discussion of the comparison of ordinary perception and hallucination. It was then noted that there is no obvious path leading from claims about the qualitative character of phenomenal experience to claims about its ontological nature. Suppose someone sees a green tree in front of her. We acknowledged earlier that it is a mistake to think that just because it is epistemically possible that her experience be hallucinatory, it is *therefore* metaphysically possible for her experience to be independent of the tree she sees. But if this inference fails, then it must be equally mistaken to argue, *from the way things appear to her*, that her experience and the tree *are* connected by a unique relation that links them intrinsically. This simple argument, which is crucial to my rejection of the intrinsic connectedness claim, is so swift that it is worth emphasizing.

Recall the principle outlined in the previous chapter, which the Direct Realist has to rely upon:

> *The Qualitative Indistinguishability Principle*: The qualitative character of the subject's experience does not, in itself, imply anything about the ontological nature of that experience; in particular, sameness of experience in the qualitative sense does not guarantee sameness of experience in the ontological sense.

The thought is that there are no entailments from claims about a subject's qualitative experience to claims about the ontological nature of the experience. How things seem cannot tell us how things actually are or must be.

But this principle cuts both ways. It may seem, subjectively, to the perceiver that her present experience is compatible *either* with there actually being an object present, *or* with mere the fact that she is suffering from a hallucination. We noted previously that this point does not, in itself, establish the metaphysical distinctness of experience and object. Equally, however, how things seem subjectively cannot show that the experience and the particular object seen *are* connected by some non-causal, intrinsic connection. The same principle applies, that an epistemic possibility about what might, or might not, be the case, does not on its own establish anything about the metaphysical analysis of the relation between a perceptual experience and the perceived object.

A fortiori, the way things seem subjectively in experience leaves open *which* of the various objects in her environment is seen, if any. This means that the subjective grounds for the intrinsic connectedness claim must collapse. However seductive or compelling the notion that we are directly aware of physical objects may be, nothing in our experience can ever establish such a view. But from this, it follows that it is totally unclear, from the standpoint of our subjective grasp of experience, what the metaphysical relation of intrinsic connectedness could be.[21]

Care must be taken here to distinguish the claim that the perceived object is some kind of *logical* constituent of the subject's overall experience, from the very different claim that the perceived object figures as a *phenomenal* constituent of the experience. In virtue of the subject's thoughts, we can allow the former claim, as noted earlier. But as we have seen, this is not enough to give the Direct Realist what he wants. At the level of concepts, the experience contains the actual object seen as a logical constituent, but this does not mean that the object, together with its observable properties, is immediately present in a phenomenal sense. The argument here shows that the first-person awareness of experience can never provide the Direct Realist with any grasp of the intrinsic connection that is supposed to hold between the phenomenal component of experience and the physical object. For the character of this phenomenal component is entirely compatible with the absence of any object. Whether or not the subject has object-involving thoughts cannot help matters here.

What then of the alternative point of view? Let us consider perception as an objective occurrence, from the standpoint of a third party investigating what is going on when a subject claims to be perceiving something. I suggest that if we adopt such an approach we find no support for the I-Direct Realism, and that instead, all the evidence points towards the causal theorist's view.

Imagine a team of scientists investigating perception and allied phenomena. Suppose that they are interested in seeing whether certain drugs interfere with the normal processes of perception, and cause hallucinations. Various drugs are given to a subject, who is positioned with her eyes open facing a display upon which objects are placed; it is also arranged for different lighting conditions to obtain during the experiment. The task under each experimental condition is simply to ascertain whether or not the subject is seeing any of the objects in front of her.

The investigators will have different kinds of evidence on which to base their conclusions:

(1) They have information about the physical conditions of the objects placed in front of the subject, whether these are reflecting light to the subject's eyes, and so on.

(2) They may acquire knowledge about the subject's brain states, about which parts of the brain are showing signs of activity.

(3) They have reports given by the subject herself about what she appears to be experiencing, and also evidence of the subject's non-verbal behaviour.

(4) By manipulating the displayed objects in various ways, and noting any correlated changes in the subject's brain states or verbal reports, they can ascertain whether there is any kind of causal dependency between the presence of the object and the subject's experience.

When they conclude, on a given occasion, that the subject is actually perceiving a particular object, they will do so on the basis of attributing to the subject an experience that is causally dependent upon that object. Thus, for example, a playing card is fixed on a poorly lit stand; only when the light is increased can the subject correctly report that it is the nine of spades; when the card is moved up and down, the subject is able to report the movement, and so on. When the subject hallucinates, there are no such reliable reports.

Notice that when investigators attribute an experience to the subject, it will be no part of their conception of the experience that it necessarily involves the perceived object as a phenomenal constituent. The subject's experience is identified by the team purely on the basis of the subject's reports, together, if necessary, with information about her brain states. Such reports acquire their meaning by virtue of the general context of the subject and experimenters, and do not depend solely upon the particular objects the subject sees. Only after checking the causal role of the object in front of the subject, can observers ascertain whether the subject is hallucinating, or in fact seeing the object. Only as the experiment proceeds, and in particular as the experimenters check for functional co-variance between the subject's reports and the properties of objects in her vicinity, does the possibility of hallucination become more remote, until a stage is reached when it can in practice be dismissed as idle. It seems natural on reflecting upon such an experiment to think of the perceiver's experience as something logically distinct from what is perceived.

Of course, in our everyday attributions of perceptual experiences to others, we do not proceed as scientific investigators. But in making such attributions, we have no additional facts to appeal to. We have only what would be available to the scientific investigators imagined above. The conclusion must be that in the ordinary case, perceptual experiences are logically distinct from the objects we perceive. As we noted earlier, it is trivially true that a *perception* of a given object X necessarily involves X (or at least a temporal stage of X). This is compatible with any theory of perception, including the causal theorist's. But the experience involved in that perception, *qua* experience, does not seem to be necessarily connected with what is perceived. The subject identifies her experience subjectively, and is able to report it, on the basis of her grasp of the general type of phenomenal content that such perceptual experiences have. No particular object external to the subject is necessary for her to understand what kind of experience she is having; the fact that it is caused by a particular physical object is merely contingent.

However, for I-Direct Realism, the causal approach sketched out above is supposed to be of little relevance to determining what goes on at the personal level, in the subject's experience. In order to defend his claim that the experience and the perceived object are intrinsically connected, the Direct Realist must discount any evidence that points to the alternative position that they are causally related, and thus logically distinct. But by eschewing appeal to causal considerations, he is deprived of any objective grounds for answering the sceptic's query about *which* particular object is perceived. As we have seen, there is a distinction to be made between the qualitative character of the subject's phenomenal experience and the ontological nature of that experience. This means that there are also no subjective grounds for ruling out the sceptic's bizarre possibilities. The I-Direct Realist is unable to provide any answer to the sceptic that doesn't amount to arbitrary fiat. Given the failure of logical/externalist considerations to account for the connection between the experience and the particular object perceived, it therefore becomes not only hard to know what sort of support there could be for the I-Direct Realist's claim that the experience and the perceived object are intrinsically connected, but also quite obscure what *kind* of connection is supposed to obtain between them. I-Direct Realism collapses into incoherence.

5 'Supervenience Direct Realism' and vehicle externalism

An alternative account of the intrinsic connected thesis attempts a closer integration with the scientific account, by appealing to some notion of supervenience, while endeavouring to retain the essential features of the Direct Realist view. I label this variant, 'Supervenience Direct Realism', or 'S-Direct Realism' for short. The claim would be that the subject's experience supervenes upon more than the events within the subject's body – in other words, the experience is considered to have an extended character, and as in some way reaching out into the world.

The S-Direct Realist argues as follows: it can be allowed that at the underlying scientific level, a complete description of the physical and physiological processes could, in principle, be provided in terms of discrete causally related stages from events involving the perceived object to events in the brain. This entire causal process is compatible with a distinct, personal level description, at which reference to the subject's experience is made; thus far the Critical Realist is in agreement. However, the upholder of S-Direct Realism advances the additional claim that the experience of the subject supervenes, not just upon the subject's bodily states, but upon the entire physical process, right back to and including the object perceived. It is concluded that the subject's experience, in perceiving an object, includes the very object seen. This is a position that has been recently canvassed by supporters of the 'extended mind' hypothesis, who include advocates of the sensorimotor contingency view; it also has been labelled 'vehicle externalism'.[22] I have no quarrel here with the extended mind hypothesis as applied to thoughts; but I shall argue here against the attempt to apply that view to the phenomenal aspect of experience.

There are serious objections to S-Direct Realism. The central objection is that there is no good reason why we should accept the claim that the experience supervenes upon the distal physical object actually seen, in addition to any events within the subject's body. For similar reasons to those advanced in the argument against I-Direct Realism, the only supervenience relations that can plausibly be defended are those based upon the subject's brain states alone. The test for whether a system of possible (experience) states E supervenes upon a conceptually distinct system B is that there can be no change in the relevant states of E without a correlated change in some (subvening) state of B. If changes in the subvening system B are sufficient for states of E to change, then we do not need to enlarge the subvening basis to include some further, separate system D. Changes in the subject's brain states display the appropriate kind of correlation with changes in the experience, so that we are entitled to make a claim about the supervenience of experiences on brain states alone; we do not need to include events outside the brain, such as the state of distal objects, in the subvening base. To do so would be like looking for a second determining cause of some event, when we have already found a cause which is sufficient to bring it about. If someone does try to claim that veridical experiences supervene upon the physical objects perceived, then we might ask: why stop at the perceived object – why not go further back down the causal chain, and claim supervenience of experience upon facts in the distant past, or into the wider environment?

There is a potential source of confusion which might obscure the force of this point. The fact that S perceives some physical object X at T logically entails the existence of X.[23] But in determining the supervenience relation for the subject S's experiences, we need to distinguish the relation fact that S perceives X, from the more simple fact that S has a certain experience, *qua* experience. It would beg the question to assume that the subject's experience essentially involves the very object X that is perceived. Both veridical and hallucinatory experiences display the appropriate correlation with the subject's brain states; nothing further is involved as a proximal cause – hence, the logical connection between the perception of X and the existence of X is irrelevant to the supervenience claim. It therefore becomes hard to see what grounds there could possibly be in favour of S-Direct Realism.[24]

The arbitrary nature of S-Direct Realism can be appreciated if we contrast two types of visual experience:

(1) Visual experiences that arise in the normal way in cases where an object is seen.

(2) Visual experiences that are caused by external objects to come about in a deviant way, so they would be properly classified as hallucinatory.

The hallucinatory experiences that occur in the second type of situation surely supervene at most only upon a person's bodily states. The question then arises: what principled ground would the S-Direct Realist have for distinguishing in this radical way between the different kinds of underlying physical situations that subvene perceptual and hallucinatory experience, so as to distinguish those complex relational states which do subvene experiences from those which do not? If the S-Direct Realist appeals to a difference in the causal paths that constitute perception and hallucinations, he is saddled with a form of the deviant causal chains problem. It is in any event quite unclear how he is to explain this difference, and without a principled non-causal way of explaining what is constitutive of seeing an object, the S-Direct Realist has no answer to the sceptic.

Perhaps one mistaken motive for S-Direct Realism stems from the complex dynamic nature of the overall perceptual process. As advocates of the sensorimotor view emphasize, perception often involves a tight 'coupling' of the perceiver's experience and the perceptual object. As I shall spell out in Chapter 7, something like this is true because of the essential nature of distal perception. The experiences that arise in distal perception are precisely those that enable creatures to be guided through an environment, so that they can track, and make use of, the objects they see. But the wrong conclusion is drawn from the fact of this coupling. This overall perceptual process will involve, from a third-person objective view, a certain kind of causal relation between subject and distal object, so that continual causal feedback from the object perceived leads to a constant updating of the subject's relative position, and so on. In the complex perceptual systems of higher mammals, this overall process involves inner states of various kinds, as has been shown by work carried out in neurophysiology and cognitive science.[25]

The third-person perspective that we have on the physical processes involved in perception should not, however, be confused with the subject's own first-person conscious perspective. From the subject's own perspective, there is an awareness of a continuous sequence of experiences, which enable the subject to act upon the environment in a coherent fashion. But all this is perfectly compatible with the idea that such experiences are inner states, causally connected with the objects the subject is tracking. These experiences supervene only upon their proximate causes, the subject's brain states. Advocates of vehicle externalism about phenomenal experience fail to pay proper attention to the difference between the first- and third-person viewpoints.

The example of the experimenters on vision given above suggests that from a common-sense standpoint, we know enough to be sure that someone is perceiving if we know that she is having a certain kind of experience which is logically distinct from, but functionally related, via some causal chain of events, to a specific object in her environment; it also makes plausible the claim that a scientific account of perception will be continuous with, and predicated upon, this idea of a common-sense functional relation, as I shall show in Chapter 7. Once we have established that such a functional relation obtains, there is nothing more we need to find out, and nothing more that we could find out. We do not need to postulate a mysterious intrinsic connection between the experience and the perceived object. All that is relevant to whether someone is perceiving would be captured by the causal account; moreover, on such an account, the subject's experiences will be conceived of as supervening only upon her bodily states. S-Direct Realism therefore has no support.

The Direct Realist view, I have argued, appeals to a relation of intrinsic connectedness between the subject's experience and the physical object perceived. A relation of such a kind is presupposed when it is claimed that an object, such as a red apple, is immediately 'present', or 'available', in my visual experience when I see it. We have examined various attempts to make clear what the relation of intrinsic connectedness between the subject's experience and the perceived object is. According to the core argument, we cannot arrive at any understanding of the relation on the basis of first-person considerations about experience. Nor can we make sense of the relation from a third-person perspective. It does not make sense, either, to claim that the relation supervenes upon the entire causal relation which holds at a sub-personal level. The direct relation that Direct Realism claims to exist cannot be coherently explicated. Since, as we have seen, externalist considerations have proved ineffectual in supporting the view, the conclusion must be that Direct Realism offers no reply to the sceptic. We cannot make sense of Direct Realist attempts to explain what links perceivers with the objects they perceive. Perceptual experiences are inner states, causally linked to the objects we perceive.

6   Replies to the core argument

In spite of these arguments, the advocate of Direct Realism may still not be persuaded. There is a natural, if inchoate, tendency to hold that ordinary veridical perception is somehow a completely direct process. The assumption is that anyone who has an experience simply knows what it is for a mind-independent object to be immediately present, and therefore what the 'direct seeing' relation amounts to. I shall explore some of the motives for this assumption in Chapters 8 and 9, when I examine in detail the claim that perceptual experience is 'transparent'. Here, however, I shall take up some other possible objections to the core argument.

Objection (1)

The sceptic's challenge cannot be taken seriously. There may be marginal cases in which it is not clear which object is seen, or whether anything is indeed seen. But in a paradigm case of seeing I know, immediately, without inference, that there is an object in front of me that I am seeing, and which object it is.

Reply

This kind of response is based upon a failure to appreciate what the metaphysical sceptic's challenge involves. It is true that in a standard case, for example, if I see a cat walk by in broad daylight, I just know immediately that I am seeing a cat. One approach to an *epistemic* scepticism about the external world consists in the idea that in certain contexts it is sufficient to respond to sceptic in a blunt fashion: I just know the cat is present, because I am seeing it; that settles the matter, and there is no more to be said.

But the metaphysical challenge I am considering here concerns very different issues. It is not denied that I often know, for sure, that I am seeing an object such as a cat in front of me. It is not denied that I see the cat directly, without inference. The problem raised by the *metaphysical* sceptic concerns *what I know* when I claim that I am seeing *this* particular object, this cat, and not some other object. It is a question of how we should *analyse* what it is to perceive a particular given object, and therefore about how my perceptual consciousness is related to the mind-independent object I perceive.

Objection (2)

Can we not simply claim that the particular object seen is whatever thing is situated in the subject's visual field; or alternatively perhaps, it is whatever object the subject is attending to in his or her visual field?[26]

Reply

We must take care to distinguish between (i) the subject's *visual field*, and (ii) the subject's *field of view*. The first is a subjective notion that relates to what the subject is conscious of at the phenomenal level, in having an experience; items such as after-images can be in the visual field. In this sense, the visual field equates to the phenomenal aspect of the subject's visual experience. The field of view, on the other hand, is a physical third-person notion about the position of external objects in relation to the subject's eyes. The core argument challenges the Direct Realist to explain what it is for a physical, mind-independent object – one that may be situated in the subject's field of view – to be in the perceiver's visual field, that is, in experience. Simply to claim that it is in the visual field does not answer the challenge. It only restates the problem.

The Direct Realist may therefore try, as an alternative, to claim that what is seen is, with certain qualifications, any physical object that is in the subject's *field of view*. The idea would be that we can explain standard cases of what seeing is in the following way: for an object X to be seen is for it to be in the subject's field of view; it must be situated, in a spatial sense, roughly ahead of the subject, and be not too small and far away. But there is a further condition required: the object must also be unobstructed – there must be no other object in the way, so that the subject is prevented from seeing it.[27] This last condition creates a difficulty. What do we mean by 'unobstructed? It is not sufficient to explain this idea in terms of solid objects. Some solid objects, such as ice, crystal and glass can lie along the line of sight, yet not obstruct vision, while other non-solid things such as smoke, and fog, and the general circumstance of poor light can interfere with vision. So we would need, as a minimum, to replace the feature which refers to the *solidity* of objects with one that refers to *opacity*. However, our grasp of the concept of opacity is based upon our grasp of the concept of seeing: an object is opaque if we cannot see through it. Hence any account along such lines will be circular.[28] If we are to make sense of the idea of an unobstructed field of view, this will be in causal terms, by reference to causal relation between external objects physically present and the subjective experience of being aware of something in one's visual field.

Objection (3)

It is a phenomenological fact that most ordinary perceptual experience reveals the immediate presence of an object. Martin, for example, claims that 'introspection of veridical perception provides evidence in favour of Naïve Realism', and he is not alone in thinking of experience in this way.[29]

Reply

There is a dilemma for those who appeal to introspective evidence, or to reflection on experience. If by 'experience' we mean unconceptualized phenomenal experience, then it cannot provide evidence of anything, as we noted in Chapter 1 when discussing Firth's views. To assume otherwise is, as Sellars points out, to succumb to a version of the Myth of the Given. If, on the other hand, the intention is to appeal to the way that experience is conceptualized, then the answer is that it depends upon the concepts employed. This point in effect returns us to the main criticism of the first-person attempt to explicate I-Direct Realism. If I conceptualize my phenomenal state as an inner sensory state, of the kind that I might be having in a hallucination, then experience does not provide evidence for naïve realism.

The claim is often made that perceptual experience is transparent – that, in having an experience, I am somehow in contact with the physical object directly. This is an objection that deserves extensive treatment, and in Chapters 8 and 9 I shall explore the reasons for this impression, and show how it rests in part on what I term a 'meta-cognitive illusion'. On the Critical Realist account, experience is not fully transparent.

Objection (4)

McDowell has claimed that seeing involves a special kind of intimate relation between the subject and what he or she sees. It is a mistake, according
to McDowell, to think of there being any mediating experience between the
subject and what is physically present. Seeing does not involve a distinct
inner experience, because, as he claims, paraphrasing Wittgenstein: 'We, and
our seeing, do not stop anywhere short of the fact.'[30]

Reply

It is significant that Wittgenstein's original formulation of the related idea,
which McDowell adapts, relates to *thinking* about an object, and not seeing
it. Wittgenstein is concerned here with the intentional nature of thought,
and is pointing out that intentional reference cannot be accounted for by
phenomenal items such as inner images, which themselves would need to be
interpreted. Suppose, for example, I am thinking about one of two identical
twins. Wittgenstein's point is that the reference of my thought is not determined by any inner conscious item. If there is any phenomenology in
thinking, it is irrelevant to the question of what makes a thought *about* a
given person, for example, about my brother in America.[31] So it is correct
to claim that in thinking about X, my thought reaches right to him, and
does not stop anywhere short, because of the lack of any essential phenomenology in thought. Nothing intervenes, in my consciousness or outside
it, between my thought about a person and that very person.

Seeing someone, however, does essentially involve phenomenal items. As
we noted in Chapter 1, that is what makes seeing so fundamentally different
from merely thinking. To see a red apple involves having the red phenomenal quality somehow immediately present in my consciousness (assuming
the experience is non-illusory). Notice, however, it does not follow from the
fact that the red quality belongs to an inner phenomenal state of the subject
that the subject is *seeing* the inner state. There is a sense, which McDowell is
right to draw our attention to, in which our seeing reaches directly to the
apple. The Critical Realist analysis accounts for this directness by claiming
that the *conceptual* component, the perceptual taking, refers directly to the
external physical object, the apple that is in the surroundings. But the perceptual taking is mediated by a nonconceptual consciousness of the *phenomenal* qualities of experience. These phenomenal qualities account for the
fact that experiences are inner states, and distinct from what is perceived. In
Chapter 9 I shall discuss in detail how these two components of experience
are unified in perception through the exercise of the imagination.

7 Conclusion

I have argued in this chapter that none of the attempts to provide a positive
account of what Direct Realism claims about the perceiving relation suc-

ceeds. It is fruitful to compare the position of the Direct Realist with the views about meaning held, in the early twentieth century, by philosophers such as Frege and Moore. They thought of meanings, or senses, as mysterious entities, inhabiting a third realm, distinct from the physical and mental worlds. What is really objectionable about this conception of meaning is that in the end such posited entities prove idle in the construction of an account of how language works. I suggest that the Direct Realist is in a similar position, except that in his case the 'idle wheel' which turns nothing in his system is not a particular entity or a monadic property, but a supposed *relation*, one that does no actual work. The direct seeing relation that is claimed to link a subject's experience with a mind-independent object is initially obscure, and ultimately unnecessary: these are characteristics of the worst kind of metaphysics. Because there is no support for the Direct Realist's view, it should be dismissed as a dogma.

To return, briefly, to the sceptic's challenge. I have argued that the causal theorist is right to claim that the subject's experience and the object perceived are logically distinct. One central feature in the causal theorist's account is therefore vindicated. However, having distinguished these two elements, the causal theorist then has the task of showing how they are related in perception; it is at this juncture that a straightforward appeal to some unspecified causal connection gives rise to the deviant causal chains problem. We shall explore the solution to this problem in Chapter 7. Before taking up the question of the precise form a causal analysis of perception should take, I will consider in the next chapter one final attempt to avoid analysing perception as involving a series of causally related stages, culminating in an inner experience. This is the sensorimotor contingency theory of perception, a view that has lately attracted considerable attention.

5   Problems for the enactive approach to perception

1 The sensorimotor contingency account of vision

A number of writers have recently developed accounts of perceptual experience that place an emphasis on the integration of perception with action. Interest in this approach goes back at least as far as Dewey's work. Dewey defended the idea that an experience is not an inner state, but an aspect of the way the perceiver is related to the environment through action. Referring to the different contexts in which one might have the experience of hearing a noise, he writes:

> If one is reading a book, if one is hunting, if one is watching in a dark place on a lonely night, if one is performing a chemical experiment, in each case, the noise has a very different psychical value; it is a different experience. In any case, what proceeds [sic] the 'stimulus' is a whole act, a sensori-motor co-ordination.[1]

Gibson, in defending his ecological view of perception, has argued for the view that perception involves the active sampling of the environment by the perceiver, and his approach has been taken up and endorsed by writers such as Francisco Varella and Evan Thompson, who advocate the 'enactive approach' to perception. Perception, it is claimed, 'is always perceptually guided activity'.[2] The fundamental idea is that experience is some kind of interaction with the environment; we should not think of experiences as distinct inner states. A variant of the enactive approach, entitled 'the sensorimotor account' has recently been defended by several writers, amongst them Kevin O'Regan, Alva Noë, and Susan Hurley.[3]

I concentrate here on the view as it appears in Noë's writings, and in particular in his recent book, since this is one of the most detailed and carefully worked out accounts from a philosophical perspective.[4] There are several facets to Noë's rich and complex account of perception. He makes a number of insightful claims about the way that our overall experience of an object is shaped by an implicit understanding of the integration of perception with action. I will take up some of these issues in Chapter 9. For now, my concern is with the basic structure of Noë's account, and whether it offers a means of replying to the core argument presented in the previous chapter. I shall argue that sensorimotor views, and similar accounts of perception in the enactive tradition, are correct to emphasize the integration of perception and action. They are wrong, however, to argue against the notion of experience as an inner state, causally linked to the perceived object.

Noë's account of seeing is deceptively straightforward. When I look at my surroundings, I normally have a sense of the presence of a variety of different objects. I may take myself to have a complex experience, full of rich perceptual detail. Noë denies that, at any given time, all the detail is present in experience in the same way. He also wishes to avoid the conclusion that our sense of the presence of detail is a complete illusion – a 'grand illusion', as some have advocated.[5] For Noë, whole objects can be visually present for a perceiver. In spelling out the broader notion of seeing a whole, detailed object, Noë makes use of a crucial contrast between what is *in view*, with what is *out of view*.[6] To take an example he discusses in several places, suppose I see a cat behind a picket fence. Not every part of the cat is visible to me at the same time; some of it is obscured, and even if it were to move from behind the fence into full view, I would still not directly see its far surface. But although in this sense not all the cat is 'in view', I form the impression that the whole cat is present. In a phenomenological sense, 'it does seem to me now as if I see the whole cat and as if the unperceived parts of the cat's body are present.'[7]

The explanation of this sense of the presence of the whole cat lies in the fact that, although I may not now have all the parts of the cat in view, I have '*access*' to the whole cat. I possess a range of sensorimotor skills. These relate to how the way I act now gives rise to further sensory stimulation, and thus further experiences of the cat ('sensory' here refers to physical input). The whole cat is present in my experience, in a broad sense, because of my implicit practical understanding of the way that 'by a movement of the eye or body I can bring bits of the cat into view that are now hidden'.[8]

The problem for this way of formulating Noë's account is that the notion of having 'access' to the details of objects in the environment appears to rely upon the idea of a primitive relation of perceptual awareness between the conscious subject and the perceived object. It presupposes an understanding of the contrast between what is *directly seen*, or *in view*, and what is *not directly seen*, or *not in view*. Strictly speaking, for Noë, what the subject 'experiences', or 'encounters' at any given time, is the way an object appears. However, the subject perceives, in the broad sense, the whole of the object, by having a mastery of the sensorimotor profile of that object. In being aware that a round plate is present, I understand how its perspectival shape would vary when I look at it from different angles. This practical understanding of changes in perspectival shape is what enables me to conceptualize the plate I see *as* round.

Appearances (or P-properties, as he calls them), for Noë, are supposed to be objective facts about things, which do not depend upon sensations or feelings. Nevertheless, for a subject to perceive an object she must be consciously *aware* of the appearance; she must have an *experience* of how it looks.[9] She must have the P-properties *in view*. Even if appearances are objective, for me to be aware of that appearance involves a state of my consciousness; my awareness of a P-property is different from your awareness of the same property.

Thus Noë's overall account of perception is constructed on two levels. At the base level, Noë appeals to a primitive notion of seeing, in which certain aspects of an external object are related to the subject's consciousness by being directly 'in view'. It is only by trading on this primitive notion that Noë can explain the broader, dispositional sense in which a whole object can be perceptually present to the subject. By altering the position of the sense organs, a subject can 'gain access' to details of an object, when further aspects of the perceived object come *into view*. This reliance upon a primitive relation between the subject's experience and aspects of the world is illustrated, for example, when Noë claims: 'To see the actual size of a thing is to see how its perspectival size varies as we move'. In this quote the second use of the word 'see' appeals to an undefined basic relation of 'seeing' that connects the subject's phenomenal experience directly to physical properties of the object perceived.

It can be argued, therefore, that Noë's account of vision amounts to a form of Direct Realism about the central notion of aspects of an object being in the subject's experience or in view, combined with a dispositional account of the broader notion of perceptual presence.[10] We have not been supplied with a genuine alternative to the central Direct Realist claim that physical objects can be immediately present in experience, at the phenomenal level. (In fact, many of Noë's remarks about the transparency of experience also seem to presuppose such an account.) Other expressions, such as 'access', 'visible', 'in sight', 'having (or losing) sight of', to which Noë appeals throughout, all presuppose the basic notion of *directly seeing* some of the sensible qualities of an object.[11] It does not help at all, of course, to claim that what is 'in view', or 'seen' in the primitive sense, is just a very small part of what is physically present at any one time. The basic fact that we have *some* 'access' from moment to moment, as a result of the movements which we make to sample the environment, is what constitutes the problem: we still need to explain what it is to have 'sight of' something actually present, *in a manner that engages with phenomenal consciousness*. If, on the other hand, having access to the detail of an object simply refers to the fact that, as a perceiver, one engages in certain patterns of physical behaviour, this cannot help us to understand what it is to be consciously aware of the sensible properties of objects.

2 The awareness of phenomenal qualities

Noë's precise view is hard to pin down, however. There is more to be said about the notion of 'access' and how this relates our perceptual awareness of the details of objects, such as their visible colours. In his recent book, Noë attempts something like a deconstruction of phenomenal consciousness. Initially, he seems to be endorsing the distinction between:

(1) being *strictly* aware of what is actually present, in an occurrent manner;

And

(2) being *potentially* aware of hidden detail, by virtue of the exercise of sensorimotor skills.

This distinction seems to be upheld in his remarks about being visually aware of a detailed scene containing a red tomato:

> The detail is visually present thanks to your possession of the skills that enable you to reach out and grasp the detail as you need it. What you experience, then, outstrips what you are *strictly aware* of now, or what you are attending to now. Crucially, you can no more grasp the whole scene in consciousness all at once, than see all sides of the tomato at once, or the occluded parts of the cat behind the fence.[12] [my italics]

He goes on, however, to deny the claim that when one perceives a colour, there is some actual or occurrent shade present in one's consciousness. Noë first notes that some of the content of perceptual experience is virtual, in the sense that it exists not in experience, but as information in the environment that the perceiver can tap into. (Here again, what it is to 'tap into' information in a *visual* manner is left unexplicated.) He then argues:

> The content of experience, I would like to argue, is virtual *all the way in*.... we cannot factor experience into an occurrent and a merely virtual or potential part. Experience is fractal, in this sense. At any level of analysis it always presents a structured field that extends outward to the periphery, with elements that are out of view.[13]

Noë tries to support this claim by a number of arguments. I do not think these succeed. As we noted in Chapter 1, no phenomenological account of colour experience can avoid a necessary commitment to there being something actually present in consciousness – a point that is independent of any issues concerning the ontological analysis of what the colour experience consists in.

Before examining Noë's arguments over this issue, let me first of all observe that unless experience can be factored into an occurrent actual component, as well as a potential component, it would be completely puzzling what the claim about 'access' to an object could amount to. A state of pure potential would not make sense of the phenomenological presence of properties. So Noë's positive view is less clear than at first sight appears. But, in any event, I do not think his arguments support his conclusion that experience is virtual all the way in.

A leading argument Noë relies upon is based on the evidence of slow Change Blindness. In such experiments, subjects are presented with what appears to be a static video image of a complex street scene. Although they do not realize it, one element in the scene is gradually changing. For example, a woman is standing next to a car, which is changing colour extremely slowly, from red, through purple to blue. Observers tend not to notice this gradual change in colour. In describing this experiment Noë states:

> ... the colour of the object you are staring at changes *while you examine it*. So long as attention is not directed to colour in particular, perceivers tend not to notice such a patent and gross change as this![14]

Change Blindness experiments show that there are limitations to what we can attend to. This is what we should expect, given the limited capacity of the channels that process perceptual input. Some of the details of these findings are, indeed, surprising. What matters, however, is how we analyse what is going on when the colour *is* attended to. As we saw in Chapter 1, there are compelling reasons for the view that there are phenomenal qualities actually present in experience, in addition to the concepts that are employed (remembering here that such concepts may include the employment of low-level classification). Before attending to the colour, the subject does not classify it; the change is at the purely phenomenal level. When the subject attends to the colour, that subject becomes conceptually aware of the slow shade change. Noticing is a conceptual activity.

Noë's comment on what goes on when I attend to a red shade in my experience is that 'there is always room for shifts in attention'. This is true, but irrelevant. Even if it were denied that the phenomenal colour is in consciousness when not attended to, we would still need to explain the fact that a phenomenal quality is present in the observer's consciousness, when the changing colour *is* attended to; the observer does not just *think* about a gradually changing shade. In analysing perceptual experience, we need to make sense of what is going on in those cases where the subject *does attend* to certain features, and when the colour is 'in sight' or 'visible'. It is hard to make sense of this basic phenomenon without recognizing that actual phenomenal qualities are somehow present in experience.

Noë's comments therefore leave unresolved the central problem raised by the claim that a part of the perceived object may be 'in view'. The challenge has been to explain the relation between the subject's experience of phenomenal qualities, and the sensible properties of physical object perceived. Noë's appeal to the fact that we can 'access' the details of the objects we see does not explain what this relation amounts to. In places the appeal to access is suggestive of a third-person perspective on experience – I have access to an object if it is before me, and my eyes are open, and I am awake, etc.[15] But this behaviourist approach provides no help in explaining how the perceived object is related to the perceiver's first-person, subjective point of view. In so far as his account relies essentially on notions such as 'directly seeing' parts of objects, or having a part of the object 'in view' or 'in sight', or 'encountering' an object, and the like, Noë's view provides no advance on the problematic Direct Realist view. Noë's account does not offer a viable alternative to the Critical Realist conclusion that experiences are inner states of the subject.

3 Experience and sensorimotor knowledge

There is, however, a further line of argument that Noë puts forward in rejecting this conception of experiences, one that is connected with his claims about the way that perception involves a subject's understanding of sensorimotor contingencies. In order to understand this notion, it is helpful to begin with Noë's views about the relation between the perceiving subject's experiences and his or her brain states. He suggests that there are good reasons for holding that perceptual experiences supervene on much more than the subject's neural states, and that for this reason we should not think of experiences as inner states, distinct from the object perceived.[16] Noë defends a version of the extended mind hypothesis:

> What I have been defending in this chapter is externalism about the vehicles of content of experience. I have been arguing that for at least some experiences, the physical substrate may cross boundaries, implicating neural, bodily, and environmental features. Just as Clark and Chalmers have argued that there is no theoretical obstacle to thinking that the vehicles of some *cognitive* processes may cross the boundaries of the skull, so I am arguing that the vehicles of some *experience* too may extend out into the world (but not that it must do so).[17]

A few pages on he makes a less qualified claim:

> In general, what determines phenomenology is not neural activity set up by stimulation as such, but the way that the activity is embedded in a sensorimotor dynamic.[18]

Noë thinks we have reasons to doubt the internalist thesis that the phenomenal aspects of the experience of seeing an object supervene upon the neural states of the perceiver alone. He denies that brain activity, on its own, is necessary and sufficient for a normal perceptual experience as of seeing an object, such as a cat or a tree in front of one. Ultimately, he concedes, the issue is not to be decided *a priori*, but is empirical; nevertheless, according to Noë it is a 'reasonable bet' that 'full-blown mature human experience does not have an exclusively neural basis'. He thinks there are good reasons for holding that rich and complex perceptual-like experiences 'depend *constitutively* on physical substrates that are not inside the head ... ' (my italics).[19]

We have already noted that Noë's views on hallucinatory experiences seem to be undermined by the empirical evidence. Complex hallucinations can occur which supervene upon the brain alone. But Noë offers a further reason for the claim that we need to look outside the brain in order to find the proximal causes of experience. On his view, perceptual experience is a temporally extended affair, involving the subject's actions in an environment. It involves the essential role of the subject's knowledge of the sensorimotor contingencies in perception. This knowledge takes the form of implicit practical mastery of the way that motor commands would lead to specific kinds of (physical) sensory stimulation of the sense organs. The subject's grasp of such knowledge, Noë suggests, is what allows us to cash out the problematic notions of 'access', and of parts of objects 'being in sight', that were criticized above.

There is, however, a pervasive lack of clarity in the writings of advocates of the sensorimotor view about the precise form of the connection between experience and knowledge of sensorimotor contingencies. It is not always made clear to what extent such sensorimotor knowledge is dispositional. Noë himself speaks, variously, of:

(1) the subject *possessing* knowledge of sensorimotor contingencies;

(2) the subject *exercising* knowledge of sensorimotor contingencies in action;

And

(3) the subject having *expectations* as a result of knowledge of sensorimotor contingencies.

In order to properly assess the sensorimotor account we need to understand the exact form in which such knowledge is supposed to be operative. Sorting out the ambiguities attaching to this issue is of paramount importance in assessing the sensorimotor view.

Consider an actual case. I see a red juggling ball on the table in front of me. The fact that I now have a phenomenal experience of red, and not of green, cannot be accounted for simply by the fact that I now *possess* some kind of implicit practical knowledge of the way that red light affects my sense organs.[20] The reason is straightforward. I also possess implicit knowledge relating to green light, and blue light, and so on. So the mere *possession* of such knowledge in the form of a standing disposition cannot account for the phenomenal nature of my current experience.

Suppose we then try to account for the nature of my experience by the fact that I am now *exercising* this practical knowledge in some way in action, as Noë sometimes claims.[21] The problem for this interpretation arises from the timescales involved. The minimal eye movements in vision are known as saccades. These occur roughly three to four times a second, that is, at intervals of approximately 200 to 300 milliseconds apart. But a subject can see and grasp the nature of what is displayed in shorter intervals of time, in around 100 to 200 milliseconds, or even less. Subjects can, for example, recognize faces in about 70 milliseconds. Grasping the gist of a complex scene, such as a party, or a harbour, or a garden, is something that people can do surprisingly quickly. Even though I do not take in everything in my field of view, I can still recognize the scene to be, say, a crowded room full of people in about 200 milliseconds.[22]

This evidence strongly suggests that subjects have some kind of perceptual consciousness before they begin to *exercise* their sensorimotor knowledge by issuing motor commands. This claim is clearly supported by the existence of hallucinations. It is also supported by experimental evidence on subjects where retinal movement is prevented, so that a constant visual input is received. It is true that in such experimental situations subjects usually report cessation of vision after a while. But it is significant that the absence of visual experience is not instantaneous. According to one recent account:

> If the retinal image as a whole is prevented from moving (by successful voluntary attempts not to move the eyes or by technical means) vision rapidly becomes blurred and the retinal image eventually fades away completely within ten seconds.[23]

This means, however, that subjects can be visually conscious for up to about ten seconds *without* acting in any way that changes visual input: long enough, if one is suitably placed, to watch someone run a 100-metre race without moving one's eyes. Crucially, the subject has a short period of time in which she has a perceptual experience, and is able to recognize the objects displayed.[24] These experimental findings all point to the same conclusion: subjects have visual experiences independently of *actually* embarking upon any courses of action, at any level of behaviour. As Milner and Goodale have observed, not all visual processing is linked directly to specific kinds of motor output.[25] More flexible information processing is required, so that at least some details of the surroundings can be stored for future planning and use (as I shall show in Chapter 7). This point means that some of the central claims of Noë's version of the sensorimotor view need to be substantially modified.

If the mere possession of knowledge of the sensorimotor contingencies is not sufficient for having an experience of a specific kind, and the actual exercise of the knowledge is not necessary, to what extent is such knowledge relevant? Noë elsewhere claims that one experiences an object *as* being of a certain kind in so far as 'in encountering it, one is able to draw on one's *appreciation* of the sensorimotor patterns mediating (or that might mediate) your relation to it' (my italics).[26] He also speaks in places of the way that seeing an object is bound up with *expectations* about our experiences.[27] This seems to me to be much nearer the mark. But it is important to note that in such passages Noë is describing a very different view from that defended elsewhere, in so far as he here appeals to dispositional factors in elucidating the sensorimotor view. What matters for visual experience is not how one is *currently* acting, not even at a very low level of retinal movement, but the nature of one's implicit beliefs relating to the way that changes in one's relation to an object *would* result in further phenomenal experiences of specific kinds.

As I shall spell out in much more detail in Chapter 9, conceptualizing an object in perception involves having specific expectations about *potential* changes at the phenomenal level. In seeing an object *as* a cat behind a fence, rather than *as* a small bush, I am in a state of preparedness; I know what further experiences to expect as a result of my own movements in relation to the object I see. Exercising the concept of a cat in experience plays a prominent and unique role in preparing me for certain kinds of changes at the phenomenal level, changes appropriate to my seeing a cat. But although what matters is having knowledge of sensorimotor contingencies in the form of expectations, it is important to note that perceptual consciousness does not consist *only* in having such expectations. Having practical knowledge relating to perception generates expectations that operate upon, and presuppose that there is a level of *actual phenomenal awareness* that exists alongside such expectations and understanding. As Noë himself states:

> Our perceptual sense of the tomato's wholeness – of its volume and backside, and so forth – consists in our implicit understanding (our expectation) that movements of our body to the left or right, say, will bring further bits of the tomato into view. Our relation to unseen bits of the tomato is mediated by patterns of sensorimotor contingency.

As we have seen, perceptual experiences contain both an occurrent phenomenal component, and also a conceptual component. The latter component involves the subject's grasp of sensorimotor contingencies, but this grasp does not occur in isolation. It necessarily involves the phenomenal component of the overall experience, which Noë is forced to acknowledge here by his employment of the expressions 'into view' and 'unseen'.

Hence, Noë's account can be criticized on two grounds. First, the practical knowledge or mastery of sensorimotor contingencies alone does not constitute experience; we need also to account for the occurrent, phenomenal component of experience. Second, it is not necessary that I actually exercise this knowledge in a practical manner, by actively exploring my environment, in order to have a conscious experience. What matters, in order that I have a fully fledged experience, is that I exercise this knowledge in a *different* sense, in now having an understanding of the way that my experiences would change as a result of movements I could make. No motor commands need be issued. Fully fledged perceptual consciousness therefore necessarily involves both the expectations generated by the mastery of sensorimotor contingencies, and also a phenomenal level to which such expectancies implicitly relate, when we take ourselves to be seeing certain sorts of features in the environment; but it does not require anything more.[28]

There is a potential for confusion here, because of the fact that, in order to have certain kinds of complex perceptual awareness, I often do need to carry out some sort of physical exploration of the scene. In order to grasp more of a complex scene, I need to explore it by redirecting my gaze, and hence taking in more information from the environment. Nevertheless, as the simple experiences illustrated above prove, it is possible to have minimal visual experiences without actively exploring a scene.

The skills theorists are quite right to emphasize the point that the information available in the surrounding scene does not all need to be stored in memory; not all the relevant information is in the region of the visual field of high acuity, where it is easy for me to attend to it, and to work out what I am seeing. So it is correct to say that, in order for me to see *fully*, or *properly*, all of what is physically in my field of view, I need physically to explore and act upon my surroundings in various ways. I redirect my gaze and I alter my focus, usually unconsciously. But in order for me to see and conceptualize an object, such as a human face, that is straight ahead of me, in the centre of my visual field, I do not necessarily have to act in any way at all. What matters, in order that I recognize what I see, is that I implicitly understand how the face might move of its own accord, or how my own movements would result in changes in the way it appears to me. As I show in detail in Chapter 9, I see the face *as* a face by exercising the concept of the face in my imagination. This involves an exercise of knowledge of sensorimotor contingencies of a very different kind. It does not necessitate actually issuing motor commands to produce further sensory input, but only implicitly knowing what *would* happen at the phenomenal level if one did so. It also involves understanding how the face might move *independently* of my own actions – an important aspect of the way I experience objects, but one which the sensorimotor account tends to neglect.

Because Noë fails to pay sufficient attention to this crucial distinction, he adopts the position he describes as 'enactive externalism': perceptual experiences supervene upon more than the subject's brain states. For Noë, it is the dynamic causal interaction between a subject and the environment that allows for experience with a given content. Neural states on their own, he suggests, are not sufficient for experience. But Noë's arguments for externalism about experience fail. As we have seen above, they fail to take account of the phenomena of complex hallucinations and of rapid visual recognition. Qualitatively similar experiences can have different distal causes. In normal perception our experiences are causally responsive, indirectly, to the objects we see at a distance from our bodies. However, taken moment by moment, experiences of the same qualitative kind can be produced by other means, for example, through having illusions of various kinds, by virtual reality systems, or in hallucinations induced by drugs or by sensory deprivation. In all these cases, the existence of an object that the subject acts upon is irrelevant. What matters for the production of the visual experience are events within the subject.[29]

Any claims about which type of physical system constitutes the subvening basis for a given type of conscious experience must ultimately rest upon evidence about correlations. The nonveridical cases cited in the previous paragraph suggest that an experience of a given kind E correlates with its proximate cause, that is, with the kind of complex overall neural state the subject has, and not with the various different distal causes that could result in an experience of that kind. There are therefore no good reasons for holding that experiences supervene upon anything more than the subject's brain states. On Noë's version of the extended mind account, the hope was that we could uphold some kind of necessary connection between the subject and perceived object, by showing how the object perceived formed part of the subvening basis for the experience. That hope cannot be sustained.

4 Time and the observer

There is, in any event, a well-known difficulty for Direct Realist theories of perception, and it creates a particular problem for any version of the extended mind view of consciousness, as far as it pertains to *phenomenal* consciousness (I am not here concerned to attack the extended mind account as far as conceptual processes are concerned).[30] This is the traditional 'time-lag' argument. Let us suppose that, despite the lack of clarity about what the direct perceiving relation amounts to, the Direct Realist were to maintain that the perceived object was indeed present, in a phenomenal sense, as a constituent of my consciousness. This position would entail a very peculiar conception of the relation between consciousness and time. The reason is that we are able to see very distant objects, such as stars. They are so far away that, in most cases, the light now causing stimulation at the retinas of humans was emitted from them many thousands or millions of years ago. On Noë's extended mind version of Direct Realism, my present conscious visual experience supervenes upon the whole scene, and must include the object I see. But if the object I am currently seeing is now no longer in existence, that version appears to be incoherent.

Imagine I am now looking up into the night sky, and see a faint yellow speck of light that I correctly take to be a star. Unknown to me, I have an experience of the star because light was emitted from that star two thousand years ago. Imagine, further, that the star ceased to exist one thousand years ago. If we take the extended mind view of *phenomenal* experience seriously, we would have to say that my present visual experience, of seeing the particular star that happens no longer to be in existence, depends constitutively on that star. But since the star no longer exists, how can my experience depend on the star in this way? What Noë means, by the term 'constitutively', is that the star is in some way a part of my *phenomenal* experience.[31] It is not simply a question of my being able to entertain a *de re* thought whose intentional content relates to *this star* that I am currently seeing. What matters is the conscious qualitative content, the yellow speck in my experience, which, small though it is, makes a difference against the surrounding dark background.

If the star has no actual existence now, how can it be a part of a conscious experience which exists in the present? Notice that the problem here has nothing to do with epistemological questions about how we can be sure whether or not there is a physical world. The problem has to do with the metaphysical task of constructing a coherent general account of the relation between the subject and what he or she perceives. We need an account of what it is now to have a *phenomenal* experience of a star that went out of existence well before I was born and became conscious. We need to explain what happened to the star between the time when it ceased to exist, and the later time when it became an item in someone's phenomenal consciousness. If it ceased to exist one thousand years ago, did it then suddenly spring back into existence at the point when I began to look in the relevant region of the sky? Where was it during the interim period? This form of externalism leads to an incoherent conception of physical things, and hence to an incoherent account of perceptual experience. Noë's only comment on the time-lag paradox is a footnote in which he raises the problem without providing an answer. He writes: 'Exactly what the role of time is in perceptual experience is tricky. Can you see the stars in the sky, even though they may no longer exist?'[32] He does not take the issue any further.

The Critical Realist has a straightforward answer. Yes, I can see a star that has ceased to exist. I see it, because that particular star caused, and is now the focus of, my present visual experience, which involves a phenomenal component. That star is a *logical* constituent of my present perceptual taking, which forms a component of my experience.[33] But the star itself no longer exists. The star is not immediately present as a *phenomenal* constituent of my experience. We make sense of these facts by admitting that the phenomenal component of my experience is distinct from the star. The former now exists, the latter does not. To avoid the time-lag paradox, we should therefore accept that conscious perceptual experiences supervene narrowly on their proximal causes, on events or sequences of events within or at the surface of the perceiving subject's body.

5 Conclusion

The upshot of these considerations is that the sensorimotor view of perception provides no help in clarifying Direct Realism; nor does it constitute a viable, distinct theory in its own right. As we have noted, the view presupposes that subjects have a first-person perspective on the world, in so far as it accepts that there is a phenomenology to perception. The sensorimotor view can help us achieve a better understanding of facts about the phenomenology of experience; it may, for example, be able to explain why colour perception is structured in the way that it is.[34] But in trying to claim that perceptual experiences are 'transparent', and not inner states of the subject, it repeats the errors exposed in the previous chapter on the Direct Realist account.[35] If, alternatively, the view tries to eliminate entirely all references to the subjective experience of phenomenal qualities, in favour of dispositions to types of motor behaviour under specified circumstances of purely physical input, then it amounts to no more than an implausible behaviourist view.

These criticisms of the sensorimotor view conclude my replies to the *ontological objection* to Critical Realism. It has been argued that we cannot make sense of the notion that perceptual experiences somehow involve a direct relation between a conscious perceiver and a physical object. Despite the various objections raised against the idea of perceptual experiences as inner states of mind, no coherent alternative view of experience has been forthcoming. There is no way we can make sense of a direct relation connecting the consciousness of the perceiving subject with the qualities of the mind-independent perceived object. Perceptual experiences are indeed inner states. The only relation that allows an answer to be made to the sceptic's challenge is a causal one. The rest of this book will consider in turn the remaining objections to Critical Realism, and show how they can be answered.

6 Perception, understanding and causation

1 The causal analysis of perception and its problems

The arguments of the previous chapters have provided reasons for accepting the Critical Realist version of the causal theory of perception. According to this general account, the analysis of the ordinary concept of perceiving involves, as an essential feature, a causal relation linking the object perceived with the subject's inner experience.

As we noted in Chapter 2, Critical Realism upholds a schematic account of perception as follows:

At a first approximation, a subject S sees a physical object X, if and only if:

(1) X exists

(2) S has an inner visual experience E, comprising:
    (a) a visual phenomenal state
    (b) a perceptual taking, an episode that involves the exercise of classificatory concepts (perhaps of a low-level kind)

(3) The object X causes E, in the appropriate manner for seeing.

Two major problems confront such attempts to elucidate the concept of perception:

First, there is a potential circularity that threatens attempts to explain perceptual notions: on the one hand, it might be thought possible to explain what it is to *perceive veridically* by reference to some kind of match or correspondence between the *content* of an experience and the scene surrounding a subject. But on the other hand, the most plausible way to explain what it is for experiences to have *content* would be to appeal to the type of experience that tends to be caused when a subject *perceives veridically* a part of the surrounding scene.[1]

Second, there is a problem concerning the relation between our pre-scientific grasp of the notion of perception and the detailed scientific understanding of perception that emerges only as a result of careful empirical investigation. Normal human beings successfully apply the concept of perception in ordinary circumstances without having any sophisticated knowledge of the physical and physiological causal processes that enable perceptual contact with the world to occur.

In defending the Critical Realist version of the causal theory, I aim to clarify the relation between our *a priori* understanding of perception, and our *a posteriori* knowledge of the causal mechanisms that underlie perception, knowledge that results from empirical investigation into the process. I shall focus upon our use of perceptual terms such as 'see', 'hear' and so on, and upon the question of how such terms refer. This will lead to a detailed account of the meaning of perceptual terms, involving a number of key features. According to the account I defend, there is a continuity between the common-sense and scientific conceptions of perception. Of course the ordinary person and the specialist differ in the extent of their knowledge of the detailed workings of perceptual mechanisms. Nevertheless, our ordinary implicit understanding of perception involves a grasp of the fact that the different modes of perception essentially involve certain causal processes, processes which have a distinctive function in guiding us to act in ways that tend towards the satisfaction of our needs. My account complements recent work in the field of animate vision which emphasizes the role of perception, especially vision, in controlling behaviour.[2] I also draw upon aspects of recent work on natural kinds, and show how some of the findings in this field have application to natural processes. When non-specialists speak of 'seeing' and hearing', etc., they are *referring to* just the same processes that scientists seek to investigate. I show how this approach avoids the circularity problem sketched above, and supports a version of the causal theory of perception, thus providing a novel solution to the well-known problem of 'deviant causal chains'.

Anti-causalists with respect to perception reject the view that the ordinary concept of perception is analysable by reference to causal notions.[3] They do not challenge the scientific accounts of perception, but distinguish the various specialist accounts of perception from the conception which any ordinary competent human possesses. Thus, for example, Snowdon, an advocate of the Disjunctive form of Direct Realism, writes:

> But one thing about conceptual analysis that is obvious, I think, and which I shall assume without argument is that it is wrong to incorporate as an element in the analysis of a concept C any condition F which can be revealed as a necessary and essential condition for the correct application of C only by arguments relying on what are, broadly, empirical considerations.[4]

On the intended interpretation of this claim, we should in consequence accept a distinction between the ordinary or common-sense concept of perception and the scientific account. The scientific account describes the *sub-personal* processes occurring at the neuro-physiological level which underlie perception, but these empirical discoveries do not contribute towards elucidating a philosophical analysis which aims to capture the sense of the ordinary or everyday concept of perception that pertains to the personal level. A philosophical analysis is, supposedly, answerable to different constraints from those affecting the scientific analysis which results from empirical research.[5]

2 The causal theorist's dilemma

If we are to defend the Critical Realist account of perception against the anti-causalist conception advocated by the Direct Realist, we need to show how the two central problems for the causal view raised above can be answered. I shall make some brief comments in Chapter 7 about the issue of perceptual content. Here I shall be taking a closer look at the problems raised by the 'deviant causal chain' objection, and precisely what this shows about our understanding of perception at the common-sense level.

The defect of the schematic analysis of perception provided above stems from the ubiquitous nature of causation. In the first place, as Price noted, there are far too many different objects causally involved in stages of the causal chain leading to a perceptual experience.[6] It is obvious nonsense to claim that a subject who has a visual experience sees every single thing that contributes causally to its production. Second, and related to this difficulty, there is the problem of the deviant causal chain hallucinatory counter-examples: there are too many different possible kinds of causal sequences which can connect objects to the brain states which underlie a person's experience.

The deviant causal chains objection has to be expressed carefully, for reasons I shall shortly point out. Here is a version of one of the many counter-examples cited: a subject S is given some sort of drug that causes her to have a visual experience *as of* a red apple as soon as light above a certain critical level of average intensity reaches her retina from the object in front of her. While under the influence of the drug the visual experiences thus caused bear no correlation to the types and positions of objects in the subject's environment. We would judge the subject's experiences to be hallucinatory. On one occasion, after having taken the drug S, opens her eyes; the object in front of her, which causes her to have a visual experience *as of* a red apple, happens by chance to be a red apple. We appear to be justified in claiming that the subject S is hallucinating on this occasion, since we believe that she would have had just the same visual experience even if she had been facing some quite different object, such as a banana, or a book.[7]

Whether we really are justified in claiming this is something we shall explore below; but the reason for classifying this case as hallucinatory appears to be bound up with the idea that the match between an external object and the content of the experience is some kind of coincidence. Hence the subject S is not seeing the apple, although the situation, as described, fits the schematic causal analysis of seeing. We assume that the causal chain that links the subject's experience with the object that it happens to match is not the causal chain appropriate for normal perception. Such cases, of which a large number have been constructed in the literature, I shall call 'DEV cases', for short. The causal theorist therefore needs to add a condition to the analysis, specifying the difference between the causal paths appropriate to genuine perception, and those which should be classified as DEV cases; and this, it is claimed, is not easy to do without introducing considerable scientific detail foreign to the ordinary concept grasped by the non-specialist.

Although this line of objection is well-known, it is important to be clear about precisely why this is supposed to create problems for the causal theorist. For one possible line of reply would be to attempt to qualify the causal claim by placing technical restrictions upon what kinds of causal links are to count in the key condition; something close to this is attempted by Chisholm in his defence of the causal theory.[8] It might seem possible, if we were able to describe in full physical and physiological detail the particular kinds of visual processes involved in different individuals from different species, that we could in theory construct a lengthy, disjunctive list of those precise conditions under which seeing is taking place. This set of conditions could not be upset by counterexample. An omniscient being need therefore have no ontological scruples about the causal theory of perception. The problem lies in our lack of omniscience, the difficulties being twofold: first, if we did just list in detail all possible cases, we would fail to achieve any general insight into the kinds of principles that unite the different cases of seeing; second, a detailed analysis of such a kind would introduce explicitly scientific notions about light waves, the structure of the retina and the optic nerve, and so on, which lie outside common knowledge. Hence the analysis would not capture the content of the ordinary commonsense concept of perception. It offers no account of how we ordinarily are able to refer to perceptual processes.

The causal theorist is therefore faced by an apparent dilemma. An analysis of perceiving that merely incorporates a simple unqualified claim that the object seen and the experience are causally linked can be upset by the deviant causal chain counter-examples. If, to avoid this problem, a detailed and specific analysis is provided, ruling out the troublesome counterexamples, the account would be beyond the comprehension of the average person who understands what perceiving is.

Believing the problem of deviant causal chains to be intractable, many philosophers have questioned the assumption with which I began. In their view, the mistake lies in the initial attempt to decompose perception into two causally related components, the subject's experience and the perceived object. Certain writers urge that mental states raise special problems, resisting a causal analysis; the most that is conceded is that if causality is involved in perception, it appears merely as a necessary condition, and does not itself contribute to an analysis of the concept, which may, it is suggested, be unanalysable.[9]

3 The generality of the deviant causal chains problem

But this pessimism is unwarranted. There are two arguments which strongly suggest that the deviant causal chains possibilities should not constitute a reason for rejecting the causal analysis. These possibilities show at most that our possession of certain concepts, including perception, involves a grasp of differences in causal processes that cannot always be made fully *explicit*. We have, nevertheless, an *implicit* understanding of the fact that two general kinds of causal chain should be distinguished: those that are appropriate to instances which fall under the concept, and those which are not.

The first argument arises from the generality of the deviant causal chains problem. Perception and other related mental concepts form a sub-class of a much wider category of concepts, whose members have in common the fact that they all relate to specific kinds of causal processes. Although such processes are implicitly identified as involving an underlying causal chain of the appropriate type, in many cases there is no connection with anything mental in character.

A single example will serve to show that deviancy is a phenomenon that extends into non-mental contexts: The process of *being poisoned* by a substance is essentially causal. Nevertheless, attempts to clarify our grasp of the corresponding concept run into problems concerning deviant causal chains, which parallel those that affect attempts to analyse concepts such as perception and action by appeal to causal connections.

To simplify what does not matter, let us interpret 'being poisoned' as restricted to cases where a substance causes a person to die, ignoring complications arising from cases of flora and non-human animals, and also cases where the outcome is illness falling short of actual death.

In a rough attempt at defining what it is for someone to be poisoned, consider the schematic:

S is poisoned by X

if and only if:

S is caused to die as a result of X being ingested by S.[10]

The chief problem facing this analysis does not stem from any marginal vagueness associated with the idea of ingesting. The difficulty is that we can construct deviant causal chain examples which fit this analysis. Here is one of the many counter-examples that could be constructed:

D1 swallows some cold liquid containing arsenic which causes a loose filling in his teeth to drop out, which chokes him to death.

The example parallels the classic deviant cases that arise in perception, where some perceptible object causes a matching experience by a non-standard means, for example via a wizard's spell, or a mad scientist's drug. A poisonous substance causes a person's death, but not in a manner we would intuitively classify as a case of poisoning. The 'match' of the poisonous nature of the substance and the final outcome of death is coincidental.

As with the counter examples to the analyses of perception and action, bizarre circumstances are imagined which fit the letter of the simple definition; but of course we would deny that the liquid *poisoned* the drinker, even if it was causally implicated in her death. Yet no-one would react to the defects of the analysis by suggesting that the fault arises from including a causal condition as part of the proposed set of necessary and sufficient conditions.[11] What the example shows is that the causal condition needs to be qualified in some way. A poison is something that causes death in the appropriate way, and not by bizarre or deviant means. A causal condition *of the appropriate kind* is essential to the concept of a *poison*, even if it proves difficult to define explicitly. A parallel point, I suggest, could be made in respect of many other concepts relating to kinds of bodily damage and nourishment.[12] The deviant causal chains problem arises quite generally, and is by no means confined to situations where the internal state caused is a *mental* state of some kind; it is not a problem specific to the analysis of perception and action. But in an obvious sense we do understand such everyday concepts such as *poison* and the like, which non-contentiously involve causality. This implies that the problem must in general admit of a solution.

4 Understanding perception and intuitions about deviancy

There is a second argument which suggests our understanding of perception is essentially causal. I shall examine this second argument in detail, since it generates further problems for the Direct Realist, problems which complement the line of argument advanced in the previous three chapters.[13]

Compare three cases where a subject has a perceptual experience as of a red apple in front of her:

Case (1)

The subject S looks at a red apple in front of her, and sees it normally. She has a veridical experience *as of* a red apple.

Case (2)

The same subject S is given a drug, so that her visual system is affected. This causes her to have an experience *as of* a red apple, which is completely independent of any visual input to the eyes. She is hallucinating; there could be a red apple in front of her, but she will continue to have an experience *as of* a red apple if it were removed.

Case (3)

This case is the deviant case cited above. S has been given some sort of drug that causes her to have a visual experience *as of* a red apple as soon as light above a certain critical level of average intensity reaches her retina from the object in front of her. Intuitively, we say that she is hallucinating, even if it is a red apple that causes her to have that kind of experience.

In the next chapter, I shall argue that a modification of Grice's original proposal will allow us to explain how our common-sense understanding of perception allows us to distinguish between those causal connections that are appropriate for normal veridical (and illusory) experience, and the deviant or non-standard causal chains that give rise to the problem cases. I shall show how the causal theory of perception is consistent with our implicit understanding of the nature of perception.

What can the anti-causalist say about the deviant chains cases? Can the causal theorist's opponent do any better in responding to the DEV problem cases? It has not been sufficiently appreciated hitherto that hallucinations in general, and the DEV examples in particular, also create a dilemma for the anti-causalist. In discussions of this issue, it is normally assumed without question that we can unproblematically recognize when a causal chain is deviant. But what are the grounds that entitle the anti-causalist in classifying Case (3) – the DEV case – as a hallucination, alongside Case (2)? By his lights, is he indeed justified in classifying Case (3) as a case of hallucination, if the experience matches the object in front of the perceiver?

It is true that many anti-causalists, in particular Direct Realists, reject the causal theorist's conception of perceptual experiences as items distinct from, and causally related to the perceived object. They argue that the type of experience that occurs in perception is a 'non-inner experience', and contains the perceived object as an ingredient.[14] Nevertheless, no matter how experiences are construed, the issue still remains: on what principled basis can the anti-causalist distinguish between those situations which involve some kind of matching hallucination, and those situations which involve genuine perceptual experiences?

At first blush it looks as if the anti-causalist can only classify the DEV case as hallucinatory if he has an intuitive understanding of what distinguishes the types of causal chain that are appropriate to perception from those that are not. Yet isn't this precisely what he denies the causal theorist? What basis therefore does the anti-causalist have for differentiating the two cases? It is only if the anti-causalist can produce grounds for classifying the Third Case as involving a *deviant* causal chain that such counter-examples can be classified as hallucination, and can be used in a direct way to undermine the causal theory.

Let us examine this problem more closely. Suppose a given DEV case involves a causal chain of type D, where D stands in for any of the large number of bizarre examples cited in the literature. In order to use D as a counter-example to the causal theory, the anti-causalist has to have grounds for a claim about the experiential situation of the following rough form:

> The causal chain of type D is deviant. It is not the kind of causal chain appropriate to normal perception. Hence any experience caused as a result of it is hallucinatory.

I shall call this the 'deviancy claim'. What then is the status of such a claim? It would appear possible, *prima facie*, to categorize it in one of three different ways:

Suppose, first that the deviancy claim is interpreted as relating to an *a priori necessity*: it is based upon purely conceptual considerations. It might, for example, be argued on purely conceptual grounds that Case (3) counts as a hallucination, because it arose by the kind of coincidence that rules out perception. This would in effect be to appeal to something close to David Lewis's account, that the matching visual experience is not part of a suitable pattern of counterfactual dependence.[15] But then the argument against the causal theorist would collapse. For if there is any purely conceptual basis by which the non-specialist can distinguish *appropriate* from *deviant* chains, then the causal theorist can appeal to precisely the same grounds himself, and incorporate them into a more sophisticated definition, which would automatically exclude the DEV cases. The causal theory of perception would be vindicated.

The anti-causalist must therefore argue that the reason for believing a given kind of causal chain D is deviant is arrived at *a posteriori*.[16] This interpretation generates two further main options. It might be held that specialists who analyse the detailed nature of seeing discover some *necessary* feature of the concept. This idea fits in with the suggestion that Grice made in his classic article defending the causal theory, when he argued that the concept of perception has a 'blank space to be filled in by the specialist'.[17] Ascertaining the precise causal mechanism underlying seeing is an empirical discovery about the nature of seeing.

But there are a number of difficulties with Grice's proposal in its original form. As Frank Jackson pointed out, we need to ensure that scientists discover the feature that is *essential* to seeing, and not merely some property that is contingently correlated with it, however strongly.[18] This objection is connected with the general criticism that Nathan Salmon and others have made of the whole notion of *a posteriori necessities*: the problem is that such claims rely upon essentialist tenets about the type of sameness relation relevant to the kind in question.[19]

Even if this problem is overcome, there is a further question of the relation of the scientific concept to the ordinary concept grasped by the layman. Grice evidently thought of these as one and the same; specialist knowledge is supposed to fill the gap in the ordinary concept. But what connects the specialist's use of 'see' with the layman's use? We cannot claim that the scientific and the ordinary accounts relate to the same process unless we can show that some special type of connection holds between them. There are two quite different ways in which such a connection might be established. In the case of natural kind terms, the connection is made via *actual samples* of the kind under scrutiny. In the simplified model originally sketched out by Kripke, an initial baptized sample of a natural kind plays a twofold role: it is the starting point in the chain of reference involving the use of the term for that kind, and it can also be transported, stored and subsequently analysed by experts, so that the inner structure which is responsible for its observable characteristics can be ascertained.[20] This is why Kripke, in defending the notion of *a posteriori necessary* truths, claims that 'the original concept of cat is: *that kind of thing*, where the kind can be identified by paradigmatic instances'.[21]

But we cannot pretend that anything like the natural kind model could be adapted for terms which apply to episodic natural processes such as *seeing*. In general, such processes cannot be stored in the same way as natural kind samples; we cannot claim that the original notion of 'seeing' is something identified in the same way by paradigmatic instances, *independently* of our conceptual grasp of the concept. Nor does it make sense to say that what counts as a case of seeing is completely determined by an inner structure in the same way that natural kinds are, even though the precise details of the causal process involved are hidden from us. We constantly apply the term 'see' to new instances of the process, because we have a conceptual grasp of the fact that seeing reliably informs us about our surroundings.

Therefore, it seems that the only way we can claim to be investigating the *same* process of seeing would be if we had some kind of conceptual handle on it. If the claim is made that the scientific use and the ordinary use are related, this must be because they share the same outline concept. I will offer a unifying account of perception along such lines in the following chapter.[22] But this would once again deny the anti-causalist what he is seeking, since on this amended Gricean interpretation, the concept of seeing will be essentially causal.

Thus both attempts to establish the *necessity* of the claim that a certain kind of bizarre causal chain is deviant support the causal theorist's contention that an understanding of the kinds of causal connection appropriate to seeing is built into our very grasp of the ordinary concept.

5   The two concept view and causality

The only option left open to the anti-causalist is to argue that the specialist's claim about the causal nature of seeing has the status of an *a posteriori contingent* statement; he must thereby reject the claim that the scientific or technical analysis of seeing relates to exactly the same notion that is involved in our ordinary understanding of the concept of seeing. There are two different concepts, albeit ones that overlap and share certain common features. Scientists have discovered, in all cases examined so far, that a certain type of causal connection of type N (involving patterns of light waves, optic nerves and the visual cortex, and so on) is correlated with all cases that count as seeing in the ordinary sense. (Perhaps scientists decide, on pragmatic grounds, to adopt a stipulative definition of seeing based upon causal relations of the appropriate type N.)

On this view, the ordinary concept is a distinct one from the scientific concept; cases of seeing in the ordinary sense are identified as genuine on grounds which are independent of any scientific knowledge. It is not *necessary* that the cases of seeing picked out by the ordinary concept involve causal connections between the object seen and the perceiver's visual experience; scientists might have found out otherwise, where the 'might' here connotes a genuine metaphysical alternative.

While this interpretation avoids an immediate capitulation to the causal theorist, it leads to paradoxical consequences. Suppose, for the sake of argument, that the anti-causalist is correct, and that causality is not a necessary condition for seeing (in the ordinary, non-scientific sense). It then follows that whether someone is seeing a particular object depends solely upon other factors; perhaps, as some anti-causalists suggest, upon the fact that the object seen is connected with a non-inner experience by being present as an actual *ingredient* of that experience. Let us call this non-causal connecting feature – partial identity, or whatever it may be – M. If M is necessary and sufficient for seeing, then even if M co-exists with an underlying causal relation R between the object and the subject's brain, seeing would still occur. It would not matter what type of causal chain links the perceived object and the subject's brain. This conclusion would follow, as a matter of logic, whatever type of causal relation is involved: the nature of the causal relation between the perceived object and the subject would simply be irrelevant to whether or not the subject is genuinely seeing.

But then it would also follow that the anti-causalist must lack a principled basis for classifying any kind of causal chain as deviant. From his perspective, there would be no non-specialist grounds for differentiating between types of causal chain. Indeed, it would be perfectly conceivable that, in Case (3), the subject S was having a non-inner experience, which involved the apple as an ingredient, and that despite superficial appearances, this was a case of genuine perception. Because all causal chains are of equal standing, for the anti-causalist, he cannot claim that the instantiation of any particular kind of causal chain is incompatible with seeing. He cannot coherently raise the possibility of 'deviant' causal chains as a problem for the causal theory. He thus has a general problem in explaining, on a principled basis, how we are able to classify an experience as hallucinatory, when there is in fact an object present which matches that experience.

This peculiar, and unintended, consequence also shows how remote the anti-causalist's conception is of the relation between the scientific and ordinary accounts of seeing from what is actually the case. For scientists take themselves to be analysing the causal conditions that enable us to see, in the ordinary sense. If the causal theory of perception is rejected, and we try to put some alternative account in its place, we would have no justification for promptly denying that some bizarre imaginary case counted as a case of seeing, on the grounds that it involved a DEV. Rather than rejecting the imaginary case out of hand, classifying it as an obvious hallucinatory situation, we would instead need to inquire further as to what other non-causal relations held between the object and the experience. The possible instantiation of bizarre and unusual causal chains would simply be *irrelevant* to the question whether someone was or was not seeing an object in the ordinary sense. But of course this does not accord with our understanding of seeing, and does not square with the natural response to DEV cases. When the features of the bizarre Third Case are outlined, we take ourselves to be justified in concluding that the subject is hallucinating, in the ordinary sense of that notion. So the insistence that causality is not part of our concept of perception is false to our actual practice, and leads to a major problem for the anti-causalist.

Nor is it any help here for the anti-causalist to modify his account by allowing that some kind of causal relation between object and experience must be involved in perception, as a further independent *necessary* – but not *sufficient* – condition, in addition to the non-causal feature M. Merely adding this further condition still leaves the anti-causalist incapable of distinguishing between those cases which are genuinely perceptual, and the DEV cases, for of course the bizarre counter-examples turn on the fact that some kind of causal link is indeed involved.

Focusing on the DEV cases therefore exposes a lacuna in the anti-causalist position when it comes to accounting for hallucinations, at least in those situations where an object is present which happens to match the subject's experience. In formal terms, the Direct Realist version of the position classifies an experience as hallucinatory if it does not contain a physical object as an ingredient. But such a description threatens to become quite *empty* if the classification of an experience as either perceptual (and therefore non-inner), or hallucinatory (and therefore inner), becomes a matter which is completely independent of the causal circumstances connecting the subject's body with his surroundings. If the causal circumstances leading to the bodily states that underlie a subject's experience are simply irrelevant, it begins to look as if the claim that a given experience is inner, or non-inner, is no more than an arbitrary fiat.

These considerations about the role of causality in perception reaffirm the conclusion of Chapter 4, that it is hard to make clear sense of the Direct Realist view. It is hard to resist the conclusion that Direct Realism is covertly appealing, all along, to the idea that causal connections of the appropriate kind are actually constitutive of veridical perception. The deviant causal chain cases do not show that we should abandon the causal theory.

Rather they demonstrate the need for a more sophisticated causal theory, a theory that shows how a grasp of the distinction between appropriate and inappropriate causal chains is involved in an understanding of the concept for perception.

6 Conclusion

We have not yet provided a satisfactory analysis of perceiving which allows a way of escaping from the causal theorist's dilemma. We have however found out something important about our understanding of perception. This understanding involves an appreciation of the fact that causality is somehow essentially bound up with the perceptual process. Moreover, we appear to have some intuitive grasp of what kind of causality is necessary for perception, and which allows us to distinguish genuine cases of perception from the deviant cases.

The problem we have been wrestling with arose from the fact that counter-examples to the simple attempt to analyse perceiving in causal terms could be constructed, involving deviant causal chains. These counter-examples lead to the causal theorist's dilemma: any causal analysis simple enough to fit our ordinary understanding of perceiving seems to be refuted by such DEV cases; any causal analysis complex enough to resist such counter-examples seems to include reference to matters of scientific detail beyond the ordinary common-sense grasp. Yet the arguments of the last two sections suggest strongly that there must be a means of avoiding the causal theorist's dilemma.

Underlying this dilemma are two presuppositions that might be thought open to question. One suggestion is that we should not assume that the notion of perceiving is determinate. It is sometimes assumed that there must always be a clear-cut answer to the question of whether a particular experience is perceptual or hallucinatory. However, the anti-essentialist arguments that stem from the work of Wittgenstein strongly suggest that the class of situations in which someone is perceiving an object, though distinctive, may still be indeterminate; there could well be some peripheral cases where there is just no clear answer to the question of whether or not someone is actually perceiving.[23] In the same way, the games of cricket and chess are distinct activities, even though neither of them comprises a completely determinate class.

Nevertheless, despite the fact that our concepts are to some degree indeterminate, we still need an account of what is distinctive about paradigm cases of perception. I shall follow Frank Jackson in assuming that there is still a need for the philosophical project of conceptual analysis, in this, as in many other, areas. Serious metaphysics requires us to show how matters described in one vocabulary are made true by matters described in another.[24] We generally agree on our classifications of situations in which people (or even animals such as dogs and bats) are *seeing* particular objects, and this agreement is not just a lucky accident. We should therefore be able to provide an account of what people know in understanding the perceptual relation, which enables them successfully to ascribe perceptual states to others, at least in central cases of perception. There must be a principled basis for our being able to make claims to the effect that someone is seeing a particular object X, and not another, possibly similar, object Y.

It is more fruitful to question the second assumption that underlies the causal theorist's dilemma. This involves the supposed requirement that the lay person should be able to articulate a full set of necessary and sufficient conditions for perceiving a particular object, even in the central cases. There is certainly an onus on the causal theorist to show, at least in broad terms, how the average person is able to grasp the difference between perceiving and hallucinating, and how, by their use of terms such as 'see', they succeed in referring to a distinctive, if indeterminate, set of perceptual situations. But there is no reason to assume that this grasp consists in direct and explicit knowledge. Instead, it is more plausible to claim that the average person has some sort of *indirect* grasp of what perception is, even though they may not be able to spell out the precise constraints on the causal path involved. Moreover, as I shall argue in the following chapter, it is hard for us to make sense of our natural responses to the deviant causal chain examples except by acknowledging the fact that people have an *implicit recognitional ability*, which is connected with an indirect grasp of the concept of perception: this ability normally enables us to distinguish between those causal chains that are appropriate to seeing, and those that are not.

Thus the Critical Realist version of the causal theory can be vindicated, *provided that* an account is offered which shows how, in principle, the average person's use of perceptual terms is indirectly connected with the indeterminate, yet distinctive, class of situations where someone is genuinely perceiving a given object. We need therefore to show how the ordinary use of perceptual terms is indirectly linked to the causal chains that scientists discover to be essential to perceiving. In the next chapter we look in detail at the way we understand perceptual processes, and how our grasp of the concept of perception can lead indirectly to knowledge of their precise causal nature.

7 A navigational account of distance perception

1 Avoiding the causal theorist's dilemma

One motive for the causal analysis of perception advocated by the Critical Realist is the failure of the Direct Realist view to provide a positive account of how the perceiver's experience is related to the physical object he or she perceives. It has been argued that no non-causal candidate can account for the link between a subject's perceptual experience and the physical object perceived. The only obstacle apparently preventing automatic acceptance of a causal theory of perception is the 'Deviant Causal Chains' objection. We have, however, seen in the preceding chapter that our understanding of perception is permeated by causal notions. Moreover, the examples of 'poison' and of terms for other causal processes show that our understanding of a concept can include a grasp of some appropriate causal condition, even though we lack explicit knowledge of the exact causal process involved. The potential threat from the deviant causal chains problem does not undermine a causal analysis in such cases.

These arguments strongly suggest that there must be some way of avoiding the causal theorist's dilemma. The general lines of any workable solution must conform to certain obvious constraints. What is required is an account that acknowledges the limited knowledge that the average scientifically ignorant members of a community have of processes such as seeing, yet also shows how their use of terms for these processes is *indirectly* related to the knowledge held by the specialist.[1] Speakers who lack a full and explicit conceptual grasp of seeing can still succeed in referring to the process, provided their use of the term is connected by some alternative means to the actual physical and physiological processes involved in seeing objects.

There are several ways in which this basic idea might be developed:

(1) First, it might be held that the precise mechanism involved in seeing can be specified indirectly by appeal to teleological notions. Thus Martin Davies has defended the view that seeing is the process involved in the use of a mechanism selected by evolution 'to produce experiences matching the scene before the eyes'.[2]

Such accounts are plagued by the well-known 'swampman' objection, which gives rise to conflicting intuitions. But in any event, this type of account is unlikely to persuade the anti-causalist objector envisaged. The appeal to past history, in order to settle what should count as the appropriate causal chain, cuts off our current practice of using perceptual concepts from those circumstances which decide their correct application. But then the meaning of terms such as 'see' becomes completely divorced from present use. Hence on the teleological view it is hard to understand how the concept of seeing employed by members of the lay community is related, even indirectly, to the specific processes involved. I shall therefore assume in this chapter that the teleological approach to the problem does not provide a satisfactory answer.[3]

(2) A second type of account of seeing was put forward initially by Grice. Grice's suggested solution was that we should specify the precise process involved in each sense modality by example. Thus he writes:

> I suggest that the best procedure for the causal theorist is to indicate the mode of connection by examples: to say that, for an object to be perceived by X, it is sufficient that it should be causally involved in the generation of some sense impression by X in the kind of way in which for example, when I look at my hand in good light, my hand is causally responsible for its looking to me as if there were a hand before me, or in which ... (and so on), *whatever that kind of way may be*: and to be enlightened on that question one must have recourse to a specialist.[4]

This attempt, as several commentators have observed, anticipates some of the ideas of the causal theory of 'direct reference' first put forward by Kripke and Putnam. It also has the virtue of making sense of the continuity between our ordinary notions of perceiving, and scientific accounts of the process. Unfortunately, in its original form Grice's proposal will not do, as we noted in the preceding chapter. If interpreted as a *definition* it is circular; if, alternatively, it is interpreted as a *commentary*, to be supported by an actual concrete example, it provides no means of ruling out the selection of a non-veridical case which would vitiate the analysis.[5]

A further objection is that Grice's account gives no indication of how to determine what is *essentially* involved in seeing; suppose the particular case selected was of someone with blue eyes: we need an account of what would allow us to dismiss this aspect as inessential. On the other hand, there are grounds (as I shall shortly show) for saying that someone with a prosthetic eye can see, and Grice's method would rule this out as a case of seeing.[6]

(3) There is a third approach to the problem, which will be developed here. The inadequacies of the two above attempts to specify the exact kind of causal mechanism involved in perception stem from their failure to recognize that perceptual terms such as 'see' do, after all, have some kind of sense

that contributes to fixing their reference. Most people have an implicit grasp of this sense, even if they are scientifically ignorant. The reference of a term such as 'see' is determined in part by our *a priori* understanding of the *dynamic role* of perceptual processes. This understanding, when applied in a given context to an individual, can be used to identify the precise physical and physiological mechanisms that essentially constitute seeing for that individual. As I shall elaborate in the next sections, recognizing this dynamic aspect of perception leads to a third type of account of seeing, which supplements Grice's original proposal.

2   A modified Gricean approach

The virtues of this dynamic conception of perception are best appreciated in contrast to the more *static view* put forward in both philosophical and psychological writings: Armstrong, for example, described perception as a process, involving the senses, which leads to the formation of mainly true beliefs about the current environment.[7] This account is paralleled in David Marr's treatment. On Marr's view, the task of perceptual theory is to show how the perceiver is able to construct, on the basis of limited and ambiguous visual input, a model of the surrounding three-dimensional scene. On this view, the focus is on perceptual *input* – upon the relation between the experience and what causes it. Perceptual experiences normally match the objects that produce them and lead to beliefs that are justified because they are arrived at by some reliable means. By contrast, most hallucinatory experiences fail to match any object in the subject's surroundings; in the deviant causal chain cases the match between experiences and the objects causing is a sheer co-incidence – it arises from a 'lucky accident' or a 'fluke'.[8] Normal perception, therefore, involves mechanisms that allow differences in experience to reflect differences in the subject's surroundings in a systematic way, enabling the subject to perceptually discriminate objects. One suggestion therefore, is that there is some kind of functional dependence between the scene before the observer's eyes and the perceptual experience it causes.[9]

A criticism that can be made of the static approach, as Clark observes in summarizing recent work in animate vision, is that it attributes an unrealistically complex level of inner representations to the perceiving subject in the explanation of action.[10] This is a point to which I shall return. But first I want to consider a more general difficulty with the approach. This concerns the problem of how to develop the broad insight, that there is some kind of functional correlation between scene and experience, into a more detailed understanding of the nature of perceiving. What needs to be clarified is the precise form of the functional dependence involved. Lewis tries to explicate the kind of functional dependence required by appealing to the way classes of physical situations match types of perceptual experiences. He first sets out his central proposal (with respect to seeing, and limiting his account to sufficiency conditions):

> If the scene before the eyes causes matching visual experience as part of a suitable pattern of counterfactual dependence, then the subject sees ... [11]

To a first approximation, if the scene had been different, then it would have caused a correspondingly different visual experience. However, as Lewis notes, many differences in scene will not lead to differences in experience, because they will not be visible. Lewis therefore claims:

> The required pattern of counterfactual dependence may be specified as follows. There is a large class of alternative possible scenes before the subject's eyes, and there are many mutually exclusive and jointly exhaustive subclasses thereof, such that (1) any scene in the large class would cause visual experience closely matching that scene, and (2) any two scenes in different subclasses would cause different visual experience.

The intuitive thought that Lewis wants to capture is, in effect, something like the following: if I see a bush at a medium distance, then there may be many different bushes which would look the same to me if substituted for it – the type of experience I have would be unchanged, and in the relevant sense each bush of a certain kind will match my experience. But if the bush were replaced by, say, a typical looking dog, then I would have a different type of experience. My experience will vary with changes in what is *visible* to me in the scene.

As already noted in the previous chapter, the appeal to 'matching experiences' is covertly circular. The reason is that we cannot know what it is for an experience to match a scene, unless we know *in general* under what conditions that experience is optimally produced in perception, and therefore provides information about. But of course, in order to know that fact, we require a way of discounting those causal links between the surrounding scene and experiences which are abnormal, or deviant; and that is precisely what is at issue.

There is in any event a further way in which Lewis's particular account leads to circularity, even if we allow the notion of matching content. Suppose a subject S is in a room, being caused by a scientist to have experiences that match the scene in the scientist's laboratory via some sort of brain implant wired up to a TV camera. The laboratory is 'before the subject's eyes', in the strictly spatial sense that S is facing in the direction of the laboratory; however, there are several other rooms with solid walls in the way. S does not see, despite the match, and despite the fact that matters are arranged so that there is a counterfactual dependence of experience and scene before her eyes. S does not see, because she cannot act in a manner appropriate to the visual experiences. If she tries to pick up a cup she thinks she sees, because of her visual experience, she will grasp at thin air. One wants to object: 'the scene is not visible to S, the walls are in the way', but this would clearly be circular – what is visible are the features that S can see in a particular situation.

Even if we help ourselves to the idea of matching, what is still lacking in the analysis is any reference to coherent output; so the case is closer to hallucinating than to seeing; there is input from an object appropriate to the inner experience, but the experience can play no useful role in guiding output. The defect of the static view is that perceptual experiences are considered in isolation, cut off from the rest of a person's mental states and behaviour. Our full concept of seeing requires both, for reasons we shall explore shortly.

Thus attempts to explain the way in which causality is involved in perception that concentrate upon a straightforward matching relation between experience and surrounding scene are doomed to failure for two reasons; first, an account of perception should say something constructive about how perceptual experiences gain their content, and cannot take the notion for granted.[12] Second, the account says nothing about the way that our perceptual experiences are essentially connected with our ability to act upon the world.[13]

There is, however, another approach to the problem of explaining functional dependence. We need to consider perception from the *dynamic perspective* typified by the approach of researchers in cognitive science and artificial intelligence. As Sellars points out, 'we were given our perceptual abilities, not for the purposes of ontological insight, but to enable us to find our way around in a hostile environment'.[14] The key idea I shall develop here starts from Evans's claim that perception involves an information-link between subject and object, which provides the subject with information about the states and doings of the object over a period of time.[15] Perceptual experiences do not occur in the isolated manner portrayed by the artificial examples of deviant causal chains that are frequently cited in the literature. Rather, experiences occur in a continuous flow, as a subject carries out a specific task focused upon visually salient objects in the local environment, responding to and guiding their actions by feedback from the environment. Consider, for example, what is involved in the cases of someone picking up a pen to write, playing tennis, cycling along a path, or climbing up a tree to pick an apple seen from the ground below.[16]

The fact that perception is a dynamic process, essentially integrated with action, is vividly illustrated in Wells's interesting short story, 'The Remarkable Case of Davidson's Eyes'.[17] In this science fiction fantasy, Wells sketches a scenario in which his eponymous hero, whilst working in a laboratory in London, is struck by a mysterious condition that affects his sight. Davidson's visual experiences undergo a drastic change, and he starts hallucinating. He appears to be witnessing events on a tropical island, yet he is unable to see his own body, which remains blundering about the environment in London, crashing into objects. He lacks a body on the tropical island he seems to see, and he lacks any sight of his actual physical surroundings in London. He is unable to causally interact with any objects on the island, although changes in his point of view of events on the island correlate with the movements of his body in London. For example, when he turns his face and body to the right in London, his view of the island swings round to the right in a corresponding way. While the bizarre condition lasts, Davidson is incapable of normal visual interaction with either environment. Much later (when the condition has passed) it transpires that an island matching the one he experienced does exist. The events he appeared to witness did in fact take place. But given his inability to connect his visual experiences with his actions, Davidson is effectively blind for the duration of his condition.

As Milner and Goodale have emphasized, echoing Sellars, vision has evolved 'to provide distal sensory control of the movements the animal makes in order to survive and reproduce ... '. Although, importantly, not all vision is linked to the direct control of objects, the visual processing system ultimately serves to guide behaviour.[18] Perception is not simply the generation of a series of static experiences: it is best understood as an extended, dynamic process, with output activity understood as an integral part of that process.

It is of the utmost importance, however, to distinguish three types of perceptually guided activity, as follows:

(1) A first type of perceptually governed activity may be termed 'simple responsive locomotion'. This comprises input-driven activity that constitutes a more or less direct response to the inflow of information from the environment, and results in the organism changing its location. Many simple organisms can register external properties such as light and use them to govern locomotion by the employment of a simple servo-mechanism. The water beetle larva (*Dytiscidae*) uses light in this way to steer towards the surface of water, where it will find air.[19] Such activity does not require internal representations or prior planning. The creature responds directly to input and to an internal need.

(2) A second type of perceptually governed activity it is appropriate to call 'grasping activity'. This includes those movements whereby an animal grabs at, or catches, an object within its immediate reach, without having to alter its location. Milner and Goodale summarize the extensive evidence for a separate pathway in the nervous system, the dorsal system, which is responsible for semi-automatic, online motor control of a range of actions. These actions include the precise calibratory movements made in grasping an object of a certain size, and hand-orienting in picking up an object. Experiments on both normal and 'blindsight' patients suggest that, in performing such finely tuned actions, subjects do not need to be visually conscious of the objects they are responding to.[20]

(3) The third type of perceptually governed behaviour differs significantly from the two modes outlined above. It is one that humans, other primates and perhaps many mammals and birds are capable of, and it essentially involves conscious experiences. This third type of perceptually governed behaviour I term 'navigational activity'. It is normally triggered when a

perceiving creature identifies some desired object beyond its reach. On the basis of assessing that object's position relative to its own body and the surroundings, the subject selects one out of a number of different possible routes through the environment in order to change its own location and make use of the perceived object. I shall first illustrate the core idea involved in navigational activity, and then elaborate it more fully.

In many situations where a creature visually identifies a source of potential benefit (or harm), no unique response suggests itself. Unlike the hungry frog that snaps automatically at a fly within its immediate sphere of control, a monkey that wishes to reach fruit on a nearby tree has many options to choose from. It may traverse a number of different possible routes to get hold of the food.

To reduce the amount of energy that would otherwise be wasted in travelling along unproductive routes, the perceiving subject needs to select, *in advance of acting*, the most efficient way through its environment. The subject needs to be able to decide upon and *navigate* a route that will lead most efficiently to its goal. Some spatially direct routes will be impossible, because of obstructions. Some possible routes will take up too much time and energy. Certain routes – climbing up the wrong tree, for example – will turn out to be dead ends.

Whereas a bee's return to its hive is largely explicable as a direct response to polarized light, no such straightforward explanation is available for navigational behaviour. A perceiving subject needs to compare, in advance, the different possible routes it could take in order to reach and make use of some identified object. The subject must plan and select one particular extended course of action, so as to reach its goal with the minimum of wasted effort. The subject will therefore rehearse, in its imagination, alternative plans for acting upon its environment, in order to see which are likely to succeed or fail. To adapt Popper's idea about the way we test our theories: the advance rejection of an imagined route, on the grounds of unworkability, prevents the subject from suffering actual loss through rashly embarking upon that route.

Navigational activity is therefore very different from simple responsive locomotion. The latter type of guided activity, which seems to apply in the case of the bee's flight and the movement of the beetle larva, consists essentially of an iterated sequence of direct responses to input from the environment: no choice or planning is involved. Navigational activity differs fundamentally from this. For the reasons argued by Milner and Goodale, it would appear to be connected with processes in the ventral system. The way in which the action is initiated cannot be fully explained by the direct pick-up of information. The important point is that the right choice of the action that initiates an extended sequence of movements through an environment will depend crucially upon the anticipation of future possible movements. For a creature to start an extended sequence of actions in the appropriate way depends upon it having some sense of how it will finally reach its target.

In consequence, to embark upon successful navigational activity requires recognition of distant targets, classification of goals, and prior planning of routes through the environment.[21] The perceiving subject, in deciding to make use of some distant target object, must first envisage and select from a number of different possible courses of action. The subject's chosen actions form a sequence that is given coherence because of the plan it follows.

In essence, navigational activity involves the following elements:

(i) The subject is able to identify an object seen beyond immediate reach: the object so identified I call *'the target object'*.

(ii) The subject has some perceptual awareness of features whereby it can steer through the environment, so as to reach the selected target object; such features may be large and distant, like the sun, or nearby – for example, a recognizable tree: such features I call *'orienting landmarks'*.

(iii) The subject will have some general awareness of the physical layout of the environment, including awareness of large scale structures that will help or hinder navigation through that environment: these I call *'neutral obstacles'*.

(iv) The subject will be aware of the fact that there are many possible routes it might navigate through the environment in order to achieve its goal. It will need to represent the alternative routes, and decide which is the most advantageous to employ. Semi-automatic responsive behaviour plays no role in deciding between such overall routes.

What is essential to such cases of seeing is a certain kind of functional dependency across time, between experience and the surrounding scene, which is governed by the action performed.[22] As Clark expresses the point, 'the emphasis has shifted from isolationist forms of problem solving towards iterated series of agent-environment interactions.' Thus, normally, when an agent sees something and is motivated to act, she performs a connected series of movements resulting in a gradual transition in the perceptible features of the overall scene. This results in a correlated set of gradual changes in the sequence of visual experiences, experiences whose contents overlap. Feedback from the environment, channelled through experience, allows a subject to fine-tune the discriminating responses which essentially characterize those actions that are dependent upon seeing. It is precisely this feature of seeing which allows someone to track relatively stable objects, and to negotiate their way successfully through an environment, even when some aspects of that environment are in flux. Such paradigmatic cases of responsive behaviour, where a subject focuses on some object or event, and manifests the fact that she sees something by her successful responses, I shall call, for convenience, 'navigational behaviour'.

The responsive behaviour typical of such navigational activity involves a pattern of focused activity directed towards a particular target object in the environment: moving towards that *target object*, selecting and manipulating it. But there are also indirect ways in which a creature's behaviour reflects a pattern of discrimination towards objects, which in human beings is particularly important in the sense of sight. When we move around our environment, we are guided by objects that we do not physically interact with in a direct manner. Sometimes we may locate an object by reference to a more prominent feature of a nearby object, so that if we temporarily lose sight of the target, we may readily re-locate it. At other times, especially in more complex longer term actions, we make use of *orienting landmarks* to guide our movements and steer by, so that we may travel in the same general direction to achieve an aim. By noting these distinctive perceptible elements of our surroundings, we are able to navigate through an environment, keeping track of our own position and of the positions of the objects that interest us. Our perception of target objects, marker features of objects and orienting landmarks plays an essential role in guiding such navigational behaviour.[23]

According to the approach I defend, the idea of navigational behaviour lies at the core of our concept of forms of distance perception such as seeing. It allows a satisfactory explication of the kind of functional dependence involved without presupposing a prior understanding of 'matching'. The navigational account explains what kind of functional dependence is at issue in perception: it is the kind of dependence which enables successful action, so that agents can satisfy their needs by making use of perceptible objects. Thus the account explains the essential connection between perception, desire and action. It also allows the identification, without circularity, of the essential causal processes that are appropriate to perception: the causal chain essential to perception for a given creature in an environment is that which connects the inner experiences with the perceptible elements and which thus enables successful action to take place.

The idea of navigational behaviour is also suggestive of a way of handling the problem of determining the contents of experiences, a problem that affects all theories of perception. The defect of simple causal theories of content is that there seems to be no clear-cut way of selecting the causal routes that are to count as relevant to determining the informational representational content of phenomenal experience. However, in successful navigational behaviour the identified distal object plays a dual causal role, as both the cause of the subject's experience, and also as the focus of subsequent navigational activity, culminating in the selection and beneficial use of that object. Appeal to this distinctive dual causal role allows a principled way of selecting those optimal conditions under which input from a distal object causes experiences of a certain phenomenal type. This complex connection, between features of the environment and the production of inner states that allow guided navigational activity, opens up the possibility that the informational representational contents of experience might be determined by reference to the way that phenomenal experiences are causally linked to, and carry information about the relevant features of the environment under such conditions. Much more would need to be said in defence of this suggestion; however, important as the issue is, I shall not pursue it further here.

Using this idea of navigational behaviour we can now return to the problem of formulating an analysis of perception. My central contention is that a grasp of the concept of seeing involves an implicit *a priori* understanding of the connection indicated above, about the way that perception is tied to action. We are unable to make sense of what it is for a creature to perceive unless we consider its actions as essentially linked to those objects it can perceive. People may not hold this knowledge in an explicit form, but when we witness someone 'blundering about' in an environment, as in Wells's example of Davidson, then we readily grasp that they cannot be perceiving the objects in their environment.

3   Understanding the sense of 'distance perception'

These considerations point to an analysis of seeing in terms of the following set of necessary and sufficient conditions:

S sees X

if and only if:

(1) X exists;

(2) S has an inner visual experience E;

(3) X causes E to occur by some causal process C;

(4) C is the process which is causally necessary for the production of suitable patterns of navigational behaviour by S with respect to objects in the environment.

In the next section we will examine the full account of the meaning of perceptual terms which fleshes out this analysis.[24] But there is a final point about the general connection between perception and action worth noting here. Our understanding of seeing as connected with potential navigational behaviour in humans and other animals belongs with our grasp of the essential differences between the categories of sentient creatures, plants and mere inanimate objects. An object such as a rock is only capable of responding to its environment in a gross mechanical way, for example by rolling downhill under the influence of gravity. No essential reference to any internal structure is normally invoked in explaining such simple movements. In contrast, navigational behaviour is in practice only explicable by reference to some kind of information-link operating through the *inner* states of a creature, in a manner that constitutes seeing. As Clark notes, although work on robotic navigation in artificial intelligence suggests that the inner representations guiding behaviour need not be as rich and complex in structure as previously thought, it is still necessary to appeal to some kind of inner representations in order to explain such action.[25]

It is true that judging by external behaviour alone, the attribution of perceptual states to a creature is defeasible. Christopher Peacocke considers a parallel case, where what appears to be a cognizing subject turns out in fact to be a complex system consisting of a marionette controlled by a computer on Mars, utilizing a vast but finite list of instructions relating possible input to output.[26] However, when we discover that this is indeed the basis for a system's behaviour, we withdraw our attribution of cognitive states to the marionette. The reason for doing so is that we no longer have grounds for thinking of the system as a unity with the appropriate kind of internal structure: there is no agent with perceptual and other mental states that contribute to the actions.

A necessary condition for genuine perception is, therefore, that the actions of the perceiver are genuine actions, causally responsive to its environment, and are not driven by a totally external source. This does not mean that a person cannot use aids, such as spectacles, or hearing devices, to enhance their perception. The point is rather that such aids may become, in a sense, part of the system that is doing the perceiving. To this extent the extended mind hypothesis seems to be correct.[27] But what drives the perceptual behaviour must be states that belong to the subject. We know that in our own case, as human beings, perception involves conscious experiences. In perceiving, we are aware of phenomenal qualities. It has been argued that experiences are inner states. Taking these considerations together points to the conclusion that a creature perceives objects in its environment, in the full sense, if its actions are prompted by inner states, including some sort of phenomenal experiences. Such experiences need to be related in the right kind of way to other mental states such as memory, belief, desire, and so on. If we know that a creature's experiences (and other mental states) are driving its navigational behaviour, as a result of being caused by the objects to which that behaviour is directed, then we are presented with sufficient evidence for the conclusion that the creature is perceiving.

In so far that the enactive approach to perception emphasizes the fact that modalities such as seeing are essentially integrated with action on an environment, it is quite correct. But there is no good reason to deny that perception in humans involves inner states of various kinds: both inner representations at the sub-personal level, involved in the complex processing of visual input, and also conscious experiences with phenomenal aspects, of the same qualitative and ontological kind that can occur in hallucination. Perception is a process essentially connected with action, but this process involves conscious experiences. For the reasons argued in Chapters 4 and 5, these experiences supervene upon what is within a person's skin.

The navigational behaviour which is in this way the hallmark of perception is therefore underpinned by a functional dependence of the overall *inner experience* on the object perceived. This in turn is dependent upon there being the appropriate type of causal chain linking the subject with what is perceived. In the final sections I show how our understanding of perception encompasses an implicit grasp of these interconnections, and how this allows a resolution of the causal theorist's dilemma.

4   Towards a more detailed account of how perceptual terms refer

The full account of distance perception I propose, which I term 'The Navigational Account', takes the above insights about the role of navigational behaviour in the concept of perception as one of its central features. According to the full account, a more comprehensive description of the use of perceptual terms within a given community covers a number of further aspects. I begin by sketching out the main elements of the account as it applies to the sense modality of seeing. I will then comment on the different elements in the account.

(1)   The term 'see' is associated by most speakers with a schematic sense, described by the conditions (1)–(4) set out in the previous section. This involves a normally implicit understanding of the fact that seeing is a *navigational* process involving the causation of visual experiences, as outlined. This is the process that enables perceivers to acquire information about their surroundings, by means of those experiences, so that they are able to move through that environment, and to act in ways beneficial to themselves, in order to satisfy their needs. An *a priori* grasp of this sense contributes to our being able to determine, in a given individual, the precise physical and physiological process that is involved when they see. As was argued in Chapter 4, visual experiences are in fact *inner* states; but I am not claiming that this ontological claim is part of our implicit understanding.

(2)   A speaker's understanding of the sense of 'see' is not normally held in the form of an explicit conceptual representation of the process, but it does involve a recognitional capacity: in particular, this capacity involves the ability to discriminate those situations where other people and animals are causally responding to objects in their surroundings in the appropriate systematic way (and hence are seeing), from those situations where they are moving around in a manner which is not responsive to perceptual input, as in Wells's story.

(3)   Speakers also associate a set of stereotypical features with seeing, which in practice contributes to their ability to say when a subject is seeing. Central to this stereotype is the fact that normally subjects face the objects they see, with their eyes open.

(4) Using their *a priori* understanding of seeing as a navigational process, experts are able, in principle, to select and investigate those situations in which a subject is seeing. They can determine experimentally the means by which a creature is able to move around its environment and make beneficial use of objects, and they can thus identify which precise physical and physiological causal processes are essentially involved when that creature sees.

(5) By complex social mechanisms of the kind first discussed by Saul Kripke and Hilary Putnam, the use by ordinary lay persons of 'see' is linked to that process investigated by experts, and knowledge of the stereotypical situations associated with seeing is passed on.

(6) Empirical investigation into the processes essentially involved when, by navigational behaviour, a given creature manifests an ability to see, will in principle allow us to judge whether the experiences that the subject has on some other occasion properly count as perceptual or hallucinatory.[28]

These different aspects of the account will now be elaborated in turn, focusing on the visual case:

(i) Understanding the word 'see' involves an *a priori* grasp of an outline sense. Seeing, in common with other modes of perception, is understood as a process involving the production of phenomenal experiences, resulting in the classification of distal objects. The experiences we arrive at through sight (and via the other senses) guide our behaviour, so that we are able to act in ways beneficial to ourselves, the better to promote our own survival. As we have already noted above, seeing is a means whereby subjects are enabled to navigate through their surroundings, and to make discriminating use of objects encountered, to their ultimate benefit. Seeing is that mode of perception in which the knowledge to facilitate such navigation and use of objects is acquired rapidly, and relates to spatial and other sensible features, such as colour, of objects at a distance from the subject.[29] It is a process which enables the acquisition of up-to-date information about the environment; being able to respond immediately to changes as they occur is essential for many kinds of actions, such as juggling, greeting a friend, driving a car, participating in sports, gathering food or chasing prey.

It is through seeing, primarily, that humans and similar creatures are able to accommodate to changes in their environment as they occur.[30] For example, the sprinting of a cheetah, or the rapid flight of a hawk, as they target, alter direction, and chase moving prey, show clearly that such creatures employ some form of perceptual mechanism in order to track their victims. If a creature is navigating through a complex environment on the basis of its present experiences, and can thus discriminate the objects in its surroundings, and track them as the overall environment changes, its experiences and the beliefs to which they give rise cannot be coincidentally related to those objects. The match between experience and object cannot be a mere 'fluke'.[31] An internal physiological process correlates the changing perceptible features of the external scene with a sequence of inner experiences whose contents overlap, allowing the anticipation and feedback necessary for successful actions. In this way the idea of systematic or functional dependence can be explicated in a satisfactory manner, avoiding the problems which beset the alternative attempts rejected earlier.

It is important to note that the subjective experiences involved in such navigating behaviour are construed in a broad sense, as involving some sort of representational states directed on to the world outside the subject. The current proposal does not appeal to a direct correlation between the object perceived and the subject's non-representational *phenomenal* states. This would be problematic for reasons argued by Akins: such correlations are hard to come by.[32] The present account is connected with what Akins terms 'the ontological project', and appeals to the representational aspect of perceptual experiences as a whole, which they have by virtue of classificatory concepts exercised. This aspect is involved when subjects use their perceptual systems to guide themselves through an objective world. Although in the purely sensational or phenomenal sense the appearances of the things we perceive may vary, our conceptual and non-conceptual representation of our surroundings is very often as of unchanging objects (although we may of course also perceive them as objectively changing; I say more about this in Chapter 9). Therefore the result of the visual process is an experience in the broad sense, that is, a state which involves conceptual representational states directed on to the subject's environment, as well as a phenomenal component.[33] It is this conceptual representational aspect of perception which allows us successfully to integrate the senses. So, for example, a bird which hears a rival give utterance to a territorial call will visually seek out the physical source which is producing the sound it hears.

If the concept of perception is understood in this way as being linked to beneficial navigational behaviour, this makes sense of the important connection between our understanding of perceptual terms and their present conditions of use, a connection that is absent on the teleological view. Our use of perceptual terms manifests an understanding of the natural link between whether a creature is now perceiving, and what it can *currently* do; if it is able to successfully navigate through a changing environment in a manner conducive to its survival over an extended period of time, then it must able to see the objects in its surroundings. The account therefore appeals to the dispositions a creature has in the present, and not to past history (I shall shortly take up the objection raised by Millikan and others, to the effect that there is no principled way to select which dispositions are to count in determining the normal use of perceptual mechanisms).

(ii) Such a grasp of the schematic sense of 'see' need not be held explicitly. It is nevertheless understood implicitly, and reflected in the speaker's recognitional capacity. We can usually recognize when other humans, or other animals, are making perceptually based selective use of objects in their environment.[34] Our understanding of the concept of perception includes an ability to discriminate between the movements of a creature that are guided by its perceptual processes, and those movements which appear to flow from some other source, such as, for example, sliding under the influence of gravity, or being pushed.

In practice, such claims about whether or not another creature is seeing a particular object are defeasible, given the limitations on our obtaining full knowledge of the situation. It is also plausible to argue that there are marginal situations where it is indeterminate whether a subject should count as seeing or not. The kinds of problematic cases raised where experiences are causally connected with objects in the surroundings via a system operated either (a) by the will of a capricious scientist, or magician, etc., or (b) by some faulty prosthetic device which only delivers accurate information for a small part of the time, are two examples that appear to fall into this category of indeterminate situations (I return to the question of deviant causal chains more fully in the final section).[35] Nevertheless, it is the appeal to the sense of the term 'see', as manifested in our recognitional abilities, that in the final analysis is decisive in determining which situations constitute a subject genuinely seeing something.

(iii) A grasp of the sense of 'seeing', applied to the behaviour of another, is often what allows us to say when another subject is seeing. But as in the case of natural kind terms, many situations involving seeing are defeasibly recognized and ascribed to others on the basis of the stereotype associated by most competent speakers with the process. This stereotype includes contingent facts relating to such matters as the position of the perceiver relative to the object seen, whether subjects have their eyes open, whether there are solid objects in between them and the things they see, and so on. Reliance on the stereotype supports such claims as 'You must have seen it, it was right in front of you'.

(iv) According to the present account there is an important continuity between the lay person's ordinary understanding of the concept, and the detailed scientific account. What drives the scientific investigation is the outline conceptual knowledge, the *a priori* grasp of the sense, and this leads to the discovery of the precise causal mechanisms that are essentially operative in any given creature when it is successfully coping with its environment.[36] We are therefore able to select paradigm cases where a creature is successfully employing its visual mechanisms so as to satisfy its needs. Specialists who investigate these cases can then discover details about the nature of the actual physical and physiological processes involved, which enable the navigational activity to take place, and can pass this knowledge on to others. The discovery, for instance, that bats employ a form of echolocation to navigate through their surroundings and catch their prey, clearly demonstrates this interplay of conceptual and empirical considerations.

The idea that there are *two* concepts of seeing, a common-sense concept, and a scientific one, is therefore at best misleading. The use of 'see' by both the scientific and the lay community refers to one and the same type of process, which enables creatures to respond to features of their environment in the manner described. What varies is the degree of understanding people have about the details of what the process involves.

(v) Putnam's idea of a 'division of linguistic labour' applies to the present model. What scientists discover, when investigating perception in humans and other creatures, are details of the processes that enable them to carry out navigational behaviour. These discoveries prompt a greater understanding of the full extent to which a creature can utilize its perceptual mechanisms, and of aspects of their exercise which may not be readily apparent. To some extent members of a community defer to the scientific knowledge of the experts. Their discoveries feed back into communally held knowledge of the stereotype. So, for example, it is now accepted that many so called desert 'mirages' in fact involve the perception of distant objects through the refraction and reflection of light, so that they appear much nearer than they really are. They are not hallucinations, but illusions of distance.[37]

There is a further social dimension in the use of perceptual terms; as noted earlier, the use of most concepts is indeterminate; to some extent their proper application is a matter for debate. Our use of perceptual terms involves a complex and subtle process of mutual persuasion and consequent adjustment about the cases we should agree are covered by a term such as 'see'. It is agreed that we can see objects in mirrors, and through a magnifying glass. But should we allow that a person sees through a compound microscope, or that they see a sub-atomic particle when they look at a cloud chamber, or that they can see objects when using some sort of prosthetic device? Should we count as seeing the case of our watching on television a football match played in another country? There is no reason to look for a determinate answer to these questions; nevertheless, it is arguable that decisions about the appropriate use of 'see' should be informed by the core idea of perception as a process, mediated by causal mechanisms, that enables perceivers to make immediate use of information about the extended environment.[38]

(vi) Identification of the detailed physical and physiological processes involved in seeing is in the first instance arrived at by reference to actual extended patterns of navigational behaviour. Such behaviour is sufficient for the attribution of seeing to the individual under scrutiny, subject to the provisos made earlier concerning the elimination of the Martian marionette cases.

However, although the manifestation of such navigational behaviour is sufficient to establish that a creature is seeing, it may not always take place. There are various situations in which visual experiences will fail to give rise to navigational behaviour. The behaviour may not fit into a coherent pattern, when, for example, the subject suffers an illusion; the subject may exhibit isolated brief stretches of behaviour which are too short for an observer to discern any specific focus of attention, or there may simply be no responsive activity on the part of the subject. A predator that has just eaten its fill may let potential prey pass by unmolested.

One attempt to decide, in principle, the question of whether the subject is seeing in these cases would be to appeal to counterfactuals about how the subject would act; the subject might be said to see if the subject would indulge in a pattern of navigational behaviour with respect to objects in the environment. But the problem is, what would ground the counterfactuals? By assumption, the subject lacks any disposition to carry out appropriate navigational behaviour in the envisioned circumstances. The suggestion therefore invites the objection that we have no principled way of selecting which counterfactuals should be appealed to, and that any attempt to so decide the issue would be arbitrary.

There is an alternative approach. The idea is that when investigating what perceiving essentially involves for a particular creature, we proceed by stages. Whether a subject – a human or some other kind of animal – is seeing some particular object X at T when it is *not* manifesting any navigational behaviour, can in principle be decided indirectly by reference to the causal processes responsible for its actions on some *other* occasion when *that same subject* is behaving in an appropriately responsive way. The Navigational Account, when fully spelt out, is an account involving a number of elements. We start from the a priori understanding of seeing as a process involving experiences that guide navigational behaviour. This fixes the reference of seeing for that subject, and enables us to discover *a posteriori* what processes are causally necessary in paradigm cases of navigational behaviour exhibited by that subject – e.g. that light waves of a certain frequency are transmitted via the back of the retina to the optic nerve, and so on. Finally, by using the knowledge about the subject's perceptual processes thus gained from such paradigm cases, we could in principle ascertain whether, in some other given case, their experiences were in fact produced by those same causal processes. As I shall argue in the next section, this multi-stage account allows a satisfactory answer to the question of which non-standard cases of visual experiences are illusory, and which are hallucinatory. It also allows a solution to the problem of deviant causal chains.

Matters of open texture arise with respect to the reference class implicitly selected for which the process of seeing is identified. Strictly speaking, what is identified is the way a given individual is seeing during the time period in which we are investigating it. But normally an assumption is made to the effect that the processes now involved are those that were involved in the past, and will go on being involved in the future, when that individual sees; and it is also usually assumed that other members of the species see in the same way as the individual under scrutiny. Such assumptions (which are in line with standard scientific practice) may be modified in the light of further information.

5 Function and malfunction

Although there is much more that can be said about the various aspects of the Navigational Account set out here, I shall restrict myself in this chapter to a discussion of two final issues. In this section I shall consider the objections made by teleofunctionalists. It follows from the Navigational Account that whether a creature is now seeing an object is a fact that is, broadly speaking, determined by the current state of that creature: either by its current navigational behaviour, or by the fact that its present visual experiences are being caused by processes similar to those causally necessary for the production of such paradigm navigational behaviour. The past history of individuals in the same species may offer some inductive support for the attribution of a perceptual state, but is not a decisive factor.

The Navigational Account of perception might therefore be considered vulnerable to the kind of criticism levelled by teleofunctionalists such as Millikan at accounts of function which appeal to current states and capacities. Millikan argues that the eyes of my 'swamp double' do not have the proper function of 'helping it to find its way about'.[39] Since her claim is that proper functions, as she defines them (by reference to actual past behaviour, subject to selectional constraints) correspond to 'functions or purposes ordinarily so-called', the implication is that my swamp double does not see. Elsewhere she inclines to the view that a person fitted with a prosthetic eye does not see unless and until she is informed about the fact, and has had time to adjust to the device and gather evidence that its use leads to true perceptual judgements.[40]

Millikan's positive claims run counter to our natural ways of explaining behaviour. Suppose I am walking beside a road and my swamp-double is suddenly created by lightning on the other side. We advance into the road to meet each other, when a truck comes round the corner at high speed. We both leap out of the way, in different directions. At the physical and physiological levels, the explanation of what goes on in our bodies differs. But there is an important similarity at the psychological level: the common explanation of the fact that we both act in much the same way is that we both *see* the truck. The Navigational Account advocated here captures this similarity, since according to it the swamp creature sees from the moment it is created. Millikan's account cannot make sense of the generality of the explanation in this kind of case.

Millikan argues that it is not possible to arrive at a determinate conclusion as to the function of a biological organ, in the absence of information about its selectional history. Dispositions cannot help us, since talk of dispositions becomes 'handwaving ... toward the relevant ceteris paribus clauses under the heading "normal conditions"'. We cannot without circularity say what normal conditions are for the different creatures which can see: the appeal to normal conditions as conditions where things operate properly is circular, and the attempt to enumerate normal conditions descriptively will fail because the geographic conditions which are normal for different creatures are quite different. Since the Navigational Account involves the identification of processes which, by implication, are those operative when the perceptual system of a creature is functioning normally, it might be thought open to objection for this reason.

However, Millikan's criticisms of appeals to normal functioning, though well taken against some non-teleological accounts, do not affect the present account. The Navigational Account does not take as its starting point an isolated bodily organ such as the eye, or any other sense organ *within* a creature. It takes as a starting point a pattern of activity of the *whole* organism, which is focused on some particular object in its surroundings. In such cases it is hard to make sense of the idea that such activity could take place without there being some kind of information-link between subject and object. The account therefore has parallels to the account that Cummins gives of functions, where the capacity of a system *as a whole* to execute some complex task is explained by the type of inner mechanism that is causally operative (given its physical make-up), in enabling it to achieve that task – in the case of perception, to maintain an information-link. The assumption is that the subject has inner experiences. So, where these inner experiences are involved in successful navigational behaviour focused upon some feature of the environment, we are entitled to claim that the different parts of the overall perceptual process all contribute to its success. What matters is the capacity of the whole organism to see, and what general processes explain this. Talk of 'function', and of 'purpose' of particular kinds of sense organs in the body, if it arises in connection with seeing, is strictly derivative.

6 Illusions, hallucinations, and deviant causal chains

Finally, I take up the more subtle questions of what differentiates ordinary seeing from cases of illusions, and from the matching hallucinations which arise in a more complicated way in the deviant causal chain cases. I do not attempt to discuss all these perceptual phenomena in full, but I shall show how the dynamic approach provides plausible ways of distinguishing between the various cases. According to the Navigational Account, we identify normal perceptual processes by starting from paradigm cases of successful beneficial action, for example where a subject sees an apple on a branch, climbs up the tree, picks the apple and eats it. Investigation of such paradigm cases will reveal the physical and physiological mechanisms which essentially underlie navigational behaviour, and hence are physically necessary when that subject sees a physical object. The question of which object is actually seen, out of the many that are causally linked with the production of the experience, is also settled by this account. A *sufficient* condition for the claim that a given object is seen is that the object is the focus of navigational behaviour; it plays a dual role, both in bringing about the inner experience that does or could initiate an extended action, and as the action's terminating point.

However, such extended action is not always initiated. To prevent misunderstanding, I should emphasize again that it is *not* claimed that subjects can *only* see those objects which can be picked up and used in the course of such navigational behaviour. We do, of course, perceive clouds, far away hills and stars. The point is that in our navigational behaviour we make use of such distant objects as orienting landmarks to guide us in moving around our surroundings; moreover, when we do so by looking at such distant items, the very same physical and physiological underlying mechanisms are employed that occur in the paradigm cases – in the cases which would in principle be selected for investigation.[41] We see whatever is causally linked to our experience by such mechanisms, when they operate in the normal way (again, as specified via the navigational paradigm). Thus the underlying process that causes me to have an experience of an apple when I see an apple in normal conditions, and as a consequence select the apple and eat it, is the same process that occurs when I am caused to have an experience as of a cloud when I look up at the sky.

Thus in the first instance the Navigational Account enables the identification of veridical, or near veridical situations, where the subject is seeing relatively normally. For it is mainly in such normal cases that a subject will be able to navigate successfully through their surroundings and make discriminating use of objects. Superficially, this might seem to raise a difficulty for the account. The process that will in principle be selected as essential to seeing apparently misses out the kinds of illusions which lead to faulty beliefs, and hence to inappropriate actions; nevertheless, illusions are still cases where something is seen.

Nevertheless, the account can be extended in a plausible way to include illusory cases. In illusions, as noted earlier, some limited information is getting through from the object. The account can be used to make this rough notion more precise. Illusory experiences share several characteristics with normal experiences. In most illusions, the subject is able to acquire accurate knowledge about some aspect of the object seen. Thus when a red object looks green under neon light, its shape and position can still be made out, and even its colour can be distinguished from several other colours – e.g. a red coach may still be distinguished from a white coach under abnormal lighting conditions. Many illusions also come by degrees: there may be a series of gradual transformations or possible intermediary cases linking the illusory experience with a normal one. A gradual alteration of lighting conditions will lead to a correspondingly gradual change in the colour appearance; an increase in the density of fog will lead by stages from a situation where the features of an object are easily visible to that where only some dim shape can be made out.

Our knowledge of which mechanisms underlie seeing explains this feature of visual illusions. The transmission of light waves is the crucial physical link connecting the object seen and events within a subject. This transmission of information can be systematically distorted. Most importantly, the systematic transformation can apply independently to distinct dimensions of the physical input. Roughly speaking, each dimension of the physical input contributes independently to the features of the experience, so usually there is some kind of correlation between distinct features of the object and distinct aspects of the experience. Thus the colour of an object can appear to change while its apparent shape remains the same, and vice versa; these in turn are relatively independent of information about the distance and direction of the object, and so on. This means that usually the resemblance between the normal case and the cases that arise from distortion is sufficiently close for us to count illusions as genuine cases where an object is perceived, even when the subject is unable to recognize the exact type of object perceived.

All this is in sharp contrast to ordinary hallucinations and, in particular, to the deviant causal chain cases. In many such cases there is no similarity at all to the causal link between the subject's experience and the object to which by some freak coincidence it is causally related. Suppose, for example, that I drink from a drugged cup of coffee, and am caused by coincidence to have a hallucinatory visual experience *as of* a cup of coffee. Here the physical mechanism that is causally responsible for the experience is quite different from that involved in both normal seeing and also in illusions, so the situation is readily classifiable as a hallucination.

In a hallucination, the production of an inner experience is normally caused by mechanisms that are quite different from those involved in normal perception; in addition, there will usually be no match between the hallucinatory experience and the main originating cause. Because of these factors, hallucinatory experiences are of no use in helping us manoeuvre around the environment. In the deviant causal chain case cited earlier, the subject has an experience *as of* a red apple, caused in part by illumination of sufficient intensity coming from the object in front of her, which by chance happens to be an apple. As far as the causal contribution of the apple is concerned in generating the experience, all that mattered was the fact that the *intensity* of light emitted was above some critical level; none of the other features – the shape of the apple, its distance, position, and colour, and so on – was relevant. This means that the subject is unable to act on the basis of the experience which results.

What allows us to categorize the situation as one involving a deviant causal chain is the fact that when a hallucinatory experience is caused, it cannot contribute to any successful action. It is because there is no causally based correspondence between properties of the object and of the experience, preserved by the underlying mechanism of light waves transmitted, and so on, that the experiences that would arise in such a deviant case could not enable the subject to navigate through the surroundings. The subject would be unable to locate the apple and eat it. We therefore are entitled to dismiss this, and other similarly deviant cases, as a coincidentally caused hallucination. In this way, knowledge of the detailed causal mechanisms which occur in normal seeing would, if all else failed, enable us to distinguish genuine perception from the deviant cases. As I have argued in this part, our ordinary use of terms like 'see' involves an indirect grasp of this knowledge; we could in principle identify the appropriate causal mechanisms, by first starting from our *a priori* grasp of the concept of seeing.

We do, therefore, implicitly recognize which kinds of causal connection are appropriate for seeing. Our *pre-scientific* grasp of the concept of perception is what, in the end, justifies us in classifying as hallucinatory the experiences caused by deviant causal chains. But it is our grasp of the function of perception that forms the basis of our understanding, not in the first instance a grasp of detailed facts about the causal chain. Nowadays, it is true, most people with a reasonable education will appreciate facts about light waves and the eye, and have some grasp of the mechanisms involved in normal perception. Because of this, they might be tempted to dismiss some seemingly weird process as intuitively deviant, on the grounds that it involves the production of visual experiences by unusual means – for example, by smell. However, in principle, *any* causal chain, no matter how intuitively bizarre it seemed, would count as a mechanism of perception – so long as it could underpin successful navigational behaviour in a creature.[42] The intuitions we appeal to in order to classify a causal chain as deviant are not based simply upon the unusual nature of the causal chain – what really matters is our appreciation of the coincidental nature of the match between cause and experience. We understand that in the deviant causal chain examples this match could not be maintained in a *dynamic* context, so the causal link would not facilitate navigational behaviour. In the case of the drugged coffee mentioned above, the visual experience as of a coffee cup cannot help us find where the cup is and pick it up.

An important consequence follows from the present Navigational Account of perception. The account appeals to the interplay of perception and action in cycles of navigational behaviour which end with the discriminating beneficial use of objects perceived. An obvious corollary of this approach is that it also suggests a solution to the problem of deviant causal chains as it affects action: the type of causal chain essential to normal action is implicitly understood as that which occurs on the output side in such cycles of behaviour involving the discriminating use of objects. The problem of deviant causal chains is solved simultaneously for perception and action.

7   Conclusion

We are now in a position to understand the proper relation between the scientific notion of perception and the everyday non-specialist understanding. It is true that no account of perception can be considered adequate if it attributes to the average layperson explicit knowledge of scientific details which can only be revealed by empirical investigation. But the account offered here does not assume that such explicit knowledge belongs to our initial grasp of the concept. Both the layperson and the scientist start from the same *a priori* grasp of the general place of the concept of perception in our overall psychology, a grasp which enables them in principle to identify those processes that are genuinely perceptual. All scientific investigation into perceptual processes presupposes a conceptual element: it is subject to the same outline constraints about the structure of the concept that the layperson accepts.

It is therefore a mistake to claim that there are two distinct concepts of perception. There is only one general concept, and it relates to the different actual (and possible) modes of perception. Construing ordinary understanding and scientific understanding of perception as continuous makes sense of our different activities, and of the connections between them. It explains how the processes selected by scientists for investigation relate to common-sense understanding: scientific work does not arise in an arbitrary manner out of some conceptual limbo, but evolves within a framework founded on our everyday practices. It also explains how we have an indirect knowledge of the kinds of causal processes that are involved in perception. The Critical Realist claim that we should analyse perception in terms of the appropriate kind of causation of inner experiences is therefore vindicated.

8 Critical Realism and the alleged transparency of experience

1 Introduction

Let us take stock of the arguments for Critical Realism up to this point. In Chapters 1 and 2 we saw that there are good reasons for analysing perceptual experiences as containing two contrasting components. Experiences contain some form of conceptual activity, which accounts for the fact that we grasp what we are experiencing, and also for the intentional nature, or 'directedness', of perception. Experiences also have what is variously called a phenomenal, or sensory, component. This later component accounts for the fact that phenomenal qualities are immediately present, as actual elements in consciousness, in a manner that differentiates such perceptual experiences from purely representational states such as thought.

As we observed in Chapters 3, 4, and 5, there are powerful arguments for the conclusion that conscious visual experiences supervene solely upon the perceiver's brain states, and are causally related to the physical objects perceived. We can no more make sense of the claim that experiences are immediately related to physical objects, than we can make sense of the analogous claim made by sense-data theorists, that in perception the subject is immediately related to a sense-datum. Conscious visual experiences are in an important sense distinct from the material objects of perception that cause them to come about.

In Chapters 6 and 7, it was argued that when we reflect upon perception from the third-person, external viewpoint, we recognize it to be a causal process that enables a creature to navigate through its surroundings. We know that when we, as human beings, perceive objects, some kind of bodily activity is at least physically necessary for perceptual processes to take place. This is part of our common-sense causal picture of what it is to be an embodied agent living in a physical world. It is the framework within which experimental inquiry into perception is conducted. This framework comprehends the idea that the perceptual processes of complex creatures involves certain kinds of subjective inner states, some of which the subject can be conscious of and report upon.

The causal analysis of perception that these considerations imply carries implications for a comprehensive account of perception, a synoptic account that pays proper consideration to the first-person, subjective point of view. When I look at a clear sky in the daytime, a blue phenomenal quality fills my visual field; this is, in actuality, a phenomenal quality of my inner experience. In having a perceptual experience, I am in some sense – to be more fully explained – aware of inner states of mind that *mediate* my consciousness of the sensible qualities of the physical objects that I perceive.[1]

In order to properly understand what is meant by the above claim, two points need to be appreciated. First, the fact that I am aware, at a non-conceptual level, of a blue quality, which belongs to my own inner sense-experience, does not entail that I am aware of it *as such*. As Sellars argued in the first part of his attack on the Myth of the Given, the ontological status of 'expanses and volumes of colour stuff' is not something they phenomenologically present themselves as having; the blue I am aware of in a phenomenal manner is immediately present to me as a phenomenal quality, and not at a conceptual level.[2] I do not necessarily classify it for what it is; indeed, as I shall show, I normally do not classify it directly in any way at all, in having concepts and thoughts relating to the sky. Second, according to the Critical Realist view I shall elaborate, the subject's perceptual thoughts are usually focused directly upon physical objects, and not upon the inner phenomenal states which prompt them.

In this chapter and the next, I focus upon an important line of criticism directed against this picture of perceptual experiences as inner states. This criticism arises from the first-person perspective. Compelling as the arguments in favour of the causal account are, the Critical Realist position has been strongly resisted on subjective, or phenomenological grounds. There is a seemingly powerful empirically based objection to the causal theory of perception, one that has been formulated in various ways. At root, the objection amounts to the claim that, in some very obvious way, the causal theory of perception does not do justice to our common-sense understanding of perceptual experience.

This objection is often expressed as a claim that experiences are 'transparent': in conscious experience I am aware of physical objects directly; I am not conscious of any inner entities that mediate my awareness of the physical objects I perceive. The causal analysis simply does not mesh with the phenomenological facts. Physical objects are immediately present in experience. We are not aware of the states of our own minds when we look at the objects in our surroundings. As Crane expresses the point, the properties we are aware of in perception, such as colours, ' . . . seem to be properties of objects, not intrinsic properties of experiences.'[3] Even when we try to examine our perceptual experiences, all we find is the world. When I inspect, or introspect, my experience of a seeing a tree, all that the experience reveals is just the very tree I am seeing in the first place. I shall call this objection the *Transparency Objection*. This conception of transparency is supposed to be consonant with the views of common-sense, and supported by phenomenological considerations.

There is a related objection, which must be distinguished from the Transparency Objection. This second objection is based upon the fact that we are able to make demonstrative references to the physical objects we see. Such demonstrative claims are based upon what is made available to the subject through perceptual consciousness. When someone demonstratively singles out some physical object in the immediate surroundings, he or she must be referring to what is present in their experience.[4] The thought is that if physical objects are not made immediately available in consciousness, then successful reference to them would not be possible. I shall show how this second objection can be overcome in the final chapter.

We need to examine the Transparency Objection in detail. My aim is to show how we can account for the apparent strength of the objection, and at the same time explain why, in the end, it should not be regarded as carrying any weight. The so-called transparency of experience, I shall argue, is a cognitive illusion of a special kind. It does not undermine the Critical Realist account of perceptual experience.

It has to be acknowledged that superficially the Transparency Objection has a certain amount of intuitive force. But as I have already pointed out (in Chapter 4), there are, necessarily, limitations on what can be concluded from such arguments. In the case of hallucinations in which subjects are genuinely deceived into thinking that they are seeing real objects, they will have exactly the same phenomenological grounds for thinking that there are physical objects immediately present to their awareness, as in the veridical case. Yet in the hallucinatory case no relevant object exists. Phenomenological considerations are not decisive; they should not be taken to override all others.

Nevertheless, the causal theorist still owes us some account of what is going on in veridical perception. There does not seem to be room, in normal circumstances, for the presence of any entity other than the physical object perceived. Hence, if the Transparency Objection is to be resisted, what is required is an account of perception that does proper justice to the phenomenology, and at the same time explains how experiences are, in actual fact, inner states. To carry out this task involves a careful examination of the precise way that concepts are united with the phenomenal component of experience by the activity of the imagination.

2 Phenomenology and the Transparency Objection

The Transparency Objection is based upon two interconnected lines of thought, which are taken to support the Direct Realist view of experience. Both involve phenomenological claims. First, when under normal circumstances I look at the physical objects around me, I see them directly. I am not conscious of basing my perceptual awareness of objects on any other prior cognitive state. The books upon the table at which I am writing are directly present to my gaze. Admittedly, in some situations I may not be able to make out clearly what kind of object I am seeing. Perhaps what I take to be a black jumper on a chair in the corner of the room is, in fact, a black cat. The dark shape half hidden in the bush in front of me could be a stag. At the end of a streak of vapour in the sky I think I can make out an aeroplane, but I am not sure. Yet in each case what I see directly are physical objects in the world: a black object on a chair in the room, some physical structure in the bush, a streak of cloud in the sky above my head. From the subjective point of view, perception *starts* with the direct awareness of the physical world. There is no inference from any non-physical intermediary entities. Perceptual consciousness relates, in most cases at least, directly to the external physical objects in our surroundings.

This suggests that we should accept a phenomenological claim roughly along the following lines:

> P1   In ordinary perceptual experience the subject is directly aware of physical objects, without drawing inferences from any states or episodes whose contents do not already include references to physical objects.

I shall refer to this claim as the 'Directness Thesis'.

The second aspect of the Transparency Objection amounts to the claim that there is no *room* for something inner in experience. There is nothing further in my experience other than the physical objects I am presented with. When I try to turn my attention away from the world, and concentrate on the nature of my own experience, there does not seem to be any change in what is present in my experience. There is no difference to what I am consciously aware of. I do not become aware of any additional entities, belonging to a different ontological kind, and with a different range of qualities. Suppose I begin by looking at the book on the desk in front of me. I am directly aware of its red cover. When I try to introspect and attend to the character of my visual experience, then I do not discover anything new, no matter how hard I try. If I turn my attention inwards, I do not discover an extra set of entities, a 'shadowy inner world' of private, non-physical entities that exist in addition to whatever is present in normal perception. When I examine my experience of seeing the red book, it is the same red phenomenal quality that is present in my consciousness. The distinctively phenomenal aspects of perceptual experience are exhausted by the properties of the physical object I directly see.

These considerations suggest that there is a second aspect of the phenomenology of perception that can be captured as follows:

> P2   When the perceiving subject introspects her perceptual consciousness, and examines the experience of perceiving a physical object, there is no change in what is present in consciousness, and no additional entity is discovered.

I shall refer to the second phenomenological claim as the 'No Duplication Thesis'.

In his discussion of the transparency of experience, Martin arrives at what is, in effect, an equivalent distinction between two aspects of the claim. He observes:

> First, as we have already noted above, introspection seems to reveal experience to have less than the sense-datum theory predicts – there does not seem to be some private entity corresponding to each object of perception, or a subjective quality to correspond to each perceived feature of such objects. Secondly, introspection reveals that there is more to the character of experience than one would anticipate on the basis of a pure sense-datum or qualia-based view.[5]

The 'more' here relates to physical objects. In veridical perception, experience is entirely made up of the presence of physical objects; there is no room in it for further kinds of entity. According to Martin, in reflecting on the character of the experience of seeing a lavender bush, ' ... it does not seem to me as if there is any object apart from the bush for me to be attending to or reflecting on ... '.[6] The two theses P1 and P2 complement each other.

In his discussion of the phenomenology of perceptual experience, Valberg argues in a similar vein. But his treatment of these issues has an additional twist. He prefaces his discussion by distinguishing between two attitudes to experience. Suppose I have the experience of seeing a book on the desk in front of me. I can reflect on the nature of experience *indirectly*, by following through the claims of reason. Valberg argues that when I adopt the reflective attitude, I am in a position to grasp the arguments for holding that perceptual experiences are inner states. My perceptual experiences belong in the common causal network that characterizes all physical things, including my own body. They are distinct from the perceptual objects that bring them about.[7]

But I am also able to consider my experiences *directly*, simply by being, as Valberg expresses the point, 'open to how things are in experience'. When we describe this second attitude, talk of 'considering' experiences might be thought out of place. Perhaps I should say: I just have my experience; I am absorbed in it. When I adopt this stance, I find that what is present in my experience is the book itself, the physical object. But there is nothing else present in the way that the book is. The idea seems to be this: when we try to account for the distinctive nature of perception, we have to acknowledge the phenomenal (or sensory) aspect of consciousness.[8] However, the item present in a phenomenal manner when I look at the book is just the very book I see. There are no other entities present that I am aware of in a phenomenal manner. So when I am *open* to how things are in experience, Valberg concludes, 'all I find is the book'.[9] Valberg's appeal to *being open* to experience thus connects with what I am here calling the Transparency Objection. The phenomenal aspect of experience is fully exhausted by the physical objects that are present, so there is no room for awareness of inner, private entities.

McDowell seems to be making a similar claim in stressing the fact that 'in enjoying experience one is open to manifest facts. ... To paraphrase Wittgenstein, when we see such-and-such is the case, we and our seeing do not stop anywhere short of the fact.'[10]

But in order to support Direct Realism, the Transparency Objection needs to be based upon something stronger than the two unqualified phenomenological claims P1 and P2. For they can be interpreted in a manner that does not entail the conception of a physical object as a mind-independent entity. For example, something very close to the Transparency Argument was originally advanced by none other than Berkeley. Consider this passage from his second dialogue, when Berkeley is developing his notorious heat-pain argument:

> PHILONOUS: What shall we say then of your external object; is it a material substance or not?
> HYLAS: It is a material substance with the sensible qualities inhering in it.
> PHILONOUS: How then can a great heat exist in it, since you agree that it cannot in a material substance? I desire you would clear this point.
> HYLAS: Hold, Philonous, I fear I was out in yielding intense heat to be a pain. It should seem rather, that pain is something distinct from heat, and the consequence or the effect of it.
> PHILONOUS: Upon putting your hand near the fire, do you perceive one simple uniform sensation, or two distinct sensations?
> HYLAS: But one simple sensation.
> PHILONOUS: Is not the heat immediately perceived?
> HYLAS: It is.
> PHILONOUS And the pain?
> HYLAS :True.
> PHILONOUS: Seeing therefore that they are both immediately perceived at the same time, and the fire affects you only with one simple, or uncompounded idea, it follows that this same simple idea is both the intense heat immediately perceived, and the pain; and consequently, that the intense heat immediately perceived is nothing distinct form a particular sort of pain.[11]

Berkeley accepts the Directness claim, P1, that objects are seen directly. In his terms, 'sensible things are those only which are perceived by sense.' (1988: 124); and it is agreed by his disputants that the senses 'make no inferences'. By arguing that what is perceived in placing one's hand near the fire is one 'simple uniform sensation', Berkeley commits himself to the No Duplication claim, P2. I cannot, according to Berkeley, make any distinction between the quality I perceive, and my experience in perceiving that quality.

Yet, for Berkeley, the objects I see are not mind-independent. Berkeley's general conclusion, of course, is that a sensible thing such as an apple – what we would term a physical object – is a collection of ideas. Thus the transparency claim threatens to cut both ways; it can be embraced by idealists, as well as by realists of different persuasions. Moore, for example, held that acts of experiences are transparent, or, as he sometimes expressed the point, 'diaphanous'; but he also held that the object I am directly aware in perception is not necessarily to be identified with a physical object. Famously, he equivocated over the ontological status of the perceptual object.[12]

It is only when the physical object perceived is interpreted as a *mind-independent* object that the Transparency Objection can be taken to support Direct Realism. This indeed is what most supporters of the objection claim. Martin is careful to speak of the argument from the phenomenal transparency of experience as concerned with the claim that 'introspection of one's perceptual experience reveals only the mind-independent objects, qualities and relations that one learns about through perception.'[13]

The realist interpretation of the transparency claim is endorsed by many writers, including those already quoted here. In his defence of Direct Realism, Smith claims: 'Perceived objects do appear simply to be there. For consciousness they have an unmediated presence.'[14] and 'We need in short, to do justice to the immediate sensory presence of physical objects to us in perception.'[15] Such objects are essentially independent of our experiences of them. Experiences involve a distinctive intentionality, whereby we are made directly aware of independent physical objects that are spatially distinct from ourselves.

Interpreted in this realist way, the claims of transparency suggest there is a conflict between the deliverances of what may broadly be called the *phenomenology* of experience, and the causal analysis of perception defended throughout this book. When we combine the Directness Thesis, understood realistically, and the No Duplication Thesis, we appear to arrive at the conclusion that the items present in my experience are just the very physical objects that I perceive, and nothing more. Perceptual experiences, on this account, are transparent. They are not inner states, aspects of the subject's perceptual consciousness, but should be understood, instead, as *conditions* for the direct consciousness of external objects. If this interpretation is correct, then there would be no room for distinct inner phenomenal states in experience.

I shall argue that the Transparency Objection does not succeed. The two phenomenological theses articulated above can be interpreted in a manner that does not entail the conclusion that experiences do not involve an awareness of inner states. In spelling out how we are able to accept them, yet avoid the Direct Realist conclusion, the distinction between Critical

Realism and the other variants of the causal theory becomes central to my overall argument.

3 The Transparency Argument

We need to distinguish between the phenomenological claims in themselves, and the argument against the causal theory of perception that is implicit in the Transparency Objection. This argument, which I shall call the 'Transparency Argument', can be reconstructed for the modality of vision as follows:

(1) In seeing the book on my desk in front of me, I have a visual experience of it.

(2) When I see the book (veridically, as in the normal case), in having a visual experience I am directly aware of a mind-independent physical object and its properties, without drawing any inferences.

(3) When I introspect my visual experience of seeing the book, I am not aware of any change to what I was previously aware of in my experience; nor am I aware of any additional, non-physical, entities that I was not already aware of before I examined my visual experience.

(4) Therefore when I see the book, there is nothing in my visual experience that I am aware of in addition to that physical object.

(5) Therefore visual experience contains no entities that I am aware of other than the physical object perceived.

(6) Therefore the causal theory of perception, understood as involving the consciousness of inner experiences that mediate the awareness of physical objects, is mistaken (at least as far as vision is concerned).

The argument starts from a straightforward stipulation about what perception involves. Premises (2) and (3) in the argument reflect the phenomenological claims P1 and P2 outlined above. Premise (2) is intended to capture the Directness Thesis, and makes the claim that the perception of an object is not inferred from an awareness of some other state; while premise (3) reflects the thesis that introspection reveals nothing new. When the perceiver shifts his or her attention, the contents of experience do not vary. Step (4) follows on from premises (2) and (3). From these claims, step (5) seems to follow logically, and this entails the conclusion of the Transparency Argument, (6), that the causal theory is false.

Now we cannot reject the phenomenological findings out of hand as simply unfounded. But as we have already observed, the fact that some hallucinations are deceptive indicates that there is a limit to how much weight we can place upon them. My aim here will be to show how we can do justice to the phenomenological insights, while maintaining the causal analysis and rejecting the Transparency Objection. We need to make clear precisely what is delivered by appeal to phenomenological considerations, and whether the conclusions drawn about the nature of visual experience are justified. Even the most enthusiastic supporter of phenomenological approaches to perception ought to accept the caveat that it may not always be easy to translate the phenomenological findings into clear-cut principles and conclusions that pertain to the kind of descriptions offered by the metaphysician and the scientist.

I shall question the conclusion that introspection cannot *in any sense* reveal a distinct inner aspect to experience, an aspect that must be distinguished from the physical objects perceived. The Transparency Objection is unsound, not because the phenomenological claims are false, but because – as I shall show – it trades on an ambiguity. There is an equivocation in the use of the term 'awareness'. To establish this, we need to unpack carefully the meanings of the No Duplication Thesis and the Directness Thesis. It turns out that the sense of 'awareness' in which we are directly aware of physical objects is not the same sense of 'awareness' that relates to the immediate presence of phenomenal qualities. The two senses of 'awareness' connect with the different aspects of experience. Once this ambiguity is pointed out, the argument from transparency collapses.

But establishing that the Transparency Argument is unsound is only part of the task facing the Critical Realist in replying to the phenomenologically based objections to the position. If a perceptual experience does genuinely involve conscious inner states, this raises questions about why it is that we do not normally appreciate this fact, and whether this implies that ordinary perceptual experience involves some kind of error. It becomes necessary to explain why having a perceptual experience does not, in any straightforward sense, involve being *mistaken* about what is phenomenally present. So the second part of the reply, which I tackle in the following chapter, has to do with showing how we can do justice to the spirit of the phenomenology, yet still accept the causal theorist's claim that the objects we see are distinct from the experiences they produce.

My strategy will be to establish the following claims. There is a sense in which experiences involve the direct manifestation of physical facts to the subject, at the cognitive level. But this is compatible with the view that the phenomenal, or sensory, component of experience is an inner state of the subject; what is immediately present in phenomenal, non-conceptual consciousness must be distinguished from the physical events that are perceived. They belong to different categories. There is indeed some conflict between the deliverances of phenomenology, and the causal analysis. But the causal analysis arises at a reflective level, when we begin to theorize about the nature of perception. Such reflection is not a normal part of our everyday perceptual dealings with the world. So questions about the conflict in our assessments of experience do not arise in ordinary perception, for reasons we shall explore in more detail in the following chapter. There is no illusion about the kinds of physical objects that we normally see, or more generally, perceive. Normal perceptual experience does not involve an error about the nature of its objects. The situation is complicated, however, by the fact that there are intellectual pressures that can lead us to misconstrue the implications of the causal analysis, and also to misconstrue the phenomenology of perceptual experience. In too swiftly accepting the claims of transparency, and their apparent implications, we can become victims of a *metacognitive illusion*. This metacognitive illusion arises because we do not fully appreciate the complexity of the way that concepts operate in experience.

4 A general problem: how can experience reveal anything?

Before we examine the Transparency Argument in detail, there is an important preliminary point that requires clarification. This concerns the manner in which the phenomenological claims, upon which the argument rests, are grounded in experience. There is a real problem about how it is that experience can support phenomenological claims of any kind at all. The problem concerns the way that such claims are related to the perceptual takings or beliefs involved in perception.

Appeals to transparency appear to involve the following thought: just by *having* a perceptual experience, the perceiver is placed in a position whereby he or she is able to *classify* the ontological category of what is manifest in experience. The nature of experience is supposed to be the kind of thing that can be discerned through introspection. However, we need to be careful here about how to express the claims of transparency. The idea seems to be that when I try to examine or reflect upon my experience, I do not discover that it is an inner entity within my consciousness, distinct from the physical objects in my surroundings. Rather, when I try to examine it, all I find is the world. Noë, another advocate of the transparency claim, argues,

> To describe sensory experience, to reflect on it, is to turn one's attention *to* the experienced world. The experience itself is transparent. There's no experiencing it. There's only encountering the world – content – as you experience it.[16]

As we noted above, on the transparency account experience is understood as a *condition* for perceptual consciousness, but is not part of the content to which that consciousness is directed. So when we speak of examining (or introspecting, or reflecting upon) experience, what is specified is some method or procedure for uncovering whatever is present to consciousness when one has a perceptual experience.

There is a central ambiguity that needs to be resolved. Whatever the process of examining experience is supposed to be, it clearly yields a conceptual state. The resulting claims, for example, that what is directly present in perceptual experience is a physical object such as a book, or a bush, and so on, are the result of the exercise of concepts on the part of the subject. So the process of examining the nature of what is made present in experience is conceptually charged. However, it is unclear at what stage in the examination of experience concepts enter into this process.

There appear to be two options open to us, if we try to analyse what the process of examining one's own experience itself involves. According to the first option, experience is interpreted narrowly, as comprising just what is present, independently of the exercise of concepts. By introspecting, the subject can become aware of the raw phenomenal (or sensory) character of the experience. A careful phenomenological investigation reveals the nature of experience as it is independently of our beliefs. Then, by reflecting on what is thus made present (perhaps in the light of background beliefs), the subject is able to classify what is present as a part of the physical world. On this view, the examination of experience is treated as a two-stage process. At the first stage, there is just raw phenomenal experience; the subject has some kind of direct, pre-conceptual awareness of what is presented to the mind. In phenomenal experience the subject is nonconceptually aware of qualities and objects, but does not classify them. Then, by examining, or reflecting upon the nature of what is presented, the subject notices and correctly identifies or classifies the phenomenal qualities, or the type of object presented. The subject rationally arrives at the belief that what is immediately present in experience is an entity of a certain kind, because of their pre-conceptual grasp of what is presented to them.

The first option is open to the fatal objection that it is committed to a version of the Myth of the Given. What is envisaged is not coherent, as was pointed out in Chapter 1. When we turn our attention inward, and reflect upon the phenomenal nature of our own experiences, we may come to notice certain features of them. But all such noticing, attending, inspecting, and so on, necessarily involves the exercise of concepts. This is because to be aware of something is to be aware of what *kind* it is. As we noted earlier, it is not possible to grasp something in experience unless one thereby becomes aware both of what sort of thing it is, and also of what it is not. Awareness of kinds is not a simple registering of phenomenal, or sensory, items in experience; it essentially involves classification (although such classification may be at a very low level). It is thus not possible to be aware of aspects of phenomenal experiences independently, and prior to, the exercise of concepts. (There are attendant problems here, about the sense in which the idea of such nonconceptual phenomenal states relates to the notion of the 'object of perception'; I shall address these at the end of this chapter and in the following chapter, and show how the phenomenal aspect of experience can play a role in perception without becoming an object either in an intentional sense, or a Moorean sense.)

As Sellars argues in the first stage of his attack on what he terms 'the Myth of the Given', we must distinguish clearly between, on the one hand, the mere *having a sensation* of something red, and, on the other hand, *being aware that* something is red, or *being aware of something as* red.[17] For Sellars, there is a radical difference between having a nonconceptual phenomenal state (nonconceptual in the sense meaning not even involving the exercise of low-level classificatory concepts) and being in a conceptual state. We cannot notice what kind of thing is in our experience without employing some concept of the relevant kind.[18] So we cannot grasp or directly designate – or attend to, single out, refer to, etc. – any item in experience, independently of the exercise of classificatory concepts of some kind. There is no bare unconceptualized experience such that we can 'pitch in, examine it, locate the kind which it exemplifies', so that we can arrive at the correct classification of that experience.[19]

To be precise, we should say that there is no *cognitive* process of any such form, beginning with some kind of concept-free introspection of the nature or kind to which a repeatable aspect of unconceptualized bare experience belongs, and proceeding, by a process that involves inferences (or that in a significant way mirrors inferential processes), to the application of concepts *to that aspect of experience*. The phenomenal and the conceptual belong to different orders, as noted earlier. The phenomenal and the conceptual stages of experience are not linked by the kinds of inferential processes that may hold between concepts. The idea that there can be a process of this sort – a process that involves some kind of inference or quasi-inference, one that can be assessed in terms of its rational credentials – is not coherent.[20]

There is, however, a *causal* process that connects the two stages in experience, by which we are led to form our perceptual beliefs. It is perfectly coherent to suppose that a phenomenal nonconceptual state can be causally related to the exercise of concepts that are operative in perception. In other words, the nonconceptual component of experience causes perceptual takings: episodes that involve concepts relating to what the subject is perceptually aware of. The subject does not make inferences from the presence of unconceptualized states, but is nonetheless prompted to entertain perceptual thoughts as a result of them.

Since we are unable to grasp directly the unconceptualized content of experience, it follows *a fortiori*, that there is no sense in which subjects can compare their own raw phenomenal states with the concepts they apply in respect of them, in order to check whether they 'match'. This point is not simply a trivial consequence of the fact that what is present in a non-conceptual phenomenal manner belongs to a different order from the exercise of concepts. The point runs deeper. The problem is that there is no neutral vantage point from which the perceiving subject can *directly* assess whether or not the concept she is exercising is the appropriate one – because there is no concept-free grasp of the phenomenal in virtue of which one can examine it in order to find out to which kind it belongs. It therefore does not make sense to say that a subject can examine her experience, understood in the narrow sense as a concept-free phenomenal state, in order to ascertain whether she is employing the correct concepts with respect to it.[21] For these reasons Sellars points out in FMPP:

... we must not suppose that if the true theory of the status of expanses and volumes of colour stuff is one according to which they have categorial status C, then they present themselves phenomenologically as having this status.[22]

It is not always clear which conception of experience is being advocated by the upholders of the transparency thesis, when they claim that an examination of experience reveals that only physical objects are immediately present in normal perception. In the course of defending his own naïve realist version of the disjunctive view, Martin has an extended discussion of the phenomenon of transparency. According to Martin:

The disjunctivist wants to claim that when a subject is perceiving veridically, then the fact perceived is itself made manifest to the subject and is constitutive of his experience.[23]

For the naïve realist, the explanation of phenomenal transparency is explained in terms of the objects of perception:

... the objects have actually to be there for one to have the experience, and indeed one may claim that they are constituents of the experimental situation.[24]

Martin goes on to claim:

When one introspects one's experience, one notes these aspects of the experimental situation and hence attends to them and can report on them.[25]

These remarks could be interpreted as a version of the incoherent appeal to the Given criticized above. The difficulty is not helped by the fact that Martin appeals in a number of places to the supposed 'match' between the perceptual judgements, or beliefs the subject forms about his experiences, and what is made manifest to him.[26] Such claims might make sense on the intentionalist analysis of experience already rejected in Chapter 1, according to which both experiences and beliefs are able to share the same propositional content. However this escape route would not be open to Martin, since he makes his appeal to the alleged transparency of experience in the course of criticizing the intentionalist account.

I am not claiming that this has to be the correct interpretation of Martin's views in the paper cited. My point, rather, is to illustrate the way that some formulations of the transparency claim are ambiguous, and leave open the precise manner in which the notion of 'experience' is to be understood. Elsewhere Martin refers to experience as 'a matter of certain physical objects being presented as just so'.[27] Here one might interpret the term 'as' to be an indication that experiences come already formed by concepts; on this wider interpretation of 'experience', the claim that subjects ought to conform their beliefs to how things are experienced is coherent.

This leads us to the second option open to the advocate of transparency. We become conscious of what our experience contains in virtue of the fact that the nonconceptual phenomenal component causes the exercise of concepts, perhaps at a low level. There is no coherent sense in which a subject can be in a conscious state involving only an unconceptualized phenomenal state. Conscious experience, on this view, should be understood in a *broad* sense as already involving concepts, at least of some low-level, classificatory kind. So when I examine what I am directly aware of, I find only physical objects, because this is the way in which I am conceptualizing my experience.

On this alternative broader interpretation of experience, it would make sense to compare experience with the beliefs they give rise to. When we introspect, we may suspend our beliefs about the surrounding world, but what we find in experience still involves some classification. The attempt to get down to a phenomenal or sensory core of experience will always involve the employment of concepts, perhaps of a primitive or low-level kind. Nevertheless, the Direct Realist will still claim that perceptual experience is transparent. When I examine my experience of the red book, I am still aware of what appears to be a physical object, with a distinctive colour and shape; I am aware of what I experience as a red book.

However, to argue in this way is to deprive the transparency claim of its force. Only if what I find when I examine my perceptual experience is answerable to the distinctively *phenomenal* nature of what is present can the claim have any relevance to the debate about the nature of perception. For it is uninformative to be told that experience gives me direct awareness of mind-independent physical objects, if what I find when I examine my experience is determined by the concepts I employ. To be sure, the concepts I spontaneously form in normal perception are concepts that relate to physical objects. But that claim is also held by the Critical Realist theory. The important point is that if our perceptual concepts are *caused* by phenomenal states, it is possible that phenomenal states and the contents of our normal perceptual thoughts belong to different ontological orders.

Thus nothing follows about the ontological nature of what is present in a phenomenal, or sensory, manner from the mere fact that, in ordinary perception, I find myself naturally disposed to think of what I am aware of in terms relating to the physical object framework. The point about the appeal to phenomenological claims was supposed to be that we could justify the transparency claim by reference to what is present in experience *in addition to* the concepts we employ. What we are given instead, on the broad interpretation of experience, is the near truism that when I employ concepts of physical objects in attending to the nature of my experience, then I find that I am aware of physical objects. The objection, in a nutshell, is that when I try to examine the nature of my normal perceptual experience, what I 'find' merely reflects the concepts I am disposed to employ. It is not surprising then, that in normal perception my experience seems to be transparent. But this leaves open the possibility that, as the Critical Realist claims, such concepts are causally prompted by inner phenomenal nonconceptual states, which are distinct from the external objects I perceive.

Now there are various complications here about the way that the phenomenal and the conceptual components of experience interrelate, which we will unravel in the next chapter. I need to make three important points of clarification at this stage.

The first point to note is that, although the Critical Realist view claims that the idea of direct inspection of the phenomenal component makes no sense, the view does hold that there are *indirect* reasons for claiming that this component comprises an inner state of the subject, and not the immediate presence of physical objects. This was the conclusion of the arguments of Chapter 4: physical objects are not present in experience as phenomenal constituents.

The second point to note is that the expression 'conceptualizing one's experience' is ambiguous. Specifically, we must distinguish between two different sorts of states, or entities, which bear some kind of relevant relation to the concepts one is currently employing in perception. These are: (i) the phenomenal component in experience that guides the concepts employed in perception and attention, and (ii) the entities – usually external physical objects – that such concepts refer to; as we shall see in Chapter 9, this means that there are *two dimensions* to the exercise of concepts in experience. This leads to the idea, as we shall see in the following chapter, that the same phenomenal experience can be conceptualized in two different ways, either as a perceptual presentation of an external object, or as an inner state, of the kind that the subject recognizes could occur without an external object being perceived.

Third, if the phenomenal and the conceptual are viewed as causally related, it follows that there is no direct constraint upon the ontological category that prompts the formation of our perceptual takings. I may have a perceptual thought about the physical object I am seeing without that object being *immediately* present in my consciousness. My perceptual thought may be causally triggered by a nonconceptual inner phenomenal state that belongs to a different category from the kind of object that enters into the content of my thought. We have evolved in such a way that inner phenomenal states trigger perceptual responses that relate directly to the physical objects around us.

In other words, in the individual case where someone perceives an object, there need be no direct *rational* constraint on the connection between the phenomenal and the intellectual components of experience. There are certainly other kinds of general constraints that are operative, in view of the fact that we are able to describe our experiences. Perceptual thoughts are not inferentially based, yet they do have presuppositions.[28] This is why, for example, I can look at someone's face and see directly, without inference, that they are joyful, sad, amused, and so on. But because of the lack of a rational constraint, there is no necessity that our phenomenal states involve entities that belong in the same category as the objects of our perceptual beliefs.

5 The Critical Realist two-component model of perceptual experience

The argument of the previous section has been that if we understand perceptual experiences to contain two components, the phenomenal and the conceptual, they must be viewed as causally related. The difference between these two components provides the basis for a relatively straightforward reply to the Transparency Argument considered earlier. For convenience, I shall repeat the argument here:

(1) In seeing the book on my desk in front of me, I have a visual experience of it.

(2) When I see the book (veridically, as in the normal case), in having a visual experience I am directly aware of a mind-independent physical object and its properties, without drawing any inferences.

(3) When I introspect my visual experience of seeing the book, I am not aware of any change to what I was previously aware of in my experience; nor am I aware of any additional, non-physical, entities that I was not already aware of before I examined my visual experience.

(4) Therefore when I see the book, there is nothing in my visual experience that I am aware of in addition to that physical object.

(5) Therefore visual experience contains no entities that I am aware of other than the physical object perceived.

(6) Therefore the causal theory of perception, understood as involving the consciousness of inner experiences that mediate the awareness of physical objects, is mistaken (at least as far as vision is concerned).

The argument trades on an ambiguity in the term 'awareness'. We can distinguish two senses of the word, corresponding to the two components of experience. In steps (2) and (3), the word is used in a sense which implies the exercise of concepts. Thus (2) is normally true because in having a perceptual thought, my thought is aimed directly at the physical object I take myself to be seeing. I have to apply concepts in my experience, and normally these refer directly, without inference, to the objects I see – books, tables, trees and also to persons and their states. Exactly how concepts are applied in experience is matter I shall examine in greater detail in the next chapter. In connection with this form of conceptual awareness I shall speak of the subject having a *direct awareness* of an object *as* belonging to a certain kind. When I look at a book in normal circumstances, I am aware of it *as* a book, without inference. When I see a friend, I may see directly that he is cheerful, and so on.

Normally, when I examine the experience I have when I see a book in front of me, I carry on exercising concepts connected with that book. Nothing in my experience changes at the phenomenal level, so I am not aware of what I experience *as* of something changing. Nor am I conceptually aware of my experience as containing anything non-physical, which it did not contain before I examined my experience, because normally I only exercise concepts that relate to physical things. Hence step (3) is also true. Because I *normally* continue to employ physical object concepts, I am not conceptually aware of anything other than the book.

Strictly speaking, there is a slight change in my overall consciousness when I examine my experience of seeing the book. Nothing needs to change at the phenomenal level, but there is a switch in the concepts I employ. I shift from thinking about the book as an objective entity, as it would be if I were not seeing it, to thinking about the way the book *appears* to me. I form a thought about how the book looks from my subjective point of view. I become conceptually aware of how it is perspectivally. But I will *probably* continue to apply concepts that relate to the physical realm.[29] I identify my experience, how the object appears, by reference to the type of object that typically produces that kind of experience. So the argument up to step (3) respects the phenomenological principles P1 and P2.

The ambiguity in the argument lies in claim (4):

(4) Therefore when I see the book, there is nothing in my visual experience that I am aware of in addition to that physical object.

In order to see anything, I need to see it *as* something – if only as a physical object of some unspecified kind, somewhere in my surroundings. But in addition to the concepts I exercise, I am conscious also of the phenomenal qualities present, at a nonconceptual level, in my experience (or, in Sellarsian terms, qualities present as attributes of my sensing state). As we saw in Chapter I, this further nonconceptual sense of awareness is what makes perception something more than mere thought. To do justice to this aspect I shall sometimes refer to that which, in the nonconceptual sense, the subject is *immediately aware* of in their experience, or to what is *immediately present* in a sense that relates to consciousness – a sense of 'present' that should be distinguished from that in which physical objects are *physically* present in the subject's surroundings. This nonconceptual sense of awareness must be contrasted with the *conceptual* sense, in which I shall speak of being *directly aware* of something as a result of the exercise of concepts.

If we understand 'aware' in the conceptual sense, this provides an interpretation of claim (4) that makes it correct. Suppose I think of my experience simply as 'an experience of a book'. There is then nothing I am *directly aware* of other than the book, because what I am, in this manner, *directly aware* of is determined by the concepts I exercise in experience. In merely thinking of my experience as an experience of a book, I have not switched my concepts to reflect the nature of my phenomenal experience as it is, intrinsically. I do not think of it as part of an inner experience, distinct from the book I am perceiving. According to the core argument presented in Chapter 4, that is what my experience of the book is – an inner, mental state. But by identifying my phenomenal state in relational terms, I may avoid acknowledging this fact about my experience. Some people might reject the arguments of Chapter 4, and hold to the view that we perceive objects directly, without intermediaries. They would then conclude that their experience, though perspectival, contained no inner entities. From the standpoint of Critical Realism they would be under a meta-cognitive illusion, one that I shall discuss further at the end of the next chapter.

But if claim (4) were to be understood in this way, as involving a conceptualization of the experience in terms connected with the book perceived, then Claim (5) does not follow. For understood in this way, (4) does not rule out the subject having a *different* kind of awareness, an *immediate* awareness of the phenomenal nonconceptual inner state that accompanies the *direct* (conceptual) awareness of physical objects. Claim (5) refers to experience in an all-embracing way, to include both the phenomenal and conceptual components. In having a perceptual experience I am *immediately* (nonconceptually) aware of my inner phenomenal state. The phenomenal qualities I am non-conceptually aware of are distinct from the properties of the physical objects that cause them; they are analogical counterparts of these physical properties.[30] I may not be aware of my inner state *as such* – I may not conceptualize it as an inner state – yet that is what it in fact is, if the core argument succeeds. There is no intelligible relation, by virtue of which the subject is immediately aware, in the phenomenal sense, of the external world of physical objects. In seeing the book, I have an inner experience, even when I only think of that experience as an experience of the book.

Spelt out more fully, the crucial steps of the argument run as follows:

(4) Therefore when I see the book, there is nothing in my visual experience that I am *directly* aware of in addition to that physical object.

(5) Therefore visual experience contains no entities that I am *immediately* aware of other than the physical object perceived.

Clarified in this way, it is clear that claim (5) does not follow from (4), when the claim in (4) is understood to refer to the direct (conceptual) awareness of the book.

Alternatively, we can understand claim (4) to involve the idea of awareness in a *nonconceptual* sense, as *immediate* awareness. But in that case claim (4) does not follow from claim (3), where awareness is understood in a conceptual sense. As I will explain in more detail in the next chapter, I may be aware of something in the conceptual sense, and exercise a concept of a physical object, even though in seeing that object my phenomenal experience belongs to a different ontological category. The existence of deceptive hallucinations supports this conclusion; these indicate that there may be a disparity between the concepts I employ in experience, and the entities I am aware of at the phenomenal level. So once again, the argument fails to go through. At some point in the argument there is always an equivocation over the meaning of 'aware'.

It follows that if experience is understood as involving two components, then the Critical Realist interpretation of the phenomenal aspect is not undermined by the Transparency Argument: according to Critical Realism, in being *directly* aware (conceptually) only of physical objects, the subject is *immediately* aware (nonconceptually) of his or her own inner phenomenal states, whether or not they appreciate this fact. As Lowe summarizes the view, using the term 'qualia' to refer to phenomenal states:

> Our qualia are just qualitative features of the perceptual experiences we enjoy when we perceive the only sorts of objects we ever do perceive, namely, 'external', physical objects ... [31]

The advocate of transparency may attempt to object to this general view of experiences by appealing to some kind of necessity attaching to our employment of physical object concepts. There is a line of thought that might be associated with Kantian considerations. The introspection of perceptual experiences supports the transparency claim, the argument runs, because the only way that we can think of phenomenal experience is in terms of the concepts that apply to the physical world. Even if I bracket my beliefs about the existence of objects, I still, perforce, have to think of what appears to me as an appearance of the kind that I get when I perceive a book.

This line of thought contains an important insight, to which we shall return in the final chapter: the physical object framework occupies a fundamental position in our thinking about experience. But this still falls very much short of what the appeal to transparency seeks to establish.

The ontology of the physical object framework is indeed central to our thinking. Looking green, as Sellars was very much concerned to argue, presupposes the concept of being green, in a physical sense.[32] But although the existence of the physical world is a presupposition of our being able to refer to our own experiences, this does not entail that we must, of necessity, always conceptualize those experiences in terms that indirectly refer to the physical objects that standardly cause them. In the individual case, how we respond conceptually to the phenomenal experiences we have can vary. It depends upon the context. We can and do apply concepts of radically different kinds to our experiences. We sometimes think of the phenomenal, or sensory, components of experiences in terms of their intrinsic nature, as *inner* subjective states, and as potentially distinct from any particular objects in our surroundings. I shall establish these claims in the following chapter. I shall spell out how an understanding of phenomenal experiences as inner states underlies much of our common-sense reflection on the nature of perceptual phenomena. There are no compelling arguments derived from our common-sense thinking about perception that rule out the Critical Realist account.

There is a second consideration here, of equal importance. Suppose that it were true that, of necessity, we always and only applied concepts relating directly to the physical objects in respect of occurrent experiences. Suppose, that is, when I have an experience, I am always prompted to have a perceptual belief whose content refers to physical objects. My perceptual beliefs would be of the form:

> That is ... a tree/apple/book/dog ... etc.

Or:

> There is ... a tree/apple/book/dog ... etc, in front of me.

Suppose further, that if I find out that I am suffering from a hallucination, my revised claim about experience always takes the form suggested by Evans:[33]

> It seems to me as though I am seeing a tree/apple/book/dog ... etc, but there is no actual physical object present.

This would not, in itself, indicate that the phenomenal aspect of experience involved a state of direct awareness of physical objects. Our perceptual thoughts could still be causally mediated by inner phenomenal states, even if those inner states never in fact become the objects of further reflective thoughts at the time that they occur.

We are now in a position to spell out the Critical Realist analysis more fully, as follows:

A subject S perceives some particular physical object X, in the full sense that includes conceptual activity, if and only if the following conditions hold:

(1) The object X exists.

(2) The subject S has an experience E, consisting of two components:
    (i) an inner phenomenal state E,

    that causes

   (ii) an episode involving concepts of at least some low-level kind – a perceptual taking – relating to a physical object.

(3) The object X causes E to come about by an appropriate causal chain C, where C can implicitly be understood (by anyone who grasps the ordinary concept of perceiving) as the kind of causal chain which sustains navigational behaviour on the part of S with respect to X.

The subject is *directly* aware, in a conceptual manner, of the physical object he or she perceives; that is, the subject forms the noninferential perceptual thought that focuses on what is taken to be perceived. Nevertheless, he or she is at the same time *immediately* aware, nonconceptually, of inner phenomenal (or sensory) states that mediate the perception of an object. Because of the nonconceptual nature of such inner states, the subject need form no thought about their status; in this sense, he or she may lack a clear grasp of the ontological structure of their experience. The phenomenological principles that were articulated earlier can be upheld because, properly understood, they do not conflict with Critical Realism.

6 Critical Realism and the phenomenological unity of perception

The advantage of the Critical Realist position is that it allows us to hold on to two apparently conflicting insights into the nature of perception. On the one hand, as was argued in Chapters 3 and 4, there are powerful arguments for the view that experiences are inner states, and that the same type of phenomenal content can be common to veridical perception, illusion and hallucination. We have, moreover, argued that there is no coherent way of making sense of the Direct Realist's claim that experiences contain the physical objects we perceive as *phenomenally presented* constituents. Inner experiences are distinct from the objects we perceive.

   Yet, on the other hand, there are a number of important considerations about the objects of perception, based upon the phenomenology of experience, upon our common-sense understanding of perception, and upon the way that perceptual experiences are integrated with actions directed on to the physical world. Perceptual experiences are intentional: they are about the physical objects, events, and other people in our surroundings. These considerations all combine to suggest that the inner experience is not the *object* of perception, where the object of perception is determined by the concepts employed directly in the perceptual thought. In some sense we do perceive physical objects directly. Critical Realism therefore holds that the inner phenomenal state and the perceptual object should not be identified; they need not be of the same ontological kind, at least not in any obvious sense.[34] They belong to different categories, and are causally connected.

   But is this a case where the offered treatment is worse than the disease? For it will be objected that the Critical Realist two-component view of experience is open to further phenomenological criticisms: if we understand experience as involving two components, which relate to distinct ontological orders, can we ever explain in a satisfactory manner the phenomenological unity of perception? To show that Critical Realism offers a means of replying to the Transparency Argument is but the first stage in the reply to the phenomenological objections to the causal theory of perception. We need to develop the theory further, to show how it provides adequate answers to further objections raised against the theory.

In his recent book, David Smith has raised a number of objections to the Critical Realist two-component theory of perceptual experience. One criticism Smith makes is that the theory is too inclusive. He cites the following case as a counter-example to the analysis of perceptual experience in terms of two, causally related, components.

> Indeed, it is presumably possible that a headache could cause me to believe that my mother is present. I should not, however, thereby be perceiving my mother – even if she were indeed present, and even if she had somehow caused the headache.[35]

In the form in which it has been defended in this book, however, the example is insufficient to defeat the causal theory. According to the Critical Realist version outlined in the previous chapter, the causal connection with the subject's phenomenal experience has to be of a kind that sustains navigational activity with respect to the physical objects perceived. Normally, headaches do not vary in a manner that reliably causes beliefs about the presence of relatives, so that one can locate them, and so on (however burdensome some of them may be on occasion). Moreover, the experiences must be of the appropriate kind so as to facilitate distance perception; they must be capable of mapping on to spatial factors such as distance and position, at least, so as to prompt true beliefs about objects in the surroundings.[36] So the subject's phenomenal experience has to be understood as visual, auditory, or something sufficiently similar in structural complexity. Such experiences may include the kind that we may assume that a bat has, using sonar, or that is triggered by the use of artificial aids in 'prosthetic vision'.[37]

Nevertheless, there is a very important phenomenological point behind Smith's objection. The perceptual experience of an object does not, after all, strike us as consisting of two entirely separate parts. The consciousness of an object is a unified state. Even if we reject the claim that physical objects are *immediately* present in phenomenal experience, we should account for the intimate link between the phenomenal and the conceptual.

When I look at a scene, I am able to single out particular features in my experience. For example, I may see two fruits next to each other; in applying the concept: *apple* to one, and *orange* to another, I am linking my concepts with what is presented immediately in a phenomenal, or sensory, manner.

So the question arises, how do the different concepts that I concurrently exercise link up with the different phenomenal features in my experience? A partial answer is that the connection between the phenomenal and the conceptual is cashed out by facts about my actions. For example, if I wish to eat an apple, the concept of an apple will figure in the mental states that led me to pick one of the fruits up, and to a change in the aspect of my overall visual experience caused by the apple.

Yet even before I carry out any action, some kind of connection is operative in my experience. There is such a thing as singling out an object in attention, in virtue of the very way that it is present in experience. Smith claims that, 'We need ... to do justice to the *immediate sensory presence* of physical objects to us in perception.'[38] Even though the Critical Realist theory does not accept that physical objects are immediately present at the phenomenal, or sensory, level as Smith alleges, it ought to explain the way that specific phenomenal structures in experience mesh with our perceptual thoughts about the objects we perceive. We may summarize this line of objection in the form of a condition that any adequate account of experience should meet, as follows:

Condition (1)

An analysis of experience should explain the way that the two components of experience are unified when I attend to an aspect of a physical object I perceive. It should account for the way that the concept I entertain applies to some specific aspect of what I am aware of, nonconceptually, at the phenomenal level, and not to the whole scene, indiscriminately.

A second, related, difficulty for the two-component account is raised by Smith. He queries how a perceptual sensation (i.e. a phenomenal state) 'can be in consciousness and yet not be an object of awareness'. Does the Critical Realist theory suggest that we simply overlook our phenomenal states? We need to give a proper account of the role of phenomenal experiences. If they are not objects of perception, it needs to be shown that they are not mere idle accompaniments of our perceptual thoughts.[39] This leads to a second condition:

Condition (2)

An analysis of experience should provide a positive account of the role of the phenomenal component of experience, while explaining why it need not become the object of perception.

There is a final problem connected with the analysis of conscious perceptual experience. On many traditional accounts of perception, it is claimed that the subject really perceives a sensation, or a sense-datum, which is mistaken for a physical object. Smith points out that both Hume, and also, more recently, Prichard, advocated views along these lines.[40] It has been alleged that Mackie argued for a similar view.[41] The idea that all perception involves some kind of mistake or error strikes many as counter-intuitive.

The kind of mistake involved in perceiving an object, if there is one, is certainly not a mistake on a par with an ordinary perceptual error about the type of physical object one is seeing. It is not the kind of mistake that is accepted once the error is pointed out – as the history of the philosophy of perception bears ample witness to. If we were constantly mistaken about the things we perceive, we would be unable to account for the successful way that we interact with the world. There is therefore a further condition that applies to an adequate account of perceptual experience:

Condition (3)

An analysis of experience should explain the unity of consciousness without imputing to the perceiving subject a straightforward error every time he or she perceives something.

In the light of the various criticisms set out above, Smith claims that the two-component theory of experience makes the connection between the phenomenal aspect of experience and the perception of physical objects unintelligible.[42] There is a phenomenological unity in experience that needs to be accounted for. Because of such criticisms, the Critical Realist analysis of perceptual experience, as elaborated thus far, should only be considered as a first stage in a full account of perceptual consciousness. The analysis needs to be developed still further. In order to show how that account can meet the three conditions specified above, we shall turn in the next chapter to a consideration of a key aspect of experience, one we have not, so far, touched upon. This concerns the crucial role played by the *imagination* in perceptual experience.

9 Imagination and the unity of experience

1 Sellars on the role of the imagination

In the late 1970s, Sellars added a further dimension to his Critical Realist theory of perceptual consciousness. In a key paper, ostensibly focusing on Kant, he spelt out the essential role played by the imagination in perception.[1] Sellars argued that the exercise of the imagination acts to bring together the conceptual and the phenomenal, or sensory, components of experience. It is through the role of the imagination that perceptual consciousness is unified.

For Kant, the imagination functions as part of the faculty of the understanding. Rosenberg, in a paper sympathetic to the Sellarsian project, elaborates the Kantian view:

> The bottom line, in short, is that the imagination is not a third faculty, correlative to sensibility (receptivity) and understanding (spontaneity). On Kant's view, the imagination just *is* the understanding. More precisely, *talk about* the imagination adverts to certain of the *roles* of the understanding in perception, certain of the ways in which it contributes to the unity of the perceptual act.[2]

Sellars develops these Kantian insights in more detail. On his later view, perceptual consciousness is still understood as comprising two basic aspects: nonconceptual phenomenal consciousness, and conceptual activity focused directly upon external objects.[3] These two components are now viewed not simply as causally connected components that make up experience, but as *unified* through the activity of the imagination. The first-person perspective on experience becomes a central concern.

The imagination – or, more strictly, the productive imagination – plays two essential roles in perception. First, through its exercise in the understanding, the subject *conceives* of the object perceived. For example, I may see the object in front of me as an apple. I take it to be an independent entity, having objective existence as a physical object, situated in some position relative to my body (remembering here, as elsewhere, that 'conceive' is being used in a broad sense, to capture low-level classification). I conceptualize what I see *as* an apple because of the physical input from that object, given my background beliefs, and prior learning. I can employ the complex demonstrative: 'This apple ... '.

Second, the productive imagination leads to the construction of what Sellars terms 'sense-image-models' of the object I see. This is a complex idea, and requires some unpacking. When I see a red skinned apple in normal circumstances, the physical input from the apple causes an inner visual phenomenal state. Immediately present in my consciousness is a red phenomenal expanse, corresponding to the facing surface of the apple. This red phenomenal experience is distinct from the apple seen, though, importantly, it does not present itself to me *as* an inner state.

The phenomenal red expanse of which I am non-conceptually aware is not an intentional object. It has *actual* existence, in the way that the mythical desired Fountain of Youth does not. As Sellars expresses it, the quantity of red 'is actually or, to use a familiar metaphor, bodily present in the experience.' But we need to say something more about the complex way in which the imagination is active in normal perception, when we see objects for what they are. Sellars addresses the question of the status of the volume of white apple flesh that the apple is seen as containing. He concedes to phenomenologists, that 'an actual volume of white is present in experience in a way which parallels the red. We experience the red as containing the white.' The use of 'as' here might make it seem as if Sellars is assigning the imagined white to the conceptual component of experience. But this is not what Sellars has in mind. Together with the imagined white of the apple, there may be, in my perceptual experience of it, further imagined features of juiciness and coolness. Sellars claims:

> But while these features are not seen, they are not *merely* believed in. These features are present in the object of perception as actualities. They are present by virtue of being imagined.[4]

So such features, which are not directly seen *of* the apple, are still importantly present, by virtue of the workings of the imagination.[5] More specifically, they are present as nonconceptual *image states* in experience.[6] They are also referred to at the conceptual level, as aspects of the physical object perceived. In a manner that parallels the analysis of the dual component view of perceiving, the imagination operates at two levels. It is a blend of imaging and conceiving.

The sense-image-model or structure of the apple comprises the totality of what is *present*, in the nonconceptual sense, in experience; it combines contributions from the senses and from the imagination. The model is, necessarily, perspectival: it represents the object seen from the point of view of the subject. Such a structure is subjective, and transient. But it is only grasped, because we exercise concepts in relation to it. I am conscious of the apple in virtue of conceptualizing the whole sense-image-model as a cool, juicy, white-containing, red-surfaced apple; an independent, non-perspectival, enduring thing.

One further, very important, element needs to be added to the analysis. Sellars speaks of the concepts we exercise in perceptual experience as connected with sets or sequences of 'sense-image-models', in the plural. To grasp the concept of an objective kind, such as an apple, or tree, or dog, in the way that enables me to apply it directly in experience, entails that I understand what it is like to perceive that object from different points of view, and through time.

This leads to what Sellars, following Kant, calls the schema of an object. The schema of an object is like a recipe that gives rise to a grasp of the possible experiences connected with that object. To change the example, to have an observational concept of a dog as an independent physical entity, I must appreciate that it is possible to see the dog from different points of view. The dog schema has to do with my implicit grasp of sequences of perspectival sense-image-models of myself looking at the dog; I must be able to envisage what it would be like, from my point of view, to look at the dog as I walk around it. I am prepared for how my experience of the dog would change. As Sellars expresses the point:

> In the first place, the productive imagination is a unique blend of a capacity to form images *in accordance with* a recipe, and a capacity to conceive of objects in a way that *supplies* the relevant recipes. Kant distinguishes between the *concept* of a dog and the *schema* of a dog. The former together with the concept of a *perceiver* changing his relation to his environment implies a family of recipes for constructing image models of *perceiver-confronting-dog*.[7]

Thus according to Sellars's model, seeing a dog *as* a dog is a complex affair.[8] At the nonconceptual level, I have an immediate awareness of visual sensations triggered by physical input from the dog; also present in my experience are images of the dog, which are combined with the visual sensations into a unified structure, a sense-image-model. At the conceptual level, my perceptual takings, in the form of demonstrative thoughts, focus on the dog itself. I conceive of this object, this animal, as an independent space-occupying thing. I am not aware, conceptually, of the sense-images-models *as such*. But my grasp of the schema of the dog enables me spontaneously to construct them in my experience. Such structures both guide and, through feedback, are guided by my conceptual interpretation of the object I take myself to be seeing. The sense-image model of the dog approximates to what some philosophers have called the non-epistemic *appearance* of the dog, understood as an inner state.[9]

It is arguable that Sellars concedes too much here to phenomenological considerations. Should we agree that the visual images of a white volume and the gustatory image of juiciness are *actually* present in my experience of the apple, in the same way as the visual redness resulting from sensory input? Why not claim that, in so far as the whiteness is imagined, it is present only as conceived, as an intentional object?

On behalf of Sellars, it could be urged in reply that an application of the Subtraction Argument, appealed to earlier in Chapter 1, supports the conclusion that at least some forms of imagination involve the production of images that have actual existence. Consider, for example the well known phenomenon of having a tune 'running through one's mind'. A certain musical phrase can lodge in one's head, sometimes even to irritating effect. To hear, internally, a tune in one's mind in such a fashion is phenomenologically quite different from merely thinking of the relation of the notes without imagining the tune. Mentally rehearsing the start of Haydn's opus 76 D minor string quartet – nicknamed, because of the repeated use of the musical interval, 'fifths' – is phenomenologically very different from thinking of, without imagining, the different intervals of a fifth as incorporated into the music. In the former case, it is arguable, the presence of inner auditory images accounts for the difference. Similar considerations apply to the visual case. Suppose I am considering a chess position on the board in front of me. There is a difference between merely thinking about a possible move, say placing a white rook on a vacant square on the seventh rank, and actually imagining, in the full-blown sense that involves the formation of visual images, the chess piece – a Staunton pattern, light brown wooden object – being on that square. Such arguments support the view that images have actual existence, and must be distinguished from the intentional objects of acts of imagining. So we can make sense of a subject's visual consciousness containing not only visual sensations, but, in addition, visual images.

Nevertheless, to acknowledge that images are the kinds of things that can have actual existence in consciousness is not the same as admitting that they are present in every case when we perceive a physical object. One may be sceptical of the view that images are as complete and extensive as Sellars in some places seems to suggest – perhaps as an unnecessary concession to the claims of phenomenology.[10] Perhaps in anticipation of eating an apple I may form an image of its white juicy centre, but I don't in corresponding fashion normally form an occurrent *image* of the whole volume of flesh contained within a dog's furry exterior.

In any case, there is a further objection that can be raised against the account. Both the exercise of the concept of a kind, and also the ability to construct various images associated with that kind, derive from the faculty of understanding. This is a *causal* explanation of how experience is unified. But we do not yet have a full explanation, from a *phenomenological* point of view, of how the two faculties are connected in the perceiver's *conscious experience*. We still have not answered Smith's objection: the connection between concepts and what it actually present in experience should be more than mere simultaneity. We need to say something further about the way that the imagination operates in guiding our expectations about the phenomenal component in experience.

It is instructive to compare Sellars's comments on this point with similar observations expressed by Strawson. In his paper on the role of imagination in experience, Strawson notes the difficulty of accounting for the way that the generality of a concept combines with the particularity of a given phenomenal experience.[11] To conceptualize a fleeting experience and take it to represent an enduring distinct object of a certain kind requires that experiences are necessarily grasped as combined with a range of other possible experiences which would count as belonging to the same object. In articulating these Kantian ideas, Strawson describes our recognitional ability as follows:

> ... the recognition of an enduring object as an object of that kind, or as a certain particular object of that kind, involves a certain sort of connection with other, nonactual perceptions. It involves other past (and hence nonactual perceptions), or the thought of other possible (and hence nonactual) perceptions, of the *same* object being somehow alive in the present perception.[12]

Strawson goes on to argue that the recognition of an object as belonging to a kind must also involve the thought of nonactual perceptions of *other* members of the same kind. It does not make sense to say that applying a concept in experience is something that I can do only once, in respect of one object. My capacity to recognize an object must extend to understanding how it looks from different points of view, or – what comes down to essentially the same point – understanding how different members of the same category look. To be capable of categorizing an object, directly in experience, as belonging to a certain kind, is to be capable of categorizing other members of the kind. Yet, as Strawson acknowledges, it is difficult to explain just what the connection is that we make between a given experience and other experiences of the same category of object. We need to cash out the metaphor of *other* possible experiences "being alive" in an experience.

In order to deal with this problem, we need, first, to make a slight revision to the basic Sellarsian model of experience, as set out above. We can develop further the role of the *schema* of a concept. When I see an object in the full, rich sense that Sellars and Strawson are discussing, I have an *implicit* awareness of possible future experiences relating to it. Seeing an object involves more than the *actual* presence of a sense-image-model of it, together with a perceptual taking. In exercising a concept at a given time with respect to the object I see, I can imagine that object's potentialities. I implicitly accept that the sense-image-model I am aware of is one out of a possible sequence of such models, those that would be present in experience were I to view the object from different locations, and in different circumstances, etc. I have implicitly held expectations about the possible courses of phenomenal experience that would result if I were to act upon the object, expectations that result from my grasp of the *schema* of the object. This means that the exercise of concepts in experience has a dispositional aspect. I am prepared for certain kinds of *transformations* to the sense-image-model I am currently experiencing. The sense in which experiences of other members of the same kind are 'alive' in my present experience consists in this preparedness: in virtue of the fact that I conceive of the object as belonging to the general kind, I have implicit expectations about the future transformations of my phenomenal experience while I am perceiving the object.[13]

It needs to be emphasized here that although I might be able to articulate some of my expectations about the phenomenal aspect of my experience (perhaps with some difficulty), these expectations do not normally occur as explicitly held beliefs. They are implicitly grasped. They arise by virtue of the concepts I exercise about the object I take myself to be seeing, but they are only dispositionally present in the form of anticipations, or forms of preparedness, in respect of the way that my nonconceptual phenomenal experience is likely to be transformed.

Importantly, these expected transformations to phenomenal experience are of two different kinds. Suppose I see the object in front of me to be a dog. In conceiving of it as a dog, I am, implicitly, prepared for transformations to my present experiences that are appropriate to experiences of a dog. Some transformations I am prepared for correspond to the changes I would expect to result from my own movements relative to the dog – if for example, I were to walk around it.[14] But others would correspond to changes resulting from what the dog might do of its own accord: I am prepared, implicitly, for the fact that the dog might get up, stretch, and walk away. In other words, there are some expected transformations which are connected with our own actions, and others that are connected with the object's own nature. Such expected transformations are essentially connected with how I conceptualize what I see. In seeing the dog as such, I am prepared for it to act like a dog; I am not, however, prepared for it to turn bright red, and float off into the sky like a balloon. For convenience, I shall sometimes speak of the expectations of transformations to the sense-image-model as expectations about the (nonconceptual) *appearance* of the object.

To analyse perceptual experience according to the revised account I am advocating does not require any fundamental change to the Sellarsian model. The perceptual experience of an object is still understood as comprising two components. The main change concerns the nonconceptual phenomenal component of experience. The revised account accepts that actual images may be generated in nonconceptual experience in the construction of sense-image-models. But the emphasis is on the way that concepts referring to external objects generate implicit *expectations* with respect to what is present in experience at the nonconceptual phenomenal level. What matters most, subjectively, when I perceive an object to belong to a certain kind, are my expectations relating to further phenomenal experiences of that object. This is to understand the role of the imagination in a more dispositional way than described by Sellars. The revised account is nevertheless in keeping with the spirit of Sellars's account, and his conception of the underlying two-fold nature of experience.[15] We can think of such expectations as forming an essential part of the notion of a sense-image-model appropriate to what is seen. These expectations form an important dimension of the exercise of concepts in experience.[16]

2 The two dimensions of the exercise of concepts

The central insight of Critical Realism is that I do *not* explicitly conceptualize the possible transformations of phenomenal experience *as such*, in ordinary perception. According to the Critical Realist view, as defended here, recognitional concepts can be seen, in effect, as involving two 'dimensions' in their employment. In exercising a concept of a recognitional kind, my cognitive awareness and my actions *refer to*, or are focused directly upon, the physical object I see – the object as it exists objectively. In addition, I have a set of *implicit expectations* about the way my phenomenal experiences of that object will conform to certain patterns when I act upon it. In being aware, nonconceptually, of my inner phenomenal states, I am guided by them in acting upon objects. Sellars is making a similar point when he writes:

> Another way of putting this is by saying that a perceptual judgement can be about a physical object without the object being referred to as *the such-and-such*, and yet also without the object being in consciousness as the colours we see are in consciousness. Thus, when Jones sees a chair, although his 'perceptual experience' is *founded on, guided by*, and *controlled* by his sensations, there is nothing in the nature of aboutness or reference which requires us to say that his 'experience' is primarily about the sensations, and only about the chair in some complicated or derived sense of 'about'. His perception is 'mediated by' the sensations, but his perception is not *about* the sensations.[17]

Even though I do not normally reflect upon my inner phenomenal states, I may manifest these expectations indirectly, in ways that I shall shortly indicate. The account I shall provide helps to make sense of the important continuities between the perceptual capacities of humans and non-human animals.

Before illustrating these ideas about the connections between concepts and phenomenal states in more detail, via a number of examples, let me summarize the Critical Realist account of perceptual experience that we have now arrived at. As we have noted, to consciously perceive an object is to classify it, by exercising concepts (perhaps low-level) of some kind. Some of the concepts we apply to an object will be inferentially based upon the exercise of other concepts. But there are some basic perceptual concepts we apply, directly and spontaneously, without inference. They contribute to what it is like to have a perceptual experience. Concepts of this kind count as observational for the perceiver. In what follows we shall be concentrating on the way that such concepts enter into experience.

Consider again a paradigm of veridical perception. I see a dog lying down in front of me, in normal circumstances. I directly recognize it to be a dog, without making any inferences (though my exercise of that particular concept is a causal consequence of my sensory stimulation, background beliefs, and the like). My exercise of the concept *dog* in relation to the phenomenal component of experience leads to an account of conscious experience that has four central features:

(1) My visual consciousness contains a nonconceptual phenomenal state, caused by input from the physical object I see. This state involves the immediate presence of phenomenal qualities. I am nonconceptually aware of a visual expanse with a certain phenomenal shape and colour, corresponding to the perspectival shape of the dog that I am seeing. Although complex, this awareness does not have the form of an Act-Object relation, as understood on Moore's analysis. It is a complex adverbial state of the subject, an objectless sensing state.[18]

(2) I have a perceptual taking, which involves a demonstrative conceptualization:

> This dog ... (is an English Setter/friendly/whitish grey in colour/lying down, etc.)

In virtue of the exercise of what, for me, is a basic perceptual concept of a dog, I recognize what I see *as* a dog. The *first dimension* of the exercise of this concept consists in this referential use. In the normal course of events I may, or may not, endorse the perceptual claim I am inclined to make.[19]

But there are two further features that belong to having a visual experience of the dog. In order to do justice to the role of the imagination we need to say more about the way that the two basic components interact:

(3) Seeing the dog *as* a dog disposes me to *imagine* of the dog more than I can actually see of it. Such imagining may lead me to have actual images of a dog in my consciousness, although it is not necessary that I form them. The images I form combine with the phenomenal state caused directly by

the dog, in the construction of sense-image-models. Hence, what is *actually* present in consciousness is a nonconceptual sense-image-model (or series of models) of the dog. These models are complex inner states, but, importantly, are not conceptualized as such. Although they guide my actions, I do not normally reflect upon them.[20]

(4) I have a set of *implicit* expectations about how the nonconceptual component of experience might change. I am implicitly prepared for transformations of the sense-image-model. (This is the *second dimension* of concept exercise.) Again, I do not normally reflect upon the possibility of such transformations to my experiences; but in acting upon the world as a result of experience, I show my implicit awareness of them. These expectations play a crucial role in normal perception, by accounting for the way in which the two components of experience are connected.

The above paradigm case of seeing, with its four central features, illustrates the Critical Realist model of perception as it applies to a standard case, where we see a familiar object under normal conditions. Most of our perceptual interaction with the world is of this kind. We perceive and act spontaneously, focusing directly upon the objects we perceive. The intentionality of perception is explained straightforwardly. It derives from the intentionality of the conceptual component, in the form of a perceptual taking. The distinctive nature of perceptual experience is accounted for by the presence of phenomenal qualities belonging to the sensory manifold, which actually exists as a conscious inner state of the subject. The two components blend smoothly in the perceptual experience of objects – in ways that I shall proceed to illustrate – without our reflecting specifically upon the exact nature of the phenomenal experiences we have.

One final clarificatory point needs to be made before I turn to an examination of the way that the model applies to a range of different cases. A central aspect of the above account, which will play a prominent role in the ensuing discussion, is the nature of the subject's demonstrative conceptualization. This need not take the form of a fully articulated judgement that the subject makes inwardly. Nevertheless, in many everyday perceptually guided actions, the subject will classify the objects he or she makes use of. In opening a door, I classify part of it as the handle which I need to turn; in picking up a spoon rather than a knife in order to eat soup on the plate in front of me, I consciously classify the object I see, in a manner that DB and other blindsight patients are unable to do. The important point is that the concepts exercised have a demonstrative aspect: they refer directly to objects in the subject's local environment.

Evans defended a plausible set of requirements for the successful demonstratively based identification of a physical object. Evans emphasizes the point that demonstrative identification is quite unlike descriptive identification.[21] For Evans, if a subject is demonstratively referring to a physical object on the basis of a perceptual experience, and independently of any background knowledge, then a number of conditions must hold. There must be an information link between the subject and the object X demonstratively referred to. But it is not sufficient for demonstrative knowledge simply that there exists some information link – for example, via a television screen – connecting the subject and the object X in a manner outside of the subject's knowledge. The subject must, according to Evans, be able to identify X in a 'fundamental way', so as to sustain 'indefinitely many thoughts' about that object. This links with a third requirement: the subject must be able to keep track of the object X, and, in particular, on the basis of the link, be able currently to locate it in egocentric space. So in standard cases of demonstrative identification of spatio-temporal physical objects, the subject must be able to *act directly* upon X.[22] Intriguingly, Evans allowed the possibility that we could make demonstrative reference to entities other than physical objects.[23]

I am not here concerned to defend all the details of Evans's account. It is hard to make sense of the denial that there must be some kind of information link between the subject and the object referred to. This condition is met, on the Critical Realist account, by the fact that the perceptually identified object is causally connected with the subject's nonconceptual phenomenal state, which in turn prompts concepts referring to that object. In the following chapter I shall take up the question of the precise form of the subject's identifying knowledge of the object referred to.

The particular aspect to which I wish to draw attention here is the requirement that the subject can, on the basis of the information link, locate the object X in egocentric space, and in consequence act upon it. To successfully refer to the object X as located 'here', or, 'over there', I must be able to reach for it, or guide myself towards it. As Evans plausibly claims, 'Where there is no possibility of action and perception, 'here'-thoughts cannot get a grip'.[24] So not only must the subject be able to think about that perceived object in a discriminating way; the subject must also be able to initiate actions directed upon that object.

Evans interprets the idea of action in this context as involving bodily movements through a public space, whereby public and egocentric spaces become united.[25] This is undoubtedly the central sense in which we think of action; it is arguable, as Evans claims, that it is necessary for reference to be made to an objectively existing entity. However, although this notion of public action may be conceptually prior, there is a coherent notion of action in which we act in the private sphere on our own subjective experiences, such as pains and after-images, for example, by attending to them. I shall argue in a later section that what is essential for reference to an entity is not so much the public nature of the potential action, understood in terms of bodily movements through public space, but the fact that reference is linked to a potential doing of an action by the subject, *simpliciter*. We shall see why the action requirement captures a central truth about our ability to refer to what is presented in experience, and also how it can be met in a satisfactory way by the Critical Realist analysis.

3 The normal conceptualization of veridical experience: concepts, expectations, and transformations of phenomenal experience

In this and the following sections I shall explore the way in which the Critical Realist model allows us to make sense of a whole range of perceptual phenomena, including various more problematic cases that we shall consider in turn. The four features of the model apply in different ways to nonstandard experiences, which differ from those that occur in normal perception. I shall also show how the model can be adapted to provide a plausible explanation of the awareness of our own hallucinatory states. This in turn will provide us with the means of replying to the objections raised at the end of the last chapter. It leads to an explanation of how, from a phenomenological point of view, experience has a unity. It also supplies us with insights into the real nature of perception that support the Critical Realist analysis.

I shall focus, in particular, on the connection between the two different dimensions, already identified above, in the exercise of a concept in experience: the referential dimension of concept employment, and the dimension arising from the subject's implicit expectations about transformations to the phenomenal component of experience. A careful examination of specific examples indicates the complex interrelations between our perceptual concepts and the phenomenal experiences to which they apply. We shall continue to concentrate mainly on examples taken from the modality of sight.

We will start with another example of a standard temporally extended perceptual situation:

Case (1): Boris walking

I see Boris as he enters near the far corner of the room. Knowing that he is a keen player, I anticipate that he will cross to the corner opposite, to watch a game of bridge in progress.

The fact that Boris walks across the room is no surprise to me. I hold some explicit expectations about what he will do. I expect that he will move to the bridge table. But these expectations about how, objectively, Boris will behave, must be distinguished from my implicit expectations about how Boris will appear, nonconceptually, in my experience – about the manner in which my perspectival sense-image-model of him is likely to change. For example, when he moves across the room, I implicitly expect that the appearance of his body will change in ways typical of a moving person. As he walks across the room, he remains a roughly constant distance from where I am situated; hence I implicitly accept that his appearance will occupy roughly the same area of my visual field.

Normally I pay no attention to such facts about appearances, which pertain to the sense-image-model I have in my experience of Boris. Nevertheless, they play an important role in visual experience, as can be seen by comparison with a second case:

Case (2): The Ames Room

The Ames Room is a special room constructed in such a way that it appears, from the particular vantage point designed for the perceiver to use, to be normally rectilinear. The room is, in fact, systematically distorted. The effect of looking, for the first time, at someone moving in an Ames Room is startling. If I see Boris walk across the back of the Ames Room, he will appear to grow or shrink radically in size.[26]

But my concept of a person is a concept of the sort of thing that does not suddenly grow or shrink in size. What is happening is something so unusual that I may well begin to reflect upon my experience. Exactly how I am able to conceptualize and reflect upon it we will presently examine. For now, the relevant point is that my attention is drawn to the nonconceptual appearance Boris presents, to the way that he appears subjectively to me. His appearance changes in unexpected ways. The implicit expectations I have about my sense-image-model of Boris are being upset.

The connection between observational concepts and implicit expectations about what is present at the nonconceptual level is reflected in cases of amodal perception, such as the case that Noë discusses:[27]

Case (3): The cat behind the fence

Suppose I see a cat half hidden by a picket fence. In one sense I do not see the whole of the cat. Parts of it are blocked from view by the slats of the fence. Yet I am directly aware, in another sense, of a whole cat being there.

According to the Critical Realist view, what is nonconceptually present in the subject's inner experience is a visual sensation, or phenomenal state, that partly represents a cat (in an informational sense). According to Sellars's later view, it may be the case that the visual sensation is filled out by an *image* I have of the cat as a whole. But there is no phenomenal, or sensory, appearance corresponding to the whole cat. It is only in virtue of the concepts I employ that I see and represent *the whole cat* (in a conceptual or referential sense). In his discussion of amodal perception, Noë accepts that there is a need to draw a distinction in experience that in some ways parallels this. He writes:

> It does not seem to me as if every part of the cat is visible to me now, even though it does seem to me now as if I see a whole cat and as if the unperceived parts of the cat's body are present ... one experiences the presence of that which one perceives to be out of view.

Noë is here using the term 'present' and 'presence' differently from the way it is used in the Critical Realist analysis. For the Critical Realist, something is present if it is immediately in consciousness, as a part of the phenomenal nonconceptual content. For Noë, 'presence' denotes a more complicated notion that is connected with the understanding. But, as we noted in the earlier discussion of Noë's views in Chapter 5, the distinction he makes between what is 'in view' and what is 'perceptually present' bears some similarities to the Critical Realist distinction. The difference is that Noë appears to interpret the former notion in a Direct Realist manner.

Even if there is no visual sensation corresponding to a whole cat in my consciousness, in another sense the whole cat is there, because of the concept I exercise of the cat. I have expectations of the way the appearance of the whole cat will change. If the cat walks beyond the end of the fence, or if I walk round it to get a different view, the appearance – my sense-image-model of the cat – will change in certain anticipated ways; but my perceptual taking, involving a concept of a cat, refers to the cat as a whole. This is what it means to say that the whole cat is, in a phenomenological sense, present. I earlier criticized Noë's formulation of the sensorimotor idea as the claim that the *actual* exercise of behaviour on the part of the subject is required for experience.[28] In the passage from which the above quote is taken, however, Noë puts forward a different version of the view, expressing it in a dispositional form that comes close to the Critical Realist position. He states:

> My sense of the presence of the whole of the cat behind the fence consists precisely in my knowledge, my implicit understanding, that by a movement of the eye, or the head, or the body I can bring bits of the cat into view that are now hidden.[29]

Nevertheless, despite the similarity to the Critical Realist account, we need to note two important differences. First, Noë here relies on the unexplained notion of certain parts being 'in view'. By appealing to this notion, Noë may appear to come close to accepting a two component view of experience. However, as was pointed out in Chapter 5, on Noë's account we are given no clear idea of what being 'in view' involves, and in places he appears to understand it in a manner that is close to Direct Realism. It is interpreted by the Critical Realist to mean, approximately, that the physical part in view is causally responsible for generating a part of the visual phenomenal state that is immediately present in the subject's conscious experience.

Second, Noë focuses exclusively on the expectations about the future course of experience that would result from movements that I initiate. This omits the fact that I am also prepared for changes in my experience that result from how the cat will move of its own accord – and my expectations of the movements initiated by the cat itself form an important part of my conceptualizing the cat as such.

The importance of our expectations of movement is illustrated by examples of 'pop-out' phenomena, as in the next case:

Case (4): The Dalmatian examples

One very striking visual phenomenon is shown by the picture of a Dalmatian dog, in which the shape of the dog merges with the background, so the perceiver may see only an array of black and white patches.

In Figure 9.1, the reader may well be able to make out the shape of the Dalmatian dog fairly rapidly, though when an example of this kind is encountered for the first time, it is not always easy for people to discern the presence of the dog. When one suddenly sees the dog against the background, one sees its legs and body, and so on, as separate from the background, and therefore capable of moving independently. The second figure (Figure 9.2) attempts to portray such possibilities of movement schematically, by highlighting the shape of the whole dog, and indicating some different possible future positions the dog could take up.[30]

In recognizing the shape in the picture as a Dalmatian dog, I am implicitly aware of it as a unified complete object, capable of moving as a whole into a different position. Experiments have confirmed the connection between recognition and awareness of the possibility of movement. In one example, a video display starts with a static image of black and white shapes, against a white background. What is in fact being displayed corresponds schematically

Figure 9.1 Dalmatian dog merging with background

Figure 9.2 Possible changes in position of the Dalmatian dog

to a Dalmatian dog, but with so much detail removed, that it is impossible to discern the presence of an animal in the absence of any movement. No creature is recognized. The display then takes on a dynamic form, as the arrangement of black and white shapes begins to alter. The moment this happens, the pattern of movement causes the immediate recognition that a Dalmatian dog is walking – an effect which is very striking.

Experiments conducted by Gunnar Johansson in the 1970s make use of this phenomenon, by displaying human figures with small spot lights attached to their joints.[31] Lighting conditions are arranged so that the bodily surfaces cannot be seen. All an observer can make out are the attached spot lights, so that when the figures are still, no bodily shape is made out; what is visible are small round circles of light against a dark background. When the figures begin to move, the recognition of a human figure is immediate. In one example, a display consists of twenty white spot lights altering their relation to each other, as the whole display moves across a screen. Although the complex moving pattern of lights on the screen is only two-dimensional, the observer cannot help but see the display *as* two people dancing around, whirling through three dimensions.[32] No effort or inference is required: the perceptual taking of the circling dancers is spontaneous. Again, the effect is very impressive.[33]

The two-component model of experience allows a satisfactory explanation of some ambiguous figures, and Gestalt grouping effects. The figure illustrated below has been the subject of some discussion:

Case (5): Rows and columns

In Figure 9.3, the two dimensional array of units can be seen in various ways, including as either a group of rows, or a group of columns:
According to Peacocke, whether we see this array as a series of rows, or, alternatively, whether we see it as a series of columns, our experience has the same positioned scenario content.[34] On the account I defend here, that is because of the fact that the two experiences share a common phenomenal

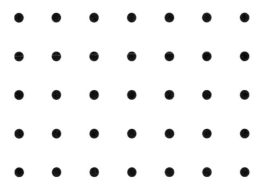

Figure 9.3 An array of elements grouped as either rows or columns

component. They each contain the same type of visual phenomenal non-conceptual state, whose informational representational content can be thus specified. In addition, the experience involves the exercise of low-level concepts of some kind (for Peacocke, representations with protopropositional content), which account for the way it is seen. When I see the array *as* a group of columns, then, according to Peacocke, my experience 'has the protopropositional content that certain elements that are in fact vertically arranged are collinear'.

On the two-component model defended here, the fact that I apply low-level concepts relating to columns means that I am more disposed to actions that are directed at columns, rather than rows – for example, if the units of the array represent counters in some game, I might be disposed to remove one entire column from the array. But there is a further dimension to concept use. Even if I form no explicit judgements, my *implicit expectations* about the phenomenal component of experience are involved. I am more prepared for certain kinds of transformations in the array than others.

Suppose I do see the array as a set of columns. In that case, I am more prepared for changes in the columns, taken as separate units; one possible change of this kind is indicated in Figure 9.4 below.

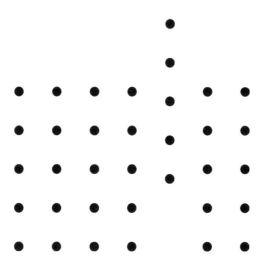

Figure 9.4 A possible change to columns in the array

Conversely, to see the array as a set of rows is to be more prepared for a transformation indicated by Figure 9.5, in which an implicit expectation of a possible movement of a row in the array is illustrated.

This fits with what Sellars has in mind when he speaks of the role of the imagination in experience. When the array is conceptualized as rows, the sense-image-model of the array contains imagined projections and movements of each row, potential and actual changes to the phenomenal com-

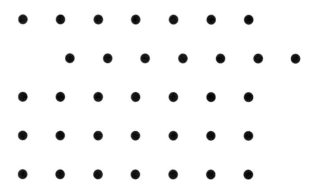

Figure 9.5 A possible change to rows in the array

ponent in experience. Consider manipulating a Rubik cube. Thinking about objectively possible rotational movements around a given axis requires seeing a given face of the cube as a set of rows, or, alternatively, as columns.[35] This is bound up with imagining the potential transformations in one's experience as the movement is carried out.

The Critical Realist two-component model is given strong support by ambiguous figures of this kind. A display or scene causes a phenomenal nonconceptual visual state. This can be conceptualized, perhaps at a low level, in more than one way. According to the account, this exercise of concepts has two dimensions. One dimension concerns the way the subject is inclined to take things to be, objectively. This referential dimension of concept employment has a certain degree of independence from the determinate form that phenomenal experience takes. That is why, in the spotlight case, the observer spontaneously sees the lighted display *as* a couple dancing, even though what is strictly present in experience is so attenuated. The second dimension has to do with the way that, implicitly, the subject expects her subjective experiences of the object to develop and transform, according to the concepts she entertains in seeing an object as an object of a certain kind.[36]

These points about the way that concepts are essentially involved in the way that we experience the world are not dependent upon the fact that the examples often make use of cartoon figures such as the duck-rabbit, and two-dimensional diagrams. They are illustrated in the following case where an ordinary three-dimensional object is seen in different ways:

Case (6): The misperceived cat

A familiar enough occurrence in everyday life is misperception. I enter a room, and see what at first glance I take to be an old black jumper on a chair. On looking harder, I suddenly realize that it is in fact a cat. This realization is connected with seeing the outline of the cat, becoming clear about which parts are its head and legs, and so on.

In contrast to the Dalmatian dog case, I actually categorize the object wrongly before making out what it is. As earlier phenomenologists and philosophers of science were keen to emphasize, I do not arrive at the reinterpretation of what I am seeing by an inferential process. I am caused to exercise a different concept in respect of my experience; this might be due in part to a top-down process, as I realize that I do not have a black jumper. Alternatively, it could be caused by a bottom-up process, as perhaps part of the shape becomes more clearly defined when my eyes adjust to the gloom. In any event, exercising the concept of a cat is necessarily connected with seeing the cat as distinct from its background, as an animal that is capable of moving independently of the chair, and moving in ways distinctive of a cat. The visual phenomenal component of the experience is 'structured' by the nature of the concept that I exercise. I have implicit expectations about how the whole cat will move as a unified object. However, as opponents of empiricism have emphasized, I do not necessarily have to conceptualize my experience *in terms of* coloured shapes.[37] There is no prior conscious awareness of a nonconceptual phenomenal core of bare sensation.

Nevertheless, as Sellars also appreciated, I may well be aware of some kinds of resemblance between my successive experiences of seeing the object on the chair first as a jumper, and then as a cat. How I experience the object is determined by the concepts I exercise, but is not just a matter of the concepts I entertain.[38] So to analyse experience as involving a nonconceptual phenomenal component that is in some sense structured by our concepts, as the two-component view maintains, makes good sense.[39] The phenomenal component accounts for what is common to the ways of seeing the cat; the conceptual component accounts for the difference.

4 Displaced perception

The distinction I am emphasizing here between the two dimensions of concept exercise is clearly illustrated by an important category of perceptual phenomena, which comprises cases of *displaced perception*:[40]

Case (7): The televised game

I am following an important game of football, by watching it live on television. In such a case, there is an obvious disparity between the images I see on the screen, and the events my thoughts and desires are focused upon, especially if I am caught up in the action of the game. It is uncontentious that my thoughts will, for the most part, be directed on to the actual players, the ball, the goalmouth, and so on, which may be many miles away from the room in which I am presently situated. Suppose I see a player taking a penalty, and scoring. My thoughts relate to how things are objectively – it may be that now the team I support has a better chance of winning. If I turn to reflect on the way things appear to me, the concepts I exercise will be of a different kind. Perhaps they relate to the image on the screen in front of me; I think that there is too much contrast in the colour, for example. Or I might reflect on matters that connect with my own subjective experience: I remove my spectacles, and notice that the way things appear is blurred. In either case, concepts of a quite different kind are employed. But for the most part, I do not reflect in either of these senses on how things appear to me. I just focus my attention on the game, even though in doing so, my thoughts about the game are guided by images of some kind that I am aware of more immediately.

Watching television lacks an important dimension when compared to normal vision. I cannot act directly as a result of what I see; or at any rate, the actions I undertake are not integrated with current visual input, so I cannot act *on* what I see. Evans considers a parallel case. A subject is physically located in a ship, exploring the seabed somewhere way below via a remotely controlled submarine, which transmits images of seabed objects back to a television screen on the ship. The subject only knows of the places portrayed by the images as the causes of those images, somewhere near the submarine; his knowledge of where those images are coming from is therefore conceptually mediated by his awareness of other facts about the submarine cameras, and so on. He does not locate what is pictured at positions he can act upon directly in his egocentric space. Hence he is not making *demonstrative* reference to the objects pictured on the screen in the nondescriptive sense defined by Evans.

But there are important recently developed forms of displaced perception in which actions are integrated with vision in ways that are much more typical of normal perception:

Case (8): Endoscopic minimal access surgery

Many surgeons now operate using a technique known as minimal access surgery (or, more colloquially, key-hole surgery). This involves using a small telescopic device and instruments 3–10 mm in diameter which are inserted into a body cavity, such as the abdomen, through small incisions. A film of the surgical procedures inside the body is relayed by a small camera mounted on the eye-piece of the telescopic device to a video screen placed adjacent to the patient, while the operation takes place. By looking at the images of the internal organs and the effector ends of the instruments on the screen, the surgeon is able to manipulate the instruments in the appropriate way using handles on their external ends.[41]

In one sense, the surgeon cannot see the instruments or the organs inside the patient's body 'directly'. The patient's skin prevents a direct view of the inside of the body. Surgeons need specific training, partly acquired through the use of simulators, in order to learn to use the image on the screen to guide the movements they make with the instruments. While most surgeons master the skills of minimal access surgery quite easily, a few prove to lack aptitude for it and cease to practise this type of surgery.

An important cause of difficulty is the lack of normal stereoscopic depth perception. The pictures on the video monitor are normally two-dimensional, whereas the instruments have to be manipulated in three dimensions.[42] However, surgeons can learn to use a number of different depth cues to ascertain the exact position to which they need to move the instruments. These include occlusion, relative size, texture gradients, and motion parallax. After training, they have practical knowledge of how to integrate their actions with what they see on the monitor, often without being explicitly conscious of such depth cues. Making the correct movements required to manipulate the surgical instruments whilst viewing the monitor becomes largely automatic, in a manner similar to that whereby a professional pianist effortlessly plays the correct notes when sight reading. Seeing becomes direct, in the sense that the perceptual thoughts as well as the actions of the surgeon focus directly upon the internal organs and the instruments, without prior inference.[43]

The important conclusion that can be drawn from these cases of displaced perception is that we are able to conceptualize our experiences in two quite different ways. When surgeons are absorbed in the complexities of an operation, the patient's body and the instruments are phenomenologically present in their visual experience. Thus a surgeon can entertain demonstrative thoughts about the patient's inner bodily organ ('that gall bladder . . .').[44] The organ is the reference of the *de re* perceptual thoughts directly prompted by looking at the monitor. The organ is also normally the focus of the surgeon's actions: in this sense, it is present, phenomenologically, in the surgeon's experience, by being present in his or her egocentric space. In Evans's terms, the surgeon can entertain genuine 'here' thoughts about the organs in the patient's body.

In a more straightforward sense, the patient's bodily organ is hidden from view, because it is inside the patient's body. In principle, someone else in the operating theatre might look at the video display and see only a reddish brown object against a background of somewhat similar colours and shapes, and be unable to interpret it; his or her concepts will relate only to images on the monitor. In actual practice, images are normally sharp, clearly coloured, and can be magnified, so that it is hard not to see what is displayed on the screen as some sort of bodily organ, made up of human flesh and blood. Potentially, the way the surgeon conceptualizes what is seen could alter. The surgeon could pause during the operation, adopt a different attentional set, and concentrate instead on how the images on the monitor appear to be blurred because the lens is fogged up.[45] But in attending to the image on the monitor *as* such, the surgeon uses a different set of concepts: one difference is that the relevant spatial concepts will be of images on a screen in two dimensions, rather than of instruments and bodily parts in three dimensional space.

Here, the fact that there are two different dimensions of concept employment is clearly illustrated. In performing the operation the surgeon exercises concepts relating to the patient's body in a manner that allows the integration of perception with action. Yet in doing so, the surgeon is actually responsive to matters that are not conceptualized. The images on the screen guide action, yet there need not be any explicit conceptual awareness of them.

In the earlier discussion of the Critical Realist model of perception, we noted that one dimension of conceptualization is constituted by the expectations I have when I perceive an object to belong to a certain kind. I am, implicitly, prepared for certain sorts of *transformations* of my present experiences, transformations that are appropriate to experiences of the kind of object I take myself to be seeing. Consideration of the kind of displaced perception that occurs in minimal access surgery suggests that I may acquire certain expectations about the future course of experience through a learning process.

The fact that some patterns of expectations are learnt does not detract from the validity of the model. It shows its applicability in different sorts of perceptual cases. When surgeons arrive at the stage of proceeding spontaneously, and directly conceptualize organs inside the bodies of patients on whom they operate, their concepts are guided by what is present in their experience while they look at the screen. The physical world with which they interact is structured into objects at the *conceptual* level, by the way that the type concepts exercised – of physical bodily parts, and so on – refer. There is a different kind of structure at the *phenomenal* level, imposed as a result of the way that the concepts exercised give rise to implicit expectations for future experience. At this phenomenal level, spatial regions of the sensory manifold are grouped together by the fact that, in perceiving an object, the subject conceives of that object as a single item, and as belonging to a certain kind. As a result, the subject is implicitly prepared for certain kinds of transformations to these regions.[46]

5 Taking stock

Before we move on to look at cases of non-standard experiences, let us take stock of the interim conclusions we have arrived at about the nature of the different kinds of visual experience of physical objects. Phenomenologists such as Merleau-Ponty have attacked traditional empiricist accounts of perception, which placed so much emphasis on sensation. But the two-component view of experience defended here must be distinguished from such traditional accounts. Perception is not *inferentially* mediated by sensations. We move about the world, taking in the objects around ourselves directly, seeing things as belonging to certain kinds, normally hardly pausing for proper thought about the way that objects appear to us. Yet sensations are still essentially involved in perceptual experience. Throughout, we are *causally* guided in our perceptual takings and our actions by the inner phenomenal states we are nonconceptually aware of.

The two-component analysis of perceptual experience does not lead to a denial of the fact that in an important sense we see whole objects, and that we can, for example, also directly see the way that the background continues behind or under an object.[47] This sense of 'directly seeing' comes close to the sense that Noë appears to have in mind when he talks about our 'sense of the perceptual presence of a detailed world'. When I suddenly become conscious of the cat *as* being on the chair, in the example given earlier, the whole cat becomes phenomenologically present to me, not just because I exercise the concept of a cat, but because in exercising it, I come to have a set of *implicit* expectations relating to my future phenomenal experiences of the cat.

So when a subject S sees an object *as* an object of a certain kind F, in this way, there are two dimensions to the exercise of concepts:

(1) To see an object as an F, S will entertain the classificatory concept of an F. The subject must think of the object she sees as an F, so that in some way the exercise of the concept can guide her potential actions.[48] For example, the exercise of the concept: *cat* may incline me to believe that there is a cat present, if I am capable of forming judgements. If the perceiving subject is an animal such as a dog, the exercise of some low-level classification may arouse a state of heightened alertness, and other processes of a similar order. However, the concepts that are entertained refer to objective features of the perceiver's surroundings – to the way things stand in relation to the perceiver, and not to how they subjectively appear.[49]

(2) S will not normally exercise concepts directly about her phenomenal experience. Some subjects may altogether lack the concept of inner phenomenal experiences. But in seeing an object, the classifying concepts S employs play a role in 'structuring' elements of phenomenal experience into wholes. In responding in a certain way to the physical object in my surroundings, I form implicit expectations about the likely transformations of the way that it appears, perspectivally, in my experience. I treat a part of the visual sensory manifold as a unity, in imagining transformations that affect a particular phenomenal region of it. My expectations shape the way that I am conscious of my phenomenal experience.

So in seeing the cat in front of me *as* a cat, the exercise of the observational concept *cat* has two dimensions. On the referential dimension, I classify what I see as belonging to the class of cats. In virtue of this aspect of the concept, I may form a few *explicit* beliefs about how the cat may move or change objectively. My exercise of the concept in this experiential context has a second dimension: it involves a responsiveness to the phenomenal component in my experience. My sense-image-model reflects potential movements of the cat. In virtue of this aspect I have many *implicit* expectations about how the cat might subjectively appear. But in seeing the cat I do not normally reflect on its appearance, on the way that things are at the phenomenal nonconceptual level in experience. If I were to do so explicitly, I would employ a different range of concepts, relating to my own subjective states, and not to the way things are objectively in my physical surroundings.

As evidenced by the cases examined above, we can now summarize a number of important conclusions about the nature of visual perception:

- A subject sees nothing without exercising perceptual concepts of some kind; these concepts may be at a low-level, and relate to very broad and basic classificatory categories, such as 'this dark shape', and so on.

- The same phenomenal level nonconceptual component of the subject's visual experience can be conceptualized in different ways.

- In exercising the basic perceptual concepts that determine the way the object is seen, the subject refers directly to the object; the application of a perceptual concept is spontaneous, and not based upon inference.

- The exercise of a concept involves a second dimension of use: although the subject does not normally form thoughts about the appearance of the object seen, he or she is responsive to phenomenal qualities of experience that are immediately present at a nonconceptual level. Such causally induced responsiveness takes the form of implicitly held expectations about the way the phenomenal qualities immediately present are likely to transform.

- As the examples of displaced perception demonstrate, what is seen is the object that is the *direct* focus of perceptual thoughts and potential action. This object need not be identical with the entities *immediately* present at the level of nonconceptual phenomenal experience.

6 The two-component model and hallucinatory experience

Sellars consistently assumes that hallucinatory and veridical experiences are ontologically on a par, in the sense defended in Chapter 4; they are inner states that differ in their causal origin. But aside from this, he rarely discusses hallucination as such. According to Rosenberg, there are reasons to doubt whether Sellars is able to provide a satisfactory account of the awareness of sense impressions *as* sense impressions.[50] He argues that on Sellars's version of Critical Realism, and more particularly on the account of self awareness sketched out in the 'Myth of Jones', developed in the last two parts of EPM, sense impressions are never experienced as such.

The point of the Jonesean story is to enable us to understand better the logic of terms that apply to inner states and episodes. This story has two parts. The first part concerns conceptual episodes such as thoughts, and also conceptualized experiences such as seeings. The second part applies to nonconceptual phenomenal states, which in EPM are referred to as 'sense impressions', and are in later work described as 'sensing states'. Each part of the story subdivides further, so that there are at least four stages involved. For Sellars, we first learn to ascribe thoughts and related conceptual episodes to other people on the basis of the context and behavioural evidence. This evidence includes verbal behaviour. But these inner episodes, though logically connected with observational terms, are not definable by reference to them; we understand them in part on the basis of a model, by analogy with overt verbal behaviour. In the second stage, we are trained into a correct reporting role when we ascribe such states to ourselves. We learn to give reasonably reliable self-descriptions of our own thoughts.[51] Such self-description is not based upon a prior noticing of the thought; as Rosenberg interprets Sellars, thoughts and other conceptual episodes do not, *as such*, have any phenomenology.[52]

In the second part of the Jonesean story, the focus is on nonconceptual phenomenal states. At stage three of the overall account, we learn the general framework of concepts for phenomenal states as it applies to other people. Part of the evidence for phenomenal states, as Rosenberg notes, is the fact that people report conceptualized states that include 'lookings' – introspectible inner conceptual episodes that they are able to avow. At stage four in the overall story, we learn to report directly our own phenomenal states. That is, we are trained to be reasonably reliable self-describers in respect of our own inner phenomenal states.

Rosenberg argues that when I report my own phenomenal states, my self-description does not involve a demonstrative claim about the phenomenal state I have. I am not conceptually aware of my phenomenal state *as* a phenomenal state. The argument seems to be this: properly understood, what the subject is aware of nonconceptually should be analysed as a *state*, a phenomenal state, perhaps of a complex kind, belonging to a subject. Sensory awareness does not involve an awareness of a distinct object that has some kind of *relation* to the subject. Therefore, there is no place for demonstrative reference to an independent phenomenal, or sensory, *object*. When a subject successfully reports their own phenomenal state, their claim is a mere avowal, made without evidence. Claims about one's own phenomenal states are not based upon a kind of inner perception, to be modelled on the observation of outer objects. If Rosenberg is correct, it would appear that Sellars never provides a satisfactory account of the phenomenology of our awareness of our own hallucinatory states.

I want to show here that we can adapt the materials that Sellars has himself provided in his later work, so as to provide a more plausible account of the phenomenology of self-awareness. It is not my aim to engage in detailed Sellarsian exegesis, but I believe it can be shown why reports of phenomenal states are more than mere avowals. The Critical Realist two-dimensional model of concept employment elaborated above need not be restricted to the perception of external physical objects. It can be adapted to cases where we become introspectively aware of our own hallucinatory experiences. The argument is that although we do not infer reports about our own sense-impressions from a nonconceptual immediate awareness of them, we can come to have introspective *conceptualized* awareness of them through the exercise of the concepts we first acquire in the Jonesean manner. In other words, once we are able to report our sense-impressions, we come to be introspectively aware of them, in a manner that bears some resemblance to outer observation, by using the appropriate concepts. As in the case of the perception of outer objects, the exercise of the imagination plays a crucial role.

The remainder of the main argument to show the compatibility of the Critical Realist analysis with the phenomenology of perception will run as follows. First, an examination of hallucinatory experience allows us to understand (a) the precise nature of what is in common to hallucinatory and veridical experiences; and (b) the nature of our introspective awareness of hallucinatory phenomenal states. Second, an examination of *deceptive* hallucinations helps us to understand the way that the concepts we exercise directly in normal *veridical* experience do not refer to what is immediately experienced. It also helps us to understand how we can respond to our own experiences in two modes: (i) in the mode of perception, and (ii) in the mode of introspection. Third, this understanding can be usefully combined with similar conclusions derived from the displaced perception case, and a further example to be discussed, the case of *double vision*. These cases support the Critical Realist account of the way that the conceptual and phenomenal components of experience are related. Our perceptual grasp of physical objects is direct, although it is mediated by an immediate awareness of nonconceptual phenomenal inner states.

At the end of Section 2 we identified four central features of conscious perceptual experience. When we analyse hallucinatory experiences, we find that the same four features apply. I begin by considering four situations in which a hallucination is recognized as such by the subject.

Case (9): The red after-image

I gaze intently at a bright, green, rectangular area on the cover of a book for about half a minute. When I look away, and let my gaze fall on a white surface, I become aware of a red patch of a similar shape. I am aware of the phenomena of after-images, so this is not unexpected. I can examine it as it slowly fades, and even as I direct my gaze on to a different background. If we count as hallucinations those perceptual experiences that are unrelated to any current sensory input from an external physical object, then the after-image is a hallucinatory image, albeit a fairly common-place and unexciting one.[53]

Case (10): Visual aura

As was noted in Chapter 4, there is a standard, relatively common form of visual aura, known as 'fortifications', which sometimes accompany migraines. It can also occur independently. This type of hallucination involves a flickering zigzag crescent of light that gradually expands and moves away from the centre of the visual field. After about twenty minutes or so it disappears off the periphery.

Case (11): A ringing noise in the ear

Only a small, though significant minority of the population experience visual aura, or experience the more complex CBS hallucinations noted in

Chapter 4. But a common enough hallucination is the phenomenon of experiencing a ringing or whistling noise in one's ear. This may, but need not, be accompanied by physical sensations in the ear, which indicate to the subject that the experience is not veridical. Yet subjectively, the sound may on occasion be indistinguishable from the faint ringing of a distant doorbell or alarm.

Case (12): Tinnitus

Sufferers from the annoying medical condition known as 'tinnitus' experience auditory hallucinations of various kinds, often in the form of high-pitched, hissing or whistling sounds, and also in the form of low-pitched, distant rumbling sounds.

In all the above cases, the assumption is that the subjects understand that they are experiencing hallucinations. A preliminary clarification is necessary in connection with this claim. According to Critical Realism, hallucinations are inner states; more specifically, they are complex objectless sensings.[54] Following from the arguments of Part I, we can understand such states, in part, as belonging to the same general kind as those that normally mediate causally between the physical input that stimulates the sense organs, and the perceptual takings that potentially guide actions directed on to external objects; we also understand them to be analogous in certain key respects to the perceptible features of physical objects. The difference between hallucinatory and veridical experiences is that in the hallucinatory case there is no physical input of the kind that can support navigational behaviour through the subject's surroundings.

One criticism that might be made of the account to be offered is based on the fact that most people lack the sophisticated kinds of concepts appealed to in the above analysis. They do not speak of hallucinatory images, and would not understand references to 'inner phenomenal states' and related notions. It should be conceded that most lay people do not ordinarily speak of hallucinatory images, inner states, and so on, even when they are attempting to describe phenomena such as migraine aura, CBS hallucinations, or phantom limb pains. But this fact does not signify a lack of concepts relating to what is inner; all it shows is a straightforward unfamiliarity with the language used by clinicians and philosophers.

Lord Brain has pointed out that many subjects describe themselves as 'seeing' what are hallucinatory images, rather than using expressions such as 'seem to see' and 'appears', and the equivalent.[55] He goes on to observe that those who lack the technical language for talking about inner phenomenal experiences are still able to use their reason to work out that they are hallucinating. They understand that the strange physical objects and animals they seem to see do not, in fact, really exist in their surroundings. They will be able to say things like 'whatever it was I saw didn't really exist'.

Phrases such as 'a strange sort of animal that was not really there', and such like, may do the job normally played by expressions devised by philosophers. Most of us, fortunately, find no need to make reference to inner states of mind in our everyday lives. So the appeal to ordinary use has no important implications for the account proposed here.

If we now examine what is going on in hallucinatory experiences, it is instructive to compare them with perceptual experiences in respect of the four central features that were found to apply in normal cases of visual perception, which were listed at the end of Section 2 above:

(1) Hallucinatory experiences, like normal perceptual states, contain a distinctive nonconceptual phenomenal component. At a minimum, this involves states with phenomenal qualities that are similar to those involved in the veridical case; from a subjective viewpoint, the simple qualities that are present in hallucinatory experience are indistinguishable from those that are present in the veridical case. Unless this was the case, we would be unable to identify and describe the intrinsic phenomenal character of the hallucinatory experiences we have. The arguments of Chapter 4 point to a stronger conclusion: hallucinatory phenomenal experiences have the same ontological status as those which occur in normal perception. In both cases, the subject is immediately aware, in the nonconceptual sense, of an inner phenomenal state.

(2) Hallucinatory experiences also involve the exercise of concepts. It is only in virtue of exercising the concept of a hallucinatory state that I become aware of the kind of hallucinatory experience I am having *as* hallucinatory. There is one significant difference between the way that concepts operate in veridical and hallucinatory experiences. In the veridical case, the concepts I exercise refer to external objects, and not to what I am immediately nonconceptually aware of; whereas in hallucinations, my concepts relate to things that, in addition, I happen to be immediately aware of. But it is important to note that the nonconceptual phenomenal state is not a *reason* for my entertaining the concepts that refer to it; as in the veridical case, the phenomenal state acts as a partial *cause*, which, in conjunction with my awareness that the situation is not normal, etc., prompts me to conceptualize the phenomenal state as hallucinatory.

The idea of a Given is as much a myth in the case of hallucinations as it is in ordinary perception. The relation between the phenomenal state and the exercise of concepts is a causal one, even when those concepts refer to the very phenomenal state that prompts them. We cannot *reason* our way to working out which concepts properly apply to our experiences, by some kind of 'careful examination' of them; or, to put the point another way, a careful examination of phenomenal experience will always presuppose the prior employment of concepts, perhaps of a rather basic kind relating to *appearances* of colour and shape.[56]

So the claim is that when circumstances lead me to believe that I cannot really be seeing the kinds of physical objects I appear to be seeing in my surroundings, I then become aware that I must be hallucinating. In doing so, I am caused by my phenomenal state to exercise a concept that refers demonstratively to that very state. Despite arguments to the contrary, which I shall explore below, there are reasons to support the thesis that we can indeed make demonstrative reference to our own phenomenal experiences.

(3) The imagination does not operate in exactly the same way in the hallucinations that I am aware of, as it does in normal veridical perception. If I am aware of a hallucinatory image as such, then I do not believe there is any more to it than what is immediately present in consciousness. Hallucinatory images can perhaps have a 'two-and-a-half dimensional' structure, as the random dot stereograms constructed by Julez suggest, but they do not have a reverse side hidden from view. Nevertheless, there are subtle ways in which the imagination is operative. Imagining how a hallucinatory image might develop over time guides the rather limited actions possible in respect of them. I could, if I were so minded, wait for an after-image of red to fade until it matched a certain colour that I am veridically seeing, and so on.

(4) Finally, and in connection with the exercise of the imagination, I have a set of implicit expectations about how the phenomenal nonconceptual component of the experience is likely to change, or not, when I act in various ways. The ways that I am able to act upon hallucinations are necessarily limited, hence compared to veridical perception such expectations are restricted in scope, yet they are still an important aspect of the way I conceptualize my own hallucinatory states. For example, when I alter the direction of my gaze, I implicitly expect the after-image that I am aware of to stay in the centre of my visual field.

Evans claims that my own nonconceptual state (which Evans calls 'the informational state') cannot become an object for me. There is nothing that constitutes 'perceiving that state', or otherwise being conscious of it, in a manner which supports demonstrative reference to it.[57] Evans's views of hallucinations, however, fail to do justice to their complex nature. We need to treat the phenomenal, or sensory, aspect of experience as a separate, nonconceptual, inner component of consciousness. Evans is right to point out that the awareness of hallucinations does not involve a relation to one's own phenomenal states of a kind that parallels the perception of independent external objects. Nevertheless, we can still directly conceptualize the phenomenal component of hallucinatory consciousness, and thus come to be aware of it through the exercise of the appropriate concepts. I will draw upon Evans's general model of demonstrative reference to show how we are able to refer directly to our own inner phenomenal states.

In the case of reference to public physical objects, Evans's model involves three basic ideas: for a subject to make demonstrative reference to an entity, she must employ a fundamental idea of the kind of entity in question, which supports indefinitely many thoughts about the object referred to; there must be an information link between the subject and the demonstrated object; and the subject must also be capable of locating the object and acting upon it directly, and not on the basis of some identifying description. As we noted earlier, Evans also allowed that demonstrative reference can be made to other kinds of entities, such as abstract objects. In these cases the requirements for demonstrative reference would have to be rather different.

If we understand hallucinations as involving an inner nonconceptual phenomenal component, it is clear that the information link requirement is met; on the Critical Realist view, there is a direct causal link from the phenomenal state to the subject's thought about it. The subject can also entertain a fundamental idea of the phenomenal state. As I argued in Chapter 1, our concept of a phenomenal state is of a certain kind of inner state, which normally causally mediates between sensory input and resulting actions. For example, I understand the phenomenal aspect of a red after-image to be the kind of state normally caused by input from a red item, and normally resulting in perceptual thoughts and actions of a discriminating kind with respect to the colours of objects. I also understand it as, in part, that which makes the difference between merely thinking about red, and actually having some kind of red experience. As we noted above, we can be trained to report such states directly.[58]

The first and second conditions that Evans specifies for the demonstrative identification of physical objects therefore can apply in the case of reference to one's own inner states. What of the third requirement, that the subject should be able directly to locate and act upon the object referred to? We do not act upon our inner states in the same way that we act upon outer physical objects. Nevertheless, there are also parallels with the action requirement. I can act upon my inner phenomenal experiences in an attenuated sense of the notion. Actions directed to my own inner phenomenal states take two main forms.

One central class of actions – or mental processes that are at any rate *doings* by the subject – arises in connection with the phenomenon of attention. Sometimes my attention is attracted by external stimuli, independently of my will. But on other occasions, directing my attention in a general way is something that I do – it is something I exert control over. In some of Mack and Rock's experiments, for example, subjects were trained to direct their visual attention away from the central point of fixation, to objects placed towards the side of their visual field.[59]

When a subject attends in this self-directed way to a hallucinatory experience, an inner item is identified directly. The subject can locate it, attend to its various features and report on them. In attending to an after-image, I direct my attention away from objects in the external world, and concentrate instead on my own inner experience. If I suffer a visual aura, I might well be prompted to think with some annoyance: 'this flickering image is preventing me from reading.' In clinical tests for tinnitus, a subject will be asked to match sounds that she hears normally with the sounds she hallucinates. Comparisons are made separately in respect of the tonal character of the sound – whether it is hissing, or whistling, and so on – and for pitch, and for volume. In cases of visual aura, subjects might be asked to describe the spatial characteristics of the inner visual state, or to draw a likeness. These various forms of attentional behaviour, and subsequent responses, are naturally explained on the assumption that subjects are thinking demonstratively about their inner states.

A second kind of action concerns the more indirect ways in which subjects can act upon their own inner states. For example, hallucinations can be indirectly manipulated in various ways. The most basic feature of hallucinations is their relative independence from current sensory stimulation. I cannot act upon my own private phenomenal states in the way that I can act upon public objects. I can, however, act in a different sense on a visual hallucinatory experience by altering the direction of my gaze, and even by shutting my eyes, so as to create a different background (shutting one's eyes changes the experienced colour of an after-image).

I can also plan ahead so as to produce an after-image. In thinking of a red after-image as an inner state of mine, I presuppose a general ontology of physical objects.[60] But as an inner state, it has distinctive attributes. It is, of course, not objectively available in the way that other kinds of state are. Wittgenstein rightly warned against modelling inner states *too* closely on outer objects. There are undoubted differences. Inner states, such as after-images and hallucinatory images of animals, are not distinct from our *phenomenal* consciousness of them. They are complex states of the subject. They have no independent existence. This means that we cannot re-identify them in the same way that we can re-identify an external object. But just as there are analogies between the perceptible features of physical objects and the intrinsic qualities of inner states, there are also important parallels between *noticing* external objects, and *attending* to inner states, such as hallucinatory images.

The examples show that when we apply concepts to our own hallucinatory images, the same two-dimensional account of concept exercise operates. The phenomenal component of my experience can become an object of my thoughts, and the focus of possible action. In addition, when I conceptualize my hallucinatory experiences *as such*, I form expectations that are consistent with my understanding of such experiences as inner states. In the case of an experience of the fortification type of visual aura, I have explicit expectations that, for example, it will alter in size and position. I probably will not attend to it all the time – indeed, like tinnitus sufferers, I will try to concentrate on other matters so as to avoid attending to it; but from time to time it may be registered again conceptually in my attentive consciousness. I am also prepared for the way that an after-image will fade, in the way that the cover of the book in front of me will not. In addition, I will have implicit expectations, for example, that my hallucinatory experiences will be unchanged when my sense-organs move relative to my surroundings. In these various ways my concepts can relate to a hallucinatory state both referentially, in a manner that treats the hallucination as an inner object, and also causally, in being guided by the state.

It will help, in clarifying this overall view of hallucinatory awareness, to distinguish between *four* different senses of the term 'object', as it can be used in connection with perceptual and hallucinatory experiences:

(1) There is, first, the *material object* of perception, the physical object that the subject perceives in having a veridical or illusory experience. This is a mind-independent entity. The material object actually exists, and is causally related to the subject's conceptual state, in the appropriate manner to support navigational behaviour, as discussed in Chapter 7. When we respond to our experiences in what Rosenberg calls 'the mode of perception', our perceptual takings focus *directly* upon the material object. It is not *immediately* present in consciousness, according to the Critical Realist account, but transcends it.

(2) The material object must be distinguished from the *intentional object*, which has quite a different mode of existence, if it can be said to exist at all. Strictly, to speak of the intentional object of a conceptual act is to give the *content* of that act – to describe how the subject conceives of what she takes to be present in having that act. As Moran points out, on Brentano's mature view, intentional objects do not even have some kind of 'inexistence'; rather they are modifications of the intending mind.[61]

(3) According to Moore's act-object analysis of sensation, the mind can stand in a unique relation of *acquaintance* to an object that is, strictly speaking, outside of consciousness. For Moore, as we saw earlier in Chapter 1, having a sensation is 'a case of 'knowing' or 'being aware of' or 'experiencing' something'.[62] But such knowledge does not take propositional form. In having a sensation of blue, the subject stands in a real relation of a distinctive kind to an *existing* blue entity, which is the *relational object* of the act of sensation. This blue *relational object* is a sense-datum, something that need not necessarily be physical, but does have actual existence. This sense-datum is not a constituent of the subject's mind. Sense-data (or, more strictly, sensibilia) are logically independent of minds. Moore specifically claims that the relation of the sense-datum to the act of sensing is not 'of one part of content to another part of content [in the subject's mind].'[63]
Analysing the having of a sensation to be a form of knowing is a version of the mongrel idea that Sellars rightly rejects.[64] A further and

major problem is that the sense-datum is supposed to be immediately present to consciousness, yet not itself a constituent in consciousness. This relation makes no sense, whether or not sense-data are construed as (in some cases) identical with physical objects, as we noted in the core argument discussed in Chapter 4.

(4) Finally, there is the idea of *sensa*, or '*objectless sensings*', that Sellars develops in his later writings on perception, in particular in his (1982 SSOP). This view can be seen as an extension of the simple adverbial view of sensation.[65] Certain complex nonconceptual phenomenal *states* – such as states of awareness of a red rectangle, in which different properties are united – can be compared in some respects to particulars, in the way that a state of the weather, such as a thunder clap, can be treated as a particular ('that low thundering'; compare also 'this snow-storm'). So what Sellars calls a sensing state is a kind of *quasi-object*, but not in virtue of being conceptualized, nor by virtue of being related to a special act of sensing.[66] It is not distinct from the subject's consciousness. It can however, be referred to by a demonstrative term, when we attend to and describe our own phenomenal states *as such* ('this after-image is red'). Unlike the physical objects we see, sensing states – or sensa – are immediately present as phenomenal aspects of consciousness. As Sellars repeatedly emphasized, they are present in conscious experience *other than as believed in*.

To conceptualize one's phenomenal state *as* a phenomenal state does not involve a relation between an act, and an object or feature that is potentially independent of the mind. In contrast to Moore's model, it involves one aspect of the subject, a conceptual state, focused upon a different aspect, a nonconceptual state that happens to be a phenomenal constituent of consciousness.

We must be careful to distinguish what is going on, when I attend to my phenomenal consciousness *as such*, from the kinds of confusions associated with the Myth of the Given, as noted in the previous chapter. It is not claimed that I infer that there is a red patch because I first grasp the bare, unconceptualized sensation of red. Rather, when I shift my attention, I am prompted to apply concepts of a different kind. When I form the belief that there is no physical object in front of me, it becomes harder for me to apply physical object concepts. I redirect my attentional set to something going on in me, which prompted the mistake – and thereby, I am *caused* to apply concepts relating to my own inner phenomenal states. My phenomenal awareness of the red patch is shaped by my use of concepts relating to my sensations. So I do not become aware of my inner phenomenal state by some problematic process of 'direct apprehension', but rather, by conceptualizing it.

This means that we need to add a fifth stage to the Jonesean account of self-awareness outlined earlier. When a subject has acquired the concept of an inner phenomenal state, and has also been 'trained' into correct reporting uses of her own sensory states, then her exercise of such concepts can begin to shape her sensory consciousness, as she becomes conceptually aware of the phenomenal aspect of hallucinatory experiences. Hence such experiences, in contrast to pure conceptual episodes such as thought, do have a phenomenology. Indeed, on the Sellarsian account, experiences have a phenomenology from the moment that we begin to employ concepts of any kind at all, in perceiving objects in the external world and classifying them.

7 Deceptive Hallucinations and Converse Cases

The above analysis allows us to offer an account of what goes on when a subject is at first taken in by a hallucination:

Case (13): The deceptive hallucinated ball

I think that I am seeing a red ball in front of me. In fact, I am hallucinating, and the ball I seem to see does not actually exist. Perhaps, unknown to me, I have been given some sort of drug such as mescaline, which affects the visual system in my brain; but the exact nature of the cause does not affect the point of the example. Mistakenly, I respond to my experience in the mode of perception. When I reach out and try to pick up the ball, my hand closes on nothing, and I then realize that there is no object there. Despite the fact that I realize I am having a hallucination, the presence of a red round shape in my visual field persists.

In a phenomenological sense, my experience changes to some extent after I realize I have been hallucinating. But any changes that occur can be fully explained in terms of the basic Critical Realist model of experience that has been outlined and illustrated in the cases already examined. I switch from using concepts that apply to physical objects, to different concepts that belong to the framework dealing with inner experiences. I now form a belief roughly to the effect that I am having an inner phenomenal experience of a red patch in my visual field.[67]

In consequence of my adopting a different conceptual framework, and now entertaining concepts about my own inner phenomenal states, there is an alteration in the pattern of my expectancies in respect of the phenomenal aspect of my experience. The phenomenal aspect itself may be largely unchanged. What is different is the way I would act as a result of being aware of the red item in my visual field. I no longer assume that there is a physical object with an exterior hidden surface, and so on. So the phenomenological differences are to be accounted for by the shift in the concepts I employ, and the expectations connected with them. Yet there are also similarities between my experiences before and after I come to realize that I am in a hallucinatory state. These are to be accounted for at the phenomenal level.[68]

It is very important to appreciate here that the red sensation is not the *object* of my perceptual taking at the initial stage while I am being deceived. Before I realize I am hallucinating, I have some kind of demonstrative perceptual thought or taking. It has an *intentional* object that is given by the expression: *this red ball*. Tye claims that the red ball I seem to see is unreal. This is correct: there is no physical red ball present. But there was, and remains, a red visual sensation in my consciousness.[69] It caused my thought about the ball I believed to exist, and perhaps also a thought that I was *seeing* a ball. Implicit expectations connected with the inner, subjective, sensations guided my thoughts and actions about the ball that I believed to have objective existence in the world, in front of me. Although the red sensation was not the focus or object of my thought, it had, and still has, actual existence. While the hallucination persists, it is an irreducible feature of reality. It is not an (in-existent) intentional object.

My demonstrative perceptual thought simply failed in its reference.[70] I did not *initially* form a thought about my phenomenal state, because my concepts purported to refer to something physical, in my surroundings. Hence it is incorrect to say that at the first stage, the object of my thought was really my own visual sensation, although I did not realize it. When I come to realize that I am hallucinating, I form a quite *new* demonstrative thought, exercising categories of a different general kind. This new attentional set does have my inner phenomenal state as its object. As we noted in the case of simple non-deceptive hallucinations, it involves a demonstrative thought focused upon my own inner state. I conceptualize my inner visual experience more directly, as an inner visual state.[71] Thinking directly about my inner sensations prepares me for actions in respect of them, as indicated above.

There is an important objection to this interpretation of hallucination that needs to be addressed. In a somewhat compressed passage in a late paper on perception, Wilfrid Sellars himself suggests that the 'ultimate referent' of the subject's demonstrative thought should be construed as the subject's sensation, or inner phenomenal or sensory state.[72] Sellars's idea is that I could be hallucinating in having the kind of experience which prompts me to claim:

This cube of pink over there facing me edgewise ... [is made of ice]

By construing the demonstrative phrase as referring to my inner sensation, we may 'save the reference' of my perceptual commitment to the existence of something pink. Sellars rightly insists that it is not true that during the time I am deceived I conceptualize my sensation (i.e. phenomenal state) of something pink *as a sensation*. Hence what he terms as the 'normal references' of perceptual takings will be physical objects. Nevertheless, he wishes to have a role for sensations as the ultimate references to which the demonstrative phrases relate, not only in cases of deceptive hallucinations, but also in cases of ordinary veridical perception.

Sellars's main argument for this interpretation is based upon the claim that it would be incorrect to deny that the perceiver is seeing anything when he hallucinates, since this would wrongly imply that he is imagining something. But is Sellars right in his understanding of what is implied by the denial? Surely it is quite in order to accept the denial of the claim that the subject is seeing, for the simple reason that he is hallucinating. There is no implication that the subject is imagining something. What would be incorrect is to deny that anything is actually present in experience, even at the purely phenomenal level.

If the analysis of reference based upon Evans's ideas is correct, then I am purporting to refer to whatever kind of thing I would act upon. I am disposed to act upon a region of physical space where I believe a ball to be. The category to which my demonstrative thought relates is governed by my potential action. It purports to refer to a physical object. Hence, in the hallucinatory case, my demonstrative thought simply fails to have a reference, for the reason that nothing fulfils the criteria based upon my potential actions. It is true that *after* I discover my mistake, the actions I am disposed to make would change: but then *so also* would my thoughts change.

It is possible that Sellars is confusing two senses of 'reason' here. The causal reason for my mistaken claim that I am seeing a pink ice cube is that I am having a hallucinatory phenomenal state of pink. But that is not a cognitive reason *for me*, which I use to infer the presence of something. We do not need to preserve the reference, in addition to explaining why I am causally prompted to form a belief about the presence of an object. For these reasons I do not want to follow Sellars in claiming that in such cases the subject's phenomenal state is the ultimate reference of the demonstrative thought. But even if I am mistaken in this, it would not, in any event, undermine the general Critical Realist analysis of perceptual experience defended in this chapter.[73]

Sellars is right to this extent: there are some contexts where I may be genuinely uncertain as to whether or not I am hallucinating. I may think demonstratively about my phenomenal experiences as states of myself, and be uncertain whether they form part of a veridical experience, or are merely hallucinatory objects. Call these 'Macbeth cases'. Such a case may give rise to a cautious perceptual taking, as Sellars illustrates, where I formulate my demonstrative thought in a different way:

> This *somehow* (a cube of pink facing me edgewise) which is a cube of pink facing me edgewise ...

In a Macbeth case, I am exercising fairly sophisticated concepts that are neutral between hallucination and veridical perception. Thus I am able to entertain the possibility that what I am aware of in a phenomenal sense may or may not be physical. But in normal situations, my concepts refer directly to physical objects. Therefore it is only by altering the concepts I employ, and by entertaining a new, distinct demonstrative thought, that I am able to refer to my hallucinatory sensations.

Case (14): The misconceived veridical case

The converse case can also occur, as other writers have also observed. I may have been given drugs that I know about, which in the past have caused me to hallucinate animals. I am then given a placebo, and I suddenly see a poodle in front of me. I think I am probably hallucinating the poodle. Unknown to me, it is a real one, and has been placed there without my noticing. I reach out, tentatively, to stroke it, and gradually become convinced of its reality. There is again a shift in the concepts I use, and accordingly, also a switch in the implicit expectations I have in respect of my experiences.

8   The perception of physical objects (1): double vision

We have examined a range of cases involving various perceptual phenomena. The conclusions derived from these cases provide support for the Critical Realist analysis of perceptual experience. Its central claims are that experiences have two components, and that what is perceived must be distinguished from what is immediately present as a phenomenal part of conscious experience. What is immediately present belongs at the phenomenal level; it is an inner state, of a kind shared with hallucinations. However, our perceptual takings – in the form of demonstrative thoughts – refer to independent physical objects. These takings, when caused in the appropriate way, determine what we perceive. This ontological discrepancy can be accommodated on the two-dimensional account of concept exercise. In order to show the plausibility of these central claims, I shall first illustrate how they apply in an atypical case of perception.

Case (15): Double vision

While seated at my desk, I look out of the window at the chimney of the house opposite. As I do so, I am aware that the window frame and its latch appear double. When I shift my focus to the window latch, the chimney behind it now appears double. There are two images of the chimney, one on each side of the latch.

Many discussions of double vision are unsatisfying, since they do not get to grips with the full complexity of the phenomenon. Austin criticizes Ayer for arguing that, if I see one piece of paper double, then two pieces of paper *really are perceived*.[74] If seeing is a relation between a subject and a physical object, then Austin is right to object to Ayer's claim. There is only the one physical object available to be perceived in the relevant sense.

Austin goes on, however, to state that double vision is 'a quite exceptional case', and 'a baffling abnormality'. Abnormal it may be, but it is not an uncommon phenomenon. If I hold an object such as a golf club straight out in front of me, I cannot focus clearly on the whole object – either the shaft near my hand is seen double, or the club head is. Austin points out that there are locutions such as 'I see the paper double', or, 'I see it as two'. Appeal to such uses, he implies, allows us to avoid referring to two entities. But aside from this, he has no satisfactory positive account to offer of the phenomenon. He completely fails to engage with the deeper question that Ayer is raising, whether we should countenance the existence of entities other than physical objects in analysing double vision.

For even though I do not *see* two physical objects (in the relevant sense) when I see the chimney double, there are at least two entities I can refer to demonstratively, which need to be distinguished from each other. As Jackson rightly points out, the contexts in which we can appeal to phrases such as 'it appears double' are rather limited.[75] There are many descriptions of features of double vision in which we make distinctions that are hard to capture in terms of statements about physical objects alone. It makes sense to say things like, 'the image on the left is fuzzier than the image on the right', and 'by altering my focus I can make the two images move further apart' and 'the appearance of the chimney is now closer to the left image of the window latch than it is to the right image of the latch'. Talk of seeing the same object double does not enable us to state such simple truths. The facts can be readily accommodated when we use the same framework of inner states that we employ when dealing with hallucinatory images. Within this framework I need to distinguish the images as different entities, since they have different properties.[76]

A potential confusion arises because there is also a sense in which, experiencing double vision, I can demonstratively think about the same object twice, as Snowdon has pointed out. He considers an experience of double vision where one image of an object is on the left, and the other on the right. We might be tempted to claim that two images of a single object present us with two distinct items, and describe the situation as follows:

(A) That-L (i.e. the leftmost of the visually presented items) is not identical with that-R (i.e. the rightmost of the visually presented items).

Snowdon suggests that we should reject this way of describing the situation, and argues:

The claim (A) is hardly self-evident. It is quite possible to say, contrary to (A), that:

(P) That-L = That-R

To sustain (P), double vision has to be thought of as involving a double sighting of a single object. On that conception the identity judgement (P) is correct. Our perception puts us in touch with a single object in such a way that we can think demonstratively about it twice.[77]

This is plausible, as far as the immediate claim about the reference to the physical object goes. However, when we think of it twice, we think of it in different ways. An appeal to the framework of inner states is required for a full account of the different kinds of claims we can make about the situation, as Jackson's examples indicate. Snowdon's account of the situation is incomplete. A full description of all the relevant facts should also include some account of the different *ways* we have of identifying the object seen twice, by virtue of the different analogue spatial aspects of the inner phenomenal state experienced. So, according to the Critical Realist view I am defending, the statement considered in (A) is ambiguous. When taken to operate at the physical object level, it is false, and should be replaced by (P). However, when interpreted as a claim about inner states, it correctly expresses the fact that my subjective visual experience is distinct from the physical object seen. It involves a spatial manifold, in which distinct parts of the subjective array can relate to the same external object. (A) thus captures important claims that we need to make when giving a full account of what occurs in double vision.

This is not a revisionary conclusion, as Snowdon seems to suggest at one point. As noted above, we are able to switch conceptual frameworks when we discover that what we at first take to be a veridical experience is in fact hallucinatory. A similar switch of frameworks is involved in treating the two images as distinct entities of some kind. The framework of inner states is implicit in the way that we sometimes think and speak of double vision. Corresponding to the two ways we have of conceptualizing the double vision case are two different sets of expectations with regard to my experience, and two different sets of potential actions. The important moral is that by shifting the framework of concepts I apply, I can extend the range of the true identificatory demonstrative judgements that I am able to make.

9 The perception of physical objects (2): the normal case

We are now finally in a position properly to assess what goes on when a subject sees a physical object in normal circumstances. Consider again the case cited at the end of the last chapter:

Case (16): Distinguishing two objects in visual experience

I see, veridically, two fruits side by side on the table. I see the one on the right to be an apple, and the one on the left to be an orange.

The conclusions we have drawn from the various cases analysed above provide the key to a proper understanding of what takes place in ordinary perception. They allow us to resolve the apparent conflict between the phenomenological directness of the perception of external objects, and the existence of mediating inner phenomenal experiences. In my normal day to day interactions with the world, I focus my thoughts on how things are, objectively, in my surroundings. But seeing an object involves more than thoughts. A full account of what is going on should do justice to the distinctively phenomenal aspect of experience. Seeing also involves perspectival experiences of objects. These experiences are interpreted, on the Critical Realist analysis, as partly constituted by inner phenomenal states. As developed here, this means that, using my imagination, I construct a sense-image-model relating to the actual and potential phenomenal experiences I have, or would have, in seeing an object of a given kind. My perceptual thoughts are guided by implicit expectations about the inner experiences I have of the objects I engage with.

Although my normal perceptual stance, in which I respond in the mode of perception to my phenomenal experiences, does not involve reflection upon either the fact that I am having perceptual thoughts, or upon my inner phenomenal states, it is perfectly possible for me to take up a stance in which I do begin to reflect upon these matters, and so to respond in the mode of introspection. I do not have to experience double vision of an object in order to alter my conceptual stance, and to switch to conceptualizing the inner experience I have in seeing it *as* an inner experience. Exactly the same considerations apply to normal vision. In seeing an apple, I can reflect on the visual experience I have in seeing that apple. Something like this occurs, I suggest, when a painter notes the comparative size that objects occupy in the visual field. If I move around the table, the apple may appear nearer to me than the orange. I can think that, objectively, the orange is larger than the apple, while at the same time noting that, subjectively, the appearance of the apple is larger than that presented by the orange.[78]

In seeing the apple next to the orange, I am directly aware of it. I interpret the use of 'directly' to mean that I am non-inferentially caused to exercise concepts in the form an occurrent demonstrative thought or perceptual taking: 'this apple is ... (good to eat ... etc.)' – a thought about the physical object I take to be physically situated in front of me. At the same time, I am immediately aware (that is, in the nonconceptual sense) of the apple's subjective appearance, at the nonconceptual level. According to the Critical Realist, this appearance is an inner phenomenal state. While the concepts in my perceptual taking relate, more or less accurately, to the apple that I see, I have an implicit set of expectations about the way that my subjective experience of it will alter. As shown by the cases of the Ames Room and the deceptive hallucination, when my expectations are confounded I may be prompted to redirect my conceptual focus, and attend to the nature of my subjective experiences.

The Critical Realist model defended here allows a reply to a general argument put forward by Snowdon against the causal theory of perception. Snowdon rejects the causal theory in favour of his own version of the disjunctive view.[79] Snowdon criticizes the causal theorist's claim that visual experiences are inner states, and distinct from the physical object seen. Suppose that in normal conditions I look at the physical scene around me, and focus my attention on some object X. Snowdon argues that if I am seeing the object X veridically, and not experiencing any kind of full or partial hallucination, then we could in theory construct a complete list of all the true identificatory judgements of every visible element in the physical scene I see, about X and the other objects present in experience. This list, according to Snowdon, will contain all the true demonstrative judgements I could then make on the basis of my current visual experience. These judgements will relate only to physical objects. There would be nothing left over in my experience, nothing else that I could be aware of and could demonstratively refer to. But if the list of such judgements is exhaustive, this entails that there cannot be any further entity present in my conscious experience that is non-physical. If this argument is correct, then there is no room in experience for any inner state, as the Critical Realist analysis holds.

But according to the Critical Realist analysis, there will be further true demonstrative judgements I can make if I alter my attentional set, and adopt a different conceptual framework. What is certainly correct about Snowdon's argument is that, in altering my attentional set, I do not bring anything new into my immediate phenomenal consciousness. In this sense, my experience remains unchanged. But in altering my conceptual framework, I apply a different set of concepts, and hence come to refer to a different *kind* of object. I shift from responding in the mode of perception, to responding in the mode of introspection. The change in conceptual frameworks is somewhat similar to the change that can occur in *displaced perception* discussed earlier, while I am looking at the video display of an operation. I can switch my attention, and consequently the conceptual frameworks I am exercising, in thinking of what I am seeing in the display, first, as a set of organs inside the patient's body, and then, a moment later, in terms of images on a screen. I could first demonstratively refer to all the organs and other objects I see, inside the patient's body; but by altering the framework I employ, I could then make further demonstrative judgements about the screen and the images displayed upon it.

Even in normal perception, I can in a similar fashion switch from attending to the physical object I see, to thinking of my phenomenal experience as an inner state. In doing so, I no longer refer directly to the object I see in the physical scene, which is distinct from my experience. Instead, I refer demonstratively to an aspect of the very phenomenal state immediately present in my consciousness. So the central claim of the reply to Snowdon is that there are further true demonstrative judgements I can make on the basis of my current visual experience, judgements that do not refer to physical objects, but to inner phenomenal states. To complete the reply, the Critical Realist has to defend a further thesis: the Critical Realist is claiming that we can make two different kinds of demonstrative judgement on the basis of a perceptual experience: judgements about what is immediately present in experience, and judgements about the external physical objects we directly perceive. So it needs to be shown how we can refer directly to physical objects, if they are distinguished from what is immediately present in a phenomenal sense. In Chapter 10 I shall explain how the Critical Realist account can make sense of our demonstrative judgements about external objects.

The key insight of the Critical Realist theory is the realization that in normal everyday perception, our perceptual thoughts are guided by implicit expectations about inner phenomenal states, without those states becoming the *objects* of our attention. The referential aspect of the concepts we employ spontaneously 'bypasses' what is phenomenally present, and focuses on the external world directly, even though it is responsive to the inner phenomenally state. As I shall now show, this model of perception meets the first condition to be met by accounts of perceptual experience set out at the end of the last chapter, which for convenience I repeat here:

Condition (1)

An analysis of experience should explain the way that the two components of experience are unified when I attend to an aspect of the physical scene I perceive. It should account for the way that the concept I entertain applies to some specific aspect of what I am aware of, nonconceptually, at the phenomenal level, and not to the whole scene, indiscriminately.

In seeing the apple to be on the right of the two fruits in front of me, I exercise the concept of an apple. This is what guides my general plan of actions. If for example, I wanted to eat an apple, I would select the object on the right. But the fact that I am seeing the fruit on the right to be the apple is also based upon my current expectations. My exercise of the concept of an apple in my perceptual taking is essentially connected with the implicit expectations I have with respect to it: I expect that object on the right to taste in a certain way if I were to pick it up and bite it; I have expectations about how it would look if it were to roll over, or if it were to be cut in half, and so on. Hence the two components of perceptual experience are unified by virtue of the two dimensions involved in the exercise of the concept of an apple.

This analysis provides us with an explanation of what it is to *attend to* a particular object. Attention is bound up with conceptualization, and this, as just noted, is bound up with the expectations I have. The external object I am attending to, in the mode of perception, is that which causes those aspects of my inner phenomenal state that I implicitly expect to transform in ways typical of the kind of object I conceptualize it as being. Similarly, when I attend to an inner state in the mode of introspection, for example to an after-image, I am prepared for the kinds of changes that are appropriate to such inner entities – that when I alter my glance, the background will change while the after-image remains in the same area of my visual field, and so on. I alter my attentional set by changing the range of phenomena I am prepared for. When concentrating on a serious game of chess, I will be running through many permutations of chess moves, pausing only occasionally to glance at the time left on my clock. I try not to allow anything else to distract me; I set my attention narrowly. This is very different from setting my attention as widely as possible to the whole of my visual field when I am out bird watching, and I am prepared to respond to the slightest flicker of movement at the periphery of my visual field.

We also have the materials to show that the second condition on any analysis of perception can be met. This ran as follows:

Condition (2)

An analysis of experience should provide a positive account of the role of the phenomenal component of experience, while explaining why it need not become the object of perception.

On the Sellarsian account, phenomenal experience does not play an idle role; it is not a mere accompaniment of the perceptual taking. It is important because it is integrated with the subject's exercise of classificatory concepts, and also prepares the subject for specific kinds of changes in experience, so as to guide further action. We noted this in the case of *displaced perception* in Section (4) above. The examples from endoscopic minimal access surgery show two things. First, that we can be guided in our actions by a nonconceptual awareness of states that are distinct from the actual objects we are manipulating; without such awareness the surgeon would be incapable of acting. Second, after the initial training period has passed, and the surgeon begins to use the video display automatically, his or her focus of attention is mainly directed onto the site of the surgery. The surgeon thinks of the task in terms of bodily parts and instrument placing, and so on. So the images on the screen which guide the actions are not the focus of the surgeon's perceptual thoughts.

Critical Realism holds that not only visually-aided perception in surgery, but in fact all perception of physical objects involves a displacement between the items that the subject is immediately aware of, and the physical objects to which the subject's perceptual thoughts are directed. The difference is a more radical one than the example of surgery appears to involve. In fact, in all cases, an implicit awareness of inner states prompts perceptual thoughts about external physical objects. Expectations in respect of the former guide actions directed on the latter. The only real difference between endoscopic surgery and normal perception is that the surgical technique involves an additional level of displacement.

The use of such analogies to explain the sense in which all perception involves the immediate (nonconceptual) awareness of inner phenomenal states is open to criticism. The objector will point out the various ways in which the parallel fails to hold. In the case of minimal access surgery, it is possible for other observers to look at the images the operating surgeon views on the video screen; they are not essentially private to the perceiver. It is possible, also, to compare directly the physical events pictured using video apparatus with the correlated images that appear on the screen; no such direct comparisons are possible between inner phenomenal states and outer objects, if the Critical Realist model of perception is correct. So it is claimed that as a consequence of the metaphysical analysis of perception upheld by the Critical Realist, epistemic differences follow. Such differences do not hold in the examples appealed to in the analogy.

These points are true, but they are ineffective as criticisms of the phenomenology and metaphysics of perception, which are the concern of this chapter. What matters is the psychological plausibility of the claim that there is an ontological gap between the perceiver's phenomenal states and the perceptual object. On any account of perception we have to accept some kind of distinction between the physical object that the subject sees, and the experience of seeing that object. What is immediately present in a phenomenal way is something that involves, in some sense, a subjective fact about the perceiver. This contrasts with the objective world to which perception gives us access. Phenomenal experience is always perspectival. Yet in most of our perceptual dealings with the world, we do not dwell on this fact. We tend to ignore the subjective element in experience. Our perceptual thoughts focus on the way that the things objectively are. On the Critical Realist view, it is claimed that the difference between the subjective experience and the objective world perceived amounts to a metaphysical difference between the types of entity involved. But since the difference is overlooked in normal perception, the fact that it encompasses an ontological distinction between inner states and outer objects does not matter. We do not normally reflect upon the difference in any event, so how it is analysed cannot be relevant to the phenomenology.

The points made here put us in a position to understand what is really wrong with the sense-datum theory of perception, where that theory is understood as distinguishing between the sense-data we immediately apprehend, and external mind-independent physical objects.[80] According to this view, sense-data are the objects we really perceive, rather than physical objects. The relation of 'apprehending' is understood as a form of perception – immediate awareness is conflated with direct perception. But this view is false on empirical grounds, for the straightforward reason that our perceptual takings are not, in the normal case, directed onto our phenomenal states as such. The demonstrative thoughts that arise in normal perception focus upon physical objects.

Sense-data, in other words, are not ordinarily the *objects* of perception, for what counts as a perceptual object is determined by the concepts we employ. From the Critical Realist perspective, both the sense-data theorist and also the Direct Realist are guilty of making the same error. They both hold the view that the entity immediately present in experience is identical with the entity that is the referent of the concepts we exercise directly in perception. These entities should not, however, be confused with each other. The fact that the Critical Realist view observes the distinction is one clear reason why it is a very different theory from the sense-data theory advanced by Russell, Ayer, and at one time by Jackson (though Jackson has now adopted a different view of experience). Moreover, Critical Realism, unlike the sense-datum theory, is not committed to foundationalism. Hence it is seriously misleading to imply, as Tye does, that Critical Realism is automatically faced with all the problems incurred by traditional sense-data accounts.[81] This is not to deny that there are *some* resemblances between sense-data, when conceived of as inner states, and the phenomenal states espoused by Critical Realism.[82]

In this section I have argued that we can give a role to phenomenal states without making them into objects, as the sense-data theory attempts to do. They are not completely idle, since they guide the exercise of concepts in experience. Thus Smith's challenge, raised in the previous chapter, is answered. It is not exactly true to say that we overlook our phenomenal states, when they are not the objects of our demonstrative thoughts. As the many examples given in the present chapter indicate, phenomenal states play an important role in experience and action, even though we do not usually form thoughts focused upon them. It is indeed quite plausible to claim that, in the case of very young children and nonhuman animals, this lack of attention to them is a necessity. Such perceiving subjects only form low-level thoughts aimed at external objects, and never attend to the inner phenomenal states that guide such thoughts, because they lack even low-level concepts relating to their own inner states.

10   Reflection and the normal perceptual stance

The final issue I shall consider has to do with the implications of the Critical Realist theory for our ordinary, common-sense thinking about perception. It has been argued that the Critical Realist analysis of experience provides the resources for an adequate reply to the Transparency Objection. It can be formulated in a way that shows how, through the exercise of the imagination, we can account for the unity of perception. The final objection to be considered is whether, according to Critical Realism, our common-sense understanding of perception is in error. It might be thought that the theory entails the conclusion that in our ordinary perceptual dealings with the world we are guilty of a pervasive mistake: we mistake our own experiences for external objects.[83]

The reply to this last objection is a subtle one. There is a sense, I shall concede, in which it is fair to say that we sometimes mistake our inner experiences for external physical objects. But this mistake is not committed in our ordinary perceptual dealings with the world. It is, rather, a mistake that arises at the reflective level, when we begin to theorize about the nature of perceptual experiences. We can then be misled about the complex ways in which physical objects are connected with our perceptual experiences. But in our normal perceptually based interaction with the world, there is no error. Properly understood, there is no conflict between the Critical Realist analysis and our ordinary ideas about perception, as these are manifested in day-to-day behaviour.[84]

In order to unpack these claims, let me begin by clarifying the distinction alluded to above, between the two different stances we can adopt with respect to perceptual experience. We should distinguish what I shall term the 'natural attitude' to the world, from our reflective level of thinking about perception and experience.

Our natural responses to the world form part of our ordinary repertoire of near spontaneous dealings with the objects around us. When I adopt the natural attitude, I simply engage with the world, without thinking about my own experiences.[85] I apply concepts of various kinds to the physical objects I encounter in experience. I classify them directly, and act accordingly, but I do not need to reflect upon my own consciousness of objects. To the extent that I think about my own situation, it is as an embodied agent, acting on the world. The natural attitude can be considered as containing our normal perceptual experiences of objects, together with the natural and straightforward actions that we base upon such experiences. This is the stance we adopt for most of the time.

This stance contrasts with what may be termed 'the reflective stance'. When I begin to reflect in more detail upon my own place in the world, I become aware of the fact that in order to perceive, I must in some sense have experiences of the world. If I and my companion see the same object, we may each have a different subjective experience of that object. If I have a sufficiently sophisticated set of concepts, I may start to think about the role of experience in perception in more detail. I need to make sense of myself not just as an embodied agent, but also as a sentient creature, having a conscious point of view on the world. It is only at the reflective level that any question about the status of experiences is raised.

The relevant point is that the responses that form part of the natural attitude do not include any reflection upon the status or contents of my experiences. The thoughts I have, and my actions, are directed on to the world around me. I take the objects I see to be directly present to me. And, in the conceptual sense of seeing, this is correct. As we have seen, Critical Realism upholds the directness of our perceptual thoughts. I directly take there to be objects in my surroundings, without inference. This is not to say I cannot justify my perceptual claims. As Sellars argued, to say that a perceptual thought is not based upon inference is *not* to say that it is without presuppositions. If asked to justify my perceptually based beliefs, I could do so by citing a number of general facts, beginning with claims about my background beliefs, and about my competence as a perceiver.[86] But in responding in the natural way by perceiving the world, I do not infer my beliefs about the world from any inner experience I have, since I do not even think about my experiences.

What is particularly important is that when I adopt the natural attitude to the world, there is a complete *absence* of any thought about my own experience in seeing an object. Since my thoughts are directed on to the objects I see, I am not concerned with my own experience. *A fortiori*, I am not cognitively aware of any distinction between my experience in seeing the object, and the object itself. At the pre-reflective level, there is no mistake involved in ordinary perception. This means that that final condition set out can also be met in a satisfactory way by Critical Realism.

Condition (3)

An analysis of experience should explain the unity of consciousness without imputing to the perceiving subject a straightforward error every time he or she perceives something.

The Critical Realist account respects the phenomenology of perception. This fits with what has already been argued. But in addition, we are able to see why Critical Realism does not impute any error to our perceptual thoughts. These concern the objects we see and their properties. We legitimately conceptualize our experiences, in the sense that we take them to be experiences of ordinary things. In adopting the natural attitude, we take ourselves to be directly seeing physical things, and also other people, and indeed their various mental states – such as their sadness, hilarity, enjoyment, annoyance, and so on. Such perceptual takings are by and large correct; there is no widespread error at this level. The natural attitude does not conflict with the claims of Critical Realism.

It could be objected that common sense includes a view about perception, and it is this view, rather than the natural attitude, which is in conflict with Critical Realism. I am in effect suggesting that common sense does not really have a view about perception; it is better thought of as a set of practices, as our general ways of acting, before we begin to reflect on such matters.

I do not, however, want to reduce the argument to a matter of trading intuitions about what is meant by 'common sense'. This would not be a satisfactory way resolving a philosophical dispute. Suppose we include in the ambit of common-sense beliefs the ordinary ways in which we categorize our perceptual experiences. We noted in the previous chapter that we often identify types of experience relationally, by reference to the kinds of objects they are normally associated with. Imagine someone who doubts whether the object she thinks she may be seeing is real. She might describe her visual experience as 'an appearance of something that looks like an aeroplane'. Such references are neutral about the ontological status of experience. They are, prima facie, compatible with Direct Realism; but they are also compatible with the Critical Realist interpretation of experience. So when we begin to reflect upon the nature of experience, there need be no conflict between these initial reflections and the claims of any theory. It is only when our reasoning becomes more sophisticated, and we begin to articulate a detailed theory about what perception involves, that claims about the ontological status of experiences are formulated.

From the Critical Realist point of view, it is only at the reflective level of theorizing about experience that we may be in error. But in theorizing at this level we have moved away from our ordinary dealings with the world, and are beginning to formulate theories of a more philosophical nature. It is not surprising, therefore, that some attempts to formulate theories about experience conflict with Critical Realism.

All in all, it is possible for the subject to conceptualize experience in at least three different ways: first, in terms of objective concepts relating directly to the independent physical things that the subject takes to be in the surroundings; second, by identifying the nonconceptual appearance of a perceived object as a subjective experience of some kind, by reference to the kind of object of which it is taken to be an appearance, but in neutral terms without commitment to the ontological status of the appearance; and third, in terms of concepts relating directly to inner phenomenal states. Strictly speaking, a mistake about the ontological status of an inner phenomenal state only occurs when I form a reflective level thought that could be expressed in something like the following way, which is in line with the Direct Realist analysis:

> My phenomenal experience of the dog I see (that is, the subjective, nonconceptual appearance the dog presents) involves only the mind-independent object I see: an objectively existing dog (or an objective, perspectival presentation of the dog); my experience is not constituted by an inner state.

Clearly, this is a pretty sophisticated kind of thought to have. It can only arise at the reflective level, when we begin to formulate philosophical theories about perception. From the perspective of Critical Realism, it is an error, but a philosophical error, and not one committed by common sense in normal perception. It arises because when we start to reflect upon the process of perception, we conflate the *directness* of our perceptual takings for the *immediacy* of the phenomenal states which guide our perceptually based actions.

11 Conclusion

The Transparency Argument exerts a powerful hold over our thinking about perception because the directness of perceptual experience makes it psychologically difficult to grasp the correct analysis of experience. The misconceptions that arise about the status of experience are the result of the fact that perceptual processes, and especially visual processes, have evolved into such wonderfully effective mechanisms for enabling us to arrive rapidly at knowledge of the world around us, the better to evade predators and to capture prey. We could not act so effectively on the world if we stopped to examine our own inner states. We take the physical objects that we see to be present in consciousness. We ignore, at a conceptual level, the phenomenal experiences that mediate our perception of them. As we have seen, the Transparency Argument is unsound, because it trades on an ambiguity in the senses of 'awareness' that it appeals to. In being directly aware, conceptually, of physical objects, the perceiver is immediately aware, non-conceptually, of inner phenomenal states.

Critical Realism does not imply that our common-sense view of perception is in error; common sense itself has no complete view about the nature of perception. In so far as there are errors, these only arise at the reflective level. They occur if it is assumed that that perception is totally direct, in the sense advocated by the Direct Realist, or if it is assumed that the Critical Realist idea is somehow in conflict with our day-to-day perceptual dealings with the world and the phenomenology such dealings give rise to. In perceiving the world, we categorize objects directly, and act accordingly. This is the natural response. It does not require philosophical justification from Direct Realism, because it is compatible with the Critical Realist view.

Perception involves inner states, but is focused upon the external objects in our surroundings. We have an understanding of the nature of perceptual experience that arises from our first-person perspective. This involves an appreciation of the fact that, by experiencing the world, we can come to know directly about the nature of the physical objects around us. The phenomenology of perceptual experience is therefore not in conflict with the Critical Realist account. It is compatible with the metaphysical gap that exists between the inner phenomenal states that are immediately present in conscious experience and the external physical objects we directly perceive.

10 Inner experience and the possibility of knowledge

1 Inner states and the perception of external objects

The central claim of this book is that perception involves conscious inner states. According to the Critical Realist analysis, an experience of a physical object comprises, in part, an inner phenomenal state of mind, a state of exactly the same ontological type that can occur in a hallucinatory experience; this state involves phenomenal qualities of which the subject is immediately aware, nonconceptually, in consciousness. Such states have one kind of nonconceptual representational content: the representational content of a phenomenal state type derives from the general relation in which such a state type stands to the properties of objects in the surroundings, by reference to which a perceiver can successfully navigate through an environment. But considered as a token, each phenomenal state in experience is logically distinct from the particular physical object perceived, that is, the distal object that produces it.

In the previous chapter it was argued that these claims can be reconciled with the phenomenology of perception. There is no conflict between the fact that, when I see an external physical object and see it directly as an object in my surroundings, in doing so I am caused to have an inner experience, one which does not contain that object as a phenomenal constituent.

In this final chapter I consider certain epistemological objections that have been raised against the general causal view of perception defended here. Each of these turns on the central claim of Critical Realism, that perceptual experiences are inner states; in each case it is alleged that this conception of experience raises serious problems for the theory. I shall argue that none of these objections succeeds against the Critical Realist version of the causal theory.

2 The possibility of reference

The first of these, to which I shall devote the most attention in this chapter, concerns the *reference* of our perceptual thoughts. It has been argued that our perceptual experiences involve concepts, which are exercised in perceptual takings. These are directed at the physical objects in our surroundings, even though we are not immediately aware of these objects. Physical objects are not parts of phenomenal consciousness, even though they may be, in a formal sense, constituents of our perceptual thoughts.

This position invites an objection along the following lines. Seated at my desk I survey a number of books on the shelf in front of me. I concentrate my attention on one of these and have a demonstrative perceptual thought:

'That red book is a copy of Sellars's *Science and Metaphysics*.'

In order for me to have a demonstrative thought of this kind, it is commonly accepted that in some sense I must know *which* particular object I am thinking of.[1] Moreover, it is necessary that I come to have this knowledge on the basis of my perceptual experience, and not purely by description. My experience is in some way *relevant* to my ability to form a demonstrative thought about the book that I see in having it. If my demonstrative thought was not somehow connected with my experience, then my thought could hardly be said to be a component of my perceptual experience. But on the Critical Realist analysis, I am, in a metaphysical sense, cut off from the book. Although I think about it *directly*, it is not *immediately* available in my consciousness. What I am conscious of in this immediate sense is a complex inner sensory state of mind, with phenomenal qualities that are distinct from the properties of the physical objects in my surroundings. So the question arises, how does my conscious experience enable my perceptual thought to refer to a particular physical object? It might well be the case that more than one book is physically present, which 'corresponds to' the experience I have, so mere correspondence alone is not sufficient to establish reference. Here the very arguments used to support the causal view in Chapters 3 and 4 might seem to threaten the Critical Realist account. There is a problem about how it is that I can succeed in forming a demonstrative thought that focuses upon the very object I am actually seeing. We need to explain how my perceptual thoughts can 'latch on' to an object that is outside my immediate experience. The Critical Realist must show that the theory does not have intolerable semantic consequences.

In the account provided in the last chapter, it was argued that there is a way that I, as a perceiver, can conceptualize my inner experience directly. Adopting a reflective stance, I can form thoughts about my experiences, as such. It might be conceded that, in this direct case, thinking about an item within my experience is not a problem. But what about reference to physical objects, which, according to the Critical Realist view, are not present immediately in experience? Up to this point, we have not explained what many take to be the central fact about reference. If I refer to a physical object, I must in some sense know which object I am referring to. The objection is that knowledge of public objects cannot be explained on the Critical Realist model, for on that account we are cut off from knowledge of the external world. The difficulty is this: my ordinary perceptual takings involve demonstratives that refer to physical objects that are logically distinct from anything present in my immediate experience. But if that is the case, how can perceptual experience make available to me the object I perceive, in a manner that allows me to grasp some essential distinguishing feature that belongs only to the particular object I see, and not to any other, so that I can single out that object referentially?

There are really three difficulties raised by this general objection. One difficulty is based upon the fact that I am cut off, epistemically, from the objects I see. So the question then arises as to how I can become perceptually aware of a physical object, and moreover, communicate with others who, like myself, have immediate awareness of only their own inner states. The second difficulty arises from the fact that, as has been argued in Chapter 4, my own inner phenomenal state has only general content.[2] In such a case, it has been objected, that inner state cannot provide a basis for perceptual beliefs that have particular content, in so far as they refer to the particular object I take myself to be perceiving. A third difficulty relates to the type of causal chain that connects me and the object I see. It has been suggested that perceivers have no clear knowledge of the causal principles that distinguish the objects they perceive and succeed in demonstratively referring to, in their everyday dealings with the world.[3]

In combination, these problems have been taken to show that reference to objects is rendered impossible on any account of experience that countenances inner phenomenal states. I will now show why this interpretation of the semantic consequences of Critical Realism is incorrect. The perceptive reader, who has followed the overall argument up to this point, will be aware that all the materials to answer these charges are already in place. I will begin by developing more fully the Critical Realist account of the way in which we succeed in referring to external physical objects.

Suppose that, on the basis of a visual experience, I form the demonstrative belief, 'that red object is a book ... '. There is one particular object that I have in mind, which I think of as the book I am seeing. In some sense – a sense that needs to be explicated – I know *which* object I am thinking of. In order for me to be thinking about some particular object as a book, I think of it as related to myself, in two ways. First, I think of it as having some location, relative to my body; for example, I may think of the object as somewhere a few feet ahead of me, slightly to the left. For the reasons discussed in Chapter 4, my belief in the egocentric location of the book is defeasible. As was shown by the example drawn from aural perception, and also by the visual cases of the submerged coin and the hall of mirrors, I may on occasion be unable to locate the object I perceive directly, and be uncertain how to act in order to select it. But second, and more importantly, I can think about the book to which I am referring on the basis of my experience as: the thing I am now seeing. This idea is implicit in my forming the demonstrative thought, and would readily become explicit if I am challenged ('Which book?' – 'That one over there, can you not see it next to the clock – I can see it clearly', etc). This may sound circular, but as we shall soon see, it can be explicated in a way that clearly shows it is not.

I need to make a clarificatory point here. At any one time I am seeing a number of objects, in the extensional sense, even if I am not conceptualizing them all. My inner phenomenal state is a complex array, and different parts of it are caused by, and correspond to, different external physical objects. So in having a visual inner experience, I am normally seeing, in the extensional sense, several objects at once. But when I form a demonstrative thought referring to a particular external object, I am usually attending, for that moment, just to that one object. As we noted in the preceding chapter, an account can be provided of what it is for me to attend to something by reference to the implicit expectations I have about changes to aspects of my phenomenal experience. Hence, in forming a demonstrative thought about a book I see, I am prepared for certain kinds of transformations to specific aspects of my experience – about how things would appear if I opened that book and turned its pages, and so on. I do not need to think *explicitly* of my experience as distinct from the object I see: as we also noted, there is a *neutral*, relational way of conceptualizing experience by reference to the typical appearance of objects in a given class. This way of picking out a *type* of experience takes into account its subjective nature, but leaves open the ontological issue of whether the experience is an inner state or a non-inner experience. In line with this idea, it is plausible to claim that when I form a demonstrative thought about an object I am seeing, such as a book, what is implicit is further knowledge of the following form:

> I am seeing *that book* (the physical object), in virtue of having a visual experience *as of* a book.

or even more fully:

> I am seeing *that book* (the physical object), in virtue of having, in *this part* of my visual experience, an appearance of something that seems to be a book.

or some such equivalent proposition, where I single out the part of my visual experience subjectively – perhaps as 'slightly to the left of the central part of my visual field'.

In what follows I shall assume as understood this qualification about which particular object I am presently attending to, out of a range of various possible objects present that I am experiencing. I shall for convenience therefore refer simply to 'the experience' that would occur when I perceive a single object; this is to be taken as relating to that aspect of my visual experience to which the relevant expectations of typical transformations apply.

The claim about demonstrative reference, then, reduced to its essentials, is this: when I demonstratively refer to an object on the basis of my present visual experience of it, I am implicitly aware that I am having some kind of experience in seeing it. My demonstrative thought is caused by my inner phenomenal experience, but it is not about that experience; as noted in the previous chapter, it refers directly, without inference, to the external object I am seeing. It is such a view about the direct role of perceptual takings that leads Sellars to claim:

> It no more follows from the fact that sensations are essentially involved in physical concept formation that physical concepts must be concepts of sensory patterns, than it follows from the fact that symbolic manipulations are essentially involved in mathematical concept formation, that mathematical concepts are concepts of symbolic manipulations. Indeed, not even the common sense concepts of *seeing a colour*, *hearing a sound*, or *feeling a pain* are concepts of sensuous immediacy. To acquire empirical concepts is (in part) to learn to respond to one's environment with these concepts.[4]

In other words, even though I have a visual experience that is an inner state, and in doing so I am aware of phenomenal qualities, my perceptual takings refer directly to the physical objects in my surroundings. In normal perception, I do not form concepts referring to my inner states, but about physical objects, such as books, that I can pick up or otherwise act upon. Nevertheless, I will be aware, implicitly, of the distinction between the physical object as it is, objectively, and my subjective experience of it. I know which object I am referring to, in the following sense: when I reflect on the matter, I realize that it is the object that I am now seeing, in having a present visual experience of a certain type.

The reason why this account is not circular derives from the navigational account of seeing defended in Chapter 7. There it was argued that we have an understanding of an outline sense of 'see' as follows:

> The term 'see' is associated by most speakers with a schematic sense. This involves a normally implicit understanding of the fact that seeing is a *navigational* process involving the causation of visual experiences. This is the process that enables perceivers to acquire information about their surroundings, by means of those experiences, so that they are able to move through that environment, and act in ways beneficial to themselves, in order to satisfy their needs. An *a priori* grasp of this sense contributes to our being able to determine, in a given individual, the precise physical and physiological process that is involved when they see.

When I see and demonstratively refer to an object, I understand that I am causally connected with it in some way. I implicitly accept that if there exists an object that I see, it causes my experience of seeing it; this will be true, no matter how I think of experience. I may analyse the experience as an inner state, or as object involving. In either case, I implicitly understand at least this: when I see something that I refer to as 'that object … ', and it really is the case that there is an object I see, it is at least *necessary* that I am causally connected with the object in question. Further, I implicitly grasp that I am causally connected to the object in whatever way it is that normally underpins successful navigational activity. I know that seeing it enables me to walk towards it and pick it up.

It is therefore true both that my demonstrative thought succeeds in picking out a unique object, and also that in some sense I know which object I am referring to. This knowledge involves an external element, since I do not know the precise details of the causal chain that is in fact physically necessary for me to see it.

With this analysis of perceptually based demonstrative reference in place, we can now examine the various criticisms sketched earlier. Smith contrasts the Direct Realist theory of perception with what he calls 'Indirect Realism'.[5] This is characterized as an account on which our perceptual thoughts refer to objects that are 'beyond what is given to us in experience', and as Smith uses these terms, clearly includes the Critical Realist view. He claims that Indirect Realism is incoherent, because it implies that subjects are only aware of the external physical realm 'indirectly'. He objects that 'we most certainly do not think of empirical objects merely as standing in some sort of relation to what we are perceptually aware of'. He claims that, according to Indirect Realism, when two people look at the same page of the same book, and refer to it by the expression 'This is a page', then their respective token utterances of the word 'this' do not pick out the same thing.

Smith's objections, however, have already been met by the arguments of the previous chapter. It is not claimed that we are perceptually aware of our own inner states. We do not think of external physical objects as of a different kind from the entities we are presently seeing. We see the physical objects in our surroundings *directly*, in so far as our experiences prompt us to have noninferential thoughts focused upon them directly. As explained above, when I and my companion use 'this' to pick out the physical object we are both looking at, our utterances have the same reference. We take ourselves to be seeing the same public object. Despite the fact that our subjective experiences are distinct, and do not contain the book as a phenomenal constituent, our perceptual thoughts refer to the same objective state of affairs. In normal circumstances this common understanding will be cashed out in our actions ('Please pass me the book' – 'Do you mean *this* book? Here it is'). Hence speakers can communicate by using demonstrative terms such as 'this' to refer to the same publicly perceptible objects.

In defending a version of Direct Realism that he calls the 'naturalized sense-data' theory, Bermudez also criticizes the idea that perception involves inner states. He claims:

the immediate objects of visual perception ... are parts of the facing surfaces of physical objects.[6]

Bermudez reverts here to one of the original meanings of 'sense-data', in which writers such as Moore allowed that sense-data could turn out, on careful analysis, to be identical with parts of the surfaces of physical objects. Understood thus as straightforwardly physical, naturalized sense-data are the immediate objects of perception, and it is assumed that there are no additional mediating inner entities that the perceiver is conscious of, in seeing an object.

Bermudez attempts to set up a dilemma for theorists who postulate some inner entity, one which it is instructive to explore.[7] He contrasts his naturalized sense-data theory with a more orthodox sense-data account of experience – which is combined with a causal theory of perception, along the lines of the theory of perception advocated at one time by Frank Jackson.[8] Sense-data, on this causal view, are interpreted as *mental* states, in the sense that they are construed as *inner* states of the perceiver.

Consider a situation where someone uses 'this' to refer demonstratively, when she sees a book. As we noted in Chapter 9, on the sense-data account – in contrast to the Critical Realist account – strictly speaking it is the inner phenomenal state that is conceptualized by the perceiving subject as a particular item, and is the 'object' of perception. According to Bermudez, there are two ways in which we could treat the referent of the speaker's utterance of 'this', in order to try to make sense of the way that we succeed in demonstratively referring to physical objects.

One view is that we might appeal to some kind of mechanism of deferred ostension. The sense-datum that the speaker is, supposedly, immediately aware of, is present as the real referent of 'this', but it is understood by the speaker and listener that the ostension is deferred onto the public object, the book, that the speaker sees. The model is of pointing to an image in a photograph, and making the elliptical reference, '*That* is my uncle'. The difficulty with this option, according to Bermudez, is that no principle governs the deferral of ostension from the sense-datum to the distal object, which causes it and which it represents, such that the speaker intends the principle, and the hearer understands it, as 'implicated in everyday reference to material objects'.

On the alternative view considered by Bermudez, the sense-datum is bypassed, and ostension 'instead latches directly onto the object represented by the sense-datum'. He rejects this account on the grounds that the immediate object of perception has no part to play in the account of demonstrative reference to the public object. The sense-datum is rendered 'otiose' in the explanation of direct perception. Thus according to Bermudez, there is no way we can explain demonstrative reference to physical objects, while maintaining the sense-data account.

It was argued previously that in ordinary perceptual cases the inner phenomenal state is not the object of the perceiver's conceptualization. It is not what the subject's perceptual taking, or conceptualization, is directly about. This is one reason for rejecting the sense-data view of perception. Yet if Bermudez's argument is supposed to show that Direct Realism is the only alternative, it must be regarded as unsuccessful, since he makes no attempt to discuss the Critical Realist account of the role of inner phenomenal states. It was argued previously that in ordinary perceptual cases the inner phenomenal state is not the object of the perceiver's conceptualization. It is not what the subject's thought is directly about. This is one reason for rejecting the sense-data view of perception. But as we have seen in the previous chapter, this does not render the inner phenomenal state idle. It is clearly not otiose in the explanation of perception; it forms an essential stage in the causal relation, in guiding the formation of our perceptual thoughts. To take Bermudez's example, I make the demonstrative judgement 'That is green', pointing to the apple in front of me, in part because I have a nonconceptual awareness of an inner phenomenal state that prompts concepts referring directly to physical objects and their colour properties.

Moreover, the precise target of Bermudez's criticism of the possible role of sense-data in deferred ostension, when he speaks of what is 'implicated in everyday reference', is loose and hard to pin down. As we noted in the preceding section, speakers need not have any *explicit* grasp of the details of the causal relation that holds between the distal object they see, and the experience they have in seeing it. That is, a speaker's understanding of the *sense* of 'see' will not allow them to *determine directly* the link between the inner phenomenal state they are immediately aware of and the physical object they are seeing in having this awareness.

However, the more modest claim made in the Critical Realist account of the sense of 'see' is that, in principle, speakers could *indirectly specify* the kind of causal relation that connects the distal perceived object, and the inner experience it gives rise to, as we saw in Chapter 7. We can therefore make sense of a form of deferred ostension in the following way. When I state, 'That is green', I (and my companion) implicitly understand the demonstrative term 'that' to refer to what I am seeing. But I am seeing whatever object it is that happens to be causally related to my experience in a manner that is the focus of, and supports my successful navigational behaviour (as we noted above). Contrary to Bermudez's claims, there is a principle which governs ostension to the distal object, one which involves an externalist element.

In this way the Critical Realist account does allow an explanation of demonstrative reference of a substantive form. By contrast, Bermudez, in common with other Direct Realists, is unable to offer a clear account of the relation he describes as 'direct perceptual contact' between the perceiver and external physical object. As we saw in the core argument of Chapter 4, this idea is ultimately empty. It is the Direct Realist who cannot explain demonstrative reference.

This takes us to the third criticism of the Critical Realist account of demonstrative reference. This criticism underlies some of the remarks made by Brewer and Eilan about the subject's reasons for making perceptual claims.[9] It turns on questions about how the perceiver's phenomenological perspective is related to her perceptual knowledge of particular objects. The pivotal claim of the core argument in Chapter 4 is that the phenomenal components of veridical and hallucinatory experiences can in principle share the same sort of intrinsic phenomenal content or character.[10] The phenomenal content that the subject is aware of belongs to a general kind of inner state; there are no grounds for saying that the particular perceived object is immediately present in experience as a phenomenal component.

Normally, when the subject identifies the informational representational content attaching to her inner phenomenal experience, she will again do this by reference to content types – as for example in describing what she sees as an appearance of a red book. The informational content of phenomenal experience that the subject grasps represents a *type* of state of affairs, and not a particular object.

But if the perceived object is not immediately present in the perceiver's conscious experience, how then can the subject's experience support her claim that she is seeing a particular object? We need to make sense of the idea that the subject's visual experience is the *reason* why she arrives at her (usually correct) demonstrative belief, to the effect that the particular object she sees is located at a certain position. The intrinsic phenomenal content and the informational representational content are grasped by the subject in a manner that is, necessarily, completely general. This may seem to lead to a problem about how the subject's experience can act as the basis for perceptual knowledge about a particular item.

In order to answer this criticism, we need, first, to appeal again to the difference between the first- and third-person perspectives. We should also clarify the precise way in which the phenomenal aspect of experience generates perceptual knowledge. When, for example, the subject sees a particular red book X, the phenomenal component of her experience may represent, generally, the type of state of affairs in which a red book-like object is at a certain position P relative to her, in a manner that is compatible with both veridical perception and hallucination. Normally, this will cause her to form the perceptual thought that there is a red book in nearby. From the subject's own perspective, she cannot be sure whether or not her experience is indeed veridical, even if she is fairly certain about how things appear to her. This means that she may be in error about whether she is having a genuine demonstrative thought about some particular object.

Considered from the external, third-person perspective, however, we are able to classify her phenomenal state differently. Although the phenomenal character, in so far as it is grasped by the subject in conceptualizing her phenomenal experience, is general, it belongs to a particular inner experience of the subject at a given time. The phenomenal component with this general phenomenal character is an inner state of affairs that is *causally* responsible for producing the conceptual component of her experience, the (demonstrative) perceptual thought. This inner state is in turn caused by the external physical object the perceiver happens to be actually seeing.

Although the kind concept exercised in the subject's demonstrative thought is thus responsive to the phenomenal component in the subject's experience, the *particular* content that it has derives from its causal ancestry – the fact that it is produced, in the appropriate causal way, by the actual object perceived, via the phenomenal component. The perceiver forms the belief that there is a particular red book located at a certain position, which she refers to by 'This ... ', but such knowledge that she has is subject to the condition that she is actually perceiving something. As McDowell concedes, it is possible that the subject is in error about the very fact that she is having a genuine thought.[11] Because of such possibilities of error over the content, it is coherent to claim that the subject takes herself to be having a demonstrative thought with a particular content, even though she may not be having such a thought. In a sense that is supported by externalist considerations, the subject knows which object she is seeing, if she is seeing an object. But whether or not she is thus in error about the existence of the particular object that she takes herself to be seeing, she is aware, in a different way, of how that the object appears to her. At the level of phenomenal consciousness she is aware of a state with a certain general character.[12]

In practice, whether there is an actual object of the relevant kind will become apparent to the subject in her subsequent actions. Such actions are *defeasible* evidence of which particular object she demonstratively referred to. Her experiences will normally guide her successfully in carrying out actions directed at the object she sees, when she picks it up or makes use of it in some other relevant way. But strictly speaking, only knowledge of the precise causal path leading to visual input can decide which object is perceived, and which is therefore the referent of the perceptually based use of 'This ... '. This point is established by the possibility of cases where a subject makes a faulty action, perhaps because she sees one of a number of very similar looking items, as in the examples of card-conjuring and the like.[13]

There is therefore a complicated story to be told about the way in which a perceiver arrives at knowledge about which object she is seeing, which appeals in part to externalist considerations. No part of it rules out the fact that a subject's perceptual takings are based upon reasons. The ultimate *explanatory* reason for her belief that she is seeing a particular red book is the very existence of the book, in front of her. This causally explains why her experience contains a red phenomenal nonconceptual state, as one component, and therefore why she forms the perceptual taking she does. As Sellars argues, merely having a phenomenal state does not, on its own, constitute a reason in any *justificatory* sense. Employing the term 'sensation' to refer to the phenomenal state, he points out:

Having sensations is having *causes of* judgements, not *reasons for* judgements. Or, better, in view of the ambiguity of 'having a reason', *having sensations* is not *knowing premises* from which one *draws inferences*. Needless to say, however, the process whereby Jones acquires concepts guarantees that when the environment evokes from him the judgement *that book is red*, he is, in all probability confronting the book, and it *is* red.[14]

McDowell and Brewer have in a similar fashion distinguished between what are, in effect, *explanatory* reasons, and the reasons a subject can be aware of, that *justify* her perceptual beliefs.[15] We have seen that the subject does not usually arrive at those beliefs in a self-conscious way. Her perceptual takings arise in a semi-spontaneous fashion, given her background presuppositions. In normal situations she will not stop to reflect upon her experiences. The concepts that arise in the course of experience lead on, in a normal context, to the endorsement of a perceptual judgement, as Sellars argued.[16] But if challenged, the subject could take stock, alter her attentional set, and examine her own phenomenal experience, using concepts that relate to those experiences as subjective states. In this way the subject can appeal to her experiences, conceptualized in the manner described in Chapter 9, in order to make explicit her own reasons, reasons that she could articulate *from her point of view*, to support her perceptual belief.[17] But as Fodor has pointed out, however, what really matters here is that the subject takes her experiences to be reasons, not merely as justifying her in *having the belief* that there is a red book, but as justifying the *content* of the claim itself: that there is a red book present.[18] On the Sellarsian account, which I do not attempt to elaborate in detail in this book, the background presuppositions help to provide such reasons.

In connection with these points about demonstrative reference, it is germane to ask whether the Direct Realist view of perceptual experience fares any better than the Critical Realist account. There is a tendency for some writers commenting on problems in this area to appeal to unclear metaphors. Expressions such as 'what experience reveals', and 'what is available in experience' are common. For McDowell and others who share the intentionalist view of experience, there is no level of nonconceptual phenomenal content; experience is conceptual through and through. Yet as we have noted in earlier chapters, the difficulty on this interpretation lies in explaining just how the contents of experiences can be made 'available' in a manner that is different from the way that such contents are presented in pure thought. To claim that in experience we are somehow 'directly open to the external world' is to make a claim that is hard to make clear sense of according to the intentionalist view of experience. The world contains physical objects and their properties, not *conceptual* items. If I think about the physical objects in the world directly, of course I exercise concepts, but what I think about is *nonconceptual*.[19] Likewise, if experience could put the perceiver in immediate contact with the world (contrary to the core argument of Chapter 4), then it would seem again to follow that the phenomenal contents of experience would be, straightforwardly, nonconceptual states of affairs – the physical objects and their properties that are, supposedly, immediately present.

If experience, in this context, is understood to refer to whatever is immediately present nonconceptually, in a phenomenal, or sensory, sense, there is no advantage to be gained by the Direct Realist position when it comes to accounting for the perceiver's demonstrative reference to the objects she sees. If the relation between the phenomenal and the conceptual components of experience is causal, then the ontological status of what is present does not constrain the category to which the concepts thus prompted refer. To claim otherwise, as Sellars notes, is one of the cluster of errors that lies at the very heart of the Myth of the Given.[20] Moreover, we do not normally conceptualize directly what is immediately present at the phenomenal level; what is present in this way simply causes our demonstrative beliefs. There is therefore no reason why those beliefs should not be about their distal causes. We have evolved to form beliefs directly about the objects in our surroundings, guided by our inner phenomenal states.

It follows from these arguments that the semantic criticism of Critical Realism does not succeed. The fact that the phenomenal component of perceptual experience is an inner state does not lead to incoherence. It does not prevent the perceiving subject from making direct reference to the external object perceived. Nor would construing experience as containing an immediate presentation of the external object, as Direct Realist theory claims, confer any advantage.[21]

3 Perceptual theories and the possibility of scepticism

Finally, I shall turn to questions about the implications of the Critical Realist theory of perception for sceptical issues concerning the justification of our beliefs about the physical world. This presents a dilemma. I cannot hope to deal with these issues fully, in the detail they deserve, in a single chapter of this book. They concern important and complex questions of a different kind from the metaphysical issues treated here. Yet traditionally, it has been claimed that epistemological problems are intimately connected with debates about the proper analysis of perception, and this assertion deserves at least some kind of answer. I shall confine myself to some general reflections about certain confusions in the traditional dialectic.

Causal theories of perception have often in the past been criticized on the grounds that they invite scepticism about the physical world.[22] This complaint is not justified. It is arguable that the normative aspects of epistemology are to quite a large extent independent of specific claims about the metaphysics of perception. It is indeed reasonable to assert that, at a very general level, epistemology and metaphysics are interconnected, so that any

account of perception that rendered physical objects completely unknowable ought to be ruled out of court. But this general epistemological
demand is still compatible with a wide variety of metaphysical positions that
allow that some kind of perceptual knowledge of the world is possible. The
thesis that perception involves inner experiences involves claims about the
proper analysis of perception, and has no particular implications for sceptical issues. Acceptance of a causal theory is not required to motivate scepticism about the external world. Nor is that theory necessarily worse off
than the rival Direct Realist account when it comes to dealing with global
sceptical claims about the existence of physical objects.[23]

We can make a *prima facie* distinction between two quite different kinds
of issue connected with perception: there are ontological issues about the
proper analysis of perceiving, and sceptical issues about how we can know
that we are perceiving. As noted in the introductory chapter, there are two
different questions that should be distinguished:

(1) What analysis can we provide of the veridical perception of a physical
    object?

(2) Does veridical perception ever take place?

These two questions are clearly quite distinct. It can also be argued that
they are largely independent from each other. The idea of perception is, as
we have seen, conceptually tied to the physical object framework. Perception
is a process, somehow involving subjective states of consciousness, which
enables a creature to move through an environment and deal successfully with
the surrounding physical objects. Questions about the analysis of this process are therefore internal to the physical object framework, and should be
addressed separately from questions about the overall status of framework.

The idea that certain ways of analysing perception are particularly prone
to the kinds of challenge raised by a philosophical sceptic is illusory. Sceptical possibilities can arise on any analysis of perceiving. It is a mistake to
suppose that Direct Realism offers a better defence against the sceptic than
the causal theory of perception. To illustrate this point I shall consider the
charge that is often made against Descartes's arguments at the start of the
Meditations.

Many writers have assumed that Descartes's initial methodological scepticism with regard to the senses rests on a causal conception of phenomenal
experience, a conception that is elaborated in the *Sixth Meditation*, and
elsewhere. Bernard Williams, for example, claims that 'the causal conception
of perception is built into the hyperbolic doubt'.[24] On Williams's view,
Cartesian scepticism involves two stages. The first stage is supposed to
involve the acceptance of a certain view about the structure of perception:
that when, for example, someone sees a physical object, that subject has an
inner visual experience, which is distinct from, but causally connected to

that physical object. In normal perception, appearances act as *mediating* entities, which are distinct from the real external objects perceived. The second stage involves noting the possibility seemingly entailed by such an account, that there may be no physical objects, of the kind ordinarily conceived, causally connected to our inner experiences. The causes of experiences may not even be physical. According to Bernard Williams, Descartes is importing into the *First Meditation* assumptions about the nature of perception that are not fully elaborated until *Sixth Meditation*.[25]

I believe that Williams's understanding of the basis for Cartesian doubt is mistaken, and that this mistake is shared by those philosophers – amongst whom McDowell is pre-eminent – who have criticized the causal theory of perception on the epistemic grounds that it is, supposedly, more prone to sceptical attack than alternative accounts of perception, such as the disjunctive view.[26] Descartes has no need of an appeal to the causal model of experience in order to support his initial scepticism, nor does he in fact make one.

On *a priori* philosophical grounds there is something questionable about the Williams's interpretation, since it is arguable that, within the realist framework that is finally embraced by Descartes, epistemic issues are largely independent of issues about analysis and ontology. Whether or not we do ever succeed in seeing physical objects is *prima facie* a distinct question from how we are to analyse what it is to perceive a physical object. No matter how one analyses perception, the sceptical issue about the existence of the external world can still be raised. Even the Direct Realist, who holds that veridical perception involves a direct relation with the physical object perceived, has to deal with the sceptical possibility that we might be perpetually dreaming or hallucinating. It may be that there are sophisticated arguments about the nature of content which can be marshalled to undermine the coherence of such scepticism. Nevertheless, there are still prima facie doubts about the existence of objects that the sceptic can raise independently of the adoption of any particular analysis of perception.

Objections can also be raised against the interpretation on textual grounds. It is important to note that the dichotomy between, on the one hand, what is within my conscious experience, and, on the other hand, what belongs in the realm of outer or external objects, is a dichotomy that, with one exception, is not invoked in the *First Meditation*; it comes into play only later on, in the *Third Meditation* and after.[27] What should strike the commentator as significant is the fact that there is a complete *absence* of any reference to the causal analysis of perception in the *First Meditation*. Descartes makes no explicit claim there that perception involves a causal link between experiences and external objects, nor does he rely implicitly on any claim to this effect. Nor is there any discussion of the sequence of causal stages in perception of the kind set out in detail in his *Optics*, or of his view that sensory states mediate our awareness of physical objects, or indeed of the notion that veridical perceptions and hallucinations share any common *ontological* features. The entire argument rests on epistemic considerations – that appearances are not necessarily any reliable guide to reality.

In the *First Meditation* Descartes does, however, rely upon two very general quasi-empirical premises: a first premise to the effect that there is a distinction to be made between appearance and reality, as the phenomena we call illusions and hallucinations (understood to include dreams) indicate; and a second premise to the effect that the appearances that occur in veridical experience are in principle phenomenologically indistinguishable from those that occur when we hallucinate, etc. There are 'no certain signs' by which we can tell them apart.

All Descartes needs to defend, in order to set up his initial scepticism with respect to the senses, is the *epistemic* claim that there can be situations which, from the standpoint of the subject, do not involve the perception of existing physical objects, but which are phenomenologically similar to those situations where the subject genuinely perceives an existing physical object. Descartes does not need to establish the *metaphysical* point that every perception of a physical object involves a separate mental element that is logically independent from what is perceived. The entire sceptical argument is independent of any analysis of perception. It is the *phenomenologically* similarity between veridical and hallucinatory experiences, not the *ontological* similarity, that drives the argument. All that the argument requires, and all that indeed Descartes actually appeals to, is the conception of an experience that falls short of a veridical perceptual experience but is indistinguishable from it: the conception, in other words, of a mere *appearance* that is not a reliable guide to reality.

On the basis of this conception of a mere appearance, Descartes presents us in effect with a short argument for the conclusion that physical objects may not exist. The argument can be reconstructed as follows:

(1) Experiences are of two kinds. When it appears to me as if I am perceiving a physical object, it might be the case either that (a) I am genuinely perceiving some physical object, or that (b) I am having a delusive experience (a hallucination or dream, etc.), and what I am aware of is a mere appearance, which is no guide to how things really are.

(2) There are 'no certain signs' which I can use to distinguish these two kinds of experience.

(3) Therefore, for all that I am aware of, *any given* experience could be delusive.

(4) Since any given experience might be delusive, it follows that they *all* might be delusive: it is therefore possible that no physical objects exist. It could be the case that all I am immediately aware of is mere

appearance, and that the totality of my experiences fails to give me any
indication of the true nature of reality.

The weakness in this argument does not relate to any account of perception, for none is presupposed. If there is a weakness, it consists in the
final extrapolation of the doubt that attaches to any individual case, to a
generalized doubt about all situations, in the step from (3) to (4). This move
certainly does not follow as a matter of logic, as has been noted by many
commentators.[28] But even if step (4) does not follow straightforwardly,
the structure of the argument raises the *prima facie* possibility that all
appearances could be delusive. A key paradoxical thought is introduced, to
the effect that I might be a creature whose experiences consist only in a
continuous train of appearances, none of which involves any immediate
relation to a physical world. All that matters for the argument is the fact
that any set of experiences, however coherent, is, *prima facie*, compatible
both with the existence of the physical world in the form assumed by
common sense and also with the existence of indefinitely many other possible worlds, including those fantastic scenarios envisaged by the sceptic.
Whether we can make sense of this generalized doubt raises deep questions
about the content of such claims, which are beyond the scope of this
book. But nothing in this formulation of scepticism turns on the analysis of
perception.

So we can note for present purposes that the doubts which precipitate the
argument derive solely from the qualitative nature of experiences, and not
from the ontology of what is immediately present in perceptual consciousness and hallucinations. What matters for the argument is the qualitative
similarity of veridical and hallucinatory experiences. This is quite independent of the ontological nature of whatever forms the immediate phenomenal
aspect of the experience.

For this reason, even if Direct Realism could be made sense of, it
would not afford an easy resolution to the sceptic's challenge. The fact that
a veridical experience simply contains a physical object as a phenomenal
constituent, if it were a fact about experience, would be insufficient. This
fact must engage with the subject's concepts in the right sort of way in
order to be available for justifying beliefs about the external world; and as
we have noted, the causal nature of the link between the two components of experience entails no necessary connection between what is present at the phenomenal level, and the concepts this leads to. McDowell
himself concedes, as he must, that 'a subject may be in error about the
contents of his own mind'.[29] Even if a veridical experience contains an
external object, this does not mean that I can thereby distinguish it from
its hallucinatory counterpart. Hence interpreting experience along Direct
Realist lines is of no avail in countering the sceptic.[30] Avoiding commitment to the causal theory does not answer sceptical issues about the
external world.[31]

4 The possibility of knowledge

The Direct Realist might argue, nevertheless, for the epistemic superiority of his analysis of perceiving in another way, attempting to raise difficulties of a different kind for Critical Realism. The two theories of perception, it might be argued, are not epistemologically equivalent because for the Critical Realist there is always a logical gap between the deliverances of experience and the reference of our normal perceptual beliefs. According to Critical Realism, our perceptual experiences are inner states. A true statement about the character of the perceiver's experience will describe a private inner world of subjective states, which have a distinct ontological status from the objects that make up the shared public world that is the focus of our normal perceptual judgements.

For this reason, the objection continues, the Critical Realist analysis of experience will always be faced with an additional hurdle that Direct Realism bypasses. The former view faces the difficult – or perhaps impossible – task of showing how, on the basis of our inner states of mind, we could ever hope to justify knowledge about an external physical world. The charge is that Critical Realism must be committed to a version of foundationalism, with all the problems that entails. Even if the Direct Realist account is theoretically open to sceptical objections, it does not face the same difficulty. By virtue of its realistic conception of experience, it is not saddled in the same way with the problem of bridging an ontological gulf between inner and outer.

So the criticism amounts to this: the two theories are on a different footing, since according to the causal theory, there is a logical gulf between experience and our ordinary perceptual beliefs about public physical objects. Critical Realism is worse off than Direct Realism, both because it is committed to a 'veil of perception' account, and also because it must embrace a foundationalist approach to knowledge.

This criticism underestimates the resources open to Critical Realism; indeed, it is guilty of misunderstanding it. The position need not be committed to foundationalism. On the particular version defended by Sellars, there is a clear line of answer to the foundationalist charge, and critics need to take this on board. The objection formulated above trades, in particular, on an ambiguity in the idea that there is some general 'basis' for our knowledge of the world. As Michael Williams points out, no-one can plausibly deny that, in some sense, the possession of sense organs, and the consequent entertaining of experiences, are causally necessary for the acquisition of inner experiences, and hence for perceptual knowledge of the world.[32] But this truism alone does not commit the theorist to an account of knowledge that conceives inner experiences to be a *justificatory* basis for knowledge of the world.

To appreciate this point, we need to refer back to the distinction made earlier, between the two senses of 'experience'. In the *narrow* sense of 'experience', there is a logical gap between the experience the perceiving subject has, and the external physical object, which the subject forms a perceptual judgement about as a result of having that experience in a normal set of circumstances. The experience is an inner state, that is in some sense an aspect or state of the perceiver. But in this narrow sense, the experience is a phenomenal nonconceptual state. So there is no question of it providing *justificatory* grounds for our perceptual beliefs about physical objects. According to the alternative *wide* sense of the term 'experience', experience comes to us in a conceptualized form, and those concepts relate directly to physical objects. There is therefore no gulf between what experience, in this wide sense, comprehends and what the world contains, since experiences already involve thoughts directly about the physical world. So on neither interpretation is there an *epistemic* gap between experience and our knowledge of the world.

The moral is this: it is one thing to accept that there exists some kind of logical gulf between the phenomenal nonconceptual states contained in experience and what our perceptual beliefs refer to; and quite another to be committed to some version of the foundationalist project of showing how beliefs about the structure of experience could generate justified beliefs about an independent reality, a world of independent physical objects that transcends our phenomenal experience. Our rational assessment of the credentials of our perceptual beliefs depends crucially upon which side of the logical gulf we set out from.[33] According to Critical Realism, in the modern form bequeathed to us by Sellars, we are inhabitants of the physical world side right from the start. That is, the 'image' or conception of the world from which we start out, and which we develop and revise with the sophisticated extensions of science, is an image of the public world of physical things and embodied agents.

On the Sellarsian view, a perceptual belief is not justified by experience, understood in the nonconceptual sense – it is directly caused by it. A perceptual belief has presuppositions, but these will all be at the level of the physical object framework. Such presuppositions relate to the subject's implied beliefs about the surrounding circumstances, and the subject's capacity as an observer, and so on. There will also be a causal-explanatory story of how the perceptual belief is produced. The justificatory starting point for an ordinary belief about a physical object in the environment consists in other beliefs about physical objects. Hence on the Sellarsian version of Critical Realism, there is no foundationalist project as traditionally understood. In the order of conceptual acquisition, beliefs about what is present in immediate experience are acquired late in the day.

For these reasons Sellars makes a distinction between the order of being and the order of knowing. Considering the example of the sense modality of sight, he writes:

> To put the matter in Aristotelian terminology, visual impressions are prior in the order of being to concepts of physical colour, whereas the latter are prior in the order of knowing to concepts pertaining to visual impressions.[34]

On the Sellarsian account of knowledge – which, as others have observed, has some similarities to the views of the later Wittgenstein – we are trained into our linguistic habits by our community.[35] This process is not a cognitive one, whereby we work out what claims we are justified in making on the basis of some private, self-contained sensory foundation. Rather, at some stage we begin to reflect on our beliefs, and come to assess them from a rational perspective. But such knowledge as we then find ourselves committed to is primarily knowledge about the physical world. It is only subsequently that we come to form beliefs about our own inner states. The adoption of the framework of beliefs about the physical world is causally prompted by our inner phenomenal states, but not justified by them. Since knowledge begins with the outer world, Critical Realism is no worse off, epistemically, than Direct Realist accounts. The fact that perceptual experiences contain an inner phenomenal element is not an obstacle to our acquiring direct knowledge of the world through perception.

5 Conclusion

The above considerations show that Critical Realism is capable of providing adequate replies to the main epistemic objections that have been levelled against the causal theory of perception. These replies conclude the detailed defence of Critical Realism that I offer in this book.

One central thought has guided my defence of Critical Realism: in order to do full justice to all its complexities, we need to consider the phenomenon of perception from two contrasting standpoints. To be successful, a theory of perception has to show how the first-person, subjective view of perceptual experience can be integrated with the third-person, objective account. We cannot argue away either viewpoint. We need to take full cognizance of both, if we wish to arrive at a coherent synoptic view.

Traditional theorists of perception of the modern period from Descartes and the British empiricists, down to many of the practitioners in the twentieth century, such as Russell, Broad, Ayer and others who argued along similar lines, were justified, in my view, in their central contention that perception involves inner conscious states. What is *immediately* present in conscious experience is not the physical object itself, but a state of the subject's mind. This claim is supported by a number of arguments, some of which have been explored here. The time-lag argument, the facts of double vision, the causal-scientific argument and, it is arguable, the argument from illusion all point to this conclusion.[36] Furthermore, as we observed in the core argument of Chapter 4, it is not possible to make sense of Direct Realism, the alternative view. Direct Realism interprets perceptual consciousness as involving a unique primitive relation to the external physical object perceived. Since this relation is not susceptible to a satisfactory explication, the only conclusion we can draw is, again, that perceptual consciousness involves inner phenomenal states.

However, traditional approaches to perception tended to concentrate too much on the first-person, subjective viewpoint; they oversimplified matters by ignoring the third-person perspective. This neglect, coupled with a distorted interpretation of the phenomenology and a simplistic model of perceptual experience that failed to acknowledge the proper role of concepts, led to overemphasis on the role of inner states. As a consequence, the positions that were embraced often resulted in epistemically disastrous forms of phenomenalism, equally unsatisfactory foundationalist accounts, or idealism.

But the many contemporary theorists who nowadays uphold the Direct Realist (or disjunctive) view, or who argue for enactive approaches to perception such as the sensorimotor account of perception, have tended to make the opposite mistake. These theorists rightly take note of the fact that our perceptual beliefs refer directly to the physical objects in our surroundings. They are, in addition, alive to the essential interconnections that hold between perception and action. But such theorists either ignore, or else downplay, the various kinds of problematic perceptual phenomena listed above. They fail to provide a satisfactory account of the nature of perception, because they fail to find perceptual consciousness puzzling enough. This leads to a parallel over-simplification in accounts of the nature of perceptual experience, in which the existence of inner phenomenal experience is simply denied, once again to disastrous effect.[37]

Critical Realism provides an account of perception that acknowledges both the essential role of inner states, and also the *directness* of perception. In the first half of this book it was argued that we must view perceptual experiences as comprising two aspects, an inner phenomenal state, and some sort of classificatory or low-level conceptual component. The navigational account of perception set out in Chapter 7 shows how we come to have an understanding of the causal nature of perception in a manner consistent with the Critical Realist view. Sellars showed in EPM and his other writings how the resulting position is not committed to foundationalism. The analysis of the role of the imagination provided in Chapter 9 indicates how the Critical Realist view can do justice to the phenomenology of perceiving.[38] As we have noted in the present chapter, a satisfactory account of perceptually based reference to an objective world can also be developed. Critical Realism is therefore able to answer all the major objections that are raised against the causal theory, and were outlined at the end of Chapter 2. It is a theory that offers the best prospects for making sense of the complex issues, both philosophical and scientific, that surround perception.

Notes

Introduction

1 See, for example the various accounts put forward in the information processing tradition; for some examples see Broadbent (1958), Treisman and Gelade (1980), Marr (1982), Pylyshyn (1984) and (2003) and recent work by Rensink (2000a and 2000b). It is important to note that it is not claimed here that the overall perceptual experience supervenes upon *input* alone; compare Hurley (1998: Chapter 9).

2 Valberg (1992: Chapter 1); for related arguments see also Robinson (1994: Chapter 6) and my own (1998); for some recent criticism see Martin (2004). I discuss the argument in more detail in Chapters 3 and 4.

3 I shall use the expression 'perceptual experience' to include veridical, illusory and hallucinatory experiences.

4 See Gibson (1966) and (1972); Gibson claims that his theory is a form of Direct Realism (1967); but note, for a critical view, Fodor and Pylyshyn (1981).

5 See, for example Thompson *et al.* (1992), O'Regan and Noë (2001), and Noë (2004).

6 As Wittgenstein points out, it is the attempt to reduce the relations between physical objects and inner states to a simple formula that leads to confusion (1953: 180). For Sellars, the various tensions in our thinking about perception originate in our common-sense thinking, but are exacerbated by the development of scientific ways of looking at the world. See, in particular, his discussion of the differences between the 'Manifest Image' and the 'Scientific Image' in PSIM (1962). Excellent discussions of Sellars's views about the conflict between the images are to be found in deVries (2005: Chapter 1) and O'Shea (2006: Chapter 1).

7 The term 'Critical Realism' has a confusing history, and has been used to apply to a number of rather different philosophical positions. Its use as a label for the specific theory of perception defended in this work derives from the American group of Critical Realists, who in the early part of the twentieth century first developed this treatment of perception in detail. This group included George Santayana, Arthur Lovejoy, and Roy Wood Sellars, the father of Wilfrid Sellars. For a presentation of their views, see Drake (ed.) (1920). For some more recent expositions of perception in sympathy with the general Critical Realist model see, for example, Mackie (1976), Millar (1991) and Lowe (1996).

8 Sellars emphasizes the contrast between the two components of consciousness in his FMPP (1981a: III, section. 2), where he writes: 'In these lectures, as elsewhere, I have been stressing the radical difference between *sensory* states and *conceptual* states, between, say, a state of sensing a-cube-of-pinkly and a state of thinking about something … '. In this book I shall use the expression 'the

phenomenal component' of experience to refer to what Sellars calls 'the sensory component'.

9 For different versions of Direct Realism see, for example, Barnes (1944–5), Dretske (1969), Snowdon (1981), McDowell (1982), Tye (2000), Martin (2002) and (2004), Smith (2002) and Campbell (2002); for recent defences of the sensorimotor contingency theory, see O'Regan and Noë (2001) and Noë (2004).

10 In Chapters 1 and 2 I shall distinguish between different kinds of conceptual classification; a creature might be said to exercise low-level concepts even if they lack self-awareness; see Smith (2002: 110), and Sellars MEV (1981b).

11 A further question often confusedly connected with these two concerns what it is to be a physical object. This raises issues connected with phenomenalism – a position I shall not be considering in this book, the reason being that, strictly speaking, phenomenalism is not an account of perception as such, but rather, a reductive theory of the whole physical framework. The concept of perception is internal to the physical object framework, broadly understood, as I shall show in Chapters 6 and 7.

12 I shall discuss these epistemic issues in Chapter 10.

13 In this I follow the philosophical approach of Wilfrid Sellars by taking the metaphysical issues as basic, in preference to the contrasting approach of writers such as John McDowell, who let the epistemological issues predominate and hence drive the analysis of perception; see, for example, McDowell (1986).

14 Compare Nagel (1986: Chapter II and *passim*).

15 Patients with Anton's syndrome have damage to the parts of the visual cortex usually associated with visual experience. They can only make guesses about what is present in their surroundings, and are unable to tell through sight even whether the room they are situated in is lit or in darkness. Yet they claim to be seeing objects normally, and confabulate their responses; see Marcel (2003).

16 I refer in particular to McDowell's discussion in his Woodbridge lectures (1998).

17 Sellars, EPM (1956). Following the standard convention in Sellars scholarship, I shall refer in the text to papers by Wilfrid Sellars by their initials; the dates are listed in footnotes.

18 I shall not, however, have anything to say about Sellars's notorious 'grain argument' here; see deVries (2005: Chapter 8).

19 For an excellent general account of Sellars's overall system, see Seibt (1990), in addition to the works by deVries (2005) and O'Shea (2006) cited above.

20 Sellars EPM (1956: Part XVI, section 62).

1 The structure of perceptual consciousness (1)

1 The basis for this classification will be elaborated in Chapter 7, in which it will be argued that distance perception is essentially integrated with patterns of extended action, involving 'navigational behaviour' that is targeted on objects of potential benefit (or harm) to perceivers.

2 As Manford and Andermann have shown, complex visual hallucinations of animals and other objects are much more common than hitherto recognized (1998). I shall discuss in more detail the claim that veridical and hallucinatory experiences can be qualitatively similar in Chapters 3 and 4.

3 See in particular Valberg (1992), Robinson (1994), and my (1998). But this is *not* to say that the experience supervenes upon input to the sense organs alone.

4 Mackie (1976: 45).

5 See, for example, Peacocke (1992), Cussins (1990), Crane (1992a), Bermudez (1998) and (2000) and the various essays collected in Gunther (2003).

6 See, for example, Bermudez (1995: 74).

7 Clark (2001). Clark makes many valuable points in this paper about the exercise of representational content in the guidance and planning of actions.

8 See Milner and Goodale (1995).

9 This use of the term 'concept' to cover such low-level concepts thus includes the leading sense of 'nonconceptual content' identified by Bermudez (1998) as explaining infant behaviour, and also Peacocke's 'proto-propositional content' (1992), as well as higher-level concepts. See also the Introduction to Gunther (2003). There is room for further confusion, however, since, according to Tye, *phenomenal* content is a form of nonconceptual intentional representational content; see his (2000: 60). I shall be contesting Tye's claim.

10 Including even other possible states of the brain or mind, as will be argued in Chapter 9.

11 See in particular the account provided by Sellars in IKTE (1978). These ideas about the way that concepts are exercised in experience will be developed in rather more detail in Chapter 9.

12 As Sellars argues, EPM (1956: Part VI).

13 I here use the term 'content' in a broad sense, to include what the subject may be conscious of in having an experience; hence by my use of 'phenomenal content' I am referring to what Block calls 'phenomenal character'; see Block (2003).

14 See Peacocke (1992). Compare also Fodor on representing without *representing as* ('The Revenge of the Given': unpublished).

15 See, in particular, the various arguments for the distinction between (i) and (ii) given in Block (2003). According to Block, phenomenal content *outruns* informational representational content.

16 On the general problem of what specifically determines the different kinds of representational content I have little to say, being inclined to agree with those philosophers who hold that external factors play an important role; it is plausible to claim that conceptual representational content is at least in part determined by the role that states with such content play in guiding actions directed towards *kinds* of objects in the environment. This question raises complex issues that are largely outside the scope of this book; I do touch very briefly on them in Chapter 7.

17 The view I subscribe to is similar to the one Millar labels 'the detachability thesis' (1991).

18 As Sellars argues in a number of places, for example SRI (1965).

19 Unless otherwise specified, I interpret 'experience' in a broad sense, to include both phenomenal (or sensory) and conceptual components.

20 Direct Realists such as Dretske have argued for a similar distinction: see Dretske (1969) and (1995).

21 For examples of the representationalist view of experience see, for example, Anscombe (1965), Harman (1990), McDowell (1994b), Tye (1996) and (2000), and Byrne (2001); more recently Jackson has also defended this view.

22 See Smith (2002: Chapter 3). I discuss Smith's views in the next chapter.

23 Bennett provides a masterly dissection of the confusions in both the empirical and rationalist traditions resulting from the appeal to such a continuum; see his discussion of Kant's views on the nature of concepts in Bennett (1974: Chapter 2).

24 Sellars, SK (1975: 306–7). Some clarifications of terminology are in order: Sellars uses the expression 'propositional content' for the most part, to include what I am here calling the *conceptual* component of experience; where Sellars uses the expression 'sensory experience', I shall usually substitute the expression 'phenomenal experience'.

25 As indicated earlier, I leave open the ontological relation between the subject's conscious experience and their underlying neural state.

26 As Sturgeon expresses the point (2000: 9).

27 Valberg (1992: 4).

28 Sellars, MEV (1981b); these ideas shall be explored further in the following chapter.

29 Peacocke (1992: Chapter 3). Many other modern theorists have made a distinction between conceptual and nonconceptual content that broadly corresponds to the distinction Sellars makes between low-level, primitive concepts, and higher-level concepts that involve some kind of a self-awareness on the part of the subject; as we have already noted, Bermudez defends a similar distinction (1998).

30 See for example Sellars's remarks at the start of the third Carus Lecture FMPP (1981a: III).

31 For example in Sellars EPM (1956: sections 16 and 22).

32 Sellars SM (1968: Chapter 1).

33 Sellars EPM (1956: section 60).

34 Sellars FMPP (1981a: III, sections 2 – 5).

35 McDowell (1998: 443–4). In point of fact, hallucinations are unlikely to share common impingements on the retina with veridical experiences, but I take it that McDowell's point is intended to refer to the inner proximate neural causes of experiences.

36 See, in particular, Levine (2001: 77).

37 Sellars EPM (1956: section 62).

38 Sellars SK (1975: 308). It needs to be remembered that by 'non-propositional', Sellars is referring to a phenomenal component that is different from any kind of conceptual state.

39 Sellars SRPC (1977b: sections IV).

40 Sellars FMPP (1981a: I, section 88).

41 Sellars FMPP (1981a: I, section 3).

42 Sellars FMPP (1981a: I, section 43 and 44).

43 The complementary strand in Sellars's attack on empirical versions of the Given involves the idea that observational claims are not inferences, yet always have presuppositions; see for example EPM (1956: Part VIII), and the illuminating discussion in deVries and Triplett (2000: Chapter 8).

44 See Wittgenstein (1953: Part I, 151–4), and Sellars EPM (1956: Part I).

45 The essential contrast between sensory states and concepts, and the dispositional nature of the latter, is emphasized by Bennett in his discussion of Kant's conception of experience (1974: Chapter 2).

46 Note especially Sellars's criticisms around section 26 of EPM (1956).

47 Sellars EPM (1956: Section 16 (ii)).

48 deVries and Triplett (2000: 38).

49 Firth makes this distinction in the course of defending the 'Percept Theory' of perceptual consciousness against traditional sense-data views (1949/50). Page references are to the version reprinted in Swartz's anthology (1965).

50 Firth (1949/50: 220).

51 Firth (1949/50: 237).

52 Firth (1949/50: 235).

53 Firth (1949/50: 236).

54 In fairness to Firth, he does express some doubts about the possibility of a full perceptual reduction. My criticisms should therefore be understood as directed against the view that it is a coherent enterprise to attempt a complete perceptual reduction.

55 Millar (1991: 26–7), makes the same point in his account of experience, an account in the Sellarsian tradition that is close to the one I advocate here.

56 It is, I believe, for reasons such as these that Sellars claims that 'I can not make sense of his [i.e. Firth's] phenomenological insights, unless he is thinking of his ostensible physical objects as (at least in part) experienced in the mode of conceptualization.' Sellars FMPP (1981a: I, section 117); compare also Sellars FMPP (1981a: I, section 152).

57 Here the criticisms Sellars levels against the traditional empiricist approach to experience are highly relevant; see EPM (1956: Part VI).

58 We shall return to explore the implications of such criticisms in Chapter 8, when assessing the claim that experience is 'transparent'.

59 Sellars EPM (1956: section 1).

60 See again the key remarks in FMPP (1981a: I, sections 43–5).

61 See deVries and Triplett (2000: Chapter 8). It can be argued that a fourth strand is also involved: that, as Sellars claims, epistemic facts cannot be analysed without remainder into non-epistemic facts: EPM (1956: Part I, Section 5, and Part VIII). There is a normative aspect to our beliefs about what we directly observe.

62 As I shall explain when discussing the 'Transparency Argument' in Chapter 8, it is important to realize that this problem is not circumvented by the adoption of a Direct Realist approach. For example, even if an overall *perceptual experience* of red contains as a phenomenal constituent the objective quality of physical redness belonging to the public object seen (or an instance of physical redness), this does not explain how the perceiver comes to apply the *concept* of the red phenomenal quality that is, supposedly, present in the overall experience. For, as we have argued, the awareness of phenomenal qualities as such does not, in itself, involve concepts. So the Direct Realist is also stuck with the same problem of abstraction, of explaining how the subject moves from having an awareness of the phenomenal quality of redness to a conceptual grasp of what is experienced. This is why Sellars's attack on the Given is not so much an attack on sense-data theories, but an attack on the whole empiricist notion of a 'direct confrontation with experience', no matter how the experience of objects is interpreted. See Sellars EPM (1956: Part 1), and also PH (1963b).

63 In his recent book Smith discusses some of the various phenomenological aspects of experience that are, it might be claimed, distinct from the phenomenal, or sensory, level: (2002: Chapter 5).

64 Sellars, SK (1975: 306).

65 Pace Armstrong (1961: 109). Compare Jackson's formulation of the argument (2000: section 6). I shall discuss Jackson's reply to the argument later in this chapter.

66 There may be some kind of similarity with vividly imagining a red shape, but that is quite a different issue; what is visualized in the imagination is not essential to my thought.

67 Sellars EPM (1956: Part XVI).

68 Sellars is not of course alone in emphasizing the importance of training – the idea plays a key role in Wittgenstein (1953).

69 I am assuming here some familiarity with the main line of Sellars's argument in the concluding sections of EPM (1956).

70 Sellars EPM (1956: section 62).

71 As deVries and Triplett observe, Sellars's account of sensory states is not straightforwardly functionalist in the way that his account of thoughts is: see their (2000: 169).

72 Sellars EPM (1956: XVI, section 61). Sellars's conception of what he here terms an 'impression' (i.e. a sensory or phenomenal state) allows for further developments in our knowledge of the intrinsic nature of such inner states, and he develops these ideas in an interesting fashion in his FMPP (1981a, III). For an

excellent discussion of Sellars's views on the nature of phenomenal, or sensory, experience, see Rosenberg (1982).

73 Strawson (1979: section I); a somewhat similar line of criticism is advanced by Evans (1982: Chapter 7). I discuss Evans's views about self-knowledge and hallucinations in Chapter 9.

74 Sellars EPM (1956: XVI, section 61).

75 For an interesting discussion of the relevance of the phenomenon of perceptual constancy, see Kelly (2001b). I consider these issues further in Chapter 4.

76 O'Shaughnessy (2000: 486).

77 Compare again Block (2003: 7), and Dretske (1995).

78 In this sense the framework we employ for making sense of our own inner states can be likened to the framework of a theory, as Sellars claims in the later parts of EPM (1956). Somewhat similar claims are defended in detail by Pears (1975: Chapter 5).

79 Millar defends an equivalent claim (1991: Chapter 1).

80 This entails that the representational content of the experience is of two kinds, as indicated in Section 1 of this chapter: phenomenal states represent, in an informational sense, the situations that typically cause them; the concepts involved in experience represent, in a different way, aspects of the scene that my thoughts are intentionally directed at.

81 Dretske has argued for a similar position over many years: see, for two examples (1969: Chapter 2), and more recently (1993).

82 See the discussion of such an example in Marcel (2003).

83 See Evans (1982: Chapter 1).

84 Fodor makes a similar criticism of the appeal to modes of presentation in his 'Revenge of the Given'.

85 For a similar line of criticism, see Jackson (2000) ('Some Reflections on Representationalism': section 6).

86 Block (2003).

87 Evans (1982: 155).

88 Jackson (2000).

89 For a more extended discussion of this phenomenon, see Milner and Goodale (1995: Chapter 3).

90 It is relevant here to compare the cases of the subjects experimented upon by Bach-y-Rita using TVSS. They report having something like visual perception without qualia; that is, they lack the usual visual phenomenal accompaniments of seeing: Bach-y-Rita (1996). As I interpret such cases, these subjects have conceptual 'takings' (or beliefs), not based upon inference, and directed at external objects or locations. These occur without being prompted by visual phenomenal states. They do, apparently, have phenomenal states of the kind that occur in touch, and, moreover, can attend to these if they choose to do so (how such attention is possible I explore in Chapter 9).

91 McDowell (1998).

92 McDowell (1998: 442, and 451).

93 McDowell (1998: 440).

94 I have argued for these essentially Wittgensteinian claims at greater length in my (1987). The point goes back to Price (1953).

95 As we shall see in examining the arguments against Direct Realism in Chapter 4.

96 There is a tendency on the part of some writers to assimilate hallucinatory objects to purely intentional objects. Tye writes in this way when he compares after-images with the contents of reports (2000: 86). The analogy is misleading, however, since what a report is 'about' need not exist in any form; but if an after-image is in consciousness, it necessarily does exist.

97 See Moore (1903), (1913–14) and (1918–19).

98 Compare Sellars BBK (1960).
99 See Bennett (1974: 16).
100 How this organization is carried out will be examined in Chapter 9, after the central claims of Critical Realism have been defended.
101 Simon and Chabris (1999).
102 There is extensive discussion of a number of different experiments demonstrating Inattentional Blindness in Mack and Rock (1998).
103 Clark (2002).
104 Mack and Rock (1998: Chapter 8); see also Fernandez-Duque and Thornton (2000).
105 See, for example, Mack (2002), Rensink (2000a) and Wolfe (1996).
106 Rensink (2000a: 22); see also his (2000b).
107 Rensink (2000a: 22).
108 Clark (2002: 188).
109 Rensink (2000c).
110 The intentionalist view of experience is also criticized, on different grounds, in Martin (2002).

2 The structure of perceptual consciousness (2)

1 Reid was perhaps the first to appreciate this point, in distinguishing between sensation and perception (1785).
2 Kant (1929: A51, B75).
3 Sellars EPM (1956: Section 45).
4 I have in mind here the 'pleonastic' sense of concept employed by Byrne (2004).
5 Sellars MEV (1981b: 337).
6 To this extent I am in agreement with Prinz (2000: Chapter 1 and *passim*).
7 On the issue of the presuppositions, see the excellent discussion in deVries and Triplett (2000: Chapter 8). An alternative account is offered by Brandom in his study guide (1997) to Sellars EPM (1956).
8 This point is independent of the ontological analysis of phenomenal experience; it applies equally to Direct Realism. Even if it were the case that in perception I was immediately aware, in a phenomenal sense, of the features of surrounding physical objects, it would only be because I conceptualized them that I could become perceptually conscious of those objects.
9 See, for example, Rensink (2000b: 1476), and the arguments in section 9 of the previous chapter.
10 Smith (2002: 94).
11 See Smith (2002: 95, 113 and 123).
12 Smith (2002: 110).
13 Smith (2002: 95).
14 Smith thus rejects what Luntley (2003) has recently termed 'the kidnapping strategy', which ties a concept to what is, in effect, currently experienced.
15 This point seems first to have been articulated by Raffman (1995). It is developed by Peacocke in his extended discussion of nonconceptual content in his (2001). Peacocke does not, however, consider the possibility of hybrid relational concepts, to which I draw attention below.
16 On this general view of the background essential for such demonstrative reference see Evans (1982: 145–53).
17 Of course the subject need not be capable of articulating the concept, since as explained, we are dealing with low-level concepts. Nevertheless, the subject's behaviour will manifest a grasp of such concepts of relational differences.
18 C. Peacocke makes a related criticism of McDowell in his (2001).

19 In his (2001b: section 4), Kelly discusses a view similar in some ways to that which I advocate here. I believe that the employment of what I term 'hybrid relational concepts' would meet the competing demands Kelly notes in respect of demonstrative concepts: that they would need to be both context-dependent, and also context-independent. Of course, nothing I say here undermines Kelly's criticisms, which I agree with, of the view that (pure) demonstrative concepts cannot in general characterize the content of perceptual experience.

20 McDowell has trouble understanding Sellars's motives for the below the line component of experience: see McDowell (1998). But by taking perceptual experience to be a unified state, an 'ostensible seeing', McDowell appears to be returning to the 'mongrel idea' that conflates sensation and knowing, and which Sellars rejects in his EPM (1956: Part 1).

21 McDowell (1994b: 51).

22 It is arguable that if we did not allow for such overall differences between successive displays, because of the differences that exist at the phenomenal level, a form of *sorites* paradox would arise when we consider a sequence of successive displays of different pairs of shades.

23 I consider some aspects of these issues further in Chapters 9 and 10.

24 See, for example Noë (2004: 2).

3   Hallucinations, illusions and the challenge of metaphysical scepticism

1 I shall for the most part continue to use the term 'Direct Realism' and its cognates in a broad sense to include disjunctivism and naïve realism. Compare Martin (2002).

2 McDowell (1994a: 192).

3 According to Martin (2004), all that we can say of a positive nature about the relation between veridical and hallucinatory experiences is that they are subjectively indistinguishable.

4 Descartes is often supposed to make a clear distinction between the subject's state of consciousness and the brain state that gives rise to it; a careful reading reveals that the distinction that Descartes makes is not clear-cut in the case of sensation. See, for example, Hatfield (1992).

5 Valberg spells out the argument in detail in his (1992: Chapter 1); see also Robinson (1994: Chapter 6).

6 Hurley (1998: Introduction and Chapter 9 passim); Hurley appears to allow that the phenomenal aspect of consciousness can be distinguished from the experience taken as a whole (1998: 150); although this phenomenal component is responsive mainly to input, it may well also depend upon other factors, for the kinds of reasons that Hurley cites.

7 See for example the work of Crick and Koch, some of which is summarized in Crick (1994), and also Gray (2004).

8 See also Sellars EPM (1956: section 36). But as we also noted, the distinction between the logical space of reasons and the empirical realm does not, for Sellars, coincide with the conscious: non-conscious distinction.

9 McDowell (1994b: 29 and 111–13).

10 For criticism of attempts to deny this obvious fact, see Robinson (1994: 88 and Chapter VI); see also Valberg's detailed argument in his (1992: Chapter 1).

11 See for example Snowdon (1981).

12 Compare Martin (1997: 82); while I accept Martin's distinction between how things seem epistemically, and how things seem phenomenally, I am claiming that the disjunctivist needs a further distinction between the qualitative character of what is presented phenomenally, and its ontological status.

13 In terms of the distinctions drawn in Chapter 1 about kinds of content, the qualitative character of experience relates to the intrinsic phenomenal content that is immediately available to the subject in experience.

14 It may well be questioned how inner experiences could share the same qualities as external objects, and clearly this issue raises further problems for Direct Realism. I shall not pursue this point here.

15 Noë (2004: Chapter 7).

16 Noë (2004: 216).

17 Noë (2004: 211).

18 See, for example, Penfield and Perot (1963).

19 See also the various similar examples cited and illustrated in Sacks (1992). I also draw here upon personal experience of such visual aura, which I understand from neurologists to be fairly typical of this phenomenon. Compare also Burke (2002).

20 Sacks, (1992: 59).

21 Some of this evidence is cited by Lord Brain (1965).

22 Manford and Andermann (1998). They suggest these hallucinations are due to cortical phenomena.

23 Ffytche and Howard (1999).

24 Armstrong (1968).

25 It may be objected that the form of seeing I have described is not purely extensional, in virtue of the fact that it is claimed that the subject must be exercising some concept. What is important for our purposes in the present chapter is that there is a basic form of seeing, by which the subject can become consciously aware of a particular object, without necessarily employing concepts at any kind of sophisticated level in order to know what individual object they are seeing, nor necessarily even employing concepts that match the stereotypical kind normally associated with that object. It is this form of seeing, employing minimal concepts, that I am calling 'extensional seeing' here.

26 See Robinson (1994: Chapter 2); and Grice (1961).

27 As will become obvious, the argument which follows is in part inspired by Kripke's important discussion of Wittgenstein's views on rule-following: Kripke (1982). The reader should be warned, however, that the argument does not parallel Kripke's in all respects. I have argued elsewhere that a sophisticated dispositional account affords a way of resisting meaning scepticism: see Coates (1997).

28 Kripke (1980: 22–3).

29 See Coates (1997) and Sartorelli (1991).

30 This sense of justification is to be distinguished from the sense which pertains to the general sceptical problem about the external world. I discuss some aspects of these issues concerning justification in Chapters 9 and 10.

31 An extreme example which shows that commonsense knowledge does not enable us to answer a question about which object is seen arises from the fact that, according to relativity, light from a distant star is affected when passing near a massive object, so that the apparent position of the star in the sky shifts.

32 I am therefore discounting idealism on the grounds that it does not provide a resolution to the problem, but rather offers a revision to the realist framework which gives rise to it. I discuss the affinities between idealism and the disjunctive view in my (1996).

33 As Valberg argues, this is part of our everyday 'causal picture of experience' (1992: Chapter 1); see also Robinson (1994: Chapter VI). It is important to note, however, that at this stage in my argument there is no assumption that brain activity alone is *sufficient* to give rise to the kind of personal level experiences which occur in perception.

34 As Grice pointed out (1961).
35 The importance of the notion of intrinsic connectedness in relation to problems of scepticism is well set out in Sprigge (1988).
36 I do not distinguish here between causal answers to the sceptic and answers which appeal to some pattern of counterfactual dependence, since arguably these accounts can be equated: see Lewis (1980). How one should classify the Aristotelian account of perception raises slightly more complex questions, depending upon matters of exegesis. It is arguable that the kind of interpretation offered by Sorabji (1992) amounts to a form of causal theory.
37 White (1961).
38 Dretske (1979).
39 Dretske (1981: Chapter 6).
40 I assume here that there is no counterpart to a 'sceptical solution' to the sceptic's challenge.
41 Compare Child's discussion of compatibilism (1994: 161).

4 The incoherence of Direct Realism

1 This is one reason for thinking that the account of natural kind terms provided by Brown (1998) needs to be amended to take account of this point.
2 As we noted in Chapter 1.
3 For a useful discussion of the individuation of content types, see Macdonald (1990).
4 We must distinguish here the subjective colour shade that I can attend to, and which is immediately present in experience, from the objective shade belonging to the external object, and which I could also form a demonstrative thought about. What matters here is the subjective experience of the colour shade.
5 This has become a familiar point since Evans introduced the notion of non-conceptual content: see Evans (1982: 229). This notion is defended in Bermudez (1998).
6 As I argued previously in my (1998).
7 Davidson (1963).
8 I am of course implicitly aware that I am *seeing* X, but the seeing relation can be accounted for in causal terms. I develop a positive account of how demonstrative reference is possible in this 'indirect' way in Chapter 10.
9 Such a view is argued by Martin; however, in connection with the ensuing argument, it should be noted that he concedes that the naïve realist view he favours may not be directly applicable to illusory cases: Martin (1997: 85). For the reasons given earlier, I do not think that the boundary between veridical and illusory cases is determinate; there is therefore a strong motivation for producing a unified account.
10 See also, on this point, the arguments in my (1998).
11 Child (1996).
12 See, e.g. Snowdon (1990: 143 and 145).
13 McDowell (1982: 478); Heidegger (1968: Lec IV). Heidegger claims that 'This face-to-face meeting is not, then, one of these 'ideas' buzzing about in our heads' (1968: 41).
14 Martin (1997: 83); compare the claims made in Campbell (2004), and also Eilan, who appeals to an unexplained 'primitive psychological relation of acquaintance' (2001: 438).
15 On this distinction, see: Macdonald (1990: 400).
16 Compare McDowell (1994b). It is not clear to me whether McDowell would want to endorse I-Direct Realism, but he appears in places to be close to it.

17 It is worth comparing Kripke's remarks (1980: 51) on the idea that meaning a certain function might be a unique kind of primitive state.
18 Compare Martin (1997: 103). There is extensive discussion of this issue in Valberg (1992), and I take up some of his claims in Chapter 8 and 9.
19 McDowell (1982: 472).
20 See the various papers in Drake (1924), Millar (1995: 86–9), and Chapter 8 of this book.
21 Part of the confusion, I believe, is caused by the fact that visual experiences have spatial depth, thus encouraging the idea that the experience gives us awareness of what is 'out there'. See, for example, McCulloch (1995: 137) for an argument based upon this idea. But since some hallucinatory experiences also display apparent depth, this feature of experience can provide no evidence for Direct Realism.
22 See, for example Noë (2004: Chapter 7), whose views I discuss in more detail in the next chapter; and also Rowlands (2003: Chapter 10). Advocates of the general idea of the extended mind view include: Clark and Chalmers (1998), and Hurley (1998).
23 In the sense that X must exist at or before T; I deal with the time-lag argument in the following chapter.
24 In connection with these points the arguments of Valberg (1992) and Robinson (1994) are highly relevant.
25 See, for example, the various theories of visual processing discussed in Pylyshyn (2003).
26 As noted at the outset, I am assuming that there is just one relevant object seen; this point does not affect the argument.
27 Compare Hyman (1994).
28 Similar criticisms are made by Byrne and Hilbert (1995) in their discussion of Hyman's (1994) account.
29 Martin (2004: 49 and 65).
30 See McDowell (1994b: 29).
31 See Coates (1987).

5 Problems for the enactive approach to perception

1 Dewey (1896: 362).
2 Thompson *et al.* (1992: section 3).
3 See in particular the paper by O'Regan and Noë (2001).
4 Noë (2004).
5 See for example the papers by Dennett (2002) and Blackmore (2002).
6 Compare Noë's remarks (2004: 68).
7 Noë (2002: 10).
8 Noë (2002: 10–11); note the similar remarks around p. 63.
9 Noë's position on the status of appearances is not, however, entirely clear. Appearances are argued at one point to be objective: 'P-properties – the apparent shape or size of properties – are perfectly real or objective ... they do not depend on sensations or feelings. ... In particular, P-properties depend on relations between the perceiver's body and the perceived object ... '; see Noë (2004: 83). However, he speaks of 'changes in sensation or appearance', as if they are equivalent (2004: 228), while earlier, in outlining the sensorimotor approach, he states that 'to perceive ... is to have sensations that one understands' (2004: 33). On the assumption that sensations are inner states, this seems to be inconsistent with the claims about the objectivity of appearances.
10 I take up the dispositional aspect of Noë's account of perceptual presence in Chapter 9.

11 Compare also the similar references to the fact that we may 'directly encounter how things are' or 'experience how it looks' op. cit. (2004: 85).

12 Noë (2004: 134).

13 Noë (2004: 134–5); compare also the views expressed on (2004: 216–17).

14 Noë (2004: 134).

15 Block claims this in his commentary on O'Regan and Noë (2001).

16 The relation between Noë's earlier view adopted in O'Regan and Noë (2001) and the later view expressed in his (2004) appears to be that whereas on the former view, perceptual experience could be reductively accounted for directly in terms of the subject's practical mastery of sensorimotor contingencies, on the latter view Noë claims he wishes to do justice to the 'phenomenological aptness' of our experience of the presence of objects. Consciousness is not eliminated, but the question of its subvening basis remains. The relevant issue is the justification for Noë's claim that the subvening basis extends outside the brain, into the environment. The situation is still further complicated, however, by Noë's claim that seeing is understanding *sensations* (2004: 33). Thus I find Noë's precise views hard to pin down.

17 Noë (2004: 221).

18 Noë (2004: 227).

19 Compare the remarks on p 210 and 218.

20 Noë appear to endorsing the 'possession' interpretation in his (2002: 10), when he claims that our sense of the presence of a cat consists in ' ... those skills – practical knowledge of the ways what we do gives rise to sensory stimulation – whose possession is constitutive of sensory perception.'

21 Compare Noë (2004: 90): ' ... perceiving is *constituted by the exercise* of a range of sensorimotor skills.' (My italics).

22 See for example, the data on visual recognition of various kinds summarized by Ballard (2002) and also by Crick (1994: Chapter 6).

23 Fischer and Weber (1993).

24 It may be hypothesized that cessation of vision is just a contingent by-product of habituation mechanisms that feature in early vision; in the case of hallucinatory visual aura, attention does not lead so readily to a parallel cessation of the visual experience.

25 Milner and Goodale (1995: 19).

26 Myin and O'Regan also seem at times to adopt this more dispositional interpretation of exercising knowledge: see their (2002).

27 See, for example, Noë (2004: 119), and also the remarks on page 117.

28 This does not mean that we self-consciously reflect upon our phenomenal experience *as such*. Rather, in conceptualizing the world around us in a certain way, our concepts are prompted and guided by what is immediately present at the phenomenal level, in a manner I shall explain more fully in Chapter 9.

29 See also my remarks in the preceding chapter about the 'coupling' of experience and object.

30 See, for example, Clark and Chalmers (1998). It is plausible to claim that extended mind accounts succeed for mental states such as thought processes precisely for the reason that there is a sense in which the essential aspects of thoughts and similar states are not present in consciousness in the way that phenomenal states are, as I have argued in my (1987).

31 This seems to be the intention behind his claim at (2004: 210).

32 Noë (2004: 245n).

33 I explain how in Chapter 10.

34 Thus the sensorimotor view may have important things to tell us that point to a solution of the so-called 'hard' problem of consciousness. This issue appears to

be the main concern of O'Regan; see, for example, the discussion of colour naming and hue in Philipona and O'Regan (forthcoming).

35 See for example the claims about transparency in Noë, Pessoa and Thompson (2000: 103), and in Noë (2004: 72).

6 Perception, understanding and causation

1 See Davies (1983).
2 For a useful discussion of this approach, see Clark (1998).
3 The Direct Realist view can also be included in the anti-causalist camp, when that view is interpreted as making the claim that we are directly aware of physical objects without being in any sense aware of distinct perceptual intermediaries such as sense impressions.
4 Snowdon (1990: 121–2).
5 One philosopher who places much emphasis on the personal/sub-personal distinction as a basis for contesting the casual theory of perception is Susan Hurley (1998).
6 Price (1932).
7 This case is an adaptation of Lewis's light meter example, given in his (1980).
8 Chisholm (1957: Chapter 10); though even Chisholm's analysis, it is arguable, can be undermined by carefully constructed deviant causal chain examples.
9 See for example Snowdon (1990).
10 Compare Ramsey (1931: 170); Ramsey's suggested definition makes reference to the fact of some poison being eaten, but the actual way in which the substance enters the body is not a crucial feature: Hamlet's father was allegedly poisoned via his ear.
11 The defect of the definition is independent of whether it is the general *kind* of substance that is considered in the attempted definition, or whether a particular *sample* of the kind is specified.
12 Indeed, it is arguable that the problem arises even more generally with respect to natural processes, and is not confined to causal relations involving people.
13 I shall draw here on the argument set out in my (2000).
14 See, for example, Snowdon (1990).
15 Lewis construes his account as a version of the causal theory (1980).
16 Snowdon appears to make a claim of this kind: (1990: 142); but I do not find his overall position on the precise relation between the scientific and ordinary concepts of seeing entirely clear.
17 Grice (1961: 144).
18 Jackson (1977: 169–70).
19 Salmon (1982: Chapter 6).
20 See Kripke (1980: 116–40 and 139n).
21 See Kripke (1980: 122).
22 Jackson argues an analogous point about the dependence on conceptual analysis of the scientific reduction of the concept of temperature in his (1998: 58).
23 Compare Lewis (1980), where he discusses two kinds of indeterminacy.
24 See Jackson (1998: 41–2 and *passim*).

7 A navigational account of distance perception

1 My use of the expression 'scientifically ignorant members of a community' approximates to the use introduced by Brown in her (1998); this refers to those members of a community – which may be all of them – who lack knowledge of the detailed processes involved in perception, whatever other scientific knowledge they might possess.

2 Davies (1983); a modification of this account has also been defended by Price (1998).

3 This particular objection against teleological accounts of our central everyday concepts is persuasively argued by Braddon-Mitchell and Jackson (1997).

4 Grice (1961: section II).

5 For related criticisms, see Strawson (1974a).

6 Jackson notes these problems in his (1977: 169–70), as does Lewis (1980); these criticisms are connected with those made by Dupré (1981) and Brown (1998) in connection with the causal theory of reference for natural kind terms.

7 See for example Armstrong (1968: 209).

8 Lewis (1980); 'matching' is intended to be cashed out in terms of information content.

9 See, for example, Jackson (1977: 170), Lewis (1980: 245), and Davies (1983: section 5).

10 Clark (1998); Clark's emphasis is different from mine, but the ideas he defends are in keeping with the analysis I defend here.

11 Lewis (1980: 245).

12 For this reason I am pessimistic about the prospects of the approach advocated by Owens (1992: Chapter 7).

13 The appeal to matching leads to a further difficulty: a complete account of seeing should explain not only veridical cases, but also illusions, in which the information acquired from the object seen may be so degraded that the appeal to functional dependence becomes problematic, and there is certainly little 'matching'. What we need to capture is the sense in which, even in an extreme illusion, the information (such as it is) 'gets through' from the particular object seen.

14 Sellars, SSOP (1982: section 89).

15 Evans (1982: 122 and 142); see also Strawson (1979) and Child (1994).

16 The importance of such feedback is emphasized by Hurley in several papers in her (1998). However, the conclusions I draw from this point are rather different from hers.

17 Wells (1895a).

18 Milner and Goodale (1995: 11).

19 The example comes from Milner and Goodale (1995: 6).

20 Milner and Goodale (1995: Chapters 5 and 6). See also Clark (2001).

21 The importance of planned perceptually guided activity is emphasized by Clark, in his (2001) and (2002).

22 In what follows I shall concentrate on giving an account of the modality of seeing, but as indicated earlier, the analysis would apply to all forms of distance perception.

23 Compare Clark (1998) for an elaboration of related ideas.

24 Remembering that we are still dealing with modes of distance perception.

25 See Clark (1998).

26 See Peacocke (1983: Chapter 10).

27 The appeal to marker features and orienting landmarks provides additional support for the extended mind hypothesis as far as the *cognitive* aspects of perception are concerned; but it does not upset the Critical Realist claim that the experience of such external features involves inner phenomenal states.

28 Thus on the two stage account put forward here, the processes which essentially underlie seeing for a creature in the actual world are fixed by whatever enables successful navigation for that creature. This idea would fit in with the two-dimensional semantics articulated by Chalmers (1996), Jackson (1998) and others.

29 Compare Jackson (1977: 170–1); I believe the emphasis that Jackson rightly places on functional spatial dependence is captured by the present account. The

precise differences between sight and other forms of distance perception would necessitate further modifications of the account, but I shall continue to ignore such points, since they do not affect the main issues.

30 As indicated earlier, I shall assume that at least some animals are able to see in the same sense that humans can; this assumption does not affect the main argument, since there are obvious parallels in human perception to the examples of animal perception that I cite.

31 Compare Strawson (1979: 51) when he notes that the fact that a person acquires information about the world through perception implies an assumption of a 'general causal dependence of our perceptual experiences on the independently existing things we take them to be of.' I should emphasize that my concern here in appealing to the processes that explain what I term 'navigational behaviour' is not to defend any particular account of the representational aspect of experience, in the sense discussed, e.g. by Cussins (1992). My project here is not concerned with the precise nature of the contents of perceptual experience as such, but with the general connections between such experiences and navigational behaviour (of the kind noted by Strawson, Evans and others), and how this connection can be used in a defence of the causal theory. The basic idea of such a connection with action is not a new: it is discussed for example in Wittgenstein (1992: 77).

32 Much the same point was argued by Sellars in PH (1967); see also Akins (1996).

33 I leave open the question of whether there could be creatures with 'super-blindsight' who lacked the phenomenal aspect altogether.

34 See the supporting empirical work of Dittrich and Lea (1994).

35 See the discussions in Lewis (1980) and Davies (1983).

36 Compare again the work of Milner and Goodale cited above (1995).

37 In his (1997), Rudd argues that our classifications are not always concerned with what science says a thing is, and that in different contexts different criteria for the correct use of a term will operate. While it is true that the context of utterance is important, it may be argued in reply that part of the overall practice in a community consists in being guided by the very general aim of seeking a synoptic view that tries to bring the different language games together, and to harmonize them where possible. Thus in our wider practice we often tend to defer, in cases of direct conflict, to the results of scientific enquiry, even though for most purposes fine scientific distinctions do not concern us (the process of resolving such conflict may be a very slow one, taking several centuries).

38 Lowe has a useful discussion of this issue in his (1996: 106–7). I believe that his key idea, that vision involves a certain kind of the *responsiveness* to its objects, is closely connected with the view defended here.

39 Millikan (1993: 18).

40 Millikan (1993: 247).

41 Note, in any event, that in an indirect way we do make use of distant stars, when we use them to orient ourselves, for example, when navigating in the nautical sense of the term.

42 It is for these reasons that we are able to say that bats perceive through echolocation.

8 Critical Realism and the alleged transparency of experience

1 Though by 'mental' here I do not preclude the identification of such inner entities with neurophysiological states of the brain.

2 Sellars FMPP (1981a: Lec I, section 78 and 79). We shall explore this point further below.

3 Crane (2003: 48).

4 This 'semantic' objection to the causal theory has been advanced by a number of writers. See for example, Snowdon (1981); and Smith (2002: 14).

5 Martin (2002); Martin construes sense-data here as not identical with physical objects.

6 Martin (2002: 381).

7 As we noted earlier in the discussion of the core argument against Direct Realism in Chapter 4.

8 As was concluded in Chapter 1.

9 Valberg (1992: 21).

10 This claim has already been noted, in Chapter 4; see McDowell (1994b: 29).

11 Berkeley (1988: 126).

12 See Moore (1903), and also (1918), and also the replies to critics in Schillp (1942).

13 Martin (2002: 378); strictly, Martin in fact advocates naïve realism; but the distinction between naïve and Direct Realism is not relevant to the point at issue.

14 Smith (2002: 69).

15 Smith (2002: 74).

16 Noë (2004: 175).

17 Sellars, EPM (1956: section 30, and also sections 6 and 7). In the second stage of Sellars's attack on the Given, which is mainly the focus of Part VIII of EPM, Sellars is concerned to argue that that the noninferential perceptual beliefs we form involve presuppositions, and we can offer justifications for them. See deVries and Triplett, (2000: Chapter 8).

18 Sellars EPM (1956: section 45).

19 Sellars EPM (1956: section 26).

20 As Sellars noted, these points about the incoherence of the idea of Givenness, so understood, are independent of ontological questions concerning the dispute between the Critical Realist and the Direct Realist; see, for example PH (1963).

21 These criticisms are not particularly new. Many philosophers working in the second half of the twentieth century who were particularly concerned with problems about the distinction between observation and theory, raised similar objections. But some of those who objected on grounds similar to those articulated above often drew the wrong moral from these kinds of criticisms of the idea of a basic Given. It does not follow from the criticisms that there is no duality within experience, as writers such as Firth claimed (1949/50) – as we noted in Chapter 1. Much of the framework within which such criticisms were often advanced presupposes it.

22 Sellars, FMPP (1981a: Lec. I, sections 78 and 79; compare also section 44).

23 Martin (2002: 399).

24 Martin (2002: 393).

25 Martin (2002: 393).

26 Martin (2002: 399, 400, and 401).

27 Martin (2002: 402).

28 This is the second part of Sellars's attack on the notion of the Given. For an excellent discussion of these issues see the extended discussion in deVries and Triplett (2000: Chapter 8).

29 The 'probably' is important here. We shall see in the next chapter how it is possible to reflect upon experience more directly, by making a shift to using concepts that apply to inner phenomenal states as such.

30 As Sellars argues in various places; see for example his SM (1968: Chapter 1). For a similar view, see Lowe (1995: Chapter 3).

31 See Lowe (1995: 61).

32 The point is made explicitly in Sellars, EPM (1956: section 18); but it is a claim that runs through his entire work.

33 Evans (1982: 227–8). As I have already argued in Chapter 1, I believe Evans is in fact wrong to claim that my inner hallucinatory state cannot become an object

for me. In the next chapter I shall explain the precise way that it can feature as an object of an introspective thought.

34 This is to interpret 'ontology' narrowly, in the sense that a conscious inner phenomenal state is in some sense a mental entity, in a way that a perceived external physical object such as a tree is not. But nothing in the Critical Realist view rules out a possible reduction of the category of inner phenomenal states to the category of physical things, understood in a broad sense. Hence Critical Realism is, prime facie, compatible with physicalism (this point is subject to the refinements of his views that Sellars develops in his later writings, in particular FMPP (1981a). See also Rosenberg (1982), and deVries (2005: Chapter 8)).

35 Smith (2002: 74).

36 Here again Lowe's remarks on structural isomorphism in his (1995: Chapter 3), and Sellars's claims about analogical predicates in his (1968: Chapter 1), and elsewhere, are relevant.

37 I have in mind the kind of artificial system involving arrays of sensors adjacent to the skin: see for example Bach-y-Rita (1972) which Smith also discusses.

38 Smith (2002: 74).

39 Armstrong once considered, and rejected, a view of this kind (1961: 116).

40 In seminars at Haverford in 1976 Sellars reported Prichard as advocating an 'under the hat' theory of perception. Sellars expressed approval, stating that his own theory was also an 'under the hat' theory, meaning that it involved the immediate awareness of inner phenomenal states, that is, sensings.

41 Some of Mackie's claims in Mackie (1976), in the course of defending Locke's version of the representative theory of perception, may be taken to endorse an error theory of perception.

42 Smith also advances some other criticisms in his rich and interesting chapter on two-component accounts. I have chosen to focus here on what I consider are the most important ones, excepting for his final criticism, which is connected with the alleged *de re* nature of perceptual judgements (2002: 84), and which I deal with in my final chapter.

9 Imagination and the unity of experience

1 Sellars, IKTE (1978). Page references are to the more accessible recent publication in (2002).

2 Rosenberg (1997). The term 'imagination' is used in a quasi-technical sense. See also Strawson, (1970: 32).

3 Where Sellars refers to the nonconceptual component of experience as sensing states, or visual sensations, I will continue to speak of phenomenal states.

4 Sellars, (1978: 422).

5 Approximately, what is seen *of* the apple are only those sensible properties that contribute directly to causing visual sensations (i.e. phenomenal states).

6 These image states may include images relating to other sense modalities besides vision, but I shall concentrate here upon visual images and the visual imagination.

7 Sellars, IKTE (1978: 424).

8 Although Sellars is ostensibly concerned with Kant's views of the role of concepts in perception, he is clearly endorsing the Kantian picture.

9 See for example the discussion in Chisholm (1957: Chapter 4), and compare also Jackson on the phenomenal sense of 'looks' (1977: Chapter 2).

10 Although in one rather compressed footnote Sellars concedes that images may be generated only occasionally, rather than continuously: see IKTE (1978: 423n).

11 Strawson (1970).

12 Strawson (1970: 43).

13 Compare also Prinz (2002: 9 and elsewhere), on the importance of connection between transformations of experience and the exercise of concepts.

14 Strawson also notes this connection with action, in discussing Wittgenstein's views on noticing aspects (1979: 47).

15 The dispositional aspect of concepts is well brought out by Bennett in his (1974: Chapter 2). The importance of this dispositional aspect is implicit in Sellars's discussion of the role of the schema of a concept.

16 As noted in Chapter 5, one point Noë appears to advance is a similar claim, in stating that 'to perceive is not merely to have sensations, or to receive phenomenal impressions, it is to have sensations one understands'; see Noë (2004: 33). On the Critical Realist account, to understand one's sensations is to exercise concepts with respect to them, in a manner that includes having expectations of the kind described.

17 Sellars, PR (1955: 205).

18 Sellars discusses the ontological structure of the sensing state in his SSOP (1982). Moore's act-object analysis is one of the main targets of the criticism of EPM (1956: Part I).

19 The precise role of endorsement is discussed in deVries and Coates (forthcoming).

20 It is possible that the imagination is in part responsible for the fact that we do not realize that objects away from the central point of visual acuity are not seen in detail. If I conceptualize what I see as a rich and complex scene, perhaps this prompts the imagination to make me think I see more detail of the world than is really present in experience. I can be visually aware of a wide expanse of, say, a flower garden in front of me, but I do not realize the extent to which the detail is lost at the periphery of my vision. Nevertheless, even when I cannot make out the detail, I am still aware of the phenomenal presence of colours and shapes, of some kind, away from the point of fixation.

21 See Evans (1982: 143).

22 Evans (1982: 143–50).

23 Evans (1982: 198). Unfortunately Evans was unable to develop this point in any detail.

24 Evans (1982: 153). An extreme case is when someone refers to a distant star; but then mariners, like ancient kings, can act in respect of stars by following them.

25 Evans (1982: Chapter 6).

26 Descriptions of the Ames Room can be found in standard texts on vision. For one illustration, see Gregory (1970: 26).

27 See Noë (2002: 8–11), and (2004: 60). Interestingly, Noë also defends a version of a two-dimensional account of perceptual content: see his (2004: 168–9).

28 In Chapter 5.

29 Noë (2002: 11).

30 The underlying point, about the connection between the recognition of a kind and the awareness of the possibility of movement as a unified object by the individual instantiating the kind, is independent of the added complication that the subject recognizes the dog in a picture; this is shown by case 6.

31 Johansson (1973).

32 This particular example is in Carsten Holler's *Punktefilm* (1998), shown at the exhibition *Eyes Lies and Illusion*, organized by L. Mannoni, W. Nekes, and M. Warner, at the Hayward Gallery, London, 2004–5. In this display, the spotlights are gradually reduced and then increased in number, adding to the effect.

33 These experimental findings throw considerable doubt on the sensorimotor contingency account of perception – it is not only the way that *our own* actions give rise to changes in experience that is relevant to the way we see things. The phenomenological presence of an object is connected with our expectations about

the way that changes in the relations between ourselves and other objects in the world, no matter how caused, have implications for experience. It may perhaps be the case that action is necessary for me to form concepts in the first place, as some experimental evidence suggests. But this is a different thesis, which concerns questions about concept acquisition, and not concept exercise.

34 Peacocke (1992: 79).

35 This simplifies somewhat the complex overall task involved, but not in ways that undermine the claim about the essential connection between seeing aspects and the imagination.

36 On the account given here, the difference between the two distinct ways an ambiguous figure is seen is accounted for by the low-level conceptual aspect of experience. But there are also good reasons for holding that there may be changes in the way that the spatial structure of a scene is interpreted at the phenomenal nonconceptual level. This is suggested by various phenomena, including some of Julez's random dot stereograms, in which the three-dimensional projected structure of the array (which has no real existence) can be seen in different ways. This raises complex issues which deserve an extended treatment, and to which I do not have space to do justice here. I hope to deal with this topic more fully in further work.

37 See, for example, Hanson (1965: Chapter 1).

38 As Sellars notes, we need to account for both the conceptual aspect, and also the descriptive core of experience; see, for example, in EPM (1956: section 16).

39 And as I have pointed out, some Direct Realist views also make the equivalent assumption; see, for example, Dretske (1969).

40 The reader should be warned that my notion of 'displaced perception' is not the same as Dretske's, although there are certain connections between them: compare Dretske (1995: 41).

41 I am much indebted to Stephen Brearley for useful information and very helpful discussions about this kind of surgical procedure.

42 More recently, operations have been performed using three-dimensional images produced by complex stereoscopic systems.

43 Though matters are not always straightforward; the surgeon may also entertain thoughts about the quality of the images, for example that they are not very sharp, or that the lens of the camera is fogged, and so on.

44 In the next chapter I show how demonstrative reference to physical objects is accommodated on the Critical Realist account of perception.

45 Sometimes both kinds of conceptualization will occur near simultaneously.

46 In this way the first-person, phenomenological account can be seen to be in harmony with third-person, scientific accounts proposed from the standpoint of cognitive science. As was noted in Chapter 1, the model proposed by Rensink appeals to two levels of representation, in which the proto-objects at a base level are taken up at a higher level in a 'coherence field'.

47 Compare, for example, the criticisms of traditional empiricist accounts in Merleau-Ponty (1962: Chapters 1 and 2).

48 In cases that are derivative from the normal perception of objects, such as seeing a cartoon figure as a rabbit, the action could be something like the selection of other similar pictures, as Wittgenstein notes in (1953: Part II, section xi).

49 As Peacocke argues in his (2003: 319), even subjects who lack a proper sense of a self can have perceptual states that have objective spatial content.

50 Rosenberg (2000).

51 Sellars (1956: section 59).

52 Rosenberg (2000: 149). As far as the essential nature of thoughts is concerned, this is surely correct, and parallels similar claims made by Wittgenstein. I argued for a similar view of the phenomenology of thought in my own (1987).

53 See Brain (1965: 51).
54 That is, as Sellars argues in his SSOP (1982), they do not involve a relation to an independent particular object.
55 Brain (1965: 58).
56 See again, the arguments advanced in Chapter 8; and see also deVries and Triplett, (2000: 38).
57 Evans (1982: 227–8). Rosenberg argues that, for Sellars, the sensing state is not an object to which the subject can make demonstrative reference (2000: 148).
58 In the final part of EPM (1956).
59 Interestingly, subjects often failed to discern objects placed at the point of central fixation under such conditions: see Mack and Rock (1998: Chapter 3).
60 It is arguable that it is this point about conceptual dependence that constitutes the central core of Wittgenstein's arguments against a Private Language. I have criticized the 'sceptical interpretation' of the Private Language arguments in my (1997).
61 See Moran (1996: 9), and also Marras (1976).
62 Moore (1903: 24).
63 Moore (1903: 24–5).
64 Sellars, EPM (1956 Part 1).
65 I do not aim to discuss here the details of Sellars's complex adverbial account. A simple adverbial account won't do – sensations cannot be interpreted straightforwardly as first order properties of a single subject, because of the 'many properties' problem. Sensational properties are co-instantiated, hence some part of the subject's phenomenal consciousness must be treated as a quasi-particular, at least; see Jackson (1977: Chapter 3). See again Sellars, SSOP (1982).
66 This sensing state is what I have elsewhere been calling a phenomenal state.
67 Precisely what new thought I form will depend upon my level of sophistication, and the concepts I employ in order to think about my experiences. I may lack clear concepts of inner states as a category, although presumably most humans understand pains to be inner states.
68 None of this is intended to rule out the possibility that there may be some top-down feedback from my conceptualization of experiences, which influences aspects of the phenomenal state; it may be that seeing an ambiguous figure as a representation of a different kind of object alters the analogue spatial properties of the phenomenal state.
69 This is not to deny that, in some way that we do not yet fully grasp, the sensation may turn out to necessarily involve the existence of events in my brain.
70 If someone preferred to express this point by saying that I never in fact had a genuine thought at all, this would not affect the point of the overall argument. What is essential is that I was *exercising concepts* relating to physical types of things; such concepts would have guided the behaviour I was disposed to make, as a result of my having made a mistake.
71 We must also be careful to distinguish what is going on here from the kinds of confusions associated with the Myth of the Given, as noted in the previous chapter. It is not claimed that I infer that there is a red patch because I first grasp the bare, unconceptualized sensation of red. Rather, when I shift my attention, I am prompted to apply concepts of a different kind. When I form the belief that there is no physical object in front of me, my inclination to employ the corresponding concepts of physical items is lessened. I redirect my attentional set to the fact that there is something going on inside of me, which prompted the mistake – and therefore I am caused to apply concepts relating to my own inner states. My phenomenal awareness of the red patch is shaped by my use of concepts relating to my sensations. So I do not become aware of my inner sensation by some problematic process of 'direct apprehension', but by conceptualizing it.

72 In SRPC (1978: section V); similar ideas are sketched by Sellars, again rather briefly, in SSOP (1982).
73 deVries (personal communication) has offered a line of thought that suggests one might interpret Sellars's claim along something like the following lines: in any perceptual act involving a putative demonstrative thought, there must be some object that could be demonstratively referred to, even if the subject's actual thought fails to demonstratively refer.
74 Austin (1962: 90).
75 Jackson (1977: 99–100).
76 Strictly speaking, they are distinct parts of a complex objectless inner sensing state of the subject.
77 Snowdon (1992: 76). I have altered Snowdon's numbering. An account of how we succeed in identifying the physical object is provided in the next chapter.
78 I thus interpret what Peacocke originally said about sensational qualities as relating to the phenomenal qualities immediately present in experience, when I conceptualize them *as such*, by adopting the framework pertaining to my inner perceptual sensations. See, for example, his example of trees seen at different distances from the observer (1983: 12, and Chapter 1 *passim*).
79 Snowdon (1981: section v).
80 The qualification is required because strictly speaking, when sense-data were first introduced and discussed at length in Moore's works, it was left open whether or not they might be identified with mind-independent objects; see for example the various essays in his (1922).
81 Tye makes this claim, incorrectly on my view, in his (2000: 84 and 112).
82 Although the phenomenal states accepted by the Critical Realist account should not be thought of on the 'act-object' model, for the reasons argued in Chapter 1.
83 This indeed is the position adopted by Sellars in his version of Critical Realism, when he claims that subjects mistake their sensing states (i.e. phenomenal states) for the surfaces of the physical objects that are seen: see his SSOP (1982: section vii). I have however already rejected Sellars's claim that the sensing state should be understood as the 'ultimate reference' of the subject's demonstrative thought in ordinary perception.
84 Although it may be the case that there is a conflict between common sense and the consequences of a Critical Realist analysis for claims about the exact nature of the sensible qualities of objects. This leads to issues connected with Scientific Realism that I do not have space to discuss further here.
85 The natural stance is connected with what Sellars terms 'The Original Image'. Only after careful reflection and refinement does this develop into what Sellars calls 'the Manifest Image'; see Sellars PSIM (1962).
86 See Sellars (1956: Part VIII), and the discussion in deVries and Triplett (2000: Chapter 8).

10 Inner experience and the possibility of knowledge

1 See, for example, Campbell (2004: 267); but compare Kelly (2004: 280).
2 That is, considered in terms of the phenomenal character that is subjectively available to the subject.
3 I shall refer below to some recent works in which specific objections along these lines are formulated.
4 Sellars, PR (1955: 205).
5 Smith (2002: 13–16).
6 Bermudez (2000a: 353).
7 Bermudez (2000a).

8 See Jackson (1977). Jackson has since revised his views, and now defends a representationalist (i.e. intentionalist), analysis of experience.
9 See Brewer (2001) and Eilan (2001).
10 See again the distinctions set out in the summary at the start of Chapter 1.
11 McDowell (1986: section 4).
12 There is a sense in which the subject's experience carries information relating to which particular object is seen. But this is different from the sense in which the phenomenal component of experience contains informational content of a representational kind, allowing for the possibility of misrepresentation. As was argued in Chapter 4, this latter notion is general in nature.
13 As we noted in Chapter 4.
14 Sellars PR (1955: 205).
15 See, for example, Brewer (1999: Chapter 5) and McDowell (1994b: Afterword, Part II).
16 Sellars EPM (1956: Parts III and VIII).
17 Compare Brewer's insistence on this point about the perceiver's own perspective (2001: 411).
18 Fodor, 'The Revenge of the Given', unpublished, footnote 35, p. 22.
19 Peacocke makes the same criticism in his (2001); McDowell however has to disagree with this point: see his (1994b: Chapter 2).
20 Sellars, FMPP (1981a: Lec. I, section 44).
21 This point was argued a while back: compare Margolis (1972).
22 See for example, Armstrong (1961: Chapter 3).
23 See, for example, Snowdon, who holds a different view from that of McDowell. Snowdon rightly notes: 'It is therefore a mistake to suppose Direct Realism is an answer to, or is in some sense a position which avoids, scepticism.' (1992: 65).
24 Bernard Williams (1978: 58).
25 Macarthur (2003: 181) has offered a similar account of the roots of Cartesian scepticism, construing scepticism of the senses as a possibility deriving from what he describes as Descartes's 'causal model of experience'.
26 See in particular McDowell's arguments in his (1986).
27 The exception is when he distinguishes between external things and entities such as thoughts and delusions, which for Descartes are obviously not in the external world; see Descartes (1641: AT VII 22–3, CSM II 15).
28 On the problems raised by this generalization, see for example Bermudez (2000).
29 McDowell (1986: 145).
30 For some cogent criticisms of McDowell's response to scepticism, which are connected with this point, see Pritchard (2005: Chapter 9).
31 For an argument along similar lines, see also Rudd (2003: Chapter 2).
32 Michael Williams (1996: Chapter 2).
33 As Michael Williams observes (1996: 73).
34 Sellars in SRI (1967: 357).
35 See, for example, Michael Williams (1996: 71).
36 I have not here discussed the 'Argument from Illusion'; for an exceptionally clear and careful statement of this argument see Smith (2002: Chapter 2). Smith himself presents an interesting response to the argument, but his way of replying to it will not be to everyone's taste. I have already indicated in Chapter 2 why I take issue with Smith on intentionality and the role of concepts in perception.
37 In both cases the over-simplification can be traced to the adoption of the problematic 'act-object' view of experience.
38 It is possible that the Critical Realist analysis of perceptual consciousness may also point us in the direction of a fuller understanding of the nature of consciousness in general. That, however, is a project for further work.

Bibliography

1 Works by Wilfrid Sellars cited in the text, with the conventional abbreviations of their titles:

Sellars, W. (1954) 'Some Reflections on Language Games', *Philosophy of Science*, 21, 204–28. Reprinted in Sellars (1963a). (SRLG)

—— (1955) 'Physical Realism', *Philosophy and Phenomenological Research*, 15, 13–32. Reprinted in Sellars (1967). (PR)

—— (1956) 'Empiricism and the Philosophy of Mind', in Feigl, H. and Scriven, M. (eds) *Minnesota Studies in The Philosophy of Science, Vol. I: The Foundations of Science and the Concepts of Psychology and Psychoanalysis*, 253–329, Minneapolis, MN: University of Minnesota Press; reprinted in Sellars (1963a). (EPM); also republished as a book with an Introduction by Rorty, R. and a Study Guide by Brandom, R. (1997), Cambridge, MA: Harvard University Press.

—— (1960) 'Being and Being Known', *Proceedings of the American Catholic Philosophical Association*; reprinted in Sellars (1963a). (BBK)

—— (1962) 'Philosophy and the Scientific Image of Man', in Colodny, R. (ed.) *Frontiers of Science and Philosophy*, Pittsburgh, PA: University of Pittsburgh Press; reprinted in Sellars (1963a). (PSIM)

—— (1963a) *Science, Perception and Reality*, London: Routledge and Kegan Paul. (SPR)

—— (1963b) 'Phenomenalism', paper presented at Wayne State University Symposium in the Philosophy of Mind in December 1962; in Sellars (1963a). (PH)

—— (1965) 'Scientific Realism or Irenic Instrumentalism: A Critique of Nagel and Feyerabend on Theoretical Explanation', in Cohen, R. and Wartofsky, M. (eds) *Boston Studies in the Philosophy of Science*, Vol. II, New York: Humanities Press; reprinted in Sellars (1967). (SRI)

—— (1967) *Philosophical Perspectives*, Springfield, IL: Charles C. Thomas. (PP)

—— (1968) *Science and Metaphysics*, London: Routledge and Kegan Paul. (SM)

—— (1975) 'The Structure of Knowledge: (1) Perception; (2) Minds; (3) Epistemic Principles', in Casteñeda, H. (ed.) (1975) *Action Knowledge and Reality*, 295–347, Indianapolis: Bobbs-Merrill. (SK)

—— (1976) 'Kant's Transcendental Idealism', *Collections of Philosophy*, 6, 165–81. Reprinted in Sellars (2002). (KTI)

—— (1977a) 'Berkeley and Descartes: Reflections on the 'New Theory of Ideas'', in Machamer, P. K. and Turnbull, R. G. (eds) *Studies in Perception: Interpretations in the History and Philosophy of Science*, 259–311, Columbus, OH: Ohio State University Press; reprinted in Sellars (2002). (BD)

—— (1977b) 'Some Reflections on Perceptual Consciousness' in Bruzina, R. and Wilshire, B. (eds) *Selected Studies in Phenomenology and Existential Philosophy*, 169–85, The Hague: Nijhoff; reprinted in Sellars (2002). (SRPC)

—— (1978) 'The Role of Imagination in Kant's Theory of Experience' in Johnstone, H. W. (ed.) *Categories: A Colloquium*, Pennsylvania: Pennsylvania State University; reprinted in Sellars (2002). (IKTE)

—— (1981a) 'Foundations for a Metaphysics of Pure Process' (The Carus Lectures), *The Monist*, 64, 3–90. (FMPP)

—— (1981b) 'Mental Events', *Philosophical Studies*, 39, 325–45. (MEV)

—— (1982) 'Sensa or Sensings: Reflections on the Ontology of Perception', *Philosophical Studies*, 41, 83–111 (SSOP)

—— (2002) *Kant's Transcendental Metaphysics: Sellars's Cassirer Lectures and Other Essays*, edited with an introduction by Sicha, J. F., Atascadero, CA: Ridgeview Publishing. (KTM)

2 Works by other authors

Akins, K. (1996) 'Of Sensory Systems and the "Aboutness" of Mental States', *Journal of Philosophy*, 93, 337–72.

Anscombe, G. E. M. (1965) 'The Intentionality of Sensation: A Grammatical Feature', in Butler, R. J. (ed.) (1965).

Armstrong, D. M. (1961) *Perception and the Physical World,* London: Routledge and Kegan Paul.

—— (1968) *A Materialist Theory of Mind*, London: Routledge and Kegan Paul.

Austin, J. L. (1962) *Sense and Sensibilia*, Oxford: Clarendon Press.

Bach-y-Rita, P. (1972) *Brain Mechanisms in Sensory Substitution*, New York & London: Academic Press.

—— (1996) 'Substitution Sensorielle et Qualia', in Proust (ed.) 1996, 81–100. Reprinted as 'Sensory Substitution and Qualia' in Noë, A. and Thompson, E. (eds) (2002).

Ballard, D. H. (2002) 'Our Perception of the World Has To Be an Illusion', *The Journal of Consciousness Studies*, 9, 54–71.

Barnes, W. F. (1944–5) 'The Myth of Sense-data', *Proceedings of the Aristotelian Society*, 45, 89–117.

Bennett, J. F. (1974) *Kant's Dialectic*, London: Cambridge University Press.

Berkeley, G. (1988) *Principles of Human Knowledge and Three Dialogues between Hylas and Philonous*, London: Penguin. Edited by Woolhouse, R. S. (1988).

Bermudez, J. (1995) 'Non-conceptual Content: From Perceptual Experience to Sub-personal Computational States', *Mind & Language*, 10, 333–69.

—— (1998) *The Paradox of Self-Consciousness*, Cambridge, MA: MIT Press.

—— (2000a) 'Naturalized Sense-Data', *Philosophy and Phenomenological Research*, 61, 353–74.

—— (2000b) 'The Originality of Cartesian Scepticism: Did It Have Ancient or Mediaeval Antecedents?', *History of Philosophy Quarterly*, 17, 333–60.

Blackmore, S. (2002) 'There Is No Stream of Consciousness' *The Journal of Consciousness Studies*, 9, 17–28.

Block, N. (2001) 'Behaviorism Revisited' (Commentary on O'Regan, K. and Noë, A. 'A Sensorimotor Account of Vision and Visual Consciousness'), *Behavioral and Brain Sciences*, 24, 977–8.

—— (2003) 'Mental Paint', in Hahn, M. and Ramberg, B. (eds) (2003).

Boden, M. (ed.) (1990) *The Philosophy of Artificial Intelligence*, Oxford: Oxford University Press.

Braddon-Mitchell, D. and Jackson, F. (1997) 'The Teleological Theory of Content', *Australasian Journal of Philosophy*, 75, 474–89.

Brain, R. (1965) 'Hallucinations' in Hirst, R. J. (ed.) 1965.

Brewer, B. (1999) *Perception and Reason*, Oxford: Clarendon Press.

—— (2001) 'Replies' *Philosophy and Phenomenological Research*, 63, 449–64.

Broadbent, D. E. (1958) *Perception and Communication*, Oxford: Pergamon Press.

Brown, J. (1998) 'Natural Kind Terms and Recognitional Capacities', *Mind*, 107, 275–303.

Burke, W. (2002) 'The Neural Basis of Charles Bonet Hallucinations: a Hypothesis', *Journal of Neurology, Neurosurgery, and Psychiatry*, 73, 535–41.

Burri, A. (ed.) (1997) *Sprache und Gedank*, Berlin: de Groeter.

Butler, R. J. (ed.) (1965) *Analytical Philosophy: Second Series*, Oxford: Blackwell.

Byrne, A. (2001) 'Intentionalism Defended', *Philosophical Review*, 100, 199–240.

—— (2005) 'Perception and Conceptual Content', in Sosa, E. and Steup, M. (eds) (2005).

Byrne, A. and Hilbert, D (1995) 'Perception and Causation', *Journal of Philosophy*, 92, 323–9.

Campbell, J. (2002) *Reference and Consciousness*, Oxford: Clarendon Press.

—— (2004) 'Reference as Attention', *Philosophical Studies*, 120, 265–76.

Castaneda, H. (ed.) (1975) *Action Knowledge and Reality*, Indianapolis, IN: Bobbs-Merrill.

Chalmers, D. J. (1996) *The Conscious Mind: in Search of a Fundamental Theory*, Oxford: Oxford University Press.

Child, W. (1994) *Causality, Interpretation and the Mind*, Oxford: Clarendon Press.

Chisholm, R. M. (1957) *Perceiving: A Philosophical Study*, Ithaca, NY: Cornell University Press.

Clark, A. (1998) 'Embodiment and the Philosophy of Mind' in O'Hear, A. (1998).

—— (2001) 'Visual Experience and Motor Action: Are the Bonds Too Tight?' *The Philosophical Review*, 110, 495–519.

—— (2002) 'Is seeing All it Seems? Action, Reason and the Grand Illusion', *Journal of Consciousness Studies*, 181–202.

Clark, A. and Chalmers, D. (1998) 'The Extended Mind' *Analysis*, 58, 7–19.

Coates, P. (1987) 'Swinburne on Thought and Consciousness', *Philosophical Studies*, 52, 227–38.

—— (1996) 'Idealism and Theories of Perception', in Coates, P. and Hutto, D. D. (1996), 59–81.

—— (1997) 'Meaning Mistake and Miscalculation', *Minds and Machines*, 7, 171–97.

—— (1998) 'Perception and Metaphysical Scepticism', *Proceedings of the Aristotelian Society, Supplementary Volume*, 72, 1–28.

—— (2000) 'Deviant Causal Chains and Hallucinations: A Problem for the Anti-Causalist', *The Philosophical Quarterly*, 50, 320–31.

—— (2004) 'Wilfrid Sellars, Perceptual Consciousness and Theories of Attention', *Essays In Philosophy*, 5, 1–25.

Coates, P. and Hutto, D. D. (eds) (1996) *Current Issues in Idealism*, Bristol: Thoemmes Press.

Cottingham, J. (ed.) (1992) *The Cambridge Companion to Descartes*, Cambridge: Cambridge University Press.

Cottingham, J., Stoothoff, R. and Murdoch, D. (eds) (1984) *The Philosophical Writings of Descartes*, Cambridge: Cambridge University Press.

Crane, T. (1992a) 'The Nonconceptual Content of experience', in Crane, T. (ed.) 1992b).

—— (ed.) (1992b) *The Contents of Experience: Essays on Perception*, Cambridge: Cambridge University Press.

—— (2003) 'The Intentional Structure of Consciousness', in Smith, Q. and Jokic, A. (eds) (2003).

Crick, F. (1994) *The Astonishing Hypothesis: The Scientific Search for the Soul*, London: Simon and Schuster.

Cussins, A. (1990) 'The Connectionist Construction of Concepts', in Boden, M. (1990).

—— 1992 'Content, Embodiment and Objectivity: The Theory of Cognitive Trails', *Mind*, 101, 651–88.

Davidson, D. (1963) 'Actions, Reasons and Causes', *Journal of Philosophy*, 60, 685–700.
Davies (1983) 'Function in Perception', *Australasian Journal of Philosophy*, 61, 409–26.
Dennett, D. (2002) 'How Could I Be Wrong? How Wrong Could I Be?', *The Journal of Consciousness Studies*, 9, 13–16.
Descartes, R. (1641) *Meditations on First Philosophy* reprinted in Cottingham, J., Stoothoff, R. and Murdoch, D. (eds) (1984).
deVries, W. (2005) *Wilfrid Sellars*, Chesham: Acumen.
deVries, W. and Coates, P. (forthcoming) 'Brandom's Two-Ply Error'.
deVries, W. and Triplett, T. (2000) *Knowledge, Mind, and the Given: Reading Wilfrid Sellars's Empiricism and the Philosophy of Mind*, Indianapolis, IN: Hackett.
Dewey, J. (1896) 'The Reflex Arc Concept in Psychology', *Psychological Review*, 3, 357–70.
Dittrich, W. and Lea, S. (1994) 'Visual Perception of Intentional Motion', *Perception*, 23, 253–68.
Drake, D. (ed.) (1920) *Essays in Critical Realism*, New York: Macmillan.
Dretske, F. I. (1969) *Seeing and Knowing*, London: Routledge and Kegan Paul.
—— (1979) 'Simple Seeing', in Gustafson, D. and Tapscott, D. (eds) (1979).
—— (1981) *Knowledge and the Flow of Information*, Oxford: Basil Blackwell.
—— (1993) 'Conscious experience', *Mind*, 102, 1–21.
—— (1995) *Naturalizing the Mind*, Cambridge, MA: MIT Press.
Dupré, J. (1981) 'Natural Kinds and Biological Taxa', *Philosophical Review*, 110, 66–90.
Eilan, N. (2001) 'Consciousness, Acquaintance and Demonstrative Thought', *Philosophy and Phenomenological Research*, 63, 432–9.
Evans, G. (1982) *The Varieties of Reference*, Oxford: Clarendon Press.
Fernandez-Duque, D. and Thornton, I. M. (2000) 'Change Detection without Awareness: Do explicit Reports underestimate the representation of Change in the Visual System' *Visual Cognition*, 7, 324–44.
Ffytche, D. H. and Howard, R. J. (1999) 'The Perceptual Consequences of Visual Loss: "Positive" Pathologies of Vision', *Brain*, 122, 1247–60.
Firth, R. (1949, 1950), 'Sense-data and the Percept Theory', *Mind*, 58, 434–65. Reprinted in Swartz, R. (ed.) (1965).
Fischer, B. and Weber, H. (eds) (1993) 'Express Saccades and Visual Attention', *Behavioural and Brain Sciences*, 16, 553–67.
Fodor, J. A. (2006) 'The Revenge of the Given'. Online. Available http://www.nyu.edu/gsas/dept/philo/courses/representation/papers/Fodor.pdf (accessed 20 July 2006).
Fodor, J. A. and Pylyshyn, Z. W. (1981) 'How Direct is Visual Perception: Some Reflections on Gibson's "Ecological Approach"', *Cognition*, 9, 139–96.
Foster, L. and Swanson, J. W. (eds) (1970) *Experience and Theory*, Amherst, MA: University of Massachusetts Press.
Gibson, J. J. (1966) *The Senses Considered as Perceptual Systems*, Boston, MA: Houghton Mifflin.
—— (1967) 'New Reasons for Realism', *Synthese*, 17, 162–72.
—— (1972) 'A Theory of Direct Visual Perception', in Royce, J. and Rozeboom, W. (eds) (1972).
Gray, J. (2004) *Consciousness: Creeping Up On the Hard Problem*, Oxford: Oxford University Press.
Gregory, R. L. (1970) *The Intelligent Eye*, New York: McGraw-Hill.
Grice, P. (1961) 'The Causal Theory of Perception', *Proceedings of the Aristotelian Society, Supplementary Volume*, 35, 121–52.
Gunther, Y. H. (ed.) (2003) *Essays in Nonconceptual Content*, Cambridge, MA: MIT Press.
Gustafson, D. F. and Tapscott, D. F. (eds) (1979) *Body, Mind and Method: Essays in Honour of Virgil Aldrich*, Dordrecht: Reidel.

Hahn, M. and Ramberg, B. (eds) (2003), *Reflections and Replies: Essays on the Philosophy of Tyler Burge*, Cambridge, MA: MIT Press.

Hanson, N. (1965) *Patterns of Discovery*, Cambridge: Cambridge University Press.

Harman, G. (1990) 'The Intrinsic Quality of Experience', *Philosophical Perspectives*, 4, 31–52.

Hatfield, G. (1992) 'Descartes' Physiology and its Relation to his Psychology' in Cottingham, J. (ed.) *(1992)*.

Heidegger, M. (1968) *What is Called Thinking*, translated by Gray, J. G., New York: Harper and Row.

Hirst, R. J. (ed.) (1965) *Perception and the External World*, New York: Macmillan.

Holler, C. (1998) Punktefilm: in *Eyes Lies and Illusion*, Mannoni, L., Nekes, W. and Warner, M., Hayward Gallery: 2004–5.

Hurley, S. L. (1998), *Consciousness in Action*, Cambridge, MA: Harvard University Press.

Hyman, J. (1994) 'Vision and Power', *Journal of Philosophy*, 91, 236–52.

Jackson, F. (1977) *Perception*, Cambridge: Cambridge University Press.

—— (1998) *From Metaphysics to Ethics*: *A Defence of Conceptual Analysis*, Oxford: Clarendon Press.

—— (2000) 'Some Reflections on Representationalism'. Online. Available http://www.nyu.edu/gsas/dept/philo/courses/consciousness/papers/RepresentationalismNYU5April00.PDF (accessed 20 July 2006).

Johansson, G. (1973). 'Visual perception of biological motion and a model for its analysis', *Perceptual Psychophysics*, 14, 201–11.

Kant, I. (1929) *The Critique of Pure Reason*, translated by Kemp Smith, N., London: Macmillan.

Kelly, S. D. (2001a) 'Demonstrative Concepts and Experience', *The Philosophical Review*, 110, 397–420.

—— (2001b) 'The Nonconceptual Content of Perceptual Experience: Situation Dependence and Fineness of Grain', *Philosophy and Phenomenological Research*, 62, 601–8.

—— (2004) 'Reference and Attention: a Difficult Connection', *Philosophical Studies*, 120, 265–76.

Kripke, S. (1980) *Naming and Necessity*, Oxford: Basil Blackwell.

Levine, J. (2001) *Purple Haze*, Oxford: Oxford University Press.

Lewis, D. (1980) 'Veridical Hallucination', *Australasian Journal of Philosophy*, 58, 239–49.

Lowe, J. (1995) *Locke on Human Understanding*, London: Routledge.

—— (1996) *Subjects of Experience*, Cambridge: Cambridge University Press.

Luntley, M. (2003) 'Nonconceptual Content and the Sound of Music', *Mind & Language*, 18, 402–26.

McAlister, L. (ed.) (1976) *The Philosophy of Brentano*, London: Duckworth.

MacArthur, D. (2003) 'McDowell, Scepticism, and the Veil of Perception', *Australasian Journal of Philosophy*, 81, 175–90.

McCulloch, G. (1995), *The Mind and Its World*, London: Routledge.

MacDonald, C. (1990) 'Weak Externalism and Mind-Body Identity', *Mind*, 99, 387–404.

McDonald, G. F. (ed.) (1979) *Perception and Identity: Essays Presented to A. J. Ayer with His Replies*, London: Macmillan.

McDowell, J. H. (1982) 'Criteria, Defeasibility, and Knowledge', *Proceedings of the British Academy*, 68, 455–79.

—— (1986) 'Singular Thought and the Extent of Inner Space' in Pettit, P. and McDowell, J. H. (eds) (1986).

—— (1994a) 'The Content of Perceptual Experience', *Philosophical Quarterly*, 44, 190–205.

—— (1994b; 2nd edn 1996) *Mind and World*, Cambridge, MA: Harvard University Press.

—— (1998) 'Having the World in View: Sellars, Kant, and Intentionality' (The Woodbridge Lectures), *The Journal of Philosophy*, 95, 431–91.

Mack, A. (2002) 'Is the Visual World a Grand Illusion? A Response', *Journal of Consciousness Studies*, 9, 102–10.

Mack, A. and Rock, I. (1998) *Inattentional Blindness*, Cambridge, MA: MIT Press.

Mackie, J. (1976) *Problems From Locke*, Oxford: Oxford University Press.

Manford, M. and Andermann, F. (1998) 'Complex Visual Hallucinations', *Brain*.

Marcel, A. J. (2003) 'Introspective Report: Trust, Self Knowledge and Science', *Journal of Consciousness Studies*, 10, 167–86.

Margolis, J. (1972) Review of Dretske's *Seeing and Knowing*, *Metaphilosophy*, 3, 53–70.

Marr, D. (1982) *Vision*, San Francisco, CA: Freeman.

Marras, A. (1976) ' Scholastic Roots of Brentano's Conception of Intentionality', in McAlister, L. (ed.) (1976).

Martin, M. (1997) 'The Reality of Appearances', in Sainsbury, M. (ed.) (1997).

—— (2001) 'Epistemic Openness and Perceptual Defeasibility', *Philosophy and Phenomenological Research*, 63, 441–8.

—— (2002) 'The Transparency of Experience', *Mind and Language*, 376–425.

—— (2004) 'The Limits of Self-Awareness', *Philosophical Studies*, 120, 37–89.

Merleau-Ponty, M. (1962) *Phenomenology of Perception*, translated by Smith, C., London: Routledge and Kegan Paul.

Metzinger, T. (ed.) (1995) *Conscious Experience*, Paderborn: Schoeningh.

Millar, A. (1991) *Reasons and Experience*, Oxford: Clarendon Press.

—— (1995) 'The Idea of Experience', *Proceedings of the Aristotelian Society*, 96, 75–90.

Millikan, R. G. (1993) *White Queen Psychology and other Essays for Alice*, Cambridge, MA: MIT Press.

Milner, A. D. and Goodale, M. A. (1995) *The Visual Brain in Action*, Oxford: Oxford University Press.

Moore, G. E. (1903) 'The Refutation of Idealism', *Mind*, 12, 433–53. Reprinted in Moore, G. E. (1922).

—— (1913–14) 'The Status of Sense-Data', *Proceedings of the Aristotelian Society*, 14, 355–80. Reprinted in Moore, G. E. (1922).

—— (1918–19) 'Some Judgements of Perception', *Proceedings of the Aristotelian Society*, 19, 1–29. Reprinted in Moore, G. E. (1922).

—— (1922), *Philosophical Studies*, London: Routledge and Kegan Paul.

—— (1942) 'A Reply to my Critics', in Schilpp (1942).

Moran, D. (1996) 'Brentano's Thesis', *Proceedings of the Aristotelian Society, Supplementary Volume*, 70, 1–27.

Myin, E. and O'Regan, K. (2002) 'Perceptual Consciousness, Access to Modality and Skill Theories', *Journal of Consciousness Studies*, 9, 27–45.

Nagel, T. (1986) *The View From Nowhere*, Oxford: Oxford University Press.

Noë, A. (2002) 'Is the Visual World a Grand Illusion', *Journal of Consciousness Studies*, 9, 1–12.

—— (2004) *Action in Perception*, Cambridge, MA: MIT Press.

Noë, A., Pessoa, L. and Thompson, E. (2000) 'Beyond the Grand Illusion: What Change Blindness Really Teaches Us About Vision', *Visual Cognition*, 7, 1–15.

Noë, A. and Thompson, E. (eds) (2002) *Vision and Mind*, Cambridge, MA: MIT Press.

Nussbaum, M. and Rorty, A. (eds), (1992) *Essays on Aristotle's De* Anima, Oxford: Clarendon Press.

O'Hear, A. (ed.) (1998) *Current Issues in the Philosophy of Mind*, Cambridge: Cambridge University Press.

O'Regan, K. and Noë, A. (2001) 'A Sensori-Motor Approach to Vision and Visual Consciousness', *Behavioural and Brain Sciences*, 24, 939–1031.

O'Shaughnessy, B. (2000) *Consciousness and the World*, Oxford: Clarendon Press.
O'Shea, J. (2006) *Sellars*, Cambridge: Polity.
Owens, D. (1992) *Causes and Coincidences*, Cambridge: Cambridge University Press.
Pashler, H. (ed.) (1996) *Attention*, London: University College London Press.
Peacocke, C. (1983) *Sense and Content*, Oxford: Clarendon Press.
—— (1992) *A Study of Concepts*, Cambridge, MA: MIT Press.
—— (2001) 'Does Perception Have Nonconceptual Content?' *Journal of Philosophy*, 98, 239–64.
—— (2003) 'Postscript: the Relations between Conceptual and Nonconceptual Content', in Gunther, Y. H. (ed.) (2003).
Pears, D. (1975) *Questions in the Philosophy of Mind*, London: Duckworth.
Penfield, W. G. and Perot, P. (1963) 'The Brain's Record of Auditory and Visual Experience: a Final Summary and Discussion', *Brain*, 86, 595–696.
Pettit, P. and McDowell, J. H. (eds) (1986) *Subject, Thought, and Context*, Oxford: Clarendon Press.
Philipona, D. L. and O'Regan, K. (forthcoming) 'Color Naming, Unique Hues and Hue Cancellation Predicted from Singularities in Reflection Properties', *Visual Neuroscience*.
Price, C. (1998): 'Function, Perception and Normal Causal Chains', *Philosophical Studies*, 89, 31–51.
Price, H. H. (1932) *Perception*, London: Methuen.
Prinz, J. J. (2002) *Furnishing the Mind*, Cambridge, MA: MIT Press.
Pritchard, D. (2005) *Epistemic Luck*, Oxford: Clarendon Press.
Proust, J. (ed.) (1996) *Perception et Intermodalité*, Paris: Presses Universitaires de France.
Pylyshyn, Z. W. (1984) *Computation and Cognition: Toward a Foundation for Cognitive Science*, Cambridge, MA: MIT Press.
—— (2003) *Seeing and Visualizing: It's Not What You Think*, Cambridge, MA: MIT Press.
Raffman, D. (1995) 'On the Persistence of Phenomenology', in Metzinger, T. (ed.) (1995).
Ramsey, F. P. (1926) 'Truth and Probability' in Ramsey (1931).
—— (1931) *The Foundations of Mathematics*, London: Routledge and Kegan Paul.
Reid, T. (1785) *Essays on the Intellectual Powers of Man*, Brody, B. A. (ed.) (1969), Cambridge, MA: MIT Press.
Rensink, R. (2000a) 'The Dynamic Representation of Scenes', *Visual Cognition*, 7, 17–42.
—— (2000b) 'Seeing, Sensing, and Scrutinising', *Vision Research*, 40, 1469–87.
—— (2000c) 'When Good Observers Go Bad', *Psyche*, 6.
Robinson, H. (1994) *Perception*, London: Routledge.
Rosenberg, J. (1982) 'The Place of Color in the Scheme of Things: A Roadmap to Sellars's Carus Lectures' *The Monist*, 65, 315–35.
—— (1997) 'Kantian Schemata and the Unity of Perception' in Burri, A. (ed.) (1997).
—— (2000) 'Perception vs. Inner Sense: A Problem about Direct Awareness' *Philosophical Studies*, 101, 143–60.
—— (2002a) 'Immediate Knowledge: The New Dialectic of Givenness', in Rosenberg (2002b).
—— (2002b) *Thinking About Knowing*, Oxford: Oxford University Press.
Royce, J. R. and Rozeboom, W. W. (eds) (1972) *The Psychology of Knowing*, New York: Gordon & Breach.
Rowlands, M. (2003) *Externalism*, Chesham: Acumen.
Rudd, A. (1997) 'Two Types of Externalism' *Philosophical Quarterly*, 47, 501–7.
—— (2003) *Expressing the World*, Chicago, IL: Open Court.
Sacks, O. (1992) *Migraine*, London: Picador.

Sainsbury, M. (ed.) (1997) *Thought and Ontology,* Milan: Franco Angelli.

Salmon, N. (1982) *Reference and Essence,* Oxford: Basil Blackwell.

Sartorelli, J. (1991) 'McGinn on Content Scepticism and Kripke's Sceptical Argument', *Analysis,* 51, 79–84.

Schilpp, P.A. (1942) *The Philosophy of G. E. Moore,* London: Cambridge University Press.

Sellars, Roy Wood (1938) 'A Statement of Critical Realism', *Revue Internationale de Philosophie*; reprinted in Hirst, R. J. (ed.) (1965).

Seibt, J. (1990) *Properties as Processes,* Atascadero, CA: Ridgeview Publishing.

Simons, D and Chabris, C. (1999), 'Gorillas In Our Midst: Sustained Inattentional Blindness for Dynamic Events', *Perception,* 28, 1059–74.

Smith, A. D. (2002) *The Problem of Perception,* Cambridge, MA: Harvard University Press.

Smith, Q. and Jokic, A. (eds) (2003) *Consciousness,* Oxford: Oxford University Press.

Snowdon, P. (1981) 'Perception, Vision and Causation', *Proceedings of the Aristotelian Society,* 81, 175–92.

—— (1990) 'The Objects of Perceptual Experience', *Proceedings of the Aristotelian Society, Supplementary Volume,* 64, 121–50.

—— (1992) 'How to Interpret Direct Perception', in Crane, T. (ed.) (1992b).

Sorabji, R. (1992) 'Intentionality and Physiological Processes: Aristotle's Theory of Sense-Perception' in Nussbaum, M. and Rorty, A. (eds) (1992).

Sosa, E. and Steup, M. (eds) (2005), *Contemporary Debates in Epistemology,* Malden, MA: Blackwell.

Sprigge, T. (1988) 'Intrinsic Connectedness' *Proceedings of the Aristotelian Society,* 88, 129–45.

Strawson, P. F. (1970) 'Imagination and Perception' in Foster, L. and Swanson, J. W. (eds) (1970).

—— (1974a) 'Causation in Perception' in *Freedom and Resentment and Other Essays* (1974b).

—— (1974b) *Freedom and Resentment and Other Essays* London: Methuen.

—— (1979) 'Perception and Its Objects' in McDonald, G. F. (ed.) (1979).

Sturgeon, S. (2000) *Matters of Mind: Consciousness, Reason and Nature,* London & New York: Routledge.

Swartz, R. (ed.) (1965) *Perceiving Sensing and Knowing,* New York: Doubleday.

Thompson, E. T., Palacios, A. and Varella, F. (1992) 'Ways of Coloring: Comparative Color vision as a Case Study for Cognitive science', *Behavioral and Brain Sciences,* 15, 1–74.

Treisman, A. and Gelade, G. (1980) 'A Feature Integration Model of Attention', *Cognitive Psychology,* 12, 97–136.

Tye, M. (1996) *Ten Problems of Consciousness,* Cambridge, MA: MIT Press.

—— (2000) *Consciousness, Color, and Content,* Cambridge, MA: MIT Press.

Valberg, J. J. (1992) *The Puzzle of Experience,* Oxford: Clarendon Press.

Wells, H. G. (1895a) 'The Remarkable Case of Davidson's Eyes' in *The Stolen Bacillus and Other Incidents* (1985b).

Wells, H. G. (1895b) *The Stolen Bacillus and Other Incidents,* London: Methuen.

White, A. R. (1961) 'The Causal Theory of Perception', *Proceedings of the Aristotelian Society, Supplementary Volume,* 35, 121–68.

Williams, B. (1978) *Descartes: The Project of Pure Enquiry,* Harmondsworth: Penguin.

Williams, M. (1996), *Unnatural Doubts: Epistemological Realism and the Basis of Scepticism.* Princeton, NJ: Princeton University Press.

Wittgenstein, L. (1953; 2nd edn 1997) *Philosophical Investigations,* translated Anscombe, G. E. M., Oxford: Blackwell.

—— (1992) *Last Writings on the Philosophy of Psychology,* Oxford: Blackwell.

Wolfe, J. (1996) 'Visual Search', in Paschler (ed.) (1996).

Index